ANCIENT IRAQ

ANCIENT IRAQ

GEORGES ROUX

THE WORLD PUBLISHING COMPANY
CLEVELAND AND NEW YORK

Published by The World Publishing Company
2231 West 110th Street, Cleveland 2, Ohio

Library of Congress Catalog Card Number: 65-18012

FIRST EDITION

Copyright © George Allen & Unwin Ltd 1964

Stock No. 2636

GBWP

PRINTED IN GREAT BRITAIN

INTRODUCTION

This is a revised version, substantially enlarged and entirely rewritten, of the series of articles which appeared between September 1956 and January 1960 in *Iraq Petroleum*, the now defunct magazine of the Iraq Petroleum Company, under the title *The Story of Ancient Iraq*. Written in Basrah with no other source of documentation than my own personal library, these articles suffered from many serious defects and were far from even approaching the standards required from a work of this nature. In my view, whatever merit they possessed resided more in the lavish manner in which they were printed and illustrated than in the quality of their content. Yet, much to my surprise, the 'Story' received a warm welcome from a large and distinguished public. From Japan to California, a number of persons who, directly or indirectly, had access to the magazine took the trouble to write to the editor or myself asking for back numbers, spare copies or reprints, and suggesting that these articles be put in book form. I have now at last complied with their wish and I must say that, had it not been for the encouragement I received from their indulgent appreciation, I would never have had the courage to embark upon such a task.

For the unexpected success of these articles I can find only one reason: imperfect as they were, they helped to fill a regrettable gap. The Tigris-Euphrates valley—the region once called Mesopotamia and now mostly in Iraqi territory—forms a large, coherent, well-defined geographical, historical and cultural unit. Throughout antiquity, its inhabitants—Sumerians, Akkadians, Babylonians and Assyrians—shared the same brilliant civilization and played the leading rôle in Near Eastern politics, art, science, philosophy, religion and literature. During the last hundred years, an enormous amount of archaeological research has been carried out in Iraq proper and in the eastern provinces of Syria. Impressive monuments have been unearthed, and museums have been filled with works of art and inscribed tablets recovered from the buried cities of Mesopotamia. No less remarkable results have been achieved in the field of philology: little by little, the two main languages of ancient Iraq—Sumerian and Akkadian—have yielded their secrets, and tens of thousands of texts have been translated and published. In university libraries, the number of books and articles devoted to one aspect or other of Mesopotamian archaeology, history and civilization is positively staggering. Yet, whilst several excellent and detailed histories of ancient Egypt, Iran, Syria, Palestine and Anatolia are offered to scholars or laymen, it is still

7

impossible to find one single recent general history of ancient Iraq in English nor, to my knowledge, in any other language.

That professional people are reluctant to undertake such a task can easily be understood. To deal thoroughly and competently with *all* the aspects of a civilization which had its roots in prehistory and lasted for more than thirty centuries would keep several scholars fully occupied for years and would fill many large volumes. Moreover, as almost every new discovery alters our knowledge of the past, even such a work would be in danger of becoming obsolete within a decade. Assyriologists and archaeologists, therefore, prefer to plough their own fields. Most of their works are only accessible to other scholars or to advanced students. Those among these specialists who aim at a wider audience write on the subjects they know best. 'Popular' books, such as Woolley's monographs on Ur, Parrot's publications on Mari, or Kramer's editions of Sumerian epics and myths cannot be too highly praised, but they are spotlights illuminating small areas in a very large picture. The layman often fails to appreciate fully their value simply because he is unable to place the sites, monuments, events or ideas described in their proper chronological or cultural context. Historians, on the other hand, have adopted precisely the opposite attitude. The works of L. King (*A History of Sumer and Akkad*, London, 1910; *A History of Babylon*, London, 1915), Sidney Smith (*Early History of Assyria*, London, 1928), A. Olmstead (*History of Assyria*, New York, 1923), B. Meissner (*Babylonien und Assyrien*, Heidelberg, 1925) and L. Delaporte (*La Mésopotamie*, Paris, 1923), excellent in their time and still very useful, though on many points outdated, have never been replaced. Instead, the French and Germans and, to a lesser extent, the British have given us, in more recent years, vast syntheses embracing either the whole of Western Asia or the entire Near East (Egypt included), or even the totality of the ancient world. E. Meyer's *Geschichte des Altertums* (1913–1937), H. Schmökel's *Geschichte des alten Vorderasien* (1957), or the chapters written by G. Contenau and E. Dhorme for *Peuples et Civilisations* (1950), by L. Delaporte for *Les Peuples de l'Orient Méditerranéen* (1948) and by G. Goossens for the *Encyclopédie de la Pléiade* (1956), or again, the monumental *Cambridge Ancient History* (1923–25) of which a revised edition is being prepared, are invaluable monuments of erudition and lack neither detail nor perspective. But it is the kind of perspective one can expect in an art gallery where even a masterpiece tends to loose its individual character among other paintings. No matter what place they give to Mesopotamia, these books fail to do full justice to the remarkable cohesion and continuity of her history and civilization.

In a modest way, the present work aims at bridging the gap between these two kinds of publications: monographs and encyclopaedias. Devoted entirely to Iraq,* it is a concise and in many respects incomplete study of the political, economic and cultural history of Mesopotamia in antiquity, beginning with the first manifestations of human presence in north-eastern Iraq during palaeolithic times, and ending with the ultimate collapse of the Sumero-Akkadian civilization, at the dawn of the Christian era. In addition, two introductory chapters purport to acquaint the reader with the geography and ecology of Mesopotamia and with the techniques and results of archaeological excavations in that country.

Ancient Iraq is not intended for scholars, but for laymen and students. Throughout the world, there exist a growing number of persons from all walks of life who are deeply interested in history in general and in the ancient Orient in particular. Cultured and eager to learn, these persons have not yet found gathered in one volume of reasonable size all the information they desire on a country which, with very good reasons, fascinates them. It is for this enlightened public that this book has primarily been written. But among those kind enough to look with indulgence upon my articles in *Iraq Petroleum* were also several university professors. In private letters and conversation, they expressed the opinion that a book written along the same lines as the articles would provide their students with a useful working instrument. In order to satisfy the requirements of this category of readers, I have enlarged on certain points, perhaps considered by many as of secondary importance, and provided each chapter with rather copious bibliographical and explanatory notes. The thought that this work could be of some help to young students of antiquity will, I hope, render the general public more tolerant to its occasional heaviness.

I have endeavoured to make this work as simple, clear and readable as humanly possible, but at the same time accurate and up-to-date. Needless to say that this was not an easy task. Writing for non-specialized readers on scientific matters is like walking on a tight rope: one is always afraid of falling into pedantism or triviality, and I am by no means sure that I have succeeded in keeping my balance all the way. In the enormous amount of material available, I had to make difficult,

* The fact that all the ancient capital cities of Sumer, Babylonia and Assyria are in Iraqi territory and that Iraq covers about three-quarters of the Tigris-Euphrates valley justifies the title of this work. It must be clearly understood, however, that several important sites mentioned are, in fact, situated in Syria or Turkey. I apologize to the Syrians and Turks and hope that they will feel no more offended than would the Belgians if part of their country was included in a history of Gaul entitled 'Ancient France'.

often heart-breaking choices, but I have taken great care to avoid over-simplification and dogmatism. History, especially where antiquity is concerned, abounds in unsolved problems, and the truth of today may be the proven error of tomorrow. I have therefore taken the liberty of discussing at some length some of the more debated problems —such as the origin of the Sumerians—and I have underlined, on almost every page, the provisional character of our knowledge. On frequent occasions, I have attempted to correlate historical events with previous events or with geographical and economic conditions. In other words, I have tried to 'explain' as much as to describe, for I feel that without such 'explanations'—no matter how tentative they are— history would be nothing but a meaningless and tedious collection of dates and data. Finally, I have given archaeology, art, literature and religion more importance than is usually expected in a work of this kind, and I have quoted as many texts as space would permit. The public nowadays wants to know how ancient people lived and what they thought at least as much as what they did, and the best way to make the past alive is perhaps to let it speak by itself.

I wish to thank all those who have helped me in this work, particularly my learned friends, Monsieur René Labat, Professor at the Collège de France, Paris, and Monsieur Georges Dossin, Professor at the Universities of Brussels and Liège, who gave me their encouragement; Mr. T. E. Piggott, former editor of *Iraq Petroleum*, who published my articles and obligingly put the blocks at my disposal; Mr. L. H. Bawden, who drew the maps with consummate skill and art; Monsieur P. Amiet, of the Louvre Museum, Dr. R. D. Barnett and the Trustees of the British Museum, Professor W. Caskel, of the University of Cologne, Dr. G. R. Meyer, of the Vorderasiatische Museum, Berlin, and Dr. Faisal al-Wailly, Director-General of Antiquities to the Iraqi Government, who authorized the publication of photographs of the monuments from their respective museums. Above all, I owe a very special debt of gratitude to Dr. D. J. Wiseman, Professor of Assyriology at the University of London, who was kind enough to read the manuscript and to offer much invaluable advice, and to my wife without whose self-sacrifice, moral support and linguistic assistance I would have been unable to write this book.

London, August 1963

CONTENTS

CONTENTS

ILLUSTRATIONS

MAPS

(all at end of book)

CHAPTER I

THE GEOGRAPHICAL
SETTING

NOWHERE, perhaps, is the influence of geography upon history as clearly demonstrated as in the group of countries which extend from the Mediterranean Sea to the Iranian plateau and form what we call the Near East. In the great deserts and equatorial forests, or in the vicinity of the poles, man is overwhelmed by a hostile nature threatening his very existence. In temperate areas, on the other hand, man is almost everywhere at home in a favourable and challenging environment. But in the arid, sub-tropical Near East, the balance between man and nature is more delicately poised. Man can live there, and even thrive, yet his various activities are largely conditioned by the relief of the ground, the nature of the soil, the amount of rainfall, the distribution of springs and wells, the course and rate of flow of the rivers. These factors exert upon him a profound influence: they mark the paths of his trade and of his military ventures, incline him to settle as a farmer or condemn him to the wandering life of a nomad, contribute to his physical and moral qualities and, to some extent, command his thoughts and religious beliefs. The history of any Near Eastern country must therefore begin with a study of the map, and the antique land of Iraq is no exception to the rule.

Since we possess no ancient treatise on geography, the following description will necessarily be based on present-day Iraq, but there is no doubt that it applies to antiquity with but minor amendments.[1] While in some parts of the country the rivers do not follow exactly the same course as they did in the past, and while regions which were once fertile are now sterile and *vice versa*, the general pattern of mountains, plains and valleys remains obviously unchanged, and a comparison between ancient and modern faunae and florae,[2] as well as the evidence obtained from geological and meteorological studies,[3] indicate that climatic fluctuations over the last six or eight thousand years have been so slight as to be practically negligible. Scientific proof of this kind, however, is almost superfluous, for any person with some knowledge of history who visits Iraq finds himself in familiar surroundings. Not only do bare mountains, stony deserts, fields of barley, palm-groves, reed-thickets and mud-flats form the landscape which ancient texts and monuments suggested, but living conditions outside the main cities are reminiscent of those of yore. On the hills, shepherds straight from Biblical ages graze sheep and goats; in the desert, tribes of bedouins endlessly wander from well to well, as of old; in the plain, peasants live in mud houses almost identical with those of the Babylonian farmers and often use similar tools, while fishermen in the marshes dwell in reed-huts and punt the high-prowed boats of their Sumerian ancestors. If the moon, the sun, the winds, the rivers are no longer worshipped, their power is still feared or welcomed, and many ancient customs and beliefs can be explained by reference to present conditions. Indeed, there are few countries in the world where the past is more strangely alive, where the historian's dead texts are provided with a more appropriate illustration.

Our field of studies is a triangle covering an area of about 130,000 square miles, limited by arbitrary lines drawn between Aleppo, lake Urmiah and the mouth of the Shatt-el-'Arab. The political frontiers of today divide this triangle between Syria and Iraq, the latter having the better share, whilst parts of Turkey and Iran protrude in the north and east. But these frontiers are recent, and the whole region constitutes, in fact, one large geographical unit having for its main axis the valleys of two great rivers, the Tigris and the Euphrates. We may therefore call it 'Mesopotamia', though the word, coined in antiquity by Greek historians, is somewhat too restricted, meaning '(the land) *between* the rivers'. Surprising as it may seem, the ancient inhabitants of 'Mesopotamia' had no name covering the totality of the country in which they lived, and the terms they used were either too vague ('the Land') or too precise ('Sumer', 'Akkad', 'Assur', 'Babylon'). So deeply embedded in their mind were the concepts of city-states and of narrow politico-religious divisions that they apparently failed to recognize the existence of a territorial unity which, to us, is obvious.

The geographical unity of Mesopotamia was matched, in pre-Christian times, by a striking cultural unity. Within our triangle flourished a civilization which, in quality and importance, was only equalled by the civilization of Egypt. According to the fashion of the day, we call it 'Chaldaean', 'Assyro-Babylonian', 'Sumero-Akkadian', or 'Mesopotamian' civilization, but it is one and the same thing. From roots set deeply in the darkness of prehistoric times, it slowly grew, blossomed in the dawning light of history, about 3000 BC, and lasted for nearly three thousand years, remaining remarkably uniform throughout, though repeatedly shaken by political convulsions and repeatedly rejuvenated by foreign blood and influence. The centres which generated, kept alive and radiated this civilization over the entire Near East were towns such as Ur, Uruk, Nippur, Agade, Babylon, Assur and Nineveh, all situated on or near the Tigris or the Euphrates, within the boundaries of modern Iraq. At the beginning of the Christian era, however, the Mesopotamian civilization, for reasons which will be detailed in due course, gradually declined and vanished. Some of its cultural and scientific achievements were salvaged by the Greeks and later became part of our own heritage; the rest either perished or lay buried for centuries, awaiting the picks of archaeologists. A glorious past was forgotten. In man's short memory, of these opulent cities, of these powerful gods, of these mighty monarchs only a few, often distorted names survived. The dissolving rain, the sand-bearing winds, the earth-splitting sun conspired to obliterate all material remains, and the desolate mounds which concealed the ruins of Babylon and Nineveh offer perhaps the best lesson in modesty that we shall ever receive from history.

THE TWIN RIVERS

Herodotus' famous sentence: 'Egypt is a gift of the Nile'[4] is often quoted. In many respects, it can also be said of Mesopotamia that it is a gift of the twin rivers. From time immemorial, the Tigris and the Euphrates have deposited their alluvium on a bed of sedimentary rocks between the Arabian platform and the

Iranian highland, creating amidst deserts a plain which, in extent and fertility, has no equivalent in the 2,300 miles of barren land stretching from the Indus to the Nile. Was this plain also claimed from the sea? In other words, did the head of the Persian Gulf reach the latitude of Baghdad in early prehistoric times, being gradually pushed southwards as millennia went by? Such is the classical theory long professed as a dogma and still to be found in most textbooks.5 A few years ago, however, a new theory was put forward, which claims that the Tigris and the Euphrates unload their sediment in a slowly subsiding basin and that, in consequence, the line of the sea-shore has probably varied very little in the course of time.6 Indeed, there are scientists who believe that, at some remote period, it might even have occupied a position farther south than the present one.7 The new theory rests upon evidence derived, in the main, from a study of surface fossils and from a reconstruction of ancient canals and river-beds as supplied by aerial photography. It has been generally well received by geologists, but most archaeologists remain sceptical, though recent surface finds in the region of Basrah8 might encourage further research in that little-known area. In any case, the solution of this interesting problem can only result from the comparison of textual, archaeological, geological and hydrographical data which are far from being immediately available, and it is wiser to leave the question open for the present.

Both the Tigris and the Euphrates have their sources in Armenia, the former to the south of Lake Van, the latter near Mount Ararat. The Euphrates, 1,780 miles long, first follows a zigzagging course across Turkey, whilst the Tigris, notably shorter (1,150 miles), almost immediately flows southwards. When they emerge from the mountains, the two rivers are separated from each other by some 250 miles of open steppe. The Euphrates, which at Jerablus is only a hundred miles from the Mediterranean, takes a south-easterly direction and leisurely makes its way towards the Tigris. Near Baghdad, they nearly meet, being a mere twenty miles apart, but they soon diverge again and do not mingle their waters until they reach Qurnah, sixty miles north of Basrah, to form the Shatt-el-'Arab. In antiquity, however, this wide, majestic river did not exist, since the Tigris and the Euphrates ran separately into the sea. This general pattern of river courses can be divided into two segments. To the north of a line Hît-Samarra, the valleys of the Twin Rivers are distinct. The two streams cut their way across a plateau of hard limestone and shale and are bordered by cliffs, with the result that the river-beds have moved very little in the course of time, the ancient cities—such as Karkemish, Mari, Nineveh, Nimrud or Assur—still being on, or close by the river banks, as they were thousands of years ago. But to the south of that line, the two valleys merge and form a wide, flat alluvial plain—sometimes called the Mesopotamian delta— where the rivers flow with such a low gradient that they meander considerably and throw numerous side-branches. Like all meandering rivers they raise their own beds, so that they flow, in certain areas, above the level of the plain, their overflow tending to create permanent lakes and swamps, and they occasionally change their course. This explains why southern Mesopotamian cities which were once on the Euphrates or on its branches are now forlorn ruin-mounds in a desert of silt, several miles from modern waterways. Changes in river-beds are extremely difficult to study in retrospect and to date with accuracy, but they certainly occurred in antiquity. It is, however, remarkable that the ancient Mesopotamians managed to keep their rivers under control, since the Euphrates followed approximately the same course for about three thousand years, passing through Sippar, Babylon, Nippur, Shuruppak, Uruk, Larsa and Ur, that is to say from 15 to 50 miles to the east of its present main channel. We still know very little about the ancient course of the Tigris in southern Mesopotamia, particularly south of Kut-el-Imara, and it is hoped that the method of ceramic surface survey developed by the scholars of the Oriental Institute of Chicago and applied by them successfully to the Diyala valley and to the central parts of Sumer and Akkad[9] will one day throw some light on this important problem of historical topography.

The climate of central and southern Iraq is of the 'dry, sub-tropical' variety, with temperatures reaching 120° F. (50° C.) in summer and an average winter rainfall of less than 10 inches. Agriculture, therefore, depends almost entirely upon irrigation. But the dimensions and profile of the plain, as well as the rate of flow of the rivers, preclude the cheap and easy 'basin type' of irrigation as practised, for instance, in Egypt where the overflow of the Nile freely inundates the valley for a time and then with-draws. Since the combined flood periods of the Tigris and the Euphrates occur between April and June, too late for winter crops and too early for summer crops, the fields must be supplied with water at man's will, and this is achieved by a complex system of canals, reservoirs, dykes, regulator-sluices and the like ('perennial irrigation').[10] To create an efficient network of canals and to maintain them against rapid silting-up are clearly colossal and unending tasks which require large labour forces and the co-operation of many demographic groups—factors which contain the germs of both local strife and political unity. But this is not all: year after year, two grave dangers threaten the Mesopotamian farmer. The more insidious of the two is the accumulation in flat, low-lying areas of the salt brought by irrigation and collected in the water-table which lies just beneath the surface. If no artificial drainage is installed—and it seems that such drainage was unknown in antiquity—fertile fields can become sterile in a comparatively short time and in this way, throughout history, pieces of land of ever-increasing size had to be abandoned and reverted to deserts.[11] The other danger lies in the capricious rate of flow of the twin rivers.[12] Whilst the Nile, fed by the great lakes of East Africa, acting as regulators, has an annual flood of almost constant volume, the volume of the combined floods of the Tigris and the Euphrates is unpredictable, for it depends upon the variable amount of rain or snow which falls on the mountains of Armenia and Kurdistan. If low waters over a few years mean drought and famine, one excessive flood often spells catastrophe. The rivers break through their embankments; the low land, as far as the eye can see, is submerged; the flimsy mud-houses and reed-huts are swept away; the crop is lost in a huge muddy lake, together with the cattle and the belongings of a large part of the population. It is a spectacle the horror of which will never be forgotten by those who witnessed the last great Iraqi inundation, in the spring of 1954. Thus Mesopotamia constantly hovers between a state of desert and gigantic swamp. This double threat and the uncertainty it creates as regards the future are believed to be at the root of the 'funda-mental pessimism' which, as we shall see, characterizes the philosophy of the ancient Mesopotamians.

Despite these drawbacks, the plain watered by the Tigris and the Euphrates is a rich farming land, and was even richer in antiquity before extensive salinization of the soil took place. The entire population of ancient Iraq could easily feed on the country and barter the surplus of cereals for metal, wood and stone, which had to be obtained from abroad. Though wheat, emmer, millet and sesame were grown, barley was—and still is—the main cereal, since it tolerates a slightly saline soil. Agricultural methods were, as might be expected, primitive: ploughing and sowing were performed at the same time by means of a wooden seeding-plough which barely scratched the surface of the fields, and the furrows were wide apart. There were two or three irrigations in summer; the main harvest was usually in April,[13] but a catch-crop was often possible after the winter rains. Yet, so fertile was the land that the figures of two- or three-hundredfold given by Herodotus and Strabo for the yield of corn[14] do not appear to be grossly exaggerated. On the basis of cuneiform texts, it has been calculated that the yield of wheat in the extreme south of Iraq, about 2400 BC, could favourably compare with that of the best modern Canadian wheatfields.[15] The hot and humid climate of southern Mesopotamia, and the availability of ample water supplies in that region also were conditions highly favourable to the cultivation of the date-palm which grows along rivers and canals, 'its feet in water and its head in the scorching sun', in the words of an Arabian proverb. We learn from ancient texts that, as early as the third millennium BC, there were in the country of Sumer extensive palm-groves and that artificial pollination was already practised.[16] Flour and dates—the latter of high calorific value—formed the staple food of ancient Iraq, but cattle and sheep were bred and grazed in the non-cultivated areas and in the fields left fallow, while rivers, canals, lakes and sea provided fish in abundance. A variety of fruit and vegetables were also grown in gardens sheltered by the palm-trees and watered by means of a very simple water-lifting instrument (*dâlu*) which is still used under its old name.[17] There is no doubt that, apart from occasional famines due to war or natural disasters, the Mesopotamians generally enjoyed a rich and varied food and were much better off, in this respect, than their neighbours of Syria, Iran or Asia Minor.

REGIONAL VARIATIONS

Up to now, our attention has been focused on the main axis of the Mesopotamian triangle, the plain between the two rivers, but if we turn to the periphery, we at once observe considerable differences in climate and landscape. Leaving aside minor local variations, four important regions can be described: the desert, the steppe, the foothills and the marshes.

Hilly in the north, dissected by deep *wadis* in the centre, flat and featureless in the south, the desert borders to the west the whole course of the Euphrates and extends for hundreds of miles into the heart of Arabia.[18] This great Syro-Arabian desert, however, was foreign to ancient Mesopotamia, and the sharp line which divides it from the Euphrates valley also marks the limit of pre-Islamic settlements. The Sumerians and Babylonians were essentially peasant-folk; unlike the Arabs, they turned their backs to the desert and remained firmly attached to the 'good land', the fertile alluvium. But they had to reckon with the uncouth nomads who attacked their caravans, raided their towns and villages and even invaded their country, as did the 'Amorites' at the beginning of the second millennium and the Aramaeans eight hundred years later. As we shall see, long chapters in the history of ancient Iraq are filled with episodes of this age-old struggle between the sedentary society of the alluvial plains and the hostile tribes of the western desert. It must be added here that desert conditions can be found in various parts of Mesopotamia itself. Not only is the desert always potentially present between the twin rivers, ready to creep in and take the place of corn fields and palm-groves as soon as rivers change their course or canals become silted-up, but large areas on the left bank of the Tigris and of the Middle Euphrates have always been dreary wastes strewn with dry wadis and salt lakes, scarcely inhabited at the best of times and by-passed by the main trade routes.

In the north-western part of Mesopotamia, beyond the thin ridges formed by Jabal 'Abd-el-Aziz and Jabal Sinjar and up to the foot of the Taurus, the plain called by the Arabs el Jazirah, 'the island', spans the 250 miles which separate the Tigris from the Euphrates. The many streams which converge and form the rivers Balikh and Khabur, affluents of the Euphrates, are spread like fans over this region, while the more than adequate winter rains are supplemented by a vast and superficial water-table fed by the snows of the nearby mountains. Cornfields and orchards stretch along the rivers or cluster around springs and wells, the meshes of this green network being filled by a steppe covered with grass at spring time and offering ideal conditions for the breeding of cattle, sheep and horses. This fertile steppe forms a natural 'corridor', a transit area between the Upper Tigris valley and the plains of northern Syria, and the amazing constellation of 'tells' representing buried cities and villages testifies that it was heavily populated in antiquity.[19]

Of particular interest for the historian is the north-eastern corner of Iraq, the foothill region between the Tigris and the mountains of Kurdistan. There, the annual rainfall varies between twelve and twenty-five inches. From a rolling plain alongside the river, the ground rises through a series of parallel folds of gradually increasing height to the rugged, snow-covered peaks of the Zagros range (altitude 8,000 to 11,500 feet) which separates Iraq from Iran. Four tributaries of the Tigris, the Greater Zab, the Lesser Zab, the 'Adhem and the Diyala, flow diagonally across the region, sometimes cutting deep gorges through the limestone ridges, sometimes zigzagging around them. The climate is hot in summer but cool in winter. The hills are now rather denuded, but here and there on their slopes can be seen a meadow or a small forest of oaks or pinetrees, whilst wheat, barley, fruit-trees, vine and vegetables grow easily on the high-lying valleys. Successively the home of prehistoric cavemen, the cradle—or, rather, one of the cradles—of farming in the Neolithic Near East, and the heart of the Assyrian kingdom, this attractive district played an important part in the history of Mesopotamia. Yet, even in Assyrian times, civilization remained confined to the cultivable land at the foot of the hills. The mountains themselves, difficult to penetrate and easy to defend, always formed a disputed borderland between the armies of Mesopotamian rulers and the 'barbarian' highlanders who, like the 'bedouins' of the western desert, coveted and threatened the wealthy cities of the plain.

At the other end of Iraq, the extensive marshes which cover the southern part of the Tigris-Euphrates delta also form a special district, widely different from the rest of Mesopotamia. With their myriads of shallow lakes, their narrow channels winding through dense thickets of reeds, their fauna of water-buffaloes, wild boars and wild birds, their mosquitoes and their stifling heat, they constitute one of the most strange, forbidding and fascinating regions of the world.[20] Although they may have varied in extent and configuration, ancient monuments and texts prove that they have always existed and indeed, the Ma'dan, or marsh-Arabs, appear to have preserved to some extent the way of life of the early Sumerians established on the fringe of the swamps, more than five thousand years ago. From an archaeological point of view, the Iraqi marshes are still largely *terra incognita*. Reports from travellers suggest that traces of ancient settlements are exceedingly rare, probably because they consisted of reed-hut villages similar to those of today, which have completely disappeared or lie buried beneath several feet of mud and water. It is hoped, however, that modern methods—such as the use of helicopters—will eventually bring about the exploration of a region which is by no means lacking in historical interest.

Thus, under an apparent uniformity, Iraq is a land of contrasts. If the northern steppe and the southern marshes can be considered as local variants of the great Mesopotamian plain, there is a striking difference in topography, climate and vegetation between the plain and the foothill region, and this difference has its counterpart in history. Throughout antiquity, a definite opposition between the North and the South—or, in terms of political geography, between Sumer-and-Akkad (or Babylonia) and Assyria—can be detected, sometimes discreet and revealed only by cultural dissimilarities, sometimes open and manifested in violent conflicts.

TRADE ROUTES

Long before they were told that a wealth of petroleum was lying beneath their feet, the inhabitants of Iraq exploited a parent-substance, bitumen, which they obtained from seepages in various parts of the country, in particular on the Middle-Euphrates, between Hît and Ramâdi. They used bitumen in many ways, not only in architecture (as mortar for brickwork and waterproof lining for bathrooms and drains), but in sculpture and inlay-work, as a material for caulking boats, as fuel and even as a drug. There is some evidence that, at least during certain periods in their history, they exported it.[21]

But bitumen was the only mineral substance at their disposal. Rich as she was in agricultural products, Mesopotamia lacked metal ores as she lacked hard stone and good timber. These materials were already being imported from abroad in proto-historical times, thus enabling a chalcolithic culture to develop in a country conspicuous for the absence of metal. Copper was first discovered, it is generally believed, in north-western Iran or in the Caucasus, and was perhaps originally obtained from Azerbai-jan or Armenia. Soon, however, were found alternative sources of supplies, such as Anatolia (which later produced iron), Cyprus and the country called in cuneiform texts *Magan*, which has been tentatively identified with the mountainous part of Oman. Tin seems to have been imported from Iran, or perhaps even Afghan-istan, before the Phoenicians, in the first millennium BC, brought it from Spain. Silver came mostly from the Taurus mountains, gold from various deposits scattered between Egypt and India.[22] Several districts of Iran could provide hard stones and semi-precious stones, and Magan was reputed for its beautiful black diorite used by the sculptors of the Third Dynasty of Ur. Ordinary timber could be found in the nearby Zagros mountains, but the valuable cedar was brought from Lebanon or the Amanus, whilst other varieties of wood came by sea from the mysterious country of *Meluhha*—possibly the ancient name of India. At a very early date, therefore, an extensive network of trade routes was devel-oped, which linked the various parts of Mesopotamia with each other and with the rest of the Near East.[23]

Within Mesopotamia, transport from one locality to another was frequently effected by water. The Tigris and the Euphrates formed convenient thoroughfares from north to south, and the larger irrigation canals could also be used as waterways between villages and cities. The advantages offered by these means of communications can readily be appreciated if one remembers that the canals themselves are obstacles to land traffic, that most of the plain is covered with thick mud in winter and liable to local inundations during the spring, and that the only pack-animal available until the camel was introduced on a large scale in the first millennium BC was the ass.

Outside Mesopotamia, two great roads led in a westerly direction towards Syria and the Mediterranean coast. These roads were of course, simple desert tracks, for the paved highways which have been found outside the gates of several cities were unlikely to go very far inland. The first road started from Sippar (near Fallujah, at the latitude of Baghdad), followed the Euphrates as far as Mari, or some other market-place in the area Abu-Kemal —Deir-ez-Zor, and, cutting straight through the desert *via* Tidmur (Palmyra), reached the region of Hom where it divided into several branches to the Phoenician ports, Damascus or Palestine. The crossing of the desert—here no more than 300 miles wide—was inconvenient in summer and exposed at all times to attacks from the nomads. Caravans and armies, therefore, usually preferred the second road, much longer but safer and well provided with water and fodder. It left the Tigris at Nineveh, opposite Mosul, ran through the steppe of Jazirah from east to west *via* Shubat-Enlil (perhaps Tell Chagar Bazar), Guzana (Tell Halaf), Harranu (Harran), crossed the Euphrates at Karkemish (Jerablus), passed through or near Aleppo and ended in the Orontes valley, with terminal branches to the Mediterranean coast and central Syria. At various points on this road, other tracks branched off in a north-westerly direction, ultimately ending in Cilicia and Anatolia. From Nineveh, it was also possible to reach Armenia and eastern Anatolia by following the Tigris as far as Diarbakr and then crossing the Taurus through narrow passes.

Communications with the east were much more difficult. The tribes dwelling in the Zagros were generally hostile, and the mountain itself constituted a formidable barrier which could only be passed at three points: at Raiat, near Rowanduz, at Halabja, to the south-east of Suleimaniyah, and at Khanaqin, on the upper Diyala. The Raiat and Halabja passes gave access to Azerbaijan and the shores of Lake Urmiah, the Khanaqin pass, to Kermanshah, Hamadan and, beyond Hamadan, the Iranian plateau. A fourth road, farther south, ran parallel with the Zagros from Dêr (near Badrah) to Susa (Shush, near Dizful), the capital-city of Elam. It met with no physical obstacle, the lower valleys of the rivers Kerkha and Karun which form the territory of Elam being merely an eastward extension of the Mesopotamian plains, but the Elamites were the traditional enemies of the Mesopotamians, and this road was more often followed by invading armies than by peaceful caravans.

The last of the great trade routes between ancient Iraq and the rest of the world was through the Persian Gulf, the 'Lower Sea' or 'Sea of the Rising Sun' as it was then called. From early Islamic times up to now, the Persian Gulf has been the 'lung' of Iraq, a window wide open on India and the Far East[24]; but the part it played in the economy of Iraq in antiquity is difficult to assess. Relations between Mesopotamia and India are attested very early in history, yet there is no absolute proof that they were effected by sea rather than by land. From the end of the third millennium BC onwards, however, frequent mentions are found in cuneiform texts of ships sailing from Ur to Dilmun (Bahrain), Magan and Meluhha, and there is ample evidence that the kings of Akkad, *circa* 2300 BC, and the kings of Assyria in the first millennium endeavoured to attract the countries which bordered the Persian Gulf within the sphere of their political and economic influence.

This brief and very incomplete description should have made it clear that Mesopotamia, contrary to what many people think, did not offer ideal conditions for the development of an original civilization. Her two rivers form a fertile delta, but they can bring disaster as well as opulence. Through considerable and sustained effort, agriculture is possible on a large scale, but metal, stone and timber are desperately lacking. Deserts and high mountains, both difficult to cross and inhabited by predatory people, surround the plain on all sides, leaving only one narrow access to the sea—a sea bordered for 500 miles by the inhospitable shores of Arabia and Persia. All considered, the northern steppe and the foothills of Kurdistan would seem to offer a more favourable environment than the great alluvial plain, and it is not by chance that these regions were the seats of the Neolithic and Chalcolithic cultures of Mesopotamia. Yet, it is in the extreme south of that country, on the fringe of the swamps, that the Mesopotamian civilization took shape. Whatever man achieved in ancient Iraq, he did it at the price of a constant struggle against nature and against other men, and this struggle forms the very thread of history in that part of the world. Before going farther, however, we must first examine the sources from which historians draw their raw material.

CHAPTER II

IN SEARCH OF THE PAST

IN order to reconstruct the past, historians make use of two kinds of documents: texts and objects—the word 'object' here covers literally any artefact, from the most elaborate building to the humblest kitchen utensil. But while objects play a comparatively small part where recent periods are concerned, they grow in importance as one moves back along the scale of time. An historian dealing, for instance, with the nineteenth century works mostly from archives and rarely bothers about the plans of churches and houses, whereas architectural details are of paramount importance for his colleague bent on, say, the Trojan war or the Athenian Republic because texts here are rare and must be supplemented by whatever information can be gained from other sources. And as historians have, in general, no direct access to such non-written documents, they have to rely upon the publications of those men whose task it is to dig up ancient cities and necropoles: the field archaeologists.

Historians of the ancient Near East are even more dependent upon archaeologists than those of classical antiquity. For, in Mesopotamia as in Egypt and Palestine, objects *and* texts lay, for reasons that we shall presently examine, deeply buried in the ground and can only be reached by means of excavation. Archaeological excavations started in Iraq in 1843 and have continued unceasingly ever since. At first the work of genial amateurs, they rose to scientific standards at the turn of this century when it was realized that filling museums with *objets d'art* was not an end in itself and that finding out how people lived was far more important. On the other hand, the very nature of their work, the fact that they were dealing with fragile material such as mud bricks and clay tablets, and the necessity, in order to reach deeper into the past, of destroying layer after layer of human occupation almost as soon as they uncovered them, obliged archaeologists to devise proper, elaborate techniques. Teams of experts trained in and sponsored by European or American museums and universities, and backed by all the resources of modern science were brought in to direct and supervise the skilled workmen who handled the pick and the spade. During the last sixty years, more than thirty sites—including practically all the main cities of ancient Iraq—have been extensively excavated and more than a hundred mounds 'sounded'. The results of this international effort are astounding. Our knowledge of ancient Mesopotamian history has been completely altered and broadened beyond all expectations. Historians, who a century ago had no other source of information than the scanty data supplied by the Bible and by a handful of classical authors, now confess that they can hardly handle the enormous amount of material put year after year at their disposal and gratefully acknowledge their debt to archaeologists.[1]

Courtesy alone would therefore justify this chapter. But other reasons have prompted us to write it. Throughout this book we shall speak of the mounds or 'tells' which represent the buried cities of ancient Iraq; we shall refer to 'levels' and 'strata'; we shall, whenever possible, give 'absolute' and 'relative' dates. It seemed to us that the reader was entitled to know from the start what we were talking about, and that the best way of satisfying his curiosity would be to summarize the objects, methods and development of what is now commonly called 'Mesopotamian archaeology'.

THE BURIED CITIES OF IRAQ

To most tourists, the first contact with the ancient sites of Iraq comes as a surprise. They are taken to a hillock rising above the plain and they are told that this is an ancient city. As they go nearer, they may find such splendid monuments as the stage-tower of Ur or the Ishtar Gate of Babylon. But in most cases, they are confronted with unsightly bits of brickwork and heaps of earth littered with broken pottery. Quite naturally, they are puzzled and wonder how this happened.

To answer this question, it should be first explained that these ancient towns were built of nothing but mud. Stone is exceedingly rare in Iraq, whereas clay is everywhere at hand. In very early times, houses were made of piled up mud (*pisé*) or of shapeless lumps of clay pressed together (*adobe*), but it was soon found preferable to mix clay with straw, gravel or potsherds, mould it into bricks, let these bricks dry in the sun and bind them together with a gypsum mortar. In that way, thicker, stronger and more regular walls could be built. Of course, kiln-baked bricks were much more resistant and durable, especially when they were joined with bitumen, but this was a costly material as wood-fuel was rare and bitumen had to be shipped from comparatively distant regions. Burnt bricks were therefore in general reserved for the houses of gods and kings, though this was by no means the rule,[2] and the vast majority of ancient Mesopotamian buildings were of simple mud bricks. The roofs were made of earth spread over a structure of reed-mats and tree-trunks, and the floors of beaten earth with sometimes a coating of gypsum. A coat of mud plaster was also usually applied to the walls.

These houses with their thick walls were relatively comfortable, being cool in summer, and warm in winter, but they required constant attention. Every summer it was necessary to put a new layer of clay on the roof in anticipation of the winter rains, and every now and then the floors had to be raised. The reason for this was that rubbish, in antiquity, was not collected for disposal but simply thrown into the street, and gradually the street level rose higher than the floor level of the houses that bordered it, allowing the rain and the filth to seep in. Earth was therefore brought into the rooms, rammed over the old floors and covered with another coat of plaster. It is not infrequent for archaeologists to find two, three or more superimposed floors in one house. Provided these things were done, mud brick buildings could last for a great many years. But then, one day something happened. Whether it was war, fire, epidemic, earthquake, flood or change in river course, the result was the same: the town was partly or totally deserted. The roofs left unattended collapsed and the walls, now exposed to weather on both faces, crumbled down, filling up the rooms and sealing off the objects left behind by the house-holders. In the case of war, the destruction was of course immediate, the victorious enemy usually setting fire to the city.

After years of abandonment, new settlers would perhaps

reoccupy the site, attracted by such things as its strategically or commercially advantageous position, the abundance of its water supplies or, possibly, a lingering devotion to the god under whose aegis it had been built. Without the means of removing the enormous mass of debris, they levelled off the ruined walls and used them as foundations for their own buildings. This process was repeated several times in the course of years and, as 'occupation levels' succeeded one another, the city gradually rose above the surrounding plain. Some sites, it is true, were abandoned early and for ever. Others, like Erbil and Kirkuk, have been more or less continuously occupied from very ancient times until now. But the vast majority of them, after centuries or millennia of occupation, were deserted at some period or another of the long history of Iraq. It is not difficult to imagine what took place then: windborne sand and earth piled up against the remaining walls and filled in the streets and every hollow, whilst rainwater smoothed off the surface of the heaped-up ruins, spreading debris over a large area and planing the flanks. Slowly but inexorably, the town took its present aspect: that of a rounded, more or less regular ruin-mound or, as the Arabs say using an old, pre-Islamic word, a 'tell'.3

The task of archaeologists is to dissect that closely woven fabric of standing or fallen walls and foundations, rubble, floors and earth-filling, to recover the plan of buildings, to collect and preserve the objects they may contain and to identify and date the successive 'levels' which constitute the tell. Depending upon the time and funds at their disposal, they use one of several methods.4

The quickest and cheapest way of knowing roughly what is in a tell is to carry out a 'sounding'. Several trenches are dug into the surface of the mound at various angles. As the trenches are deepened, objects such as pottery are collected for dating purposes and a record is made of the floors and the segments of walls encountered. This method is obviously imperfect and should only be used for preliminary surveys or for comparatively unimportant sites. A variety of sounding often applied to high and narrow tells consists of cutting a long trench, not on the surface but on the side of the mound from summit to base, just as one cuts into a Christmas pudding. An impressive series of levels can be detected in this way, but it is practically impossible to circumscribe any building.

Another method, in theory perfect, is to divide the surface of the site into squares, dig up each square in turn until a certain depth is reached and start all over again for the second horizontal 'slice'. The objects found in each square and in each layer are carefully numbered and plotted on maps. As the work goes on, monuments gradually take shape. This very slow and expensive method is rarely used. The only example of it that we can quote for the Near East is Byblos (Jebail), on the Lebanese coast, where excavations of this kind have been in progress since 1926⁵ As a rule, archaeologists use what may be called 'extended sounding'. A certain area is carefully selected on the surface of the tell and a trench dug. But as soon as walls are encountered, they are followed and denuded on both faces until the whole building is unearthed. Several areas are treated in the same way and may or may not join together. Whenever desirable, digging is pushed in depth underneath the uppermost and, consequently, more recent buildings which are necessarily destroyed in order to bring to light their predecessors. In one or two points, a shaft or 'test-pit' may be sunk down to the virgin soil, giving a cross-section of the mound, a summary as it were of its various occupation levels. Some parts of the site remain, of course, untouched, but this is of little importance if the main monuments such as temples and palaces and a selection of private houses have been unearthed. Nimrud, Babylon, Uruk, Ur, Nippur and all the main sites of Iraq were or still are excavated by this method with, in the main, highly satisfactory results.

DATING THE PAST

Dating the monuments and objects discovered can be very easy or very difficult. Obviously, a building whose bricks are stamped with the inscription: 'Palace of Sargon, King of Assyria' is *ipso facto* dated, provided we know when King Sargon reigned. But this is the exception. By far the majority of objects found in archaeological excavations—and indeed the totality where prehistory is concerned—bear no inscription. In such cases, dating can only be approximate and 'relative', and is based on such criteria as shape, dimensions and style. The cumulative experience derived from the excavation of many a tell has taught archaeologists that bricks of a certain size, vases of certain shapes and decoration, weapons of a certain type, sculptures of a certain style, etc., are exclusively or predominantly found at a certain level and, grouped together, form what is called a 'cultural unit' or 'cultural stratum'. If only one of these objects is inscribed with a 'date', or if it is found in close and indisputable relation with a monument which is otherwise dated, then the whole cultural unit easily falls in position within the scale of time. If not, attempts are made to correlate the period during which these objects were in use with more ancient and more recent periods. To take an example, in a number of southern Mesopotamian sites, a certain category of painted vases (the so-called Jemdat-Nasr pottery) appears immediately *below* a cultural stratum characterized, among other things, by 'plano-convex' bricks (i.e. bricks of which one side is flat and the other rounded) and immediately *above* a cultural stratum where plain, dark or red ceramic predominates. Various inscriptions enable us to date the plano-convex bricks to the third millennium BC (Early Dynastic period: c. 2800–2350 BC). The plain pottery is undated but forms part of the cultural unit called 'Uruk' after the site where it was first identified. The Jemdat-Nasr stratum can therefore be given a 'relative' date. It is intermediate in time as in space between the Uruk period and the Early Dynastic period and ends about 2800 BC. How long did it last is another matter, but there are means of forming rough estimates.

When dealing with history, it is of course necessary to express dates in figures, and it is not without interest to examine how these are obtained and to what extent we can trust them.

The ancient Greeks counted from the first Olympiad (776 BC), the Romans from the foundation of Rome (753 BC); the Moslems date from the *hijra* (AD 622) and we have our own Christian era. But the ancient Mesopotamians had no such fixed chronological system until late in their history, when they adopted the Seleucid era (311 BC). Before that time, they simply referred to the years of reign of their rulers. These could be expressed in three ways: (1) the years of the reign were given in plain figures, e.g. 12*th year of Nabû-na'id* (*Nabonidus*), *King of Babylon*; (2) or, within each reign each year was defined by some important event such as

35

victories, royal weddings, construction of temples, etc., e.g. *Year (when) Uruk and Isin were conquered*; (3) in Assyria only, each year of a king's reign was named after some high official of the kingdom (eponyms or, in Assyrian, *limmu* system).

These dating systems could only be of practical value for the Mesopotamians themselves if they possessed for each king a list of his year's names or a list of eponyms, for each dynasty a list of its kings with the duration of their reigns, and finally a list of the successive dynasties which ruled over the country. Such lists existed and several of them have fortunately survived. Here are some examples:

Date-list of king Hammurabi of Babylon.[6]

(Year 1) Hammurabi became king.
(Year 2) He established justice in the country.
(Year 3) He constructed a throne for the main dais of the god Nanna in Babylon.
(Year 4) The wall of (the sacred precinct) Gagia was built.
(Year 5) He constructed the *en.ka.ash.bar.ra* (?).
(Year 6) He constructed the *shir* (?) of the goddess Laz.
(Year 7) Uruk and Isin were conquered.
(Year 8) The country Emutbal (was conquered).

It will be seen from this list that the date quoted above is the seventh year of King Hammurabi.

King List B, covering the First Dynasty of Babylon.[7]

Sumuabi, king, 15 years.
Sumulail, 35 years.
Sabu, his son, same (i.e. king), 14 years.
Apil-Sin, his son, same, 18 years.
Sin-muballit, his son, same, 30 years.
Hammurabi, his son, same, 55 years.
Samsuiluna, his son, same, 35 years.
etc.

Limmu-list (fragment).[8]

Shulman-ashared, King of Assyria, (campaign) against Urartu. (Shalmaneser).
Shamshi-ilu   field-marshal   against Urartu

Marduk-rîmani	chief cup-bearer	against Urarṭu
Bêl-lishir	high Chamberlain	against Urarṭu
Nabû-ishid-ukin	*abarakku*	against Itu'
Pân-Assur-lamur	*shaknu*	against Urarṭu
etc.		

The time-range of these lists varied. Some were restricted to one place and one dynasty.9 Others, like the king list B just quoted, included several dynasties which reigned—at least apparently—in succession. Others were even more ambitious and embraced very long periods and dynasties of several kingdoms. Such is the famous 'Sumerian King List' reconstructed by Th. Jacobsen which ranges from the mythical rulers 'before the Flood' to King Sin-magir (1827–1817 BC) of the First Dynasty of Isin.10

To express such dates in terms of Christian chronology would have been impossible but for Claudius Ptolemeus (Ptolemy), a Greek from Alexandria who, in the second century AD, appended to one of his books a list of all the kings of Babylon and Persia from Nabonassar (747 BC) to Alexander the Great (336–323 BC). This list, known as 'Ptolemy's Canon', not only gives the length of each reign but the outstanding astronomical events that marked some of them. Now, it so happens that by putting together several Assyrian tablets we can reconstruct a long, uninterrupted *limmu*-list covering the period between Adad-nirâri II (911–891 BC) and Ashurbanipal (668–631 BC), and this *limmu*-list also gives the main astronomical phenomena of these times. Between 747 and 631 BC, the *limmu*-list and Ptolemy's Canon coincide, and so do the eclipses, the movements of stars, etc., that they mention. Moreover, astronomers have found that an eclipse of the sun which, in the *limmu*-list is said to have occurred in the month of *Sivan* (May–June) of King Ashur-dân's tenth year, actually took place on June 15, 763 BC, and this is precisely the date arrived at by proceeding backwards and adding together on the list the years of each reign. The absolute chronology of Mesopotamia is therefore firmly established from 911 BC onwards.11 The chronology of early periods rests upon more fragile foundations. In theory, it should be possible to work it out from king lists and dynastic lists, but these have proved to be often misleading. Not only do they show significant differences, but they contain a number of gaps, or scribal errors, or they give as successive dynasties which, in fact, partly overlapped or were contemporary. One should not therefore be surprised to find different figures in different textbooks and occasional changes of opinions. For instance, the accession date of King Hammurabi was given as 2394 BC seventy years ago (Oppert, 1888), 2003 after the first world war (Thureau-Dangin, 1927), and varies now between 1848 (Sidersky, 1940) and 1704 (Weidner, 1951), depending on the calculations of the various scholars. As the date of Hammurabi is the keystone of the chronology of the second and third millennia BC, its lowering has had very important consequences, especially as regards the relationship between Mesopotamia and the surrounding countries.[12]

We cannot leave this subject without mentioning the attempts made recently to put chronology on a more scientific basis by means of physical methods, and in particular, the Carbon 14 or Radiocarbon method developed by Professor W. F. Libby of Chicago in 1946.[13] Its principle is briefly as follows: all living organisms contain ordinary carbon of atomic weight 12 and a radioactive isotope of carbon of atomic weight 14 which is formed in the upper layers of the atmosphere through the action of cosmic rays on nitrogen, falls upon earth and is absorbed by vegetation and ultimately by animals. The ratio of carbon 14 to carbon 12 remains fixed throughout life: one billionth of a gram for every gram of ordinary carbon. After death, when no more carbon 14 is absorbed, that part of it which is in the organism decreases slowly and regularly by reverting to nitrogen. As the curve of disintegration, or 'half-life' curve of carbon 14 is known (this is about 5,568 years), it is possible to find the date at which the organism died and consequently its age. This method can be applied to organic matter such as bone, wood, charcoal, shells, reeds, etc. found in archaeological excavations. But its usefulness is limited by a number of factors, in particular a 'standard deviation' (error of counting random radioactive desintegration) and an unavoidable margin of error. This means that although it is invaluable for prehistory where variations of several hundred years matter very little, it is practically of no help when precise historical chronology is required.

ARCHAEOLOGICAL RESEARCH IN IRAQ

The transformation of once flourishing cities into tells was more rapid than one might think.[14] Herodotus, in the middle of the fourth century BC, sees Babylon still alive, but neglects to visit Nineveh, destroyed a century and a half before, and Xenophon leading 10,000 Greek mercenaries across Mesopotamia in 401 BC passes near the great Assyrian capital without even noticing it.[15] Four centuries later, Strabo speaks of Babylon as of a town in ruins, 'almost completely deserted'.[16]

A thousand years went by. As the blanket of dust over the ancient cities grew thicker and thicker, their memory gradually faded away. Arab historians and geographers still knew something of Iraq's glorious past, but Europe had forgotten the East. The peregrinations of Benjamin of Tudela in the twelfth century and the travels of the German naturalist Rauwolff four hundred years later were isolated episodes. It was not before the seventeenth century that western interest in oriental antiquities was awakened after an Italian nobleman, Pietro della Valle, not only gave an entertaining account of his journey across Mesopotamia but brought back to Europe, in 1625, bricks found at Ur and Babylon 'on which were writing in certain unknown characters'. Gradually, it dawned upon academies and royalty that here was a field worth investigating. For the first time, in 1761, a scientific mission was sent out east by the king of Denmark with orders to gather as much information as possible in various fields including archaeology. The numerous inscriptions copied at Persepolis by its leader Karsten Niebuhr—a mathematician by profession—were put at the disposal of philologists who were soon at work deciphering the mysterious writing. From then on, nearly all the individuals who visited or lived in the Orient made a point of exploring ruins, collecting 'antikas' and copying inscriptions. Prominent among them are Joseph de Beauchamp, a distinguished French abbé and astronomer (1786), Claudius James Rich, a Resident of the East India Company and British Consul General in Baghdad (1807), Sir James Buckingham (1816), Robert Mignan (1827), James Baillie Fraser (1834) and that extraordinary army officer, sportsman, explorer and philologist, undoubtedly the greatest of all, Sir Henry Creswicke Rawlinson (1810–95). We should also mention here at least one important government-subsidized expedition of the early nineteenth century—the British 'Tigris–Euphrates Expedition' of F. R. Chesney (1835–6), which studied the course of the two rivers and collected a wealth of information on the country around them.

With the exception of the two holes dug by de Beauchamp and Mignan at Babylon, all these men confined their activities to the examination and measurement of the ruins as they saw them and were far from imagining what those 'desolate mounds' concealed. But in 1843 Paul Emile Botta, Italian-born French Consul in Mosul, started at Khorsabad the first archaeological excavations in Iraq, discovered the Assyrians and opened a new era. Almost at once (1845), an Englishman, Sir Henry Layard, followed his example at Nimrud and Nineveh, and soon a number of tells were excavated. In 1877, Emile de Sarzec, French Consul in Basrah, having heard of some statues found by chance at Telloh, near Nasriyah, decided to dig there and discovered the Sumerians. Thus, within thirty years a hitherto unknown civilization was revealed to the world, astonished to learn that Mesopotamia could yield nearly as many treasures as Greece or Egypt. Botta, Layard, Sarzec, Loftus, Smith, the pioneers of that heroic period were all amateurs in every sense of the term. They had no experience and little method. Their main object was to discover and send to the museums of their respective countries, statues, bas-reliefs, inscriptions and *objets d'art* in general. They had no time for mud bricks and broken pots, destroyed much and preserved little. But they opened the road and, despite obstacles of all sorts, they worked with an energy and enthusiasm which have never been surpassed.

Meanwhile, in the libraries of Europe, no less enthusiastic but more patient scholars were engaged in the fantastic task of deciphering the written documents which by then were pouring by the thousand into the museums. The history of this intellectual adventure cannot be outlined here, even briefly. Suffice it to say that the decipherment of the Assyro-Babylonian language, begun in 1802, was considered assured in 1847, and that by 1900, the other language of ancient Mesopotamia, Sumerian, was broadly comprehended.[17]

The entry on to the stage by the Germans at the turn of the century heralded a new approach to excavation work. Robert

Koldewey at Babylon (1899–1917) and Walter Andrae at Assur (1903–14) introduced strict, even meticulous techniques in a domain where luck and intuition had long reigned supreme. The German method was soon generally adopted and the twenty years between the two world wars witnessed what should perhaps be considered as the most brilliant and fruitful period in the history of Mesopotamian archaeology. These were the days when Woolley was digging Ur and its celebrated Royal Cemetery (1922–34), when Heinrich and his team were working at Uruk, Parrot at Mari, the British at Ubaid, Nineveh, Arpachiyah and Chagar Bazar, the Americans at Tepe Gawra, Nuzi and in the Diyala valley, and both the British and the Americans at Kish and Jemdat-Nasr. One by one, large and small tells were opened up and yielded their secrets. The main features of Mesopotamian history were defined piece by piece and beyond history older, fascinating cultures appeared which threw new light on the origins of civilization in that part of the world.

During this time, Iraq had emerged as a nation. Baghdad had now its own museum. Young Iraqi archaeologists had been trained, and excavations, far from coming to a complete standstill during the second world war, continued—with the most interesting results at 'Uqair (1940–1), Hassuna (1943–4) and 'Aqar Quf (1943–5). The war over, work was resumed by the Germans (Lenzen) at the huge site of Uruk, by the Americans (Heines and MacCown) at Sumer's religious capital, Nippur, by the French (Parrot), at Mari, the metropolis of the Middle Euphrates. Mallowan, on behalf of the British Museum, reopened Nimrud, the Assyrian military capital-city which had not been touched for over seventy years. Seton Lloyd, Taha Baqir, Fuad Safar for for Iraq Museum dug up three virgin sites: Eridu, one of the most ancient sacred cities of Iraq, Harmal, a modest mound unexpectedly rich in texts, and Hatra, the strange capital of a pre-Islamic Arab kingdom. Recently, the Japanese in Jazirah and the Danes in the Zab valley have joined in a field where international co-operation has always been practised on a large scale. At the time of writing, all the main cities of ancient Mesopotamia and a number of less renowned towns have been or are being excavated. But more than 6,000 tells from the Taurus to the Persian Gulf await the diggers—enough to keep busy several generations of archaeologists and epigraphists. And as though, in our search for the past, we were proceeding backwards, after the Assyrians, after the Babylonians, after the Sumerians, after the nameless peoples of the fourth and fifth millennia BC, the Stone-Age of Iraq has now been brought under the searchlight. Despite inevitable gaps in our knowledge, it has at last become possible to write a complete history of ancient Mesopotamia, starting from those very remote days when men chose the hills and caves of Kurdistan for their dwellings and left behind them the humble tools of chipped flint which betray their presence.

CHAPTER III

FROM CAVE TO FARM

ONLY twelve years ago, textbooks and scientific journals alike were silent on the prehistory of Iraq. Archaeological work had been concentrated on the Mesopotamian plain where prehistoric remains, if they ever existed, would be by now buried under a very thick layer of alluvium. The lowest levels of several tells had supplied enough material for historians to build up a sequence of five 'proto-historic' cultures which announced and explained the dawn of the Sumero-Akkadian civilization about 2800 BC, but all these cultures belonged to the late Neolithic and to the Chalcolithic ages and covered, at the most, a couple of thousand years. Prehistory proper, the Stone Age of Iraq, was practically unknown. True, a few worked flints had been found on the surface in various parts of Iraq and, as early as 1928, Professor D. A. E. Garrod, the lady archaeologist well known for her studies in prehistoric Palestine, had visited Kurdistan and found palaeolithic artefacts in two caves near Suleimaniyah, but these discoveries attracted little attention outside a small circle of specialists. Twenty years were to elapse before Professor R. J. Braidwood publicized the Neolithic site of Jarmo and aroused enough interest to promote further research in this long neglected field. Since then, the American excavations at Barda-Balka, Palegawra and Karim-Shehir (1951), the survey of the Zab basin by the Oriental Institute of the University of Chicago (1954–5) and the startling discoveries made by Dr R. Solecki in Shanidar Cave since 1951 have contributed considerably to our knowledge of Iraq's most ancient past and filled a much regrettable gap in Near Eastern prehistory.

In order to make our description of this new development in Mesopotamian archaeology clearer, a few words should first be said about the terminology used by prehistorians.[1]

The Old Stone Age, or Palaeolithic period, coincides with the geological period called Pleistocene because it is for geologists the most recent (*pleistos*) chapter in the long history of the earth. The Pleistocene, which started about half a million years ago and ended in about 10,000 BC, witnessed—at least in Eurasia and North America—four great advances and retreats of the polar ice-cap, four 'glacial periods' each of them lasting for several tens of thousand of years, separated by three 'interglacial periods' of no less considerable duration. It is generally assumed that, in contrast with the 'glacials' and 'interglacials' of the northern hemisphere, 'pluvials' (i.e. periods of very heavy rains) and 'interpluvials' occurred in tropical regions. Glacials and pluvials began and terminated very gradually and were punctuated by long spells of comparatively warmer or drier climate (interstadials). For absolute dating, we may refer to the following tentative figures proposed by Professor F. E. Zeuner:[2]

The First Glacial started about   600,000 years ago
The Second Glacial started about 500,000 years ago
The Third Glacial started about 250,000 years ago
The Fourth Glacial started about 120,000 years and began to
terminate about 20,000 BC.

Throughout this time men existed, sometimes living in the open, sometimes finding refuge in caves, always relying for their food on the game they hunted and on the wild fruit and roots they gathered. These men are known to us from their skeletons— exceedingly rare and fragmentary for very early periods—but mostly from the tools and weapons which they made out of stone, bone or ivory. In the language of prehistorians, stone implements of a particular site form an *industry*, and similar industries form a *culture*. Each culture has been given a name, derived from the site where it was first discovered or defined. Broadly speaking, there were two great trends in the techniques of stone work: either the core of a flint or chert nodule was reduced by chipping to a more or less ovoid object called 'coup-de-poing' or 'hand-axe', or the flakes detached from the core were worked by skilled hammering to the shapes of scrapers, cleavers, burins, points and the like. The distinction between core cultures and flake cultures, however, is more theoretical than real as, on many a site, core and flake techniques were practised simultaneously.

The Palaeolithic period is divided into three sub-periods termed Lower, Middle and Upper Palaeolithic.

Three main primitive cultures called Abbevillian, Clactonian and Acheulian form in Europe the Lower Palaeolithic which extends in time from the first glacial to the third interglacial and covers 300,000 or 400,000 years. They are essentially hand-axe cultures and differ from each other in the use of core or flake techniques and in minor details which need not concern us. The human remains associated with these cultures are at first those of ape-like creatures, but true human beings not very different from *Homo Sapiens* appear during the last stages of the period.

From the flake techniques of the preceding age derive the Levalloisian and Mousterian cultures which characterize the Middle Palaeolithic (second half of the third interglacial to last stages of the fourth glacial). This is the classical age of the cave-dwellers, the best known representative of which was the brutish 'Neanderthal man' now extinct.

The main features of the Upper Palaeolithic period which started about 35,000 years ago are the increasing diversity and complexity of flake techniques (Aurignacian and its Chatelperronian and Gravettian varieties, Solutrean and Magdalenian cultures in Western Europe), the development of bone, antler and ivory work, and the expression of magico-aesthetic tendencies, particularly in the superb Magdalenian rock paintings of France and Spain. The skill possessed by the several races of fully developed *Homo Sapiens* roaming Eurasia and North Africa led to the fabrication of an increasing number of small tools and weapons, and the blade industries of the Upper Palaeolithic gradually merged into the microlithic cultures (Capsian in Africa, Azilian and Tardenoisian in Western Europe) of the Mesolithic, or Middle Stone Age. Finally, the invention of agriculture and the domestication of animals, a revolution which reached Europe about 3000 BC but originated at a much earlier date in the Near East, mark the beginning of the Neolithic period, or New Stone Age.

Such is the frame into which we must now fit the prehistory of Iraq.

THE PALAEOLITHIC OF IRAQ

Although there is some evidence of cyclic glaciation in the Taurus and Zagros mountains, the great ice-sheet which four times covered a great part of Eurasia never reached as far south as the Near East. Iraq stood at the junction of areas subjected to sub-glacial and sub-pluvial conditions, and the climatic changes which took place in that country during the Pleistocene were never as dramatic as in other parts of the world. Nonetheless, they indirectly modelled its physiographical features. The level of the Persian Gulf fluctuated with the variations in the polar ice-cap, rising when it retreated, falling when it advanced, and this in turn influenced the profile of the rivers and their eroding action. On the other hand, phases of heavy rains accompanied by active erosion alternated with dry periods marked by extensive deposition of silt and gravel in the river beds. In one region at least of the Kurdistan foothills, four such successive cycles have been identified and connected with the last two glacials and interglacials.3 Hard as it is to imagine, there were times when large rivers flowed across the desert, when the Tigris and the Euphrates were perhaps as broad as the Amazon and when the two Zabs and the Diyala, carrying ten times as much water as they do now, were cutting deep and wide valleys into the ridges of Kurdistan. Throughout most of the Pleistocene both the western desert and the foothill region of Iraq were grassy steppes and uplands benefiting from a comparatively temperate and uniform climate and offering highly favourable conditions to the existence of prehistoric men.

No evidence of pure Lower Palaeolithic cultures has yet been found in Iraq. The most ancient traces of human presence in that country were discovered in 1949 by Dr Naji-al-'Asil, then Director-General of the Iraqi Department of Antiquities, at a place called Barda-Balka, one and a half miles north-east of Chemchemal, between Kirkuk and Suleimaniyah.4 There, around a megalith of Neolithic age, were palaeolithic flint tools lying on the ground. A sounding made in 1951 by two American scholars traced their origin to a once open 'workshop' or 'camp site' now buried under three to five feet of silt and gravel.5 The flint implements consisted of heart-shaped or almond-shaped hand-axes and of side-scrapers made out of flakes. There were also limestone 'pebble-tools', i.e. round pebbles from which one or two flakes had been struck off so that they could be used for scraping. This industry has strong affinities with the Acheulian, Tayacian (a derivative of Clactonian) and Mousterian cultures and has been attributed to the beginning of the Middle Palaeolithic period, that is to the very first stages of the last glacial, about 120,000 years ago.

A further step into the Middle Palaeolithic is represented by the mixed Levalloiso-Mousterian industry discovered in 1928 by Miss Dorothy Garrod in the lowest level of the 'Dark Cave' of Hazar Merd, about 12 miles south of Suleimaniyah.[6] But nowhere is the true Mousterian better illustrated than at Shanidar Cave excavated since 1951, by Dr R. Solecki, of the University of Michigan.[7]

Shanidar Cave is a rock shelter in the southern flank of the Baradost mountains overlooking the valley of the Greater Zab, not far from the small town of Rowanduz. It is still used in winter by Kurdish shepherds. Digging through its floor, Dr Solecki was able to reach a depth of 45 feet and to identify four occupation levels. In level D, the lowest and thickest (28 feet), successive layers of hearths and ash deposits mixed with bones and flint implements proved that the cave had been inhabited at various periods in Middle Palaeolithic times. The stone artefacts consisted of points, scrapers and borers typical of the Mousterian culture in its last phase. Animal bones were those of ox, sheep and goats suggesting a moderately cold climate, and there were numerous tortoise shells. But of special interest are the four human skeletons which level D contained: that of a 6-months-old child found in 1953, and those of three adults found in the 1956-7 season. The bones of the child and of two of the adults were in poor condition, but the skull of the fourth skeleton—a man about 35 years old, 5 feet 3 inches tall—could be restored with a fair degree of accuracy.[8] It exhibited all the features of the Neanderthal man: the thick bones, the massive chinless jaw, the sloping forehead, the prominent brow-ridges, and there is every reason to believe that the other individuals belonged to the same race. Dr D. T. Stewart who examined these remains could also diagnose that the arm of one of the Shanidar men, already crippled from birth, had been later amputated with a crude flint knife.9 All these people, it seems, were killed by huge blocks falling from the roof of the cave, though by no means at the same time. Three skeletons are believed to be about 45,000 years old while the fourth one, stratigraphically lower, might be as old as 60,000 years.

Level C of Shanidar Cave takes us well into the Upper Palaeolithic period. Through carbon 14 tests effected on the charcoal of its hearths, it has been possible to fix its lower and upper limits at 'more than 34,000 years' and 'about 25,500 BC' respectively. The stone material was of the blade-tool type characteristic of the Aurignacian cultures. As it contained some well-made gravers of unusual form, Dr Solecki has proposed for this industry the name of 'Baradost' or 'Baradostian' from the mountains in which the cave opens. The upper part of level C and the greater part of level B, immediately above, yielded samples of the same industry, but with a tendency for the artefacts to be undersized (microliths). This late Aurignacian or 'extended Gravettian' culture is represented in several paleolithic sites of Northern Iraq. Small round scrapers and 'pen knife' blades, and bladelets with deeply notched edges in particular were found in abundance in the cave of Zarzi, near Suleimaniyah, by Miss Garrod6 and in the cave of Palegawra, 20 miles to the east of Chemchemal, by B. Howe.10 They also occur in various caves explored by Professor Braidwood and his co-workers in 1954-5, especially Kaiwanian and Barak, west and south of Rowanduz.11 It appears that some at least of these small objects could be hafted and used as weapons to kill wild horses, deer, goats, gazelles, sheep and swine which then lived in a still cool but already drier country.

The Palaeolithic men of Iraq were not isolated. Through the Syrian desert—where Stone Age artefacts have been found in various places—they were in contact with the Palaeolithic men of Syria-Palestine, and it is not by chance that the flint industries of the two countries have so many strong resemblances. They also had commercial intercourse with the Anatolian plateau and the Iranian highlands. The material of Shanidar D and Hazar Merd, for instance, is almost identical with that of Bisitun Cave in Western Iran and in many points similar to that of Korain Cave in Turkey. In Upper Palaeolithic times, the men of Shanidar made some of their tools of obsidian (volcanic glass), the nearest source of which was in the Lake Van district in Armenia. Indeed, from camp to camp, stone-working techniques spread as far away as Europe if we are to believe with some authorities that the Aurignacian culture originated in the Near East. Yet, Iraqi Kurdistan, because of its semi-secluded position in a corner of the 'Fertile Crescent', retained its own characteristics. According to Solecki, the 'Baradost' industry is unique in the Near East, and the Neanderthal men of Shanidar, though somewhat more recent than those of Mount Carmel, do not, like the latter, seem to have mixed with or evolved towards Homo Sapiens, and remained 'conservative' in their physical characteristics. Finally, the Solutrean and Magdalenian cultures which, in Western Europe, succeeded the Aurignacian and flourished in late Palaeolithic times never reached Iraq—nor, for that matter, any other part of Western Asia. In those countries, the passage from Aurignacian to microlithic (Mesolithic) was direct, and the Mesolithic was but a short step from the Neolithic revolution.

MESOLITHIC AND NEOLITHIC

Microliths—those small flakes worked to an infinite variety of shapes—betray a stage in man's evolution when he became dexterous enough to perform minute tasks and clever enough to kill his prey at a distance (arrows). In the Near East, microlithic cultures apparently derived from the blade industries of the late Aurignacian in such a gradual way that it is practically impossible to fix a starting point for the Mesolithic period which they characterize. If dates are wanted, 10,000 BC (the lower limit of Shanidar B level as determined by radiocarbon tests) can be taken as a rough estimate.

It is equally difficult to say when the Mesolithic ended. Classically, it was succeeded by the Neolithic, or New Stone Age, but the distinction between the two periods is somewhat fallacious. The Neolithic, which ends with the first appearance of metal, begins with a revolution in man's feeding activities—the cultivation of plants and the domestication of animals—and *not* with the introduction of new techniques in stone work.[12] Microlithic tools were used for a very long time by Neolithic farmers before disappearing. Furthermore we cannot, with the material at our disposal, pinpoint the crucial passage from a food-gathering to a food-producing economy. It can be argued that hoes could be used for uprooting as well as for tilling, sickles for reaping naturally growing or deliberately grown wheat, querns and mortars for grinding and pounding wild seeds or even mineral pigments; and who can decide whether bones of sheep or cattle belonged to wild or to domesticated animals? All considered, our best criterion is perhaps the presence on a site of permanent habitations, for agriculture ties man to the land. But here again, it is not always easy to draw a firm line between the stone huts of hunters for whom agriculture was an occasional activity and the farms of fully settled peasants.

What appears clearly from the evidence available today is that the Neolithic revolution took place by progressive steps in the Near East some time around 7000 B C, much earlier than anywhere else, probably because the Near East offered the most favourable climatic conditions and was the only part of the Old World where emmer wheat and barley grew wild. Exactly where agriculture was 'invented' is still an unsolved problem, for both Iraq and Palestine can at present claim to possess 'the most ancient of all villages'. Iraq, however, has over Palestine the advantage of having four sites situated close together in its north-eastern region, which illustrate the transition from pure Mesolithic to indisputable Neolithic.

The first site is Shanidar level B which yielded microlithic flint and obsidian tools, 'very carefully and expertly chipped', together with hammer stones, rubbing stones and mullers: a typical Mesolithic cave-site with no convincing evidence of agricultural activity.

The second site, Karim-Shehir, six miles east of Chemchemal,[10] covers two acres and consist of one occupation level only, just below the surface. The flint artefacts, microlithic in character, are associated with objects which can be regarded as agricultural tools: flint sickle blades, chipped-and-ground stone hoes and milling stones. In addition, a very irregular pebble pavement spread over the whole area suggests hut floors, though no plans of habitations are recognizable. If Karim-Shehir was, as it is thought, a camp site of semi-nomads, it represents a very early stage in the development towards sedentary life.

A more permanent type of agricultural community probably occupied the third site, Mlefaat.[13] In that small mound near the Kirkuk-Erbil road, were found pit-houses, some of them surrounded by walls of piled-up stones and paved with pebbles. The tools consisted mostly of stone celts and mortars.

A gap of unknown duration separates Mlefaat from our fourth site, Jarmo, not far from Chemchemal. Jarmo was excavated by Professor R. J. Braidwood, of the University of Chicago, in 1948, 1950-1 and again in 1955.[14] The 23-feet high artificial mound rests on top of a very steep hill and is formed of fifteen layers of superimposed habitations. Ten of these layers are characterized by the absence of pottery and belong to the same 'pre-ceramic Neolithic' cultural stratum. The inhabitants of Jarmo lived in square, multi-roomed houses built of pressed mud (pisé), with mud-ovens and baked-in clay basins sunk in the ground. They ate with bone spoons, sewed with bone needles, and their stone spindle-whorls show that they could weave or plait flax and perhaps wool. They used microlithic and normal-sized flint and obsidian blade tools, in particular sickles made of flint fixed with bitumen to a wooden backing. But most of the heavy objects lying about in the rooms, such as axes, celts, saddle-querns, hand-rubbers, mortars, pestles and vases were of limestone, often beautifully ground. These objects together with carbonized grains of wheat and barley leave no doubt about the agricultural activities practised at Jarmo, while 95 per cent of the animal bones found were those of domesticable—if not already domesticated—animals: sheep, cattle, pigs and dogs. These people adorned themselves with simple clay or stone necklaces, grooved bracelets of marble and shell pendants, buried their dead under the floor of their houses and modelled clay figurines of animals and of a steatopygous, pregnant woman, the 'Mother Goddess' who presumably embodied for them the mysterious forces of fecundity. Pre-ceramic Jarmo was first dated by radiocarbon tests on snail shells about 4750 BC, but further tests on charcoal gave higher figures and Professor Braidwood now takes 6500 BC as a more likely date.[15]

Thus, 3,500 years at least before Europe, northern Iraq was the scene of the Neolithic revolution, the most important perhaps of all times. On the foothills of Kurdistan watered every winter by the Atlantic rains, man ceases to be a wandering hunter depending for his living upon his luck and skill and becomes a farmer attached to the small piece of land from which he obtains a regular food supply. Out of clay he builds himself a house. He invents new tools to perform new tasks. He secures in sheep and cattle a permanent and easily available source of milk, meat, wool and hide. At the same time his social tendencies develop, for the care and defence of the land call for close co-operation. Each family probably erects its own farm, cultivates its own field, grazes its own flock and makes its own tools; but several families are grouped together and form a hamlet, the embryo of a social organization. Later, other revolutions will occur: metal will replace stone, villages will grow into cities, cities will be united into kingdoms and kingdoms into empires. Yet, the essentials of life, the labour of man bent over mother earth and enslaved to the cycle of seasons has not changed since those remote days.

The absence of pottery in ten out of fifteen levels singles out Jarmo as one of the most primitive agricultural communities and an exception among the other Neolithic sites explored in Western Asia, since practically all of them have yielded some kind of ceramic. The only other notable exception is Jericho near the Dead Sea, 600 miles from Jarmo, where Miss Kathleen Kenyon has recently unearthed a large and quite remarkable pre-ceramic Neolithic settlement with houses built of mud bricks—and not of simple *pisé*—and a strong city-wall of undressed stones.[16] Moreover, Jericho seems to be older than Jarmo in absolute chronology if we accept the figure of 6800 B C given by radiocarbon tests. The objects found in the two sites, however, have very little in common and no influence of one upon the other is detectable. It would appear therefore, that the Neolithic revolution took place at different dates and under slightly different forms in various parts of the Near East.

The potsherds present in the upper levels of Jarmo, the large 'grain bins' of archaic Tell Hassuna (see next chapter), the 'milk jars', 'husking trays' and bowls of baked clay found at Tell Matarrah[17] are the first examples in Iraq of the last invention of Neolithic men. This early pottery is, as expected, purely utilitarian, coarse, badly fired, fragile and unattractive. But portable clay vessels no doubt were soon in great demand, and oriental potters were not slow at perfecting their technique. At the same time, the creative ability inherent in their art prompted them to indulge in various forms of decoration. The burnished, painted and incised ceramic which soon appears on most of the Near and Middle Eastern Neolithic sites is not always of high artistic value. Nor does it represent an important cultural progress. But it is of immense interest to archaeologists and marks for them the beginning of a new era. Easier to recognize and to identify than plain pottery, decorated earthenware plays in archaeology the same part as fossils play in geology. It is the hall-mark of late prehistoric cultures and helps us in our attempt to reconstruct the complex pattern of large-scale cultural relationships and ethnic movements which fills the next two thousand years of Mesopotamian prehistory.

CHAPTER IV

FROM VILLAGE TO CITY

THUS, five thousand years before Christ, the Zagros foothills and the Tigris basin in the north of Iraq are occupied by Neolithic farmers and cattle-breeders living in small villages of pressed mud, using stone-age tools, practising stone-age magic and grouped, it seems, into independant social units hardly larger than clans or families. About two thousand years later, however, history begins, this time at the other end of Iraq, in the southern part of the Tigris-Euphrates valley. There, we are confronted with a highly organized and complex society. The country is divided between several states centered by comparatively large cities, and the master of each state is a god ruling through a prince of his choice. Agriculture, based upon canal irrigation, produces enough surplus to feed a population of specialized priests, civil-servants, scribes and artisans. Writing is known and put to many uses. Architecture, sculpture and metal-work display signs of exceedingly skilled, often brilliant craftsmanship. Religion, which governs public and private life, embraces a formidable pantheon, and the whole economy of the city-state revolves around the temple of its chief god. Such is, in brief, the picture offered by the Sumerian civilization, at the beginning of the third millennium BC. Needless to say that the twenty centuries which witnessed the formation and birth of this civilization are of exceptional interest and deserve the closest attention.

The story of the passage from Neolithic to History cannot yet be told in full detail because our information is still scanty and sporadic. At least we know that it took place within Iraq itself. Forty years of archaeological excavation have discredited the old theory according to which the Sumerian civilization had originated in some mysterious and remote country and had been imported into Mesopotamia fully fledged. We can now trace back each of its elements to one stage or another of Iraqi prehistory, and it appears that, while some were brought in by foreign invasion or influence, others had roots so deep into the past that we may call them indigenous. Like all civilizations, the Sumerian was a mixed product whose shape was, to a large extent, determined by the mould into which the components were poured.

Because written documents are lacking, the peoples behind the scene must remain nameless. We know that two main linguistic-ally distinct human groups—Sumerians and Semites—lived in southern Mesopotamia in early historical times; yet, we cannot say with certainty when they appeared and what part they played in this slow, spasmodic development. All we have to solve our problems are material remains which speak for themselves, but which are of little value when it comes to detecting political events and ethnic movements. In this respect, pottery is perhaps the most useful relic, for it is found in abundance on all sites and lends itself to comparative studies. Although changes in pottery styles may be due to a variety of reasons and do not necessarily indicate a change of population, the ceramic criterion handled with caution, is a fairly reliable index of relations between different cultures. It should never be forgotten that ancient Iraq was no more a closed country than is modern Iraq. It was open to influences from all points of the compass and capable, in turn, of influencing the surrounding areas. Whether such exchanges were purely commercial and peaceful, or whether they were tied with military campaigns or ethnic migrations is a very difficult problem. All we can say is that the last part of pre-history was probably a period of considerable instability among the populations of the Near East. No doubt, as the climate in that part of the world became increasingly drier, a large number of hunting tribes must have left the mountains or the deserts and tried to settle, if necessary by force, within the horns of the 'fertile crescent' where a more secure way of life awaited them.

The long span of time that we are about to enter, those centuries when Mesopotamia was pregnant, so to speak, with Sumer, form what some archaeologists call 'proto-history'. Proto-history has been divided into five great periods, each of them characterized by a distinctive cultural assemblage, and named after the site where this assemblage was first identified. They are, in chronological order:

the Hassuna-Samarra period,
the Halaf period,
the Ubaid period,
the Uruk period,
the Jemdat-Nasr (now often called 'Proto-literate') period.

As we shall presently see, these divisions do not actually apply to the whole country under study. The first two cultures are restricted to the North, the last two, to the South. Moreover, the reader should be warned that all is not as clear in practice as it is on paper, and that scholars are still divided on the question of the exact limit between the Uruk and the Proto-literate periods and even on the name which should be given to the latter. But we shall leave out academic discussion of this kind and concentrate on describing, one by one, the successive culture-periods of proto-historic Mesopotamia.[1]

THE HASSUNA-SAMARRA PERIOD

The site, typical of this period, is Tell Hassuna, 22 miles south of Mosul, excavated in 1943-4 by the Iraqi Directorate of Antiquities under the direction of Seton Lloyd and Fuad Safar.[2] There, resting on the virgin soil, were coarse pottery and implements suggestive of a Neolithic farming community, presumably living in huts or tents, for no trace of buildings was found. But, overlying this primitive settlement were six layers of houses, progressively larger and better built (levels Ib–VI). In size, plan and building material, these houses were strangely similar to those of present-day northern Iraqi villages. Around a courtyard, six or seven rooms were arranged in two blocks, one block serving as living quarters, the other as kitchen and stores. The walls were made of adobe, the floors paved with a mixture of clay and straw. Grain was stored in huge bins of unbaked clay sunk in the ground up to their mouth, and bread was baked in domed ovens resembling the modern *tanur*. Mortars, flint sickle-blades, stone hoes, clay spindle-whorls and crude figurines were present. Large jars kept inside the houses contained the bones of deceased children accompanied by tiny cups and pots for after-life refreshment while, strangely enough, much liberty seems to have been taken with the disposal of adult skeletons piled up in the corner of a room, thrown in clay bins 'without ceremony', or buried in cist graves without the usual funerary gifts.

All this reminds of Jarmo, but the presence of decorated pottery indicates a somewhat higher cultural stage and permits interesting comparisons between Hassuna and other parts of the Near East. Briefly, the ceramic material of Hassuna falls into three categories termed by the excavators 'archaic', 'standard' and 'Samarran'.

The *archaic* pottery ranges from level Ia to level III and is represented by: (1) tall, pear-shaped jars of coarse clay. This home-made, strictly utilitarian type of ceramic is found on prac-tically all sites of Neolithic western Asia and yields little informa-tion; (2) bowls of a finer ware, varying in colour from buff to black or red according to the method of firing, with a surface 'burnished' by rubbing with a stone or bone. There is little doubt that this pottery was imported into Iraq from the west, more precisely from the 'isthmic' region between Turkey and Syria (Sakje-Gözü in the Amanus mountains, Mersin in Cilicia, the 'Amuq plain around Antioch) where it is found in abundance; (3) bowls and jars with a glossy surface and a simple, geometric decoration in red colour. This archaic painted pottery apparently originated in Syria-Palestine and spread eastwards. Samples of it have been found as far away from Hassuna as Jericho and Megiddo in Palestine.

Here is therefore positive evidence for a community of culture in the whole area of the 'Fertile Crescent', from the Dead Sea to the Tigris, with a main focus along the Mediterranean. Moreover, the skulls from Hassuna which have been studied belong, like the skulls of Byblos and of Jericho, to 'a large toothed variety of the long-headed Mediterranean race'[3] and suggest an underlying unity of population. Yet, the so-called '*Hassuna standard ware*', predominant in levels IV to VI, is peculiar to northern Iraq and seems to be an essentially local product. The decoration, restricted to a small part of the vessels, consists of simple designs (straight lines, triangles, cross-hatchings) effected by the application of a matt brown paint on a matt background and/or by shallow incisions. The forms are limited to globular jars with straight necks and to bowls with a round or flat base. The whole fabric is original, perhaps, but rather crude.

In the upper levels of Hassuna, however, the clumsy products of the local potters are mixed with a truly sumptuous crockery, unexpected in such primitive surroundings, which bears the name of *Samarra ware* because it was first discovered in a prehistoric cemetery underneath the houses of the famous Abbassid capital.[4] Both decoration and forms are here remarkably elaborate. On the pale, slightly rough surface of large plates, around the rim of carinate bowls, on the neck and shoulder of round-bellied pots are painted, not only a variety of geometric designs arranged in neat, regular horizontal bands, but representations of scorpions, birds, fish, antelopes and even human beings. These motives are conventional, but perfectly well balanced and treated in such a way that they give an extraordinary impression of movement. Undoubtedly, the people who modelled and painted these vessels were great artists. In all probability, they had come, not from the west, but from that great province of painted pottery: Iran. The limited diffusion of the Samarran ceramic, however, evokes the image of small groups of perambulating craftsmen rather than of conquerors: it occurs only in the Upper Tigris valley, from Samarra to Nineveh, in Upper Jazirah (Tell Halaf, Tell Chagar Bazar) and at one point of the Euphrates valley, Baghuz, opposite Abu-Kemal.[5]

Thus, the humble village of Hassuna offers an excellent illustration of the various influences to which Neolithic Iraq was subjected. Stimulated by this double current from the East and from the West, endowed with an artistic sense of their own, the Mesopotamians, after an unknown number of years, went a step further on the path of cultural development.

THE HALAF PERIOD

The second period of proto-historic Mesopotamia takes its name from Tell Halaf, a large mound overlooking the Khabur river near the village of Ras-el-'Ain, on the Turko-Syrian frontier. There, just before the first world war, a German archaeologist, Max Freiherr von Oppenheim, came upon a thick layer of beautifully painted pottery immediately below the palace of an

Aramaean ruler of the tenth century BC. The discovery was not published until 1931.[6] At that time, little was known of Near Eastern prehistory, and the date of Oppenheim's 'Buntkeramik' was the subject of much controversy. During the following years, however, the excavations conducted by Professor M. E. L. Mallowan at Nineveh,[7] at Tell Arpachiya near Mosul,[8] and at Tell Chagar Bazar in Jazirah[9] put the 'Halaf period' in its proper chronological context and supplied a complete picture of its cultural assemblage.

Although purely Neolithic in its tool equipment, the Halaf culture offers a number of new and very distinctive features. The settlements are still of village type and size, but cobbled streets at Arpachiya indicate some kind of municipal caretaking. The houses are larger and better built than those of Hassuna. Pisé or adobe remain in use, but the first mud bricks appear, at least in the Khabur basin. Undoubtedly, the most outstanding monuments of the new period are the buildings called *tholoi* (plural of *tholos*) by analogy with the tombs of Mycenae of much later date, which they resemble. Ten such tholoi were found at Arpachiya, approximately two for each occupation level. They are vaulted, beehive-shaped structures of pisé resting on circular stone foundations, 13 to 32 feet in diameter. To some of them is appended a long, rectangular antechamber built in the same material. Contrary to the Mycenaean tholoi, those of Mesopotamia rose above the ground and contained no bones nor grave furniture. In fact, they were completely empty and, for this reason, it is very difficult to imagine what their exact function was. Several theories have been propounded, but none of them is very convincing. Their small number, their central position, the care with which they were built and rebuilt, the accumulation of burials and of votive objects around them suggest that these monuments played an important rôle in the life of the community. They may well have been shrines or religious buildings of some sort; alternatively, one may think of secular buildings, of 'town halls' where the notables of the village met to take important decisions. There are at present, in the marshes of southern Iraq, lofty and often handsome reed-houses called *mudhifs*, that serve a similar purpose.

No less interesting than the mysterious tholoi are some of the small objects found in abundance at Arpachiya and elsewhere. We allude, in particular, to steatite pendants of various shapes and to small stone discs with a loop at the back engraved with straight lines or criss-cross patterns. These objects, probably worn on a string around the neck, were impressed on lumps of clay fastened to baskets or to jar stoppers as a mark of ownership. We have here the very first examples of the stamp-seal, and the stamp-seal is the forerunner of the cylinder-seal, a typical and, in many respects, important element of the Mesopotamian civilization.[10] Also characteristic of the Halaf period are stone maceheads, amulets in the form of a bull's head, a bull's hoof or a double-axe, and terra-cotta figurines of a dove and a 'Mother-Goddess'. The latter—no doubt a legacy from Palaeolithic times—has now quite distinctive traits. The woman is usually represented squatting—perhaps in the position of accouchement—her knees sharply drawn up, her arms encircling her heavy breasts. The head is reduced to a shape-less lump, but the body is 'naturalistic' and covered with painted stripes and dots which may represent tattooings, jewellery or clothing. It is probable that these figurines were talismans against the hazards of childbirth or against sterility rather than actual images of a goddess.

Last but not least comes the pottery and, in this domain, the progress over the preceding cultures is quite striking. It can be said without exaggeration that, during the Halaf period, the ceramist's art reached a degree of perfection never attained before or after in Mesopotamia. The Halaf ware is made by hand in a fine, ferruginous clay slightly glazed in the process of firing. The walls of the vessels are often very thin, the shapes varied and dar-ing: round pots with large flaring necks, squat jars with rolled out rims, beakers, footed chalices, large and deep 'cream bowls' with a carinated, angular profile. The decoration lacks perhaps the bold movement of the Samarra ware, but it is perfectly adapted to the shapes, minutely executed and pleasant to the eye in the manner of Persian rugs. On a cream or peach 'slip' is laid, first in black and red, later in black, red and white, a closely woven pattern that covers most of the vessel. Triangles, squares, checks, crosses, scallops and small circles are among the favourite designs, though flowers, sitting birds and crouching gazelles are also encountered. Most characteristic of all and perhaps loaded with religious symbolism are the double-axe, the 'Maltese square' (a square with a triangle on each corner) and the *bukranum*, or stylized bull's head.

In spite of obvious Iranian influences, the Halaf pottery is essentially a local product. From its centre of origin, around Nineveh, we can follow its diffusion in a westward direction, along the caravan route which leads to the Mediterranean *via* the Khabur (Brak, Chagar Bazar, Halaf), the Balikh (Tell Aswad), the Euphrates (Karkemish), Syria, Cilicia and even Lycia. But the connections of the Halaf culture do not stop there. Before its great antiquity was recognized, some scholars thought that the polychrom ceramic of Tell Halaf was of Greek origin.[11] This is certainly not true, though there is no doubt that it has some affinities with the Neolithic painted wares of continental Greece. The *tholoi*, on the other hand, have parallels in Cyprus (Khirokitia), in Crete (Messara plain) and, at a later date, in the Peloponnesus (Mycenae), and it is certainly not by chance that the mother-goddess, the dove, the double-axe and the *bukranium* are the standard cult objects both in Minoan Crete and in pre-Hittite Anatolia.[12] Migrations from the East, unity of culture, or community of origins? The time has not yet come when such major problems can be solved.

THE UBAID PERIOD

After what looks like several centuries of existence, the Halaf culture at the peak of its development came to an abrupt end. In one or several waves, invaders coming, it seems, from south-western Iran[13] brought into Iraq a new culture which bears the name of a small site only four miles from Ur 'of the Chaldees', al-'Ubaid.[14] This name is significant, for it implies that the South, as well as the North, is now involved. For the first time, Mesopotamia appears as a cultural and perhaps political unit.

To be sure, there are indications that the southern half of Iraq was already inhabited during the Halaf period. Recent geological studies coupled with archaeological research have shown that the Tigris-Euphrates delta was formed much earlier than was formerly believed, and the classical picture of the Ubaid folk moving into the plain and settling on muddy islands 'just emerged from the receding sea' must be revised. In 1937-9, for instance, the German expedition digging at Uruk found at a neighbouring place called Qal'at Hajj Muhammed a painted ceramic which, in fabric and decoration, was different from the standard Ubaid ware.[15] This settlement, it should be noted, had been buried under ten feet of alluvium and was only exposed in the bed of the Euphrates at low water. Then came the extraordinary discovery made by the Iraqi Directorate of Antiquities at Eridu in 1946-9.[16] Eridu (Abu Shahrain, 16 miles south-west of Ur) was one of the most sacred cities of ancient Mesopotamia, being the earthly residence of Enki, the god of subterranean waters and one of the main deities of the Sumerian pantheon. The ruins are now marked by low mounds and sand dunes at the foot of a much dilapidated 'ziqqurat', or stage-tower, erected—as inscribed bricks tell us—by the kings of the Third Dynasty of Ur, about 2100 BC. But, under a corner of this ziqqurat, Fuad Safar and his team unearthed an impressive series of seventeen temples built one above the other in proto-historic times. The eight upper temples were elaborate buildings dating from the Uruk and Ubaid periods; the poorly preserved remains of temples IX to XIV below them yielded a mixture of Ubaid and Hajj-Muhammed-like ceramic, and finally, still deeper, appeared temples XV, XVI and XVII (the latter reduced to fragments of walls). In many respects, the earliest temples differed from anything hitherto known in southern Iraq. They consisted of one single, rather small square room with an altar facing the entrance; they were built of long, prismatic mud-bricks bearing deep thumb impressions and, above all, they contained a painted pottery which, in the opinion of experts, closely resembled the Hajj Muhammed ceramic, but was also loosely related to the Halaf and Samarra wares.[17] Clearly then, the site had been occupied long before the Ubaid period began by a people somehow connected with the 'Halafians' in the north. Another inescapable conclusion was that the same religious tradition had been handed down from century to century on the same site, from the fourth millennium BC until well into historical times. Perhaps one day other deep soundings, at Nippur for instance— the city of another great Sumerian god, Enlil—will yield similar results.[18] The more we dig, the more we find that the Sumerian civilization was very deeply rooted into the past.

The hall-mark of the Ubaid culture is, as usual, the painted pottery. Even easier to identify on a site than the Halaf pottery, it is somewhat cruder and less attractive. The clay, frequently overfired, varies in colour from buff to green. The paint is matt, dark-brown or bluish-black, the decoration confined as a rule to only a part of the vessels. Though occasional plants, animals and broad sweeping curves are not without elegance, the monotony of the standard motifs (triangles, striped or cross-hatched bands, broken or wavy lines) betrays a lack of imagination. Yet, the fabric is fine, some specimens seem to have been made with a slow wheel or 'tournette', and spots and loop-handles appear for the first time. Among the most typical forms are a bell-shaped bowl, a jar with a basket handle, and a lenticular vessel with a long spout called 'tortoise-shell'. This pottery is found throughout Mesopotamia with but slight regional variants, but there are marked differences between the North and the South as regards the rest of the Ubaid cultural assemblage.

The words 'clay and reed' would aptly qualify the Ubaid culture in southern Iraq. As stone is rare in that part of the country, its use was limited to heavy tools, blades and personal ornaments. All other objects were made of terra cotta, including the so-called 'clay nails' (in fact, probably pounders), crescent-shaped clay sickles, and even axes, adzes and knives. The 'mother-Goddess' type of clay figurine—a slim standing woman with a snake-like head crowned with a coil of hair made of bitumen—was very popular, and there were figurines of men as well. A number of houses, the majority perhaps, were frail structures of reed matting, supported by wooden poles and plastered or not with clay. One such 'hut' (or rather, a partitioned courtyard annexed to a brick building such as can be seen today in and around Basrah) was found at Eridu, amazingly well preserved. But bricks were widely used for more elaborate buildings. At Eridu, again, the temples belonging to the Ubaid period were built of large mud-bricks set in clay mortar, and consisted of one long, rectangular *cella* with smaller rooms at each angle. At one end of the *cella*, against the wall, was a low platform which probably supported the statue of a divinity, while at the other end stood a brick altar or offering table. Externally, the walls were decorated with shallow buttresses and niches that caught the light and broke the monotony of the plastered brick-work. Let us note this decoration: it has an obscure but definite religious meaning and persists throughout history as a distinctive feature of practically all Mesopotamian sanctuaries.

If we now turn to the North, we are confronted with a somewhat different picture. The site here is Tepe Gawra, 15 miles northeast of Mosul, excavated from 1931 to 1938 by an American expedition.[19] This high and narrow mound comprises eighteen levels which range from the Halaf period to the middle of the second millennium BC, the Ubaid period being represented by levels XIX to XII. At Tepe Gawra, reed habitations are unknown and all the houses are made of bricks. Stone, on the other hand, is frequently used, and stone stamp-seals, very rare in the south, are here quite numerous; they now bear, instead of linear designs, representations of animals and of human beings arranged in what may perhaps be considered as mythological scenes. Metal objects, in small number, appear for the first time and their presence, almost exclusive to this site, can probably be accounted for by the proximity of the mining districts of Armenia, Azerbaijan and the Caucasus.[20] But other characteristics peculiar to the North cannot be explained by geography alone. Thus, if the three temples around a courtyard which form a majestic 'acropolis' in Gawra level XIII closely match the Eridu temples in many respects, two *tholoi* betray persisting traditions, as does the 'Mother-Goddess', sitting and painted in the Halaf period style. More important perhaps, the burial customs at Eridu and at Gawra are completely different. At Eridu, in a large cemetery just outside the village, adults and children alike are buried lying on their backs in graves lined and covered with bricks. At Gawra, most of the graves are simple inhumation pits grouped around the temples, and the bodies lie contracted on one side; children are buried in urns. This, among other things, suggests that the bearers of the Ubaid culture were in a minority in the North.[21] Subjected but not eliminated, the descendants of the 'Halafians' still probably formed a large part of the population, whereas the South was entirely 'Ubaidian'. In the next chapter, we shall see how the gap between the North and the South gradually widened and how the South took the lead in the march towards civilization.

These regional differences, however marked, do not alter the

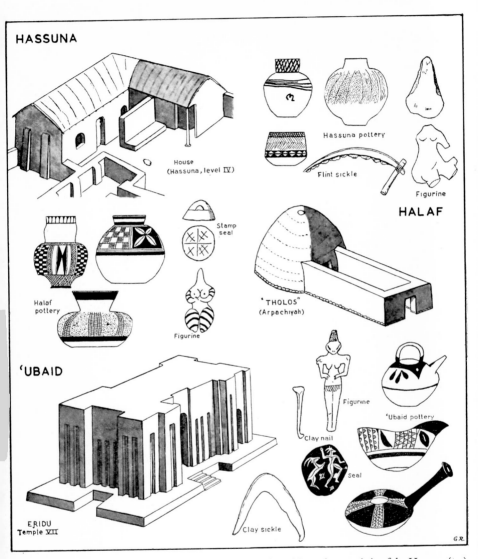

PLATE 3. Buildings, pottery, clay figurines, seals and other objects characteristic of the Hassuna (*top*) Halaf (*centre*) and 'Ubaid (*lower*) periods.

C. The votive stone vase from Uruk (3 feet 7 inches high). The carving represents Inanna, the goddess of love and fecundity, receiving sacrificial offerings. (Proto-literate period.)

PLATE 4

A. Life-size face of a woman, queen or goddess found at Uruk. It is flat at the back and was probably attached to a statue. (Proto-literate period.)

B. Archaic pictographic tablet from Kish. (Proto-literate period.)

fundamental unity of the Ubaid culture. Imported first, it seems, into the Mesopotamian delta, it expanded along the twin rivers and eventually spread over Jazirah and northern Syria. The Taurus and the Zagros mark its limits, but neither of these mountains offered an insuperable barrier to commercial intercourse. The reality and extent of this trade is attested by the presence of metal at Tepe Gawra, of obsidian near the Persian Gulf and of amazonite (a semi-precious stone found only in India) at Ur. Although probably no more than a simple form of basin irrigation was practised in the southern plain, the supply of food was sufficient to support a fast-growing population. The new settlements, extremely numerous, were situated along the main rivers or on their branches and communicated with each other by water, as illustrated by the clay models of boats found at Ur and at Eridu. Because, on most sites, the Ubaid stratum was only reached at the bottom of narrow test-pits it is impossible to say whether these settlements were hamlets, villages or small towns. But it is remarkable that all the main cities of ancient Sumer sprang from them. Another fact has yet wider implications: of all the buildings of the Ubaid villages, the temple was always the largest and best constructed; moreover, the same religious architectural traditions were maintained on the same spot from the Ubaid period to early historical times, that is, for almost a thousand years. Thus, the Sumerian city progressively grew, not around a palace or a castle, but around a shrine. In all probability, the temple was already the hub around which economic and social activities revolved. We do not feel entitled, at this early stage, to pronounce the word 'Sumerians', but we must recognize that the Ubaid period prepared the ground for the development of the Sumerian civilization.

CHAPTER V

BIRTH OF A CIVILIZATION

As the reader will have noticed, we have abstained from giving 'absolute' dates to the proto-historic periods. The reason is that, until the results of radio-carbon tests become available, any attempt to establish a chronology rests upon such inadequate grounds as the depth of occupation levels or the time we think it must have taken for a culture to develop and to degenerate. As a very rough estimate, one can perhaps assume that the Hassuna and Halaf periods occupied the whole of the fifth millennium BC, while the Ubaid period, apparently very long, covered the first six or seven hundred years of the fourth millennium. When we come to the final stages of proto-history, however, correlations with Palestine and Egypt[1] make things comparatively easier and the following tentative dates can be advanced:

Uruk period	3300–3100 BC
Proto-literate period	3100–2800 BC

During these five hundred years, the cultural development which, up to then had been slow, progressed at a quicker pace and finally the Sumerian civilization blossomed. But this took place only in the south of Iraq. The northern part of that country followed a different course and, though not exactly 'barbarian', lagged behind in many respects. Several reasons concurred to endow the south with such a privilege. We have seen how superficial the Ubaid influence had been in the north, and it is just possible that the peasants of the Upper Tigris were more con-servative, less open to progress than those of the Lower Euphrates. On the other hand, rivers and canals isolated to some extent the southern half of Iraq from the periodical devastating raids of nomads and highlanders. But the decisive factor was no doubt the enormous common effort required by artificial irrigation, for it implies the existence of co-ordinating authorities at least on a regional scale and must have led to an early concentration of power and wealth in a few hands and on a few points. Some villages became more important and richer than the others. Around their temples—already, we assume, the centres regulating the whole economy—gathered that part of the population that lived for them and from them: priests of various ranks, of course, but also storekeepers, overseers, guards, foremen, architects, masons, carpenters, tinsmiths, potters, stone-cutters and so on, and these villages slowly grew into towns. In that way, southern Mesopotamia passed from a rural to an urban type of social organization eminently suitable to artistic achievements and technical progress. The geographical factors that made life harder in the South than in the North made it also more civilized. This process, incidentally, was not restricted to Mesopotamia: the archaic civilizations of Egypt, India and China, were also born in broad valleys and were founded on river irrigation.

The passage from village to city coincides in Iraq with the appearance of new pottery forms, the invention of the potter's wheel, the replacement of the stamp-seal by the cylinder-seal and several other developments culminating in the invention of writing, shortly before 3000 B C. These changes are so important that, in the opinion of several scholars, they can only have resulted from a foreign invasion. Yet, if invaders are postulated, it is surprising how little we know of them. Their country of origin, their numerical importance, the road they followed and the form taken by their intrusion are questions either unanswerable or open to much controversy. On the other hand, a close examination reveals no drastic changes in social organization, no real break in architectural or in religious traditions. We are confronted here, not with a sudden revolution, but with the final term of an evolution which had started in Mesopotamia itself several centuries before.

The culture-period resulting from these new conditions is attested only on a few sites of southern Iraq. Among them, Uruk —the site after which it was named—remains the most important. It is therefore at Uruk itself that we must study the 'Uruk culture'.

THE URUK CULTURE

The ruins of Uruk (biblical Erech, modern Warka) rise impressively, in a desert area about half-way between Baghdad and Basrah, not far from the small Arab town of Samawa. In antiquity, Uruk was dedicated to two divinities: An (or Anu), the sky-god, and the goddess of love, Inanna, better known under her Semitic name Ishtar. In the middle of the ruins, around a mud-brick ziqqurat, stands the temple of the goddess, E-Anna ('the House of Heaven'), a vast complex of buildings and courtyards constantly rebuilt and enlarged from prehistoric times to the Achaemenian domination. The temple of Anu, more modest, lies in another part of the city. It is mainly in these two areas that the German archaeologists who have been digging at Uruk-Warka since 1928 unearthed before the war the remains characteristic of the new culture: temples, pottery, cylinder-seals and tablets.[2]

The archaic temples of Uruk were very similar in plan to those of the Ubaid period at Eridu already described: the buttressed façade, the long *cella* surrounded by small rooms, the doors on the long side testify to the persistence of architectural traditions as well, probably, as of belief and cult. In E-Anna six such sanctuaries were discovered. They were arranged in pairs in three successive layers, a fact that has led Professor H. Lenzen to suggest that they were dedicated not only to Inanna, but also to her consort the fertility-god Dumuzi.[3] Particularly remarkable were the lowermost levels with their enormous temples—one of them, built on limestone foundations, measured 260 by 100 feet—and their extraordinary 'mosaic building'. The latter consisted of a large courtyard extending between two sanctuaries and bridged by a raised portico of eight massive brick columns, eight feet in diameter, arranged in two rows. The side walls of the courtyard, the columns themselves and the platform on which they rested were entirely covered with a coloured pattern of geometrical design formed by the flat end of terra-cotta cones, three or four inches long, which had been painted in black, red or white and then stuck into the mud plaster. This original and very effective type of decoration was widely used during the Uruk and Protoliterate periods, and loose clay cones can still be picked up by the thousand in the ruins of Warka. The colour, when preserved, has lost its brightness, but little effort is required to imagine what a fresh cone-mosaic façade must have looked like in the glaring oriental sunlight. This taste for colour is also manifest in the use of wall painting. One of the archaic temples of E-Anna, the so-called 'Red Temple,' owes its name to the pink wash which covered its walls, and at Tell 'Uqair, 50 miles south of Baghdad, the Iraqi Directorate of Antiquities excavated, in 1940–1, a temple of the Uruk period decorated with frescoes, which, when discovered, were 'as bright as the day they were applied';4 human figures, unfortunately damaged, formed a procession, and two crouching leopards guarded the throne of an unknown deity. All these temples, it must be noticed, rested on low brick platforms, as did the temples of the Ubaid period at Eridu. But with time the platform became higher, tending to be more important in size than the building itself. Here, in all probability, is the origin of the ziqqurat, the stage-tower topped by a shrine so typical of the Mesopotamian civilization in historical times.5 This evolution is illustrated by the Anu temple of Uruk where six temples built in succession were finally included in a truly monumental platform rising fifty feet above the plain. At the top of this platform are the remains, amazingly well preserved, of a sanctuary dating to the late Uruk period, the so-called 'White Temple'. And to stand between these walls, at the very place where officiated, five thousand years ago, the priests of the sky-god, leaves the visitor with an unforgettable impression.

The magnificence of this architecture tends to dwarf the other forms of art. Yet the seal impressions of the Uruk period are little masterpieces. At that time, the stamp-seal was almost completely superseded by the cylinder-seal, a small cylinder of stone bored throughout and engraved on the outside which would, when rolled on clay, repeat the motif *ad infinitum*. The earliest cylinder-seals were engraved with great skill and their subjects arranged with considerable ingenuity. But their value is not only artistic: they are almost the only objects of that period that are alive with people and give us an inkling of their occupations. For instance, a cylinder-seal representing a massacre of prisoners bespeaks war, while the frequent occurrence of cattle walking in herds, gathered around their pens or attacked by lions evokes the farmers' main preoccupation. Mysterious ceremonies performed by naked priests are also frequently represented. We have here for the first time, besides an art in miniature, a source of information which, at all periods, will prove useful to the historian of ancient Mesopotamia.

At first sight, it is surprising to find how much artistic sense was lavished on the decoration of buildings and on stone-cutting and how little on ceramics.[6] Among the pottery—unpainted as a rule —of the Uruk period, only a few jet black and highly polished pieces, and possibly the red-slipped vessels are fairly pleasant to look at. The remainder, either plain or grey slipped and burnished, is dull. Cups with handles, and jars or bottles with long, often curved spouts, obviously copy metal-work, but the common forms are rarely elegant. Perhaps the availability of bronze and silver vessels as well as the invention of the potter's wheel which enabled mass production are responsible for the decadence of a once flourishing art. However, the possibility of this ceramic being foreign to Mesopotamia and imported by trade or invasion cannot be altogether excluded.

But the Uruk period witnessed another novelty immensely more important than the wheel, the cylinder-seal or the cone-mosaic decoration, an epoch-making invention comparable only to the invention of agriculture in Neolithic times. It is towards the end of the period, in the archaic temples of E-Anna in Uruk, that writing appears for the first time in the form of pictographic tablets.[7]

The writing used in Mesopotamia throughout history and known as 'cuneiform' was originally—as all primitive writings, past or present—a collection of small, simplified drawings, or *pictograms*. The earliest texts from Uruk and elsewhere are already too complex to represent the first attempt made by men to preserve their thoughts, and in all probability the first pictograms were engraved on wood or painted on skins or leaves. But such media must have disintegrated long ago in the humid subsoil of Iraq and the only documents that have survived are written on clay. The process of writing was in itself very simple: the scribe took a lump of fine, well washed clay and shaped it as a small, smooth cushion, a few inches square. Then, with the end of a reed stalk cut obliquely, he drew lines dividing each face of the cushion into squares and filled each square with incised drawings. The 'tablet' was then either baked or left unbaked. Baked tablets are nearly as hard as stone; old, unbaked tablets crumble into dust between the fingers, but if they are collected with care, allowed to dry slowly in the shade and hardened in an oven, they become almost indestructible.

The earliest texts in our possession were written in Sumerian.[8] This language being largely monosyllabic, writing was based, as in Chinese, on the principle: one object or idea equals one sound equals one sign. The first pictograms were therefore extremely numerous (more than 2,000). Some of them represent objects easy to identify, such as agricultural tools, vases, boats, heads of animals or parts of the human body, while others appear to be purely conventional. But because it is very difficult to represent abstract ideas graphically, one pictogram was often used to express several words and could be read in several ways. For instance, a foot would not only mean 'foot' (pronounced *du* in Sumerian), but also ideas related to the foot such as 'to stand' (*gub*), 'to go' (*gin*), 'to come' or 'to bring' (*tum*). Reciprocally, some concepts totally unrelated but pronounced with the same sound were grouped under the same sign. Thus, the sign of the bow was used for 'bow' (*ti*), but also for 'to live' (*ti* or *til*). Normally, in classical Sumerian, the correct reading of a sign is indicated either by the context or by other signs called 'phonetic complements', 'determinatives', or 'grammatical particles'. But the archaic texts had nothing of this kind. Moreover, the signs were laid down in apparent disorder, and some of them, used only in ancient periods, were later abandoned so that their phonetic value (or values) is unknown. For these reasons, we cannot *read* the pictographic tablets. All we can say is that they have all the characteristics of economic documents (lists of workmen, lists of goods, receipts, etc.) and could not tell us what we would like to know above all: the events that took place during the Uruk period.

THE PROTO-LITERATE PERIOD

In 1925, an eminent Oxford assyriologist, Stephen Langdon, discovered at Jemdat Nasr, between Baghdad and Babylon, a distinctive pottery consisting, in the main, of large thick jars decorated with geometrical or naturalistic designs in black and/or red paint applied directly on the buff clay.[9] Later, the 'Jemdat Nasr ware' was found, always in small quantities, on other southern Mesopotamian sites and was taken as the hall-mark of a cultural period immediately preceding history, the so-called 'Jemdat Nasr period'. As research progressed, however, it was found that a few pots can hardly make a culture and that, if a dividing line had to be drawn, the invention of writing was a much better landmark. Hence the term 'Proto-literate' proposed by the Chicago school of orientalists and adopted by a number of scholars.[10]

We say 'period' and not 'culture', for between the cultural elements of the Proto-literate period and those of the Uruk period there is no fundamental difference, but simple variations in style and quality. Architectural remains are rare but sufficient to prove the absence of drastic changes in the plan and decoration of temples; only the stress is now put on their platforms, and the cone-mosaic decoration generally applied in panels instead of covering every inch of the walls. Cylinder-seals carry the same religious and secular scenes, though these tend to become stereotyped and conventional. Writing is more and more in use, but the pictograms are less numerous, less 'realistic' and are often used for their phonetic value alone. The bulk of the ceramic is identical to the plain Uruk pottery and the rare 'Jemdat Nasr ware', apparently of Iranian inspiration, may represent nothing more than a transient local fashion. The wheel, the plough (depicted on tablets) were certainly invented before, and stone and metal vessels are obviously the products of a long tradition. All things considered, sculpture represents perhaps the only original contribution of the new period to the progress of the arts.

Practically unknown before, sculpture suddenly appears, soon reaches a high degree of perfection and is applied with passion to a large variety of objects, Lions attacking bulls, heroes mastering lions, sullen boars, peaceful ewes and rams are carved in relief or in the round on stone vases and bowls, on troughs, on mural plaques and on the back of the rare stamp-seals that have survived. Also from that time date the first statuettes of worshippers offered as *ex-votos*, so frequent in early historic Sumer. And a rather crude basalt stele found at Warka, which represents two bearded men killing lions with spear and arrows, is the oldest known ancestor of the famous Assyrian hunting scenes. If all this is not always of excellent quality, two objects—both found at Uruk—are as yet without rival in the whole world for that period.[11] One is a 3-feet high alabaster vase carved in low relief with perfect skill, where the goddess Inanna is shown receiving gifts from a man of high rank, perhaps a priest, a chief or even a god. This vase was already regarded a valuable *objet d'art* in antiquity, for it had been repaired with metal clips. The other masterpiece is an almost life-size mask of a woman made of marble. The eyes are unfortunately missing, but the face is modelled with that mixture of delicate realism and sensitivity which is rarely found before the classical period of Greek sculpture.

Progress in techniques, achievements in art, writing, all these are the symptoms of a fully mature civilization which should be called without hesitation 'Sumerian'. Born and bred in southern Iraq, this civilization radiated over the entire Near East and exerted a deep influence on the other oriental cultures. We can well imagine that the as yet undeciphered 'Proto-Elamite' script on clay, which appears about that time in nearby Elam (southwest Persia), was inspired by the archaic Sumerian writing or invented by a related people. But it is more difficult to understand through which channel and in what circumstances Egypt borrowed from Mesopotamia.[12] Yet the late prehistoric graves of Naqadah have yielded typical Mesopotamian Proto-literate cylinder-seals, and the object itself was adopted by the Egyptians who engraved it with their own traditional designs and, having no clay tablets on which to roll it, used it for centuries as an amulet. Similarly, favourite Mesopotamian motifs such as hunting scenes, lions devouring cattle, or beasts with long, intertwined necks were copied by Egyptian sculptors just as the Egyptian architects of the First Dynasty built their royal tombs with the recessed façades of the Mesopotamian temples. Indeed, some authorities believe that the Sumerian pictograms antedate the earliest hieroglyphs and may well have inspired their inventors. This one-way influence is the more remarkable since contacts between the two great focuses of civilization in the Near East have always been surprisingly rare and superficial throughout ancient history.

Strangely enough, in Mesopotamia itself the archaic Sumerian civilization remained localized to the southern half of the country. True, faint traces of it were detected at Mari, on the Middle Euphrates,[13] and Professor Mallowan in 1938-9 excavated at Tell Brak, in the Khabur basin, a typically 'Proto-literate' temple on a platform, which he calls the 'Eye Temple' because it contained thousands of small stone idols engraved with a pair of staring eyes.[14] But Tell Brak stands out as an exception and perhaps represents a colony of southern Mesopotamians detached from their homeland. For obscure reasons the rest of Jazirah and the Tigris valley long remained impervious to the progress realized a few dozen miles further south. Throughout the Uruk and most of the Proto-literate period, for instance, the inhabitants of Tepe Gawra fought with maces and slings, continued to use stamp-seals, made their pottery by hand and ignored writing, though they drove in four-wheeled chariots and buried their chiefs with a wealth of grave furniture unequalled in the south at that time. The 'Gawra culture' was eventually replaced by the 'Nineveh culture' (level 5 of the deep sounding at Nineveh) characterized by a wheel-made, rather attractive, painted or incised pottery and by Sumerian weapons and seals. But by that time, Sumer had already entered history, and the whole of the Early Dynastic period (*circa* 2800-2400 BC) was to elapse before the first written documents appeared in the North in the wake of the Akkadian conquerors.[15]

The gap between the North and the South, opened at the end of the fourth millennium, was never entirely filled in ancient history. After the Akkadians, successively the Sumerian kings of the Third Dynasty of Ur and Hammurabi of Babylon held under their sway the Upper Tigris and the foothills of Kurdistan. Yet, from their inscriptions one forms the impression that these districts were considered somewhat foreign and culturally inferior. The Hittite raid on Babylon (1595 BC) and the long period of semi-anarchy that followed the Kassite domination put an end to the political supremacy of the South. The North then took its revenge and the kings of Assur and Nineveh ruled over the whole of Mesopotamia. But the Babylonians never willingly accepted government by these 'barbarians' and repeatedly tried to shake off the yoke, while the mighty monarchs of Assyria themselves, who piously collected the old Sumerian texts and regularly took

part in the New Year Festival of Babylon, implicitly acknowledged their debt to a very ancient and venerable civilization.

THE SUMERIAN PROBLEM

Who are these Sumerians, whose name can now be pronounced
for the first time and who are going to occupy the stage of history
for the next thousand years? Do they represent a very ancient
layer of population in prehistoric Mesopotamia, or did they come
from some other country, and if so, when did they come and
whence? This important problem has been debated again and
again ever since the first relics of the Sumerian civilization were
brought to light, nearly a century ago, and is still with us. The
most recent discoveries, far from offering a solution, have made
it even more difficult to answer, but at least they have supplied
fresh and solid arguments to an old debate and it is in this new
light that the 'Sumerian problem' should be examined.[16]

The word 'Sumerian' comes from the ancient name of the
southern part of Iraq: *Sumer* or, more exactly, *Shumer*, usually
written in cuneiform texts with the signs KI.EN.GI.[17] At the
beginning of historical times, three ethnic groups lived in close
contact within that region: the Sumerians, predominant in the
extreme south from approximately Nippur (near Diwaniyah) to
the Persian Gulf—the Semites, predominant in central Mesopotamia (the region called *Akkad* after 2400 B C)—and a small, diffuse
minority of uncertain and mixed origin to which we can attach
no definite label. From the point of view of the modern historian,
the line of demarcation between these three components of the
first historical population of Mesopotamia is neither political nor
cultural, but linguistic. All of them had the same institutions; all
of them shared the way of life, the techniques, the artistic traditions, the religious beliefs, in a word the civilization which had
originated in the extreme south and is rightly attributed to the
Sumerians. The only reliable criterion by which we can separate
and identify these three peoples is therefore their language.
Stricto sensu, the appellation 'Sumerians' should be taken as
meaning 'Sumerian-speaking people' and nothing else; similarly,
the 'Semites' were those who spoke a Semitic dialect; and indeed
we would be unaware of the existence of the third ethnic element

were it not for a few strange, non-Sumerian and non-Semitic personal names and place names which occur here and there in the texts. This, incidentally, explains why all efforts to define and to assess the relations between Sumerians and Semites in other fields than philology are doomed to failure.[18] Another point should be made quite clear: there is no such thing as a Sumerian 'race', neither in the scientific nor in the ordinary sense of the term. The skulls from Sumerian graves that have been examined are either dolicho- or brachy-cephalic and indicate a mixture of the so-called Armenoid and Mediterranean races, the latter being somewhat predominant.[19] As for the physical features depicted on monuments, they are largely conventional and have therefore no real value. The big, fleshy nose, the enormous eyes, the thick neck and flat occiput long considered to be typical of the Sumerians also belong to the statues of individuals bearing genuine Semitic names found in the almost exclusively Semitic district of Mari, while more realistic portraits such as those of Gudea, the Sumerian governor of Sumerian Lagash, show a short, straight nose and a long head.

Philology alone is often a good index of ethnic relationship. Thus the Greeks, the Hittites and the Indo-Aryans, though dispersed over a wide area, were related to each other through the Indo-European languages they spoke, and probably came from a common homeland in southeastern Europe. But in the case of the Sumerians, philology is of no help. The Sumerian language is 'agglutinative', which means that it is formed of verbal radicals modified or inter-connected by the apposition of grammatical particles. As such, it belongs to the same category as numerous dialects spoken from Hungary to Polynesia. Yet it bears no close resemblance to any known language, dead or living. The Sumerian literature presents us with the picture of a highly intelligent, industrious, generally peaceful and deeply religious people, but offers no clue as to its origins. Sumerian myths and legends are almost invariably drawn against a background of rivers and marshes, of reeds, tamarisks and palm-trees—a typical southern Iraqi background—as though the Sumerians had always lived in that country, and there is nothing in them to indicate clearly an ancestral homeland different from Mesopotamia.[20]

We are therefore obliged to fall back on archaeology, that is to say on the material elements of the Sumerian civilization. The question here is: among the various ethnic groups responsible for the successive proto-historic cultures of Mesopotamia, which can be identified with the Sumerian-speaking people of history? Put in this way, the problem is, of course, insoluble since we do not know what languages were spoken in Mesopotamia before the Uruk period. Whatever answer is given, it can only rest on broad generalization, intuitive thinking or mere guesswork. On this question scholars in general are divided into two groups: for some, the Sumerians came to Mesopotamia during the Uruk or the Proto-literate period: for others they were already there in Ubaid times at the latest. We cannot enter here into a detailed discussion but, personally, we are rather inclined to agree with the tenets of the second theory. True, the Sumerian *writing* appears for the first time at the end of the Uruk period, but this does not imply that the Sumerian language was not spoken before. Again, there are in ancient Mesopotamian literature place names that are neither Sumerian nor Semitic, but do they necessarily represent the traces of an older and exclusive population? As for the change in pottery style which marks the beginning of the Uruk period, who can say with certainty whether it was brought about by invasion, foreign influence or a purely local change of fashion? In fact, in all respects except pottery, the Uruk culture appears as the development of conditions that existed during the Ubaid period. The persistence of religious traditions throughout, in particular, is remarkable. To take only one example among many: the thick layer of fish bones which covered the floor of the Ubaid temples at Eridu[21] offers a near certitude that the deity worshipped there was already the Sumerian water-god Enki.

Can we go further back into the past? If we accept ceramics as a reliable criterion, the Ubaid folk appear to have come from Iran and other signs indicate that, in the north of Iraq at least, they behaved as conquerors and imposed their law upon older populations. But the 'Eridu ware', on the other hand, suggests that the first inhabitants of the South were in some way related to both the Ubaidians and the northern Halafians, as if these were two branches from the same stock. And the Halafians, in turn, may well have descended from the Neolithic farmers of Hassuna and Jarmo. Thus, the more we try to push back the limits of our problem, the more it thins out and vanishes in the mist of pre-history. One is even tempted to wonder whether there is any problem at all. The Sumerians were, as we all are, a mixture of races and probably of peoples; their civilization, like ours, was a blend of foreign and indigenous elements; their language belongs to a linguistic group large enough to have covered the whole of Western Asia and much more. They may well, therefore, represent a branch of the population which occupied the greater part of the Near East in early Neolithic and Chalcolithic times. In other words, they may have 'always' been in Iraq and this is all we can say. As one of the most brilliant orientalists once put it: 'The much discussed problem of the origin of the Sumerians may well turn out to be the chase of a chimera.'[22]

CHAPTER VI

THE GODS OF SUMER

WHATEVER the real origin of the Sumerians, there is no doubt that their civilization sprang from the prehistory of Iraq itself. It reflected the mood and fulfilled the aspirations of the stable, conservative peasant society which has always formed the backbone of that country; it was 'Mesopotamian' in origin and in essence. For this reason, it survived the disappearance of the Sumerians as a nation about 2000 BC and was adopted and carried over with but little modification by the Amorites, Kassites, Assyrians and Chaldaeans who, after them, ruled in succession over Mesopotamia. The Assyro-Babylonian civilization of the second and first millennia is therefore not fundamentally different from that of the Sumerians, and from whatever angle we approach it, we are almost invariably brought back to a Sumerian model.

This is particularly true of religion. For more than three thousand years, the gods of Sumer were worshipped by Sumerians and Semites alike; and for more than three thousand years, the religious ideas promoted by the Sumerians played an extraordinary part in the public and private life of the Mesopotamians, modelling their institutions, colouring their works of art and literature, pervading every form of activity, from the highest functions of the kings to the day-to-day occupations of their subjects. In no other antique society did religion occupy such a prominent position, because in no other antique society did man feel himself so utterly dependent upon the will of the gods. The fact that the Sumerian society crystallized around temples and was first organized on a theocratic basis had deep and lasting consequences. In theory, for instance, the land never ceased to belong to the gods, and the mighty Assyrian monarchs whose empire extended from the Nile to the Caspian Sea were the humble servants of their god Assur just as the governors of Lagash who ruled over a few square miles of Sumer were those of their god Ningirsu. This, of course, does not mean that economics and human passions did not play a part in the history of ancient Iraq as they did in the history of other countries; but the religious motives should never be forgotten nor minimized. As an introduction to the historical periods which we are about to enter, a brief description of the Sumerian pantheon and religious ideas will surely not be out of place.[1]

THE SUMERIAN PANTHEON

Our knowledge of Mesopotamian religious and moral ideas derives from a variety of texts—epic tales and myths, rituals, hymns, prayers, incantations, lists of gods, collections of precepts, proverbs, etc.—which come, in the main, from three great sources: the sacerdotal library of Nippur (the religious centre of Sumer), and the palace and temple libraries of Assur and Nineveh. Some of these texts are written in Sumerian,[2] others are Assyrian or Babylonian copies or adaptations of Sumerian originals even though, in a few cases, they have no equivalent in the Sumerian religious literature discovered so far. The dates when they were actually composed vary from the end of the third millennium to the last centuries before Christ, but we may reasonably assume that they embody verbal traditions which go back to the Early Dynastic period (*circa* 2800–2400 BC) and, possibly, even earlier, since a number of Sumerian deities and mythological scenes can be recognized on the cylinder-seals and sculptured objects from the Uruk and Proto-literate periods. Before these, positive evidence is lacking, but the unbroken continuity of architectural traditions, the rebuilding of temple upon temple in the same sacred area suggest that some at least of the Sumerian gods were already worshipped in southern Iraq during the Ubaid period.

With the gradual development of civilization in lower Mesopotamia a class of men emerged who had the leisure to ponder over the great problems of origins, of good and evil, of death and after-life. The formulation of religious ideas and their casting in myth form were certainly slow processes, carried out by several 'schools' of priests simultaneously; but somehow, in the end, a

PLATE 5. From the 'Royal Cemetery' of Ur. A harp found in the 'Great Death Pit' and partly restored. Beneath the bearded bull's head, made of solid gold, is a set of shell plaques engraved with scenes of animal life.

PLATE 6. The so-called 'standard' from the Royal Cemetery of Ur. The two sides and the ends of this prismatic object are decorated with panels of shell, lapis-lazuli and red limestone set in bitumen. On the 'war side', shown here, Sumerian soldiers are fighting and naked prisoners are brought to the King.

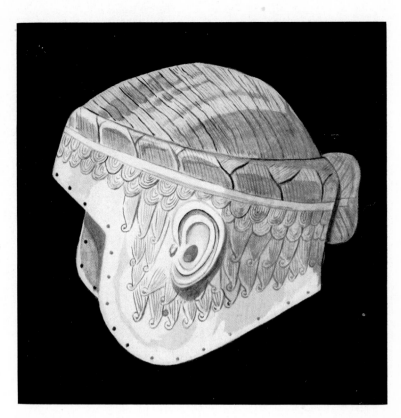

PLATE 7

A. From the Royal Cemetery of Ur. The gold helmet of Meskalamdug.
This ceremonial helmet reproduces the hair-dress of the time and is made of
one sheet of 15 carat gold.

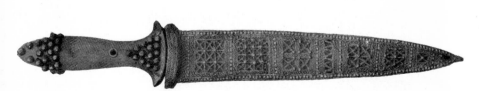

B. From an anonymous grave of the Royal Cemetery of Ur. A gold dagger
with a hilt of lapis-lazuli, in its gold sheath.

PLATE 8
A. Gold tumbler from
the Royal Cemetery
of Ur.

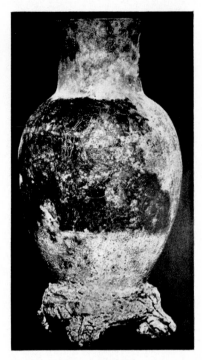

B. The silver vase of Entemena, *ensi*
of Lagash (from Telloh.)

C. Votive plaque from
Telloh, portraying
Ur-Nanshe, an early
ensi of Lagash, with
his family.

general agreement on principles was reached, and while each city retained its own patron-god and its own set of legends, the whole country worshipped a common pantheon. The divine society was conceived as a replica of the human society of Sumer and organized accordingly. The heavens were populated with hundreds of supremely powerful manlike beings, and each of these gods was assigned to a particular task or a particular sphere of activity. One god, for instance, had charge of the sky, another of the air, a third one of the sweet waters and so forth, down to the humble deities responsible for the plough, the brick, the flint or the pickaxe. In fact, the expressions 'had charge of' and 'were responsible for' are misnomers, since the Sumerians believed that every element, every category of objects possessed a dynamic personality, a set of active properties, a 'will' of its own, and it was these forces immanent in nature which the gods embodied.3 These gods, like the Greek gods, had the physical appearance and all the qualities and defects of human beings: they were highly intelligent but could run out of ideas; they were good in general, but also capable of evil thoughts and deeds; they were subject to love, hatred, anger, jealousy and all other human passions; they ate and drank and got drunk; they quarrelled and fought and suffered and were wounded and could even die—i.e. go and live in the Netherworld. In brief, they represented the best and worst of human nature on a superhuman scale.

The gods of Mesopotamia were not all of equal status. A number of them were relatively unimportant deities entitled, at the most, to a small chapel at the corner of a street. Others, such as Shara and Zababa—respectively the patron-gods of Umma and Kish—were only really great in their own city-states, just as governors are great in their provinces. Yet others, though more especially worshipped in certain towns, were by virtue of their nature the objects of a general cult. Such were, for instance, the moon-god Nanna (called Sin by the Semites), the patron-god of Ur, and his son,4 the sun-god Utu (Semitic Shamash), the patron-god of Sippar and Larsa. Both dispelled darkness, a quality which, taken figuratively, affected every human being, for while the moon-god read into the dark future and 'knew the destinies of all', the sun-god 'lay bare the righteous and the wicked' as it flooded the earth with blinding light. To the same category belonged Ninurta, the warrior-god, the 'Mother-Goddess' Ninhursag, and the great goddess of love and procreation Inanna —better known to the public under her Semitic name Ishtar— together with her husband Dumuzi. Dumuzi (the Tammuz of the Semites) deserves special mention because it was for a long time believed that he was a vegetation-god who died and was resurrected every year, symbolizing the disappearance of grass and grain in the summer and their reappearance in the spring.[5] This belief was founded upon a series of Babylonian texts known as 'Tammuz lamentations' which deplored in poetic style the death of the god, upon a misunderstanding of the Sumero-Akkadian myth of 'Inanna's (or Ishtar's) descent to the Nether-world',[6] and upon what is known from late sources of the cult of Adonis-Tammuz as practised by the Phoenicians towards the end of the first millennium BC. In recent years, however, an improved reading of the Sumerian epic tales and a thorough revision of all the material available have led such eminent scholars as Kramer, Jacobsen and Falkenstein to the conclusion that Dumuzi was never resurrected at all, that he was not released from the Nether-world by Inanna but taken there by force in order to take his wife's place and prevented from returning to earth.[7] It would seem, then, that the idea of a 'dying and resurrected god', so dear to some historians of religion, has to be abandoned—at least as far as Dumuzi-Tammuz is concerned. Yet it cannot be denied that this god, now considered as a purely 'chtonic' deity, was closely associated with vegetation, flocks and cattle, and his union with the goddess of love can be regarded as a typical example of the Fertility Cult practised by all the peoples of the Near East since Neolithic times. But it must be emphasized that, in the country of Sumer, the power of procreation was not the privilege of one single divine couple. What Inanna and Dumuzi did for Uruk, their main residence, other gods—not necessarily endowed with a strong agrarian or sexual character—could do for other cities, and it is now generally admitted that each city-state ensured the fertility of its own fields and the fecundity of its own people and cattle by means of a Sacred Marriage between its patron-god and one of its goddesses. This marriage, celebrated once a year in the spring, formed an essential part of the New Year Festival which will be described later in detail. (See below, Chapter XXIV.)

Finally, we come to the three male gods who stood as dominating figures in the vast Sumerian pantheon: An, Enlil and Enki.

An (Anu or Anum in Akkadian) embodied 'the overpowering personality of the sky'[8] of which he bore the name, and occupied first place in the Sumerian pantheon. This god, whose main temple was in Uruk, was originally the highest power in the universe, the begetter and sovereign of all gods. Like a father he arbitrated their disputes and his decisions, like those of a king, brooked no appeal. Yet An—at least in the classical Sumerian mythology—did not play an important part in earthly affairs and remained aloof in the heavens as a majestic but somewhat pale figure. At some unknown period[9] and for some obscure reason, the patron-god of Nippur, Enlil, was raised to what was in fact the supreme rank and became in a certain sense the national god of Sumer. Much later, he himself was in turn wrested of his authority by the hitherto obscure god of Babylon, Marduk; but Enlil was certainly less of an usurper than Marduk. His name means 'Lord Air' which, among other things, evokes immensity, movement and life (breath), and Enlil could rightly claim to be 'the force in heaven'[10] which had separated the earth from the sky and had thereby created the world. The theologians of Nippur, however, made him also the master of humanity, the king of kings. If An still retained the insignia of kingship, it was Enlil who chose the rulers of Sumer and Akkad and 'put on their heads the holy crown'. And as a good monarch by his command keeps his kingdom in order, so did the air-god uphold the world by a mere word of his mouth:

'Without Enlil, the Great Mountain,
No city would be built, no settlement founded,
No stalls would be built, no sheepfolds established,
No king would be raised, no high priest born . . .
The rivers—their floodwaters would not bring over flow,
The fish in the sea would not lay eggs in the canebrake,
The birds of heaven would not build nests on the wild earth,
In heaven, the drifting clouds would not yield their moisture,
Plants and herbs, the glory of the plain, would fail to grow,
In fields and meadows, the rich grain would fail to flower,
The trees planted in the mountain-forest would not yield their
    fruit . . .'[11]

The personality of the third greater god is far more subtle and complex. Enki literally means 'Lord Earth', but possibly because the earth without water cannot bear fruit, Enki soon became the deity of the sweet waters that flow in rivers and canals, rise in springs and wells and bring life to the Mesopotamian delta. In fact the Semites called him Ea, a Sumerian name which can be translated as 'House (or Temple) of the Waters'.[12] Of the life-giving fluid, Enki had all the qualities: ubiquity, limpidity, purifying and fertilizing properties, but also—as we shall see in the Adapa legend—deceiving mobility and treacherous charm. Enki-Ea, the tutelary god of Eridu, was above all the god of intelligence and wisdom, 'the broad-eared one who knows all that has a name'. He stood as the initiator and protector of arts and crafts, of science and literature, the patron of the magicians, the Great Teacher and the Great Superintendent who, having organized the world created by Enlil, assured its proper functioning,

> 'The "big brother" of the gods, who generates prosperity,
> Who budgets the accounts of the universe,
> The ear and the mind of all the lands.'[13]

There were many other important Sumerian gods, some of whom will be met in the following chapters. But An, Enlil and Enki were the greatest of all. They ruled the world through authority, force and wisdom as it should be ruled and formed the supreme triad responsible not only for the regular functioning of the cosmos but also, as we shall presently see, for its creation.

TALES OF CREATION

The Mesopotamians imagined the earth as a flat disc surrounded with a rim of mountains and floating on an ocean of sweet waters, the *abzu* or *apsû*. Resting on these mountains and separated from the earth by the atmosphere (*lil*) was the sky vault along which gravitated the astral bodies. A similar hemisphere underneath the earth formed the Netherworld where lived the spirits of the dead. Finally, the whole universe (*anki*: sky-earth) was immersed, like a gigantic bubble, in a boundless, uncreated, primeval ocean of salt

water. The earth itself consisted of nothing more than Mesopo-
tamia and the immediate neighbouring regions; in its centre stood
Babylon for the Babylonians and, probably, Nippur for the
Sumerians.

How and by whom had the world been created? The answers
to this question varied, no doubt because they were founded on
different traditions.[14] One legend stated that Anu had created the
heavens and Enki the *apsû*, his abode. Another legend attributed
the creation of the universe to the general assembly of all the gods,
and yet another to only four great gods acting collectively. The
beginning of an incantation against the 'worm' responsible for
toothaches says that Anu created the sky which created the earth
which in turn created the rivers, the rivers the canals, the canals
the marshes and the marshes the worm. But this sounds rather
like the nursery rhyme 'The house that Jack built' and should
perhaps not be taken too seriously. More interesting is a version
from the town of Sippar according to which the great Babylonian
god Marduk had 'built a reed platform (or raft) on the surface of
the waters, then created dust and poured it around the platform',
because this is actually how the marsh Arabs of southern Iraq
make the artificial islands upon which they erect their reed-huts.[15]
In general, the Sumerians believed that the primeval ocean,
personified by the goddess Nammu, had begotten alone a male
sky and a female earth intimately mixed together. The fruit of
their union, the air-god Enlil, had separated the sky from the
earth and, with the latter, had engendered all living creatures.
The theory that the ocean was the primordial element from which
the universe was born, that the shape of the universe had resulted
from the forceful separation of heaven from earth by a third party
was generally adopted in Sumer, Babylonia and Assyria, and
forms the basis of the most complete and detailed story of creation
that we possess: the great Babylonian epic called from its opening
sentence *Enuma elish*, 'When on high . . .'. But the Babylonian
genesis has still wider philosophical implications; it describes the
creation not as a beginning but as an end, not as the gratuitous
and inexplicable act of one god, but as the result of a cosmic
battle, the fundamental and eternal struggle between those two
aspects of nature, Good and Evil, Order and Chaos.

Enuma elish is a long poem in seven tablets originally composed during the Old Babylonian period (beginning of the second millennium), though all the copies found so far were written during the first millennium B C. In most copies the main part is played by Marduk, the patron-god of Babylon, but an Assyrian version substitutes the name of Ashur, the national god of Assyria, for that of Marduk. On the other hand, Marduk is once called in the poem 'the Enlil of the gods', and as we know that Marduk had usurped the rank and prerogatives of the Sumerian god Enlil, we can confidently surmise that the hero of the epic was originally Enlil, as in the Sumerian cosmogony already mentioned.[16]

The Mesopotamian story-writers took their inspiration from their own country. If we stand near the present Iraqi sea-shore, at the mouth of the Shatt-el-'Arab, on a misty morning, what do we see? Low banks of clouds hang over the horizon; large pools of sweet water, seeping from underground or left over from the river floods, mingle freely with the salty waters of the Persian Gulf; of the low mud-flats which normally form the landscape no more than a few feet are visible; all around us, sea, sky and earth are mixed in a nebulous, watery chaos. This is how the authors of the poem who, no doubt, had often witnessed such a spectacle, imagined the beginning of the world. When nothing yet had a name, that is to say when nothing had yet been created, they wrote, Apsu (the sweet waters), Tiamat (the salt waters) and Mummu (the clouds[17]) formed together one single confused body:

'Enuma elish la nabû shamamu . . .
When on high the heaven had not been named,
Firm ground below had not been called by name,
Naught but primordial Apsu, their begetter.
(And) Mummu (and ?) Tiamat, she who bore them all,
Their waters commingling as a single body;
No reed-hut had been matted, no marsh land had appeared;
When no gods whatever had been brought into being,
Uncalled by name, their destinies undetermined—
Then it was that the gods were formed within them.'

In the landscape already described, larger patches of land emerge from the mist as the sun rises, and soon a clear-cut line separates the sky from the waters and the waters from the earth. So, in the myth, the first gods to emerge from the chaos were Lahmu and

Lahamu, representing the silt; then came Anshar and Kishar, the twin horizons of sky and earth. Anshar and Kishar begot Anu and Anu, in turn, begot Ea (Enki). At the same time or shortly after- wards, a number of lesser deities were born from Apsu and Tiamat, but of these gods the poem says nothing except that they were gay, turbulent and noisy. They 'troubled Tiamat's belly' and disturbed their parents so much that they decided to destroy them. When they heard of this plan, the great gods Lahmu and Lahamu, Anshar and Kishar, Anu and Ea were shocked and amazed: 'they remained speechless', thinking, no doubt, that the exuberance of Life was preferable to the peace of a sterile Confusion. However, 'Ea the all-wise' soon found a means of wrecking the evil scheme. He 'devised and set up a master design': he cast a magic spell upon Mummu and paralyzed him; in the same way, Apsu was put to sleep and slain. After this double victory Ea retired in his temple, now founded on the abyss of sweet waters (apsû) and with his wife Damkina engendered a son, Marduk, who possessed out- standing qualities:

'Perfect were his members beyond comprehension . . .
Unsuited for understanding, difficult to perceive.
Four were his eyes, four were his ears;
When he moved his lips, fire blazed forth.
Large were all four hearing organs,
And the eyes, in like number, scanned all things.
He was the loftiest of the gods, surpassing was his stature;
His members were enormous, he was exceedingly tall.'

Meanwhile, Tiamat was still alive and free. Delirious with rage, she declared war on the gods. She created a number of fierce dragons and monstrous serpents 'sharp of tooth, unsparing of fangs, with venom for blood', and placed one of her sons, Kingu, at the head of the gruesome army. The gods were terrified. Anshar 'smote his loins and bit his lips' in distress, and declared that Kingu should be put to death. But who was to do this? One after another, the gods all declined to fight. Finally, Marduk accepted under one condition: that he be made their king. 'Set up the assembly,' said he, 'proclaim supreme my destiny, let my word, instead of yours, determine the fates.' The gods had no alternative but to agree. They met in a banquet and, slightly inebriated, they endowed Marduk with the royal powers and insignia. Marduk chose his weapons: the bow, the lightning, the flood-storm, the four winds, the net. He clad himself with 'an armour of terror, a turban of fearsome halo' and, mounted on his storm-chariot, went forth alone to fight the forces of Chaos. At the sight of him, the army of monsters disbanded. Kingu, their chief, was captured. As for Tiamat, she was caught in Marduk's net and, as she opened her mouth, he at once blew the four winds into her stomach. Then, he pierced her heart with an arrow, smashed her skull with his mace and, finally, split her body open 'like a shell fish'. Half of her 'he set up and ceiled it as sky', the other half, he placed beneath the earth.

After his victory, Marduk put the universe in order. Having, in the new sky, fixed the course of the sun, the moon and the stars, he decided to create mankind:

> 'I will establish a savage (*lullu*), "man" shall be his name.
> Verily, savage-man I will create.
> He shall be charged with the service of the gods
>   That they might be at ease!'

On Ea's advice, Kingu was put to death and with his blood, Marduk and his father fashioned the first human being. Thereafter, Marduk divided the gods into two groups: three hundred of them to dwell in heaven, three hundred to live on earth side by side with humanity. As a reward for his victory, the gods built Marduk's great temple in Babylon, Esagila, and, assembled in another great banquet, they 'proclaimed his fifty names'.

Childish as this story may sound, it was loaded with grave significance for the Babylonians. To their deeply religious minds it offered a non-rational but nevertheless acceptable 'explanation' of the universe. Among other things, it described how the world had assumed its alleged shape; it made good the fact that men must be the servants of the gods; it accounted for the natural wickedness of humanity, created from the blood of evil Kingu; it also justified the exorbitant powers of Marduk (originally Enlil) by his heroic exploit. But above all, it had, like the Sacred Marriage, a powerful magical virtue. If every year for nearly two millennia *Enuma elish* was recited by the priests of Babylon on the fourth day of the New Year Festival, it was because the Babylonians felt that the great cosmic struggle had never really ended and that the forces of Chaos were always ready to challenge the established Order of the gods.

LIFE, DEATH AND DESTINY

The commerce of men with the gods, like the commerce of men between themselves, had its degrees. If the King of Babylon was directly under Marduk's orders, the Babylonian peasant was in closer contact with Ashnan, the barley-god, or Shumuqan, the cattle-god, than with Anu or Enlil. Besides, there were enough deities to cater for the important events of life; whenever required, an invocation and an offering of dates would propitiate Gula, the goddess of childbirth, or Pasag, the protector of travellers. In case of dire emergency, the greater deities could be approached through the clergy or, more directly, through the offices of the 'personal god' who, like a guardian angel, always stood at the side of every man or woman.

Sumerians, Babylonians and Assyrians looked up to their gods as servants look to their good masters: with submission and fear, but also with admiration and love. For kings and commoners alike, obedience to divine orders was the greatest of qualities, as the service of the gods was the most imperative of duties. While the celebration of the various festivals and the performance of the complicated rituals of the cult were, of course, the task of priests, it was the duty of every citizen to send offerings to the temples, to attend the main religious ceremonies, to care for the dead, to pray and make penance, and to observe the innumerable rules and taboos that marked nearly every moment of his life. A sensible man 'feared the gods' and scrupulously followed their prescriptions. To do otherwise was not only foolish but sinful, and sin—as everyone knew—brought on man's head the most terrible punishments. Yet, it would be wrong to think of the Mesopotamian religion as a purely formal affair when hymns and prayers disclose the most delicate feelings and burst with genuine emotion. The Mesopotamians put their confidence in their gods; they relied upon them as children rely upon their parents, they talked to them as to their 'real fathers and mothers' who could be offended and punish but who could also be placated and forgive.

Offerings, sacrifices, the observance of religious prescriptions were not all that the Mesopotamian gods required from their worshippers. To 'make their hearts glow with libation', to make them 'exultant with succulent meals'[18] was certainly deserving, but it was not enough. The favours of the gods went to those who led 'a good life', who were good parents, good sons, good neighbours, good citizens, and who practised virtues as highly esteemed then as they are now: kindness and compassion, righteousness and sincerity, justice, respect of the law and of the established order. Everyday worship your god, says a Babylonian 'Counsel of Wisdom', but also:

'To the feeble show kindness,
Do not insult the downtrodden,
Do charitable deeds, render service all your days . . .
Do not utter libel, speak what is of good report,
Do not say evil things, speak well of people . . .'[19]

As a reward for piousness and good conduct, the gods gave man help and protection in danger, comfort in distress and bereavement, good health, honourable social position, wealth, numerous children, long life, happiness. This was not perhaps a very noble ideal by our standards, but the Sumerians and Babylonians were contented with it, for they were practical, down-to-earth people who loved and enjoyed life above everything. To live for ever was the dearest of their dreams, and a number of their myths—in particular Adapa and the Gilgamesh cycle (see next chapter)— aimed at explaining why man had been denied the privilege of immortality.

But only the gods were immortal. For men, death was ineluctable and had to be accepted:

'Only the gods live for ever under the sun,
As for mankind, numbered are their days,
Whatever they achieve is but wind.'[20]

What happened after death? Thousands of graves with their funerary equipment testify to a general belief in an after-life where the dead carried with them their most precious belongings and received food and drink from the living. But such details of the Mesopotamian eschatology as we can extract from the myth 'Inanna's descent to the Netherworld' or the Sumerian cycle of Gilgamesh are scanty and often contradictory.[21] The 'land of no return' was a vast space somewhere underground, with a huge palace where reigned Ereshkigal, the Sumerian Persephone, and her husband Nergal, the god of war and pestilence, surrounded by a number of deities and guards. To reach this palace, the spirits of the dead had to cross a river by ferry, as in the Greek Hades, and take off their clothes. Thereafter, they lived a wretched and dreary life in a place:

> 'Where dust is their food, clay their sustenance;
> Where they see no light and dwell in darkness,
> Where they are clad like birds with garments of wings,
> Where over door and bolt dust has spread.'[22]

Yet we learn from other sources that the sun lit the Netherworld on its way round the earth, and that the sun-god Utu pronounced judgement on the dead, so that they were probably not all treated with the same severity. It would seem that the Sumerian idea of hell was as vague as ours, and that a great deal of this literature is just poetical embroidery on a loose theme.

Death, however, was not the Mesopotamians' sole preoccupation. They had, like us, their share of disease, poverty, deception and sorrow, and like us they wondered: how could all this happen when the gods ruled the world? How could Evil prevail over Good? Of course, it was often possible to put the blame on man himself. So tight was the network of rules and prohibitions that surrounded him that to sin and offend the gods was the easiest thing to do. Yet there were occasions when the irreproachable had nevertheless been punished, when the gods seemed to behave in the most incomprehensible way. A Babylonian poem called *Ludlul bêl nemeqi*, 'I will praise the Lord of Wisdom', pictures the feelings of a man, once noble, rich and healthy, now ruined, hated by all and afflicted with the most terrible diseases. As it turns out, in the end the god Marduk takes pity on him and saves him; but our Babylonian Job had had time to doubt the wisdom of Heaven. Bitterly he exclaimed:

'Who knows the will of the gods in heaven?
Who understands the plan of the underworld gods?
Where have mortals learnt the way of a god?
He who was alive yesterday is dead today.
For a minute he was dejected, suddenly he is exuberant.
One moment people are singing in exaltation,
Another they groan like professional mourners ...
I am appalled at these things; I do not understand their
significance.'[23]

But the famous Babylonian 'pessimism' was much more than a temporary outburst of despair. It was metaphysical in essence, not ethical, and had its roots in the natural conditions which prevailed in Mesopotamia itself. The Tigris-Euphrates valley is a country of violent and unexpected changes. The same rivers that bring life can also bring disaster. The winters may be too cold or rainless, the summer winds too dry for the dates. A cloudburst can, in a moment, turn a parched and dusty plain into a sea of mud, and, on any fine day, a sandstorm can suddenly darken the sky and blow devastation. Confronted with these manifestations of supernatural forces, the Mesopotamian felt bewildered and helpless. He was seized with frightful anxiety. Nothing, he believed, was ever sure. His own life, the life of his family, the products of his fields and of his cattle, the rhythm and measure of the river floods, the cycle of seasons and indeed the very existence of the universe were constantly at stake. If the cosmos did not revert to confusion, if the world order was nonetheless maintained, if the human race survived, if life came again to the fields after the scorching heat of the summer, if the moon and the sun and the stars kept revolving in the sky, it was by an act of will of the gods. But the divine decision had not been pronounced once and for all at the origin of all things; it had to be repeated again and again, particularly at the turn of the year, just before that terrible oriental summer when nature seems to die and the future appears loaded with uncertainty. The only thing man could do in these critical circumstances was to provoke the decision of the gods and secure their goodwill by performing the age-old rites that ensured the maintenance of order, the revival of nature and the permanence of life. Each spring, therefore, a great and poignant ceremony took place in many cities and especially in Babylon: the *akîtu* or New Year Festival, which combined the Sacred Marriage of the gods, the great drama of Creation and the annual reinstatement of the king, and culminated in the gathering of all the gods who solemnly 'decreed the Destinies'. Only then could the king go back to his throne, the shepherd to his flock, the peasant to his field. The Mesopotamian was reassured: the world would exist for another year.

CHAPTER VII

AN AGE OF HEROES

I F the Sumerians were not short of theories as to the origin of
the universe, they were regrettably more discrete about their
own origins. There is, it is true, a myth[1] which alludes to a
pure, clean and 'bright' land where death, disease and sorrow
were once unknown, where:

> 'The raven utters no cries,
> The *ittidu*-bird utters not the cry of the *ittidu*-bird,
> The lion kills not,
> The wolf snatches not the lamb,
> Unknown is the kid-devouring wild dog . . .'

in the myth, this wonderland is called *Dilmun*, a country which,
n historical texts, is generally equated with the island of Bahrain,
in the Persian Gulf.[2] But the name 'Dilmun' here probably stands
for any far-off and imaginary place rather than for Bahrain itself.
Moreover, there is nothing in the Dilmun myth to suggest that
this country was ever the homeland of the Sumerians. In reality,
the Sumerians, like most ancient peoples, saw their country as the
hub of the universe, and themselves as the direct descendants of
the first human beings. They used the same ideogram for *kalam*,
'The Country' (i.e. Sumer) and for *ukù*, 'people in general' and
'the people of Sumer' in particular. Significantly, the other ideogram for 'country', *kur*, pictures a mountain and was originally
used in connection with foreign countries only. Clearly the
Sumerians identified themselves with the earliest inhabitants of
Mesopotamia, and indeed with the initial population of the earth.
How then did they imagine their own 'prehistory'?

FROM 'ADAM' TO THE DELUGE

In the preceding chapter, we have seen how, in the great Babylonian Epic of Creation, the first and nameless 'savage-man' had

been created from the blood of the evil god Kingu. Other myths3 refer to the making by the gods of one or two human beings either from clay or from the blood of minor deities, or both. But nowhere are we told what happened to these Adams or Eves. Up to now, Sumerian literature has offered no close parallel to the biblical story of the Lost Paradise, and to find a Mesopotamian account of the Fall of Man, we must turn to the Babylonian—and therefore relatively late—legend of Adapa.4

Created by the god Ea (Enki) as 'the model of men', Adapa was a priest of Eridu who fulfilled various tasks in Ea's temple, the most important being to supply his master with food. One day, as he was fishing on the 'great sea', the South Wind suddenly blew with such violence that his boat capsized and he himself was nearly drowned. In his anger, Adapa uttered a curse whereby the wings of the South Wind—that big demon-bird—were broken and for a long time 'the South Wind blew not upon the land'. It so happens that the south(-easterly) wind is, in southern Iraq, of capital importance to agriculture, for it brings what little rain there is in winter and, in summer, causes the ripening of the dates.5 When the great god Anu heard what Adapa had done, he was naturally much angered and sent for the culprit. But Ea came to Adapa's aid. He told him that upon his arrival at Anu's gate in heaven he would meet the two vegetation gods, Dumuzi and Ningishzida (whom Adapa, it seems, had indirectly 'killed' by suppressing the South Wind) but, if he clad himself in mourning and showed signs of grief and contrition, the two gods would be appeased; they would 'smile' and even speak to Anu in Adapa's favour. Anu would then no longer treat Adapa as a criminal but as a guest; he would, after Oriental fashion, offer him food and water, clothes to put on and oil with which to anoint himself. The last two Adapa could accept but, warned Ea:

'When they offer thee bread of death,
Thou shalt not eat it. When they offer thee water of death,
Thou shalt not drink it . . .
This advice that I have given thee, neglect not; the words
That I have spoken to thee, hold fast!'

Everything happened as Ea had said, even beyond expectation, for Anu, touched no doubt by Adapa's repentance and sincere confession, offered him instead of the food and drink of death the 'bread of life' and the 'water of life'. But Adapa, following strictly his master's advice, refused the gifts that would have rendered him immortal. Whereupon, Anu dismissed him with these simple words:

'Take him away and return him to earth.'

Whether Ea's proverbial foresight had failed him, or whether he had deliberately lied to Adapa is difficult to determine. But the result was that Adapa lost his right to immortality. He lost it through blind obedience as Adam lost it through arrogant disobedience. In both cases, man had condemned himself to death.

The biblical parallel, however, goes no further for the time being, for even if we see in Adapa a Mesopotamian Adam,[6] we are lacking that long line of posterity which, in the Bible, links the first man with the Hebrews' true ancestor, Abraham. The Sumerians were not possessed of the passion for genealogy that was characteristic of the nomadic Semites. They viewed their own history from a different angle. The gods, they reasoned, had created mankind for a definite purpose: to feed and serve them. They had themselves fixed the details of this service, they had 'perfected the rites and exalted the divine ordinances'. Humanity, however, was but a great, rather stupid flock. It needed shepherds, rulers, priestly kings chosen and appointed by the gods to enforce the divine law. At some remote date, therefore, almost immediately after the creation of mankind, 'the exalted tiara and the throne of kingship' were 'lowered from heaven', and from then on a succession of monarchs led the destinies of Sumer and Akkad on behalf of and for the benefit of the gods. Thus was justified by reference to the most distant past the theory of divinely inspired kingship, current in Mesopotamia from the third millennium onwards. Yet some modern scholars hold different views. They believe that the original political system of Sumer was a 'primitive democracy'. Monarchy, they say, developed comparatively late in proto-history, when the chief warriors, formerly elected by an assembly of citizens for short periods of crisis, took over for good the control of the state.[7] This is a very interesting theory but, in our view, only a theory, and it has been argued that assemblies (*ukin*), as far as we can judge from the texts at our disposal, appear

B. The statue of Ebih-Il, an official from Mari, is one of the finest pieces of Early Dynastic sculpture. The name is Semitic, but the attitude and costume, as well as the sculptor's technique, are typically Sumerian.

PLATE 9

A. Fragment of the Stele of the Vultures, representing the army of Eannatum, *ensi* of Lagash (Telloh.)

PLATE 10

A. Basalt stele from Uruk, 32 inches high, representing a hero hunting lions. (Uruk or Proto-literate period.)

B. This beautifully worked bronze head, three-quarters life size, was found at Nineveh and is presumed to be a portrait of king Sargon of Akkad (*circa* 2371–2316 B.C.)

to be purely consultative bodies summoned by the king on rare occasions, and without real power. As far as we can go back in the past, we see nothing but monarchs second only to the gods.

We possess, by chance, a document that gives us an uninterrupted list of kings from the very beginnings of monarchy, down to the eighteenth century BC. This is the famous 'Sumerian King List' compiled from about fifteen different texts and magnificently edited by Th. Jacobsen in 1939.[8] This document is invaluable: not only does it embody and summarize very old Sumerian traditions, but it provides an excellent chronological frame in which can be placed most of the great legends of the Sumerian heroic age. For the Sumerians, like the ancient Greeks, Hindus and Germans, had their heroic age, their age of demi-gods and superhuman kings who stood on equal terms with the gods and performed fantastic feats of valour. Only now do we begin to realize that some at least of these heroes are only half-mythical and belong, in fact, to history.

According to the Sumerian King List, kingship was first 'lowered from heaven' in the city of Eridu, a remarkable statement if we remember that Eridu has yielded traces of the most ancient Sumerian settlement in southern Iraq (see above, Chapter IV). Then, after no less than 64,800 years during which only two kings reigned in Eridu, kingship, for some untold reason, was 'carried' to Bad-tibira (three kings, one of them the god Dumuzi himself, 108,000 years). From Bad-tibira, it passed on successively to Larak (one king, 28,800 years), to Sippar (one king, 21,000 years) and to Shuruppak (one king, 18,600 years).[9] These incredible figures, strangely reminiscent of Adam's posterity in the Bible, have no hidden significance; they simply express a widespread belief in a golden age when men lived much longer than usual and were endowed with truly supernatural qualities. But an even closer comparison with the Old Testament is called for by the brief and astonishing sentence which follows the mention of Ubar-Tutu, King of Shuruppak, and closes the first paragraph, as it were, of the Sumerian King List:

'The Flood swept thereover.'

Here we feel irresistibly compelled to interrupt our narrative and examine one of the most controversial and fascinating problems of Mesopotamian archaeology and mythology: the problem of the Great Flood.

THE GREAT FLOOD

In 1872, George Smith, a pioneer of British assyriology, announced to an astonished world that he had discovered, among the many tablets from Ashurbanipal's library in the British Museum, an account of the Deluge strikingly similar to that given in the Bible (Genesis vi. 11–viii. 22). The story he had in hand was but an episode from a long poem in twelve tablets known as the Gilgamesh Epic of which we shall speak later. The hero of the epic, Gilgamesh, King of Uruk, is in search of the secret of immortality and eventually meets Ut-napishtim, the only man to have been granted eternal life and the son, incidentally, of Ubar-Tutu of Shuruppak. This, briefly, is what Ut-napishtin tells Gilgamesh:[10]

At some indefinite date, 'when Shuruppak was already an old city', the gods decided to send a deluge in order to destroy the sinful human race. But Ea took pity on Ut-napishtim and secretly speaking to him through the thin wall of his reed-hut, advised him to tear down his house, abandon his possessions, build a ship of a certain size, take with him 'the seed of all living creatures' and prepare himself for the worst. The next day, work was started on the ark and soon a huge cubic, seven-decked vessel was ready, caulked with bitumen and loaded with gold, silver, game, beasts and Ut-napishtim's family, relations and workmen. When the weather became 'frightful to behold', our Babylonian Noah knew that the time for the deluge had come. He entered the ship and closed the door. Then, 'as soon as the first shimmer of morning beamed forth, a black cloud came up from out of the horizon,' announcing the most terrible tempest of wind, rain, lightning and thunder that man had ever witnessed. The dykes gave way, the earth was shrouded in darkness; even the gods were panic-striken and regretted what they had undertaken:

'The gods cowered like dogs and crouched in distress.
Ishtar cried out like a woman in travail . . .
"How could I command war to destroy my people,
For it is I who bring forth my people" . . .

The Anunnaki gods wept with her;
The gods sat bowed and weeping . . .
Six days and six nights
The wind blew, the downpour, the tempest and the flood
    overwhelmed the land . . .'

On the seventh day, however, the tempest subsided. Says Ut-napishtim:

'I opened a window and light fell upon my face.
I looked upon the "sea", all was silence,
And all mankind had turned to clay.'

The ark landed on mount Nisir,[11] but no land was visible beside
the rock that held fast the ship. After a week had elapsed, Ut-napishtim
sent forth a dove, but she came back; he sent forth a
swallow, but she also came back; he sent forth a raven, but the
raven found land and did not return. Ut-napishtim then poured
a libation on top of the mountain and offered a sacrifice of sweet
cane, cedar and myrtle:

'The gods smelled the savour,
The gods smelled the sweet savour,
The gods gathered like flies over the sacrificer.'

If Ishtar, in particular, was delighted, Enlil, who had ordered the
deluge and whose plans were frustrated, was filled with anger
and put the blame on Ea. But so well did Ea plead his own cause
and the cause of mankind that Enlil's heart was touched. He
entered the ship and blessed Ut-napishtim and his wife, saying:

'Hitherto Ut-napishtim has been but a man,
But now Ut-napishtim and his wife shall be like unto us gods.
In the distance, at the mouth of the rivers, Ut-napishtim shall
    dwell.'

Needless to say, George Smith's publication of this story made
headlines in the newspapers of the time. As new cuneiform texts
became available, however, other versions of the Flood legend,
less complete but older than the Gilgamesh version (written at

Nineveh in the seventh century BC) were discovered. The name of the hero varied. In a Sumerian text from Nippur dated about 1700 BC, he was called Ziusudra, while in a Babylonian epic of slightly later date, he was called Atrahasis, 'Exceedingly Wise', probably a nickname for Ut-napishtim himself.[12] But, allowance being made for other minor variations, the theme was always the same: a gigantic Flood had swept over the earth and all but one (or two) human beings had perished; in the long history of mankind, the deluge marks a definite break and the replacement of one race of men by another. The resemblance with the biblical story is, of course, striking; furthermore, it seems probable that the Hebrews had borrowed from a long and well established Mesopotamian tradition. Quite naturally, the question arose: are there traces of such a cataclysm in Mesopotamia?

The first and, so far, the only archaeologist to answer positively was the late Sir Leonard Woolley. Between 1929 and 1934, in the course of his brilliant excavations at Ur, Woolley sank two deep 'test-pits' near the wall of the inner city, within the area of the famous 'Royal Cemetery' (Early Dynastic period). Having crossed several occupation levels, he came upon 'eleven feet of clean, water-laid silt' practically free from remains of any kind. Immediately above and below this sterile level were potsherds and various objects pertaining to the Ubaid culture and, at the bottom of the pits, the virgin soil. 'Eleven feet of silt', reasoned the archaeologist, 'would probably mean a flood no less than 25 feet deep; in the flat, low-lying land of Mesopotamia, a flood of that depth would cover an area about 300 miles long and 100 miles across.' There was therefore evidence of 'an inundation unparalleled in any later period of Mesopotamian history', and the flood which at Ur had submerged the settlement of the Ubaid period was boldly equated with the Flood with a capital F, the biblical Deluge.[13] This, added Woolley, was not surprising since we know that Abraham 'went forth from Ur of the Chaldees' (Genesis xi. 31) and could well have brought with him into Canaan the saga of the Flood, no doubt as popular in Mesopotamia in his days as the Knights of the Round Table in mediaeval England.

This was almost too good to be true, and no one but Woolley, in scientific circles, took the 'discovery' very seriously, for neither the extent, nor indeed the reality of a flood can be deduced from the depth of mud deposited in a limited area. According to Woolley's theory, the surface covered by the Flood would have encompassed practically the whole of southern Iraq. Yet, Eridu, only 15 miles from Ur and lying somewhat lower, has yielded no trace whatsoever of a flood. Layers of silt, it is true, were found on various other sites, but they vary widely in thickness as well as in chronological position. The 'flood level' of Kish, for instance, belongs to the Early Dynastic and not to the Ubaid period, and the same applies to the thin alluvial deposits found at Uruk, Lagash and Ut-napishtim's own city, Shuruppak.[14] All these 'sterile' levels have been interpreted as local inundations rather than traces of a *general* flood. We can therefore conclude that archaeological excavations in Iraq have afforded no evidence of a cataclysmic Deluge. But what then is at the root of the Mesopotamian legend? Various explanations have been put forward. It is, for instance, possible that a legend born in one or several cities affected at some time or another by an exceptionally severe inundation, was stretched to the size of a universal Flood by oriental imagination. Alternatively, one can think of a major cataclysm such as a tidal wave or a hurricane involving Mesopotamia and striking the imagination of its inhabitants. But these theories do not account for two important facts: (*a*) the Sumero-Babylonian as well as the biblical stories put the stress on heavy rains rather than on river inundation, and (*b*) the legend of the Flood does not belong only to the Near East, but also to a vast number of countries in all parts of the world.[15] We have therefore the choice between two explanations: either the Flood is a pure myth, invented by the primitive peoples to 'cancel' a large 'slice' of the past,[16] or the flood really existed but in very early prehistorical ages. The torrential rains which, in sub-tropical countries like Iraq, took the place of glaciations during the Pleistocene period were witnessed by man. The memory of these rains could perhaps have been handed down from generation to generation through verbal tradition and eventually transformed into a single legendary catastrophe. Both theories can be defended, but we shall probably never know the truth, and the Deluge, like the lost continent of Atlantis, will remain for ever an unsolved mystery.

DYNASTIES OF SUPERMEN

After the Flood, says the Sumerian King List, kingship was again 'lowered from heaven', this time in Kish, a city now represented by an important group of tells, about 10 miles due east of Babylon.[17] The first 'dynasty'* of Kish comprises twenty-three reigns with an average duration of 1,000 years per reign. If we omit one king whose name could not be read by the scribe who compiled the list from old tablets, we observe that, out of twenty-two monarchs, twelve bear Semitic names or nicknames, such as *Kalbum*, 'dog', *Qalumu*, 'lamb', or *Zuqaqip*, 'scorpion'; six have Sumerian names and four have names of unknown origin. This is important because it shows the mixture of ethnic elements in southern Iraq at an early date, the predominance of Semites in the region of Kish, and the absence of rivalry between Sumerians and Semites within the same city-state.[18] As we shall see in the next chapter, we have good reason to believe that this dynasty was at least partly historical and should be placed shortly after 2800 BC. Yet one of its kings is expressly designated as a mythical figure: 'Etana, a shepherd, the one who ascended to heaven', and as it happens that we possess Babylonian and Assyrian tablets which give us more details about Etana, we can enlarge on this point.[19]

The Etana legend starts like a fable. The serpent and the eagle lived on the same tree and helped each other as good neighbours should. But the eagle one day devoured the young of the serpent. The serpent went weeping to the sun-god Shamash who prompted the following stratagem. The serpent hid in the belly of a dead ox, and when the eagle came to devour the carcase, the reptile took his revenge: he caught the big bird, broke his 'heel', plucked him and threw him into a pit. Now, a certain Etana who had no children and was desperately in need of the 'plant of birth' which grows only in heaven, also cried to Shamash, and Shamash advised him to rescue the eagle, win his friendship and use him as a vehicle to fly to heaven. This Etana did. 'Upon the

---

* The word 'dynasty' in Mesopotamian history should not be taken as meaning a royal *family*, but a succession of kings ruling over the same city-state for a period of time. The Sumerian King List mentions only the dynasties which ruled, one after the other, over the *whole* country of Sumer.

eagle's breast he placed his breast, upon the feathers of his wings he placed his hands, upon his sides he placed his arms' and, in this uncomfortable position, he took off for a breathtaking flight. Gradually, he saw the earth shrink to the size of a furrow and the sea to the size of a bread basket. But when land and sea were no longer visible, Etana panicked: 'My friend, I will not ascend to heaven!' he shouted and, loosening his grip, he plunged, head down, towards the earth followed by the eagle. Our text, unfortunately, breaks off at this crucial moment, but we can assume that Etana reached his goal, for not only did he live a respectable 1,560 years, but, according to the King List, he had a son and heir called Balih.

The Sumerian King List gives the impression that the last king of the first dynasty of Kish, Agga, was defeated in battle by the first king of the first dynasty of Uruk; but we know that the two dynasties overlapped and that Agga, in fact, was contemporary with the *fifth* king of Uruk, Gilgamesh. We owe this information to a short Sumerian poem[20] which describes how Agga sent an ultimatum to Gilgamesh demanding that Uruk submit to Kish, how the ultimatum was rejected and Uruk besieged and how, at the sight of mighty Gilgamesh peering over the wall, the enemy was overwhelmed with fear and 'cast itself down'. In the end it was Agga who became the vassal of Gilgamesh, and Kish which submitted to Uruk, as indicated in the King List. Yet if the predecessors of Gilgamesh did not rule over the whole country of Sumer but only over Uruk, they were prominent figures all the same, since we have in order of succession: Meskiaggasher, son of the sun-god Utu, who 'went into the sea and came out (from it) to the mountains'; Enmerkar, 'the one who built Uruk'; divine Lugalbanda, a 'shepherd', and finally, Dumuzi, the vegetation-god called here 'a fisherman'. The deeds of two at least of these heroes and demi-gods are now familiar to us owing to the recent publication of four Sumerian epic tales which once formed parts of a 'cycle of Enmerkar' and of a 'cycle of Lugalbanda'.[21] All these legends revolve around the usually strained relations between Uruk and Aratta, a far-away country separated from Sumer by 'seven mountains' and probably to be located in western Iran.[22] In one of these tales we are told at length of the considerable difficulties encountered by Enmerkar in obtaining gold, silver, lapis-lazuli and precious stones from the Lord of Aratta, either by threats or in return for grain, a situation which must have repeated itself again and again in the long history of Mesopotamia, and which perhaps underlies the endless wars between that country and mountainous Elam. In another tale we see Uruk besieged by the MAR.TU folk, i.e. the nomadic Amorites of the Syrian desert who, as will be told later, settled in Iraq and took over from the Sumerians at the beginning of the second millennium BC. If we could be sure that these legends reflected the political situation as it was at the dawn of history and not at the date when they were actually written down (about 1800 BC), we would find in them matter of considerable interest for the historian.

Finally, we come to Gilgamesh, the fifth king of the first dynasty of Uruk and the son, we are told, of the goddess Ninsun and of a high priest of Kullab, a district of Uruk. Gilgamesh, whose exploits are reminiscent of those of both Ulysses and Hercules, was the most popular of all Mesopotamian heroes and appears in the form of a brawny, bearded man fighting bulls and lions on a very large number of monuments, from the cylinder-seals of the Proto-literate period to the sculptured reliefs of the Assyrian palaces. Like Enmerkar and Lugalbanda, he had his own cycle of Sumerian legends, apparently unconnected episodes of his life, of which five are known to us.[23] But this is not all. Early in the second millennium, a long poem with Gilgamesh as hero was composed, which amalgamated some of the older Sumerian legends with new material. The resulting 'Gilgamesh Epic' has, by chance, survived practically complete, and as it is without any doubt the masterpiece of Assyro-Babylonian literature and, indeed, one of the most beautiful epic tales of the ancient world, we must at least try to give a brief summary of it, referring the reader to several excellent translations which have been published.[24]

THE STORY OF GILGAMESH

'He who saw everything to the ends of the world', as the title of the poem has it, Gilgamesh was two-thirds god and one-third man. He was supremely strong, brave and handsome, and cared much for Uruk, his city. The Babylonians admired in particular the strong wall which he had built around it—perhaps the six miles long wall of Early Dynastic times that still encircles the ruins of Warka. Yet his arrogance, his ruthlessness and depravity were a subject of grave concern for the citizens of Uruk. They complained to the great god Anu, and Anu instructed the goddess Aruru to create another 'wild ox', a 'double' of Gilgamesh, who could challenge him and distract his mind from 'the warrior's daughter and the nobleman's spouse' whom, it appears, he would not leave in peace. So, out of clay Aruru modelled Enkidu, a huge, brutish, hairy creature who lived in the steppe among the wild beasts:

> 'With the gazelles he feeds on grass,
> With the wild beasts he jostles at the watering places,
> With the teeming creatures, his heart delights in water.'

Now, one day a hunter saw Enkidu at a distance, and understood why his traps were always torn up and his pits filled and why the game kept slipping out of his hands. He reported the matter to Gilgamesh who set a trap of another kind against the wild man. A woman, a prostitute was sent forth to the steppe with orders to seduce Enkidu and convert him to civilized life. The harlot had no difficulty in fulfilling the first part of her mission. She then took Enkidu by the hand 'like a mother' and led him to Uruk, where he soon learnt to bathe, anoint himself with perfumed oil, eat bread and indulge in strong drinks. But while in Uruk, Enkidu heard that Gilgamesh was once more going to exercise his *ius primae noctis* in the communal house and bravely barred his way. A terrible fight ensued which ended in mutual affection and peace, Gilgamesh having found a companion of his own stature and Enkidu a master: 'They kissed each other and made a friendship.'

The exuberant Gilgamesh, however, was anxious to make himself a name, and persuaded Enkidu to accompany him to the vast and remote Cedar Forest, abode of Huwawa (or Humbaba), a frightening giant 'whose mouth was fire, whose breath was death'. Having prepared their weapons and prayed to the gods, the two friends left Uruk and, covering in three days the distance it normally took six weeks to accomplish, they reached the Cedar Forest:

'They stood still and gazed at the forest,
They looked at the height of the cedars . . .
From the face of the mountains
The cedars raise aloft their luxuriance,
Good is their shadow, full of delight . . .'

Having caught the guardian unaware, they entered the forbidden
land, and already Gilgamesh was felling tree after tree when
Huwawa rose in anger and would have massacred the two
adventurers if Shamash had not come to their rescue; he sent all
the eight winds against Huwawa who, paralysed, acknowledged
himself beaten and begged for his life. But Gilgamesh and Enkidu
cut off his head and triumphantly returned to Uruk.

Following this exploit, the goddess Ishtar herself fell in love
with Gilgamesh and offered to marry him. But Gilgamesh would
have none of it. Reminding the unfaithful goddess how she had
treated her numerous lovers, from Tammuz for whom she had
'ordained wailing year after year' to the shepherd and the gardener
whom she had turned into wolf and spider, he abused her in the
most outrageous terms:

'Thou art but a brazier which goes out in the cold,
A backdoor which does not keep out blast and windstorms,
A waterskin which soaks through its bearer,
A shoe which pinches the foot of its owner!'

Bitterly offended, Ishtar asked Anu to send the Bull of Heaven
to ravage Uruk. But after the Bull had knocked down man after
man, Enkidu seized it by the horns whilst Gilgamesh thrust a
sword into its neck, and as Ishtar was cursing the ruler of Uruk,
he tore off the beast's right thigh and tossed it in her face.

Such impudence was more than the gods could stand. They
decided that one of the pair should die. Enkidu, therefore, was
seized with a long and painful disease and, having reviewed his
past life, cursed the harlot and dreamed of the sombre Netherworld, he passed away, mourned by his companion for seven
days and nights 'until a worm fell out of his nose'.

The death of Enkidu affected Gilgamesh deeply. For the first
time the fiery and fearless King of Uruk realized the full horror

of death. Could he also disappear like this? Could he not escape the dreadful fate of the human race?

> 'Fearing death I roam over the steppe;
> The matter of my friend rests heavy upon me.
> How can I be silent? How can I be still?
> My friend, whom I loved, has turned to clay.
> Must I, too, like him, lay me down
> Not to rise again for ever and ever?'

Gilgamesh decided to meet Ut-napishtim, the man who survived the Deluge, and obtain from him the secret of immortality. First, he had to cross the mountain of Mashû, the vast and dark mountain of the setting sun whose entrance was guarded by scorpion-men; but they took pity on him and let him pass. On the other side of the mountain he met Siduri 'the barmaid who dwells on the edge of the sea', and Siduri's advice was to stop worrying and wandering and to enjoy life. Yet, touched by his sorrow, she told him where Ut-napishtim could be found: on the other side of an immense and dangerous sea barred by 'the waters of death'. Our hero did not hesitate. He enlisted the help of Urshanabi the boatman, crossed the sea and finally met Ut-napishtim who told him his own story, the story of the Flood. Could Ut-napishtim do something for Gilgamesh? Yes, he should get hold of a certain thorny plant which grew in the depths of the ocean, the plant of life. Gilgamesh, like a pearlfisher of the Persian Gulf, tied heavy stones to his feet, dived and picked the plant. Alas, on his way home, while he lay asleep near a spring, a snake came out from the water and carried away the precious harvest. There would be no eternal life for Gilgamesh. The conclusion implicit in the story is as pessimistic as Ut-napishtim's address to our hero:

> 'Do we build houses for ever?
> Does the river for ever raise up and bring on floods?
> The dragon-fly leaves its shell
> That its face might but glance at the face of the sun.
> Since the days of yore there has been no permanence;
> The resting and the dead, how alike they are!'

Such is—briefly outlined and unfortunately robbed of its poetical fragrance—the story of Gilgamesh, the most famous epic tale, probably, in the ancient Near East, judging from the numerous Assyro-Babylonian 'editions' and from the Hittite and Hurrian translations that have come to us. Gilgamesh-the-hero is, of course, a myth. But what of Gilgamesh-the-king? A few years ago one would have strongly doubted his existence; today there are good reasons to believe that a king of that name actually ruled over Uruk, though definite proof is still lacking. For some time we have had the impression of standing at the moving, ethereal border which separates fiction from reality; we have now the certitude that the time of Gilgamesh corresponds to the earliest period of Mesopotamian history.

CHAPTER VIII

THE EARLY DYNASTIC PERIOD

HE history of ancient Iraq, like its prehistory, is divided
into periods, each of them characterized by important
political changes and, occasionally, by major or minor
variations in the social, economic and cultural fields.
The first of these periods covers part of the third millennium
and ends with the conquest of Sumer by the Semitic King of
Akkad, Sargon, *circa* 2400 B C. For this reason, it is often called
'Pre-Sargonic', though the term 'Early Dynastic' is now generally
preferred, at least among English-speaking scholars.

When exactly does history begin in Iraq? The question is of
more than academic interest and deserves to be examined. We
know that the only chronological scale at our disposal, the
Sumerian King List, is made up of part legend, part history. Just
when does it become historical and trustworthy? When do we
cease to be confronted with legendary heroes, to meet kings who
really existed? Clearly, the answer is: when we have in hand an
authentic inscription from one of the early rulers of Sumer
mentioned on the List; and the higher the position of this prince
in the dynastic lines, the earlier the starting point of history.

For a long time, however, we were denied such a document.
Until the first world war, our knowledge of the Pre-Sargonic
period was almost entirely derived from the excavations carried
out, between 1877 and 1909, by the French at Lagash, nowadays
Tell Luh or Telloh, a large mound near the Shatt-el-Gharraf,
35 miles due north of Nasriyah.[1] Beside very remarkable
works of art, these excavations have yielded a number of inscriptions which have made it possible to reconstruct in fairly great
detail the history of Lagash and to draw a list of its rulers, from an
early 'date' in the third millennium to about 2000 B C.[2] Unfortunately the information thus obtained was restricted to one city only

and, still worse, to a city whose princes did not figure on the Sumerian King List, no doubt because they were never considered as having ruled over the whole country of Sumer. To base the early history of Mesopotamia on the Lagash sources only was as hopeless a task as to reconstruct the history of England from the archives of Canterbury and the list of the Dukes of Kent.

Now, in the winter of 1922–23, Sir Leonard Woolley was digging at al-'Ubaid, near Ur, the site which has given its name to one of the proto-historic periods of Mesopotamia. Beside the prehistoric cemetery, there was at Ubaid a mud-brick platform which once supported a small but richly decorated temple. The sanctuary itself had been completely destroyed in antiquity, but large parts of its decoration, including magnificent bronze sculptures and reliefs, had been thrown away by the enemy and lay buried in the dust at the foot of the platform. It was among this precious 'rubbish' that Woolley found a marble tablet with an inscription.[3] It read:

'To (the goddess) Ninhursag, A-anne-padda, King of Ur, son of Mes-anne-padda, King of Ur, for Ninhursag built (this) temple.'

A-anne-padda was otherwise unknown, but it was easy to identify his father, Mes-anne-padda, with the founder of the First Dynasty of Ur mentioned in the King List as having succeeded the First Dynasty of Uruk. Thus for the first time, one of those archaic Sumerian rulers, previously held as mythical, was proved to have actually existed. But we now have even better. Only four years ago, a German assyriologist, Dr D. O. Edzard, found in the Baghdad Museum a fragment of a large alabaster object of un-known origin bearing a short inscription written with very archaic signs:

'Me-bárag-si, King of Kish'

This monarch, as Edzard proved,[4] was none other than En-me-barage-si of the King List (*en* being a title which could be omitted), twenty-second king of the 'legendary' First Dynasty of Kish and the father of Agga who, as we have seen, fought against Gilgamesh. Moreover, a year later, the sumerologist S. N. Kramer was able to demonstrate, with the help of a text known as the 'Tummal inscription', that Gilgamesh was a contemporary of Mes-anne-padda of Ur.5 From all this, we may conclude: (a) that Gilgamesh, King of Uruk and presumed hero of the famous epic, in all probability existed, and (b) that Enmebaragesi, King of Kish, father of Agga and remote successor of Etana, is the earliest Sumerian monarch known with certainty to this date. The arrangement of dynasties in the light of this discovery can be found in chronological table II, at the end of this book.

Is it possible to be more precise and to give 'absolute' dates? The chronology of the third millennium is still extremely vague and controversial. But, if we accept the dates 2371–2316 for Sargon of Akkad—in accordance with Sidney Smith's chronology—and work out our dates backwards, we come to about 2700 BC for Enmebaragesi of Kish. This date, for the time being, can be taken as a tentative starting point for the history of ancient Iraq.6

THE SUMERIAN CITY-STATES

Because our attention is now focused on Sumer, we are tempted to forget what a small country Sumer really was: ten thousand square miles, a little less than the area of Belgium, the size of four or five English counties. Life was concentrated along the rivers and canals, and since the Euphrates followed then a more easterly course than it does at present, the 'cradle of civilization' was, in fact, a long and narrow strip of land extending from approximately the latitude of Baghdad to the swamps that bordered the shores of the Persian Gulf.

This country was divided between several politico-religious units which we call 'city-states'. Each city-state consisted of a city with its suburbs and satellite towns and villages, and of a certain territory, including gardens, orchards, palm-groves and fields, which belonged to the city or rather, as we shall see, to its gods. The open, uncultivated steppe between the irrigated areas served as pasture land and was called in Sumerian edin, a word from which the biblical term 'Eden' might well derive. The area covered by the average city-state is unknown, but a figure of 1,800 square miles has been advanced for Lagash, whose total population for this period is estimated at about 30,000–35,000 people.7

During the Early Dynastic period no more than thirteen cities
are attested from literary sources for the whole country of Sumer.
They are, from north to south: Sippar, Kish, Akshak, Larak,
Nippur, Adab, Umma, Lagash, Bad-tibira, Uruk, Larsa, Ur and
Eridu. But archaeological excavations have shown that other
important towns existed in other parts of Mesopotamia and that
they were under strong Sumerian cultural influence. This is the
case, for instance, of Assur (Qal'at Sherqat), on the Tigris, and of
Mari (Tell Hariri), on the Euphrates, respectively 250 and 300
miles as the crow flies from Nippur. Lacking written documents,
we do not know to what ethnic group the first inhabitants of
Assur belonged, but the objects discovered by the Germans before
the first world war in its archaic Ishtar temple are typically
Sumerian.[8] The same applies to Mari, though here we know from
personal names in local inscriptions that we are in the heart of a
Semitic district. The French excavations at Mari, before and after
the last war,[9] have brought to light a number of pre-Sargonic
monuments, including at least four temples and a ziqqurat. One
of these temples, dedicated to the goddess Ninni-Zaza, contained
a conical monolith or *baetyl* which would have been at home in a
Semitic sanctuary of ancient Palestine. Yet panels of shell and
mother-of-pearl figurines set in bitumen strikingly similar to
those found at Ur and Kish decorated these temples, and the
Semitic kings and citizens of Mari who offered to their gods
delicately carved statuettes of themselves, wore the traditional
Sumerian woollen skirt and were portrayed bearded and with
shaven head in the Sumerian attitude of prayer: hands clasped
in front of the chest. Similar though much cruder statuettes were
also found, in the early thirties, by the Oriental Institute of
Chicago's expedition digging at Tell Asmar (Eshnunna), in the
Diyala valley, and indeed Tell Asmar, together with the neighbouring sites of Khafaje (ancient Tutub) and Tell 'Aqrab, have
supplied archaeologists with more information on the Early
Dynastic period than the cities of Sumer proper where very
ancient buildings lie, as a rule, hidden under the ruins of more
recent monuments.[10] Thus we can follow, at Asmar and Khafaje,
the constant rebuilding of temples along different plans but always
with the same material: the cushion-shaped 'plano-convex' bricks,
often laid obliquely in 'herringbone style', which are the hall-mark

of the period throughout Mesopotamia. We can admire at Khafaje a temple on a platform standing in an extraordinary oval enclosure. We can reconstruct the appearance of these early Mesopotamian towns, with their small houses closely packed together and their narrow, winding streets. We can recognize in the 'scarlet ware' of the Diyala valley, with its vivid but fragile decoration of human figures and animals, the last offspring of the prehistoric painted pottery. We can even play with the clay chariots used as toys by the children of those remote times. Yet, interesting as this is, we must return to the literary sources from Sumer proper if we want to form an idea of the political, social and economic organization of the Early Dynastic city-states.[11]

Each Sumerian capital of state was formed of several agglomerations or boroughs, and each borough had as its centre a temple. The city as a whole and the territory under its jurisdiction were under the protection of one particular god, who not only protected but *owned* the state. For instance, Lagash *belonged* to Ningirsu, son of Enlil, as Ur belonged to Nanna, the moon-god, and expressions such as 'the field of Ningirsu' or 'Ningirsu's, victory over Shara (god of Umma)' should not be taken metaphorically but in the strictest sense of the term. Naturally, the inhabitants of the city-state also belonged to the god or, more precisely, to the god of the borough in which they lived, and were divided into groups called 'the people of Ningirsu', 'the people of Baba', etc. There were only two categories of citizens, freemen and slaves, but it should be noted that slaves, recruited in very limited number and only from prisoners of war, played a negligible part in the economy of Sumer during the Early Dynastic period.

The citizens could possess, and dispose freely of houses, gardens, fish-ponds, asses, sheep and goats. They had their own furniture and tools and a limited quantity of silver. A number of them also owned some land, though such properties were probably small. Almost all the land and cattle belonged to the gods, that is to the temples. Each temple possessed its own fields and pastures (the main temple having, of course, the greater share) which were exploited by its own people. The cultivated land was divided into three parts: one part was 'the land of the Lord' (*gána-nì-en-na*) and, as such, was worked by the whole community for the sole benefit of the temple; another, 'the food land' (*gána-ku-ra*) was allotted to the dependants of the temple for their support, and the third part, 'the plough land' (*gána-apin-la*) was let out to tenants against one-seventh or one-eighth of the harvest. The temples, therefore, disposed of important revenues which they either consumed or redistributed, stored in anticipation of famine, or exchanged against goods imported from foreign countries, such as metal, wood or stone. As, in addition, they had permanently at their disposal the entire population of the city-state, they could undertake the building of sanctuaries and fortifications, the digging of canals and other large-scale operations requiring a vast number of labourers. The beneficial rôle played by the temples as economic regulators and promoters of public works explains and justifies their exorbitant powers.

All this required considerable planning, control and book-keeping, and we touch here on one of the most surprising aspects of this civilization. Far from being 'primitive', the Sumerian society of Early Dynastic times was thoroughly organized, one is even tempted to say over-organized. The Sumerians were meticulous people with 'bureaucratic' minds. They have left us thousands of payrolls, vouchers, lists, labels and other records which make tedious reading but are invaluable as a source of information. We learn for instance from the economic texts found at Telloh (Lagash) and Fara (Shuruppak)[12] that the entire working population of these cities was regimented and enrolled in various 'corporations', some of them necessarily quite small. For instance, there were separate shepherds for male and female asses, and separate groups of fishermen according to whether they fished in sweet, brackish or sea-water, and even the snake-charmers formed a distinctive trade headed by a 'chief snake-charmer'. Merchants and artisans, similarly organized, worked partly for the citizens and partly for the temples, though the commerce with foreign countries was entirely regulated by the latter. An army of scribes, controllers, inspectors, overseas and other officials, directed by a chief inspector (*nu-bànda*) and by a superintendent (*agrig*) under the leadership of the high priest of each temple (*sanga*), kept running the huge state machinery. If a label should be attached to a society like this, where most of the means of production lay in the hands of a clergy-controlled state, but where personal property nevertheless existed, perhaps the words 'theocratic socialism' could be accepted, bearing in mind that ready-made formulas are, of necessity, approximate and often misleading.

EARLY SUMERIAN RULERS

Above the high priests of the different temples was the ruler of the city-state, the 'shepherd' chosen by the city god and responsible to him. In the archaic texts from Uruk, the ruler is called *en*, a title usually translated by 'lord' but implying, in fact, the highest sacerdotal functions. As the *en* resided in the temple compound, it seems reasonable to assume that he was the high priest of the city god, the head of the temple around which the Sumerian city had grown in prehistoric times. During the Early Dynastic period, however, the ruler was known either as *ensi*, 'governor', or *lugal*, 'king'. *Ensi* is written—and was until recently read—PA.TE.SI, a compound ideogram probably meaning 'the chief' (PA) who delimits (SI) the temple precinct (TE).¹³ *Lugal* simply means 'great (GAL) man (LÚ)'. The difference between the two titles is not easy to appreciate, but it is generally believed that the *lugal* was an independent ruler, or a sovereign commanding more than one city-state, whereas the *ensi* was the vassal of a *lugal*. The ruler's wife, known as *nin*, 'lady', played an important part in the religious and public life of the city. The *lugal* and the *ensi* lived in a palace (*é-gal*, 'great house') distinct from the temple. Two such palaces were excavated in southern Iraq: one at Kish, the other at Eridu.¹⁴ Both were very similar in plan: they consisted of two large buildings side by side with numerous rooms opening on to courtyards, and one of these buildings was surrounded by a thick double wall. In the Kish palace was a majestic hall with a row of four columns down the centre.

The ruler administered the property of the city god and governed the state on his behalf, combining the functions of war leader, chief justice, head of the clergy and minister of public works. One of his most sacred duties was the building and restoration of temples, in consequence of the belief that humanity had been created for the service of the gods and that the ruler was but the first of their servants. Innumerable inscriptions refer to such building activities, and from Ur-Nanshe, an early King of

Lagash, to Ashurbanipal, in the sixth century BC, several Mesopotamian princes were portrayed in stone or bronze with a basket
on their head, carrying bricks for the new temples. There is also
no doubt that the city chief played a leading rôle in the New Year
Festival and, on many occasions, acted as the male god in the
Sacred Marriage ceremony. Indeed, there is reason to believe that,
early in the third millennium, during the 'heroic age' of Enmerkar,
Lugalbanda and Gilgamesh, certain Sumerian royal couples were
considered as 'living gods' or, more correctly, as human duplicates
of the gods representing on earth the divine couple to which the
city-state belonged. This, at any rate, appears to be the best
answer to the important problems raised by the most startling
discovery ever made in the course of Mesopotamian excavations,
the Royal Cemetery of Ur.

A detailed description of the Royal Cemetery cannot be given
here; it should be read in the excellent articles and books written
by Sir Leonard Woolley on this fascinating subject.[15] None but
the discoverer himself could effectively convey the feeling of
excitement that seized him and his team as gold literally oozed
from the earth under their picks, and as marvel after marvel was
brought to light. None but this outstanding archaeologist could
describe the delicate and painstaking removal, the patient and
skilled restoration of the magnificent objects, ornaments and
weapons that accompanied the dead: the gold vessels and daggers,
the gold and lapis-lazuli statuettes of a ram 'caught in a thicket',
the gold and silver animals' heads which decorated the harps, the
gold head-dress of queen Shub-ad, and, above all perhaps, the
splendid gold helmet of Mes-kalam-dug—to quote only the main
pieces. Woolley's dramatic evocation of these strange funerals
where musicians with their harps. soldiers with their weapons and
court ladies in gorgeous attire willingly followed their masters
into the awesome pits where they were drugged to a painless
death never fails to leave the reader with a poignant, unforgettable
feeling of horror, mingled with wonder and admiration.

But the Royal Cemetery of Ur presents the historian with very
difficult problems. There is no doubt that it belongs to the dawn
of history, to the period immediately preceding the First Dynasty
of Ur (*circa* 2650 BC). There can also be no question but that the
people so lavishly buried could be other than kings, queens and

princes. In the sixteen royal tombs several inscriptions were found, most of them on cylinder-seals, but two names only, Mes-kalam-dug ('The hero of the good land') and A-kalam-dug, are followed by the title *lugal*, 'king', and two other names, those of Nin-banda, wife of Mes-kalam-dug, and of Shub-ad, spouse of an unknown monarch, are qualified by the title *nin*, 'queen'; and while the fact that all but two tombs had been plundered in antiquity might account for the absence of other royal inscriptions, this absence is nevertheless disconcerting.[16] Even more puzzling is the practice of collective burials involving from three to seventy-four attendants—practically a whole royal household. It is attested on a smaller scale in other countries and in other times—in Egypt during the First Dynasty, among the Scythians and the Mongols, in Assam, and even among the Comans of southern Russia as late as the thirteenth century AD[17]—but nowhere in Mesopotamia outside Ur. Again, it can be argued that practically all the royal tombs in ancient Iraq were found plundered and that we have no written description of a royal funeral. Yet this silence about a ceremony which must have been of paramount importance is surprising, and can only be explained by assuming that royal burials with human sacrifices fell into disuse at a very early date, probably during the Early Dynastic period. But why this sacrifice? The only text in our possession alluding to a king going to the grave with his retinue is, significantly, a Sumerian epic tale known as 'the death of Gilgamesh'.[18] Now, we know that Gilgamesh and Mes-kalam-dug lived at approximately the same time, and we also know from other sources that Gilgamesh was considered to be a god of the Netherworld. This would tend to confirm the theory first propounded by Woolley that Mes-kalam-dug, A-kalam-dug, Shub-ad and the other anonymous kings and queens of the Royal Cemetery were more than monarchs: they were gods, or at least, they represented the gods on earth and, as such, were entitled to take their court with them into another life, a life no doubt incomparably more enjoyable than that of the ordinary human being.

If the Kings of Mesopotamia ceased early to be 'substitute gods', they always retained some of their priestly functions. Yet the general trend throughout history was towards a gradual separation of the Throne from the Temple, and this development started in Pre-Sargonic times. Already, about 2500 B C, Entemena, ensi of Lagash, was no longer high priest of that city, for on a beautiful silver vase which he dedicated to Ningirsu, an inscription expressly mentions: 'In those days Dudu was priest (*sanga*) of Ningirsu.'[19] There were even times when the ruler and the priests were, it seems, in open conflict. About a century after Entemena, Urukagina, the last prince of Lagash, tells us in a famous inscription[20] how he, as champion of the gods, put an end to the abuses that existed before his reign: inspectors of the ruler interfered in all affairs, fantastic taxes were levied on burials and, apparently, on weddings, houses were bought below their price by rich officials, corruption was rife and the poor suffered much; but, more important, the king was building up vast estates, his 'onion and cucumber gardens' encroached on the best fields of the gods and were tilled by oxen and asses belonging to the temples. Urukagina revoked many officials, reduced taxation and 'reinstated Ningirsu' in the buildings and fields of the ruler:

'He freed the citizens of Lagash from usury, monopoly, hunger, theft and assault; he established their freedom.'

But these reforms, if they were applied at all, had no lasting effect, for it was under Urukagina's reign that Lagash and the rest of Sumer fell into non-Sumerian hands.

OUTLINE OF HISTORY

To reconstruct the sequence of events during the Early Dynastic period is not an easy task. Not only are historical texts proper extremely rare and usually concise, but the coexistence of several local 'dynasties' and the part played by some rulers not mentioned in the King List add considerably to the difficulty. We shall therefore aim at nothing more than a brief outline of Pre-Sargonic history, warning the reader that many points in our reconstruction are highly controversial.

When the first royal inscription, that of Enmebaragesi (*circa* 2700 B C), appears, the First Dynasty of Kish had already reigned supreme for several generations, with the result that the title 'King of Kish' had become almost synonymous with 'King of the Country, King of Sumer'. If we can trust the Tummal inscription, it was Enmebaragesi who built the first temple of Enlil in Nippur, and soon Nippur—which was never the seat of a dynasty—was taken by the Sumerians as their religious capital, the Rome or the Mecca, as it were, of their country. At first, *lugals* and *ensis* from nearly all city-states competed in sending to Enlil's temple the most valuable presents, but towards the end of the period it became necessary for the rulers to be 'elected by Enlil in Nippur' if they were to be acknowledged by other princes as their suzerains; the possession of Nippur became the condition *sine qua non* of supremacy in Sumer. This custom has never been fully explained. We know that Enlil was the greatest god of Sumer and Nippur his city, but Anu, before him, had held this position and it is perhaps permissible to wonder whether Enlil did not owe his rise to the supreme rank to the fact that he was the god of Nippur. Both Kish and Nippur, it should be remembered, lay in the north of Sumer and their territories must have spanned the space between the Tigris and the Euphrates, then considerably closer to each other at that latitude than they are now. These two cities, therefore, commanded the great trade routes that went down the Twin Rivers, from Anatolia, Armenia and Azerbaijan to southern Iraq, the 'bronze routes', as well, perhaps, as the main irrigation canals. Whoever controlled them controlled the commerce and industry of Sumer, and this might well account for the importance attached to their possession.

According to the legend, Gilgamesh of Uruk obtained the submission of Agga of Kish and put an end to his dynasty, but in actual fact the real successor of Kish as a leading state was Ur. On seal impressions found at Ur, Mes-anne-padda styles himself 'King of Kish', and his two sons probably possessed Nippur since they restored its temple. The wealth of Mes-anne-padda's predecessors, displayed in the sumptuous grave furniture of the Royal Cemetery, indicates that Ur had long been a prosperous city, and what remains of the Early Dynastic buildings at Ur itself and Ubaid confirms this impression. But after a century or so, Ur lost its hegemony. From the mountains which border Iraq to the east descended hordes of Elamites, and the two foreign dynasties of Awan and Hamazi imposed their law upon at least part of Sumer. This was not the first episode in the long series of wars between Mesopotamia and Elam which were to last, from then on, for two thousand years: it is said in the King List that Enmebaragesi 'carried away as spoil the weapons of Elam', and the stories of Enmerkar and Lugalbanda suggest that the conflict had its roots in prehistoric times.

At this point our attention becomes centred upon Lagash, not only because its ruins have yielded more historical texts than any other city, but also because one of its rulers is about to play an important part in a country profoundly disorganized by two invasions. Like his grandfather Ur-Nanshe, Eannatum, *ensi* of Lagash (*circa* 2550 BC) was a great builder of temples and digger of canals; in addition, circumstances made of him a great warrior. He purged Sumer from the Elamite bands and protected its eastern flank by conquering, if not, as he claims, 'Elam the great mountain that strikes terror, in its entirety', at least several towns on the border of Elam. He overthrew Ur and Uruk and 'added to the princeship (*nam-ensi*) of Lagash the kingship of Kish'. But the war about which we are best informed is a localized conflict, the war against the city of Umma (Tell Jokha), 18 miles only from Lagash.[21] The bone of contention was a certain field called Gu-edin which lay at the limit between the two states and which was claimed by both. Already, several generations before Eannatum, a certain Mesilim, King of Kish—perhaps identical to Mes-anne-padda, King of Ur and of Kish[22]—had acted as referee and set up his stele as boundary stone in that area. But now:

'The ensi of Umma, at the command of his god, raided and devoured the Gu-edin, the irrigated land, the field beloved of Ningirsu. . . . He ripped out the stele and entered the plain of Lagash.'

The infantry of Lagash, armed with long spears and protected by heavy shields, met in battle the soldiers of Umma. Eannatum won:

'By the word of Enlil, he hurled the great net upon them and heaped up piles of their bodies in the plain. . . . The survivors turned to Eannatum, they prostrated themselves for life, they wept. . . .'

The fight ended in a peace treaty. The ensi of Lagash 'marked off the boundary with Enakalli, the ensi of Umma; he restored Mesilim's stele to its former place' and levied on Umma a heavy tax in barley. Eannatum's victory—or rather the victory of Ningirsu, the god of Lagash, over Shara, the god of Umma—was commemorated by a masterpiece of early Sumerian sculpture, unfortunately found in fragments, the stele 'of the Vultures', so called because of the birds of prey that tear up the corpses of the vanquished. Towards the end of his reign, Eannatum had to fight a coalition of the men of Kish and Mari led by Zuzu (or Unzi), King of Akshak.[23] Although he claimed victory, there is little doubt that this war marked the end of the small empire he had built.

The century following Eannatum's death is rather confused. It appears that En-shakush-anna, King of Uruk, and Lugal-anne-mundu, King of Adab (nowadays Bismaya, 16 miles north of Tell Fara[24]) successively occupied Kish and Nippur, and were recognized as suzerains of Sumer. But their authority was challenged by the rulers of Mari. According to the Sumerian King List, six kings of Mari ruled over Sumer for 136 years. This figure is certainly exaggerated, but the fact that sovereigns from a city so far away in the north-west reigned at all in southern Iraq is an indication of the state of semi-anarchy prevailing at that time in the region. In Lagash, under Eannatum's nephew Entemena, war broke out again with Umma whose ruler was backed by 'foreign kings'—perhaps the Kings of Mari. In a long inscription on two clay cylinders, Entemena recalls what happened in the past, tells us how he 'slew the Ummaite forces up into Umma itself', then stood firm against the pretensions of the new ensi of Umma, 'that plunderer of fields and farms, that speaker of evil', and dug a boundary ditch as a permanent frontier between the two rival cities. We also know from other sources that Entemena concluded a 'brotherhood pact' with his powerful neighbour Lugal-kinishe-dudu of Uruk who had united Uruk and Ur into a single kingdom, and that his reign ended in peace and prosperity. But a few years later, the situation deteriorated again in Lagash. The priests of Ningirsu seized the throne and occupied it for about two decades, enlarging, as we have seen, their personal properties at the expense of the gods. They were overthrown by Urukagina, famous for his social reforms, but Urukagina reigned only eight years. An energetic and ambitious ensi of Umma, Lugal-zagge-si, marched against Lagash, took it and destroyed it, thus avenging two centuries of defeat. On the smouldering ruins of the city, an unknown scribe sat later to write a lamentation which has come down to us:[25]

'The men of Umma have set fire to the (temple) Antasurra, they have carried away the silver and the precious stones. . . . They have shed blood in the temple E-engur of the goddess Nanshe; they have carried away the silver and the precious stones. . . . The men of Umma, by the despoiling of Lagash, have committed a sin against the god Ningirsu. . . . As for Lugal-zagge-si, ensi of Umma, may his goddess Nidaba bear his mortal sin upon her head!'

But the curse had no immediate effect. After Lagash, Lugal-zagge-si took Uruk and established himself as king of that city. He then proceeded to conquer the rest of Sumer and apparently succeeded. Indeed, on a vase dedicated to Enlil in Nippur, he claims conquests embracing the whole of Mesopotamia as well as Syria:

'When Enlil, king of all sovereign countries, had given him the kingship over the nation (Sumer), had directed upon him the eyes of the nation, made all sovereign countries wait upon him, and made (everyone) from where the sun rises to where the sun sets submit to him; then he drew toward himself the feet of (everybody) from the Lower Sea (Persian Gulf) (along) the Tigris and the Euphrates to the Upper Sea (Mediterranean). From where the sun rises to where the sun sets, Enlil let him have no opponent. All sovereign countries lay (as cows) in pasture under him; the Nation was watering (its fields) in joy under him; all the dependent rulers of Sumer and the ensis of all independent countries bowed to him before his arbitral office in Uruk.'[26]

It is difficult to believe that Lugal-zagge-si possessed in fact such an empire. Perhaps this is no more than a piece of grandiloquence; perhaps the King of Uruk had managed to obtain the submission or the alliance of the Semites of Mari who, in turn, might have held the Semites of Syria under their political influence. In any case, the 'Sumerian Empire' of Lugal-zagge-si lasted no longer than his reign: twenty-five years. A newcomer, a Semitic prince, Sargon of Akkad, gave both the fatal blow.

CHAPTER IX

SEMITIC INTERLUDE

THROUGHOUT the Early Dynastic period, the Sumerian rulers competed and struggled for supremacy over a dozen cities and a few square miles of irrigated land: Sumer. The sea-shore to the south and Kish to the north marked the limits of their ambitions, and Mari and Assur were, it seems, as foreign to them as Elam. But about 2400 BC, Semitic princes from central Iraq altered the course of events. Not only did Sargon and his successors subdue all the Sumerian city states, but they conquered the whole Tigris–Euphrates basin as well as parts of the adjacent countries, embarked on expeditions in the Persian Gulf, and built the first great Mesopotamian empire. For the first time since the prehistoric Ubaid period, the two halves of Mesopotamia, till then connected only by loose cultural ties, were bound together as one large nation extending from the Taurus to the 'Lower Sea', from the Zagros to the Mediterranean. To the people of the times, this territory appeared immense; it encompassed 'the Four Regions of the World', it was 'the Universe'. The Sargonic empire was to last for about two hundred years and to collapse under the combined pressure of the Zagros tribes and internal rebellion, but it had set an example never to be forgotten. To reconstruct the unity of Mesopotamia, to reach what we would call its natural limits, became the dream of all subsequent monarchs, and from the middle of the third millennium until the fall of Babylon in 539 BC, the history of ancient Iraq consists of their attempts, their successes and their failures to achieve this aim.

Who, then, were those Semites who made such a brilliant entry into history?

THE SEMITES

The adjective 'Semitic' was coined in 1781 by a German scholar, Schlözer, to qualify a group of closely related languages, and subsequently the people who spoke these languages were called 'Semites'. Both words come, of course, from Sem, son of Noah, father of Ashur, Aram and Heber (Genesis x. 21–31) and alleged ancestor of the Assyrians, Aramaeans and Hebrews. Among the Semitic languages, Arabic is today the most widely spoken; then come Ethiopic and Hebrew recently revived in script. Others, like Akkadian (Babylonian and Assyrian), or the Canaanite dialects, are dead, while Aramaic survives, much altered, in the liturgic tongue of some Oriental Churches (Syriac) and in the dialects spoken by small, isolated communities in the Lebanon and northern Iraq. All these languages have many points in common and form a large and coherent family. One of their main characteristics is that almost all the verbs, nouns and adjectives derive from radicals usually composed of three consonants. The insertion of long or short vowels between these consonants gives precision and actuality to the concept expressed by the radical in a general way. Thus, in Arabic, the radical *ktb* conveys the vague idea of 'writing', but 'he wrote' is *kataba*, 'he writes' *yiktib*, 'writer' *kâtib*, etc. Languages of this type are called flectional and contrast with languages such as Sumerian, which are of the agglutinative type.

As long as they are used for linguistic purposes, the words 'Semitic' and 'Semite' are convenient and acceptable to everyone. But because the Semitic languages, before the great Islamic expansion, were spoken in a limited area, a number of authors have considered the Semites as a particular race, or rather—since the concept of a Semitic race is rejected by modern anthropologists—as an homogeneous community of persons sharing, not only the same language, but also the same psychology, laws and customs and the same religious beliefs. In other words, the Semites are taken to be one great single 'people'. Is this view justified? The problem is, of course, of extreme importance to our subject and must be examined.[1]

The area inhabited by the Semitic-speaking peoples in ancient historical times consists of the Arabian peninsula and its northern appendages: the Syrian desert and the Fertile Crescent. It is a well defined, compact region, limited on all sides by seas and high mountains. According to the classical theory, all Semites were originally nomadic tribes living in the central part of this area. At various intervals, large groups of them left the Syro-Arabian desert to settle, peacefully or by force, in the peripheral districts, mostly Mesopotamia and Syria–Palestine. They were:

—the Akkadians in Mesopotamia during the fourth millennium BC;

—the Western Semites (Cananeo-Phoenicians and Amorites) in Mesopotamia and Syria–Palestine during the third and second millennia;

—the Aramaeans all around the Fertile Crescent in the twelfth century BC;

—the Nabataeans and other Pre-Islamic Arabs, from the second century BC to the sixth century AD;

—and finally, the Moslem Arabs from the seventh century AD.

This theory holds good—especially for the last three ethno-linguistic groups—inasmuch as it describes in broad outline a certain sequence of events. In detail, however, it cannot be accepted without serious amendments. To consider the Syro-Arabian desert as the centre of diffusion of the Semites is out of the question. Only the Yemen, parts of Hadramaut and Oman, and a few oases in Arabia proper offer favourable living conditions, and it is extremely doubtful whether the great desert of central Arabia was inhabited at all between the Palaeolithic ages—when it was not a desert but a savanna—and the first millennium BC. Life in extensive desert areas presupposes large-scale seasonal migrations in search of pastures, but only short-range migrations were possible before the widespread use of domestic camels in the Near East from the twelfth century BC onwards.[2] Before that time, the nomads, who rode on asses and practised sheep-rearing, were much more restricted in their movements than the bedouins of today, and could not wander far beyond the limits of the grassy steppe which extends between the Tigris and the Euphrates and at the foot of the Zagros, the Taurus and the Lebanon. There they were in close and constant touch with the agricultural populations which bought their sheep and supplied them with grain, dates, tools, weapons and other utilitarian objects and amenities. The relationship between nomads and peasants could take various forms.3 In general, the two groups met regularly in villages or on the market-place, outside the gates of the city, and exchanged goods, together, no doubt, with a number of ideas. Then the nomads returned to the steppe, perhaps only a few miles away. Occasionally, individuals left the tribe to find work in the towns as mercenaries, craftsmen or merchants. Sometimes a family, a clan, or a whole tribe would acquire (or be granted) land, and devote itself partly to agriculture, partly to sheep-breeding. Not infrequently the local governments exercised some control over the nomads, using them in particular as auxiliary troops whenever required. But in times of political unrest, the situation could be reversed: tribes or confederations of tribes waged war against the sedentary society, ransacked the towns and occupied a territory, large or small, where they eventually settled. The sedentarization of the nomads was therefore a slow, almost continuous process with occasional episodes of armed intrusion. It took the form, not of an outward movement from the desert centre to the fertile periphery, but of a series of short- or medium-range movements within the periphery itself, from the steppe to the irrigated land. Thus, the Fertile Crescent and possibly parts of the outskirts of the Arabian peninsula appear as the true home-land of the Semitic-speaking peoples. They were there, as far as we can judge, from prehistoric times, but they *reveal* themselves to us at different periods, either because they adopt some sort of writing, or because, at a given moment, they become militarily active or politically influential and are mentioned in the written records of the civilized sedentary society.

Because most nomadic tribes in the ancient Near East spoke Semitic languages, it does not necessarily follow that all Semitic-speaking people were nomads. The failure to recognize this point has resulted in a great deal of confusion. The features attributed, rightly or wrongly, to the 'Semites' in general—their 'spirited, impatient, mercurial, and emotional type of mentality',4 their 'monotheistic, anti-mythological and anti-ritualistic religious ideas',5 their socio-political concepts revolving around the tribe—all this applies in fact only to the *nomadic* Semites and results, to a great extent, from their particular way of life. But, if some of the

Arabs, Aramaeans and Western Semites fall within this category, we have no proof whatsoever that the Akkadians in Mesopotamia—nor, for that matter, the Cananeo-Phoenicians in Syria–Palestine—were originally nomads. As to Mesopotamia, we do not know when the Semites first entered the country, if indeed they entered at all. Attempts have been made to correlate one or the other of the great ethnic migrations of proto-historic times with a Semitic invasion, but the wide divergence of opinions among scholars on this subject is tantamount to a confession of ignorance.[6] Semitic personal names and a few texts written in Semitic language appear during the Early-Dynastic period,[7] and their geographical distribution suggests that the Semites were in a minority among the Sumerians of the south, but were powerful and active, if not predominant, in the region of Kish. Judging from the Mari inscriptions and from later documents, it seems fairly certain that they already formed the greater part of the population of northern Iraq. From the Sargonic period onwards, the central part of Mesopotamia, from Nippur up to perhaps Hît and Samarra, including the lower Diyala valley, was called 'the country of *Akkad*', this name being usually written with the Sumerian ideogram URI. We may therefore call the earliest Semites of Mesopotamia *Akkadians*. Their language, also called Akkadian, constitutes a particular branch of the semitic family, and they wrote it with the cuneiform script invented by the Sumerians to express their own language—a delicate and awkward adaptation since the two languages are as unrelated to each other as, say, Chinese and Latin. While a number of Sumerian words passed into Akkadian, the Sumerians borrowed a limited amount of Akkadian words such as *hazi* 'axe', *shám*, 'price', or *súm*, 'garlic'. This is about all the sources available at present enable us to say. But it must be pointed out that not one single Sumerian text refers to the Akkadians as enemies, invaders or nomads. And although it is possible, albeit not quite proven, that the social organization and political system of the Akkadians differed from those upon which the Sumerian city-state was founded, it appears clearly that the Akkadians practised agriculture, lived in villages and towns and shared the way of life, the religion and the culture of the Sumerians. So far as we know at the present time, the only obvious difference between the

Akkadians and the Sumerians is a linguistic one; in all other respects, these two ethnic groups are indistinguishable. The Akkadian domination in Sargonic times changed the course of history; it did not fundamentally alter the predominantly Sumerian character of the Mesopotamian civilization.

SARGON OF AKKAD

The reign of Sargon made such an impression on the Sumero-Akkadians that his personality was surrounded with a lasting halo of legend. A text written in Neo-Assyrian times (seventh century BC) describes his birth and early childhood in terms reminiscent of Moses, Krishna and other great men:

'My mother was a changeling (?), my father I knew not.
The brothers of my father loved the hills.
My city is Azupiranu, which is situated on the banks of the Euphrates.
My changeling mother conceived me, in secret she bore me.
She set me in a basket of rushes, with bitumen she sealed my lid.
She cast me into the river which rose not over me.
The river bore me up and carried me to Akki, the drawer of water.
Akki, the drawer of water, took me as his son and reared me.
Akki, the drawer of water, appointed me as his gardener.
While I was a gardener, Ishtar granted me her love,
And for four and . . . years I exercised kingship.'[8]

This is, at best, strongly romanced history, though we learn from more reliable sources[9] that the man who was to call himself *Sharru-kín*, 'the righteous (or legitimate) king', was of humble origin. The cup-bearer of Ur-Zababa, king of Kish, he managed —we do not know how—to overthrow his master and marched against Uruk where reigned Lugal-zagge-si, then overlord of Sumer. Lugal-zagge-si, who had fifty ensis under his command, was defeated, captured, brought to Kish 'in a dog collar' and exposed at Enlil's gate. Thereafter, the usurper attacked Ur, Lagash and Umma; everywhere he was victorious and of every town he 'tore down the walls'. To show that he had conquered

Sumer in its totality, he made a symbolic gesture, a gesture which will later be repeated by other monarchs on other shores: he washed his weapon in the Lower Sea, the Persian Gulf.

Sargon could have contented himself with the prestigious title 'King of Kish', but he had other ambitions. Somewhere on the Euphrates, he founded a new capital, Agade—the only royal city of ancient Iraq whose location remains unknown[10]—wherein he built a palace as well as temples for his tutelary goddess, Ishtar, and for Zababa, the warrior-god of Kish. The major innovation of the reign, however, was the ascendancy given to the Semites. Akkadian governors were appointed in all important Sumerian city-states, and Akkadian became, as much as Sumerian, the language of official inscriptions. Yet the religious institutions of Sumer were respected: Sargon's daughter was made a priestess of Nanna, the moon-god of Ur, and by calling himself 'anointed priest of Anu' and 'great ensi of Enlil', the King of Agade proved that he did not wish to break with ancient and respectable traditions.

Having consolidated his political and moral authority over Sumer, and having considerably increased his army, Sargon launched several military campaigns in at least two directions: across the Tigris towards Iran, and along the Euphrates towards Syria. To the east, he met with strong resistance: the troops of four rulers of south-western Persia led by the King of Awan. The enemies were eventually defeated and, their chief having been killed on the battlefield, Sargon appointed as his vassal the submissive ensi of Elam whose town, Susa, was raised from the rank of a modest market-place to that of a capital-city.[11] In so doing, the King of Akkad could hardly have foreseen that a governor of Elam would contribute to the fall of his own dynasty, or that the name of Susa would, for centuries to come, be symbolic of Mesopotamian defeat and humiliation. The campaign to the north-west appears, wrongly perhaps, almost as an armed promenade: Sargon says that at Tutul (Hît), he 'prostrated himself in prayer before Dagan' (the grain-god worshipped all along the Middle Euphrates) and that 'Dagan gave him the Upper Region: Mari, Iarmuti and Ibla as far as the Cedar Forest and the Silver Mountain'. Iarmuti and Ibla, certainly in northern Syria, have not been located with certainty, but the Cedar Forest stands for the

Lebanon or the Amanus, and the Silver Mountain for the Taurus range. As both names indicate, Sargon had secured a supply of wood and precious metal which could now be floated freely and safely down the Euphrates to Sumer and Akkad.

This is as far as the authentic sources—Sargon's own inscriptions—take us. We can, however, consider as certain one or several unrecorded northerly campaigns along the Tigris, at least as far as the latitude of Mosul, since tablets written in Akkadian language begin now to appear in that region, and since a magnificent bronze head, usually taken as portraying Sargon himself, was found at Nineveh.[12] But what are we to think of the several chronicles, omens and literary compositions of later date which give us a detailed and often poetic description of Sargon's campaigns and conquests? Where, for instance, does history end and legend begin in the text known as 'the Epic of the King of the Battle' which shows the king of Akkad advancing deep into the heart of Asia Minor to protect merchants from the exactions of the King of Burushanda?[13] We can accept successful campaigns in Kurdistan and, perhaps, expeditions on the Persian Gulf as far as Oman, but can we really believe that Sargon 'crossed the Sea of the West' and set foot in Cyprus and Crete? The figure of the first great Mesopotamian conqueror enflamed the ancient writers' imagination. For them, the king who had said:

'Now, any king who wants to call himself my equal,
  Wherever I went, let him go!'[14]

was perfectly capable of having conquered 'the world'. Yet, extreme scepticism is as undesirable as extreme credulity, for most of these stories must contain at least a grain of truth.

The glorious reign of Sargon lasted for no less than fifty-five years (circa 2371–2316 BC). 'In his old age', says a late Babylonian chronicle,[15] 'all the lands revolted against him, and they besieged him in Agade.' But the old lion still had teeth and claws: 'he went forth to battle and defeated them; he knocked them over and destroyed their vast army'. Later on, we are told, 'Subartu—i.e. (the nomadic tribes of) Upper Jazirah—in its might attacked, but they submitted to his arms, and Sargon settled their habitations, and he smote them grievously.'

THE AKKADIAN EMPIRE

The events which darkened the last years of Sargon announce the general revolt which broke out in Sumer and in Iran after his death. His son and successor, Rimush, repressed it with extreme vigour, but his authority was challenged even in his own palace: after only eight years of reign (2315–2307), 'his servants', says a Babylonian omen,[16] 'killed him with their tablets'—which is proof that the written word was already a deadly weapon! Rimush was replaced by Manishtusu, perhaps his twin brother as his name 'Who is with him?' might suggest.[17]

The main event in Manishtusu's reign (2306–2292) was an expedition across the Persian Gulf. It is described as follows:

'Manishtusu, King of Kish, when he had subjugated Anshan and Shirikum (in SW. Iran), he crossed the Lower Sea in ships. The kings of the cities on the other side of the sea, 32 of them assembled for battle. He defeated them and subjugated their cities; he overthrew their lords and seized the whole country as far as the silver mines. The mountains beyond the Lower Sea—their stones he took away, and he made his statue, and he presented it to Enlil.'[18]

Whether these 'mountains beyond the sea' were those of Oman or of Persia is a moot point, but the goal of the expedition is clearly stated, and if we look at the situation in Mesopotamia at that time, we understand the reasons behind it. The northern regions had been crossed by the armies of Sargon, but not effectively occupied. The populations of Jazirah and northern Syria were free again. Farther north, a people which will later play an important part in the history of ancient Iraq, the Hurrians, occupied the great half-circle of the Taurus mountains, from Urkish, north of Karkemish, to the country of Namar, around Lake Van, and perhaps as far south as the Upper Zab.[19] Their eastern neighbours, the Lullubi, were entrenched in the Shehrizor plain, near Suleimaniyah. Below the Lullubi, around Hamadan in the central Zagros, were the savage Guti and, farther south, the turbulent tribes around Elam. All these peoples were on anything but friendly terms with the Akkadians, and as they held all the passes leading from Anatolia, Armenia and Azerbaijan to Mesopotamia, the latter was cut off from its traditional supplies of copper, tin and silver. The 'bronze routes' were closed, and the Akkadians had only two alternatives: either to secure other sources of metal, such as Oman or south-eastern Persia, or to fight in the north.

Narâm-Sin ('Beloved of Sin'), the son of Manishtusu, chose war and, at least for a while, was rewarded with success. To the title of 'King of Agade', he could proudly add those of 'King of the Four Regions (of the World)' (*shar kibrat 'arbaim*) and 'King of the Universe' (*shar kishati*). Furthermore, his name was preceded by the star, the ideogram for 'god', read in Sumerian *dingir*, in Akkadian *ilu*. Thus, the king had become a god, like Lugalbanda and Gilgamesh. Megalomania? Certainly not, for the mighty Assyrian kings of the first millennium BC were never deified. But we must confess that the deification of a limited number of monarchs in ancient Mesopotamia is a strange practice not yet fully understood. Perhaps the most likely explanation is that the divine title was taken only by those sovereigns who played the part of the male god in the Sacred Marriage ceremony of the New Year Festival.[20]

Narâm-Sin was of the same stamp as his grandfather Sargon and, like him, became a hero of legend. His long reign (2291–2255) was almost entirely filled with military operations, and they all took place at the periphery of Mesopotamia. In the west, he 'slew Arman (Aleppo?) and Ibla with the weapon of the god Dagan' and 'he overpowered the Amanus, the Cedar Mountain'.[21] In the north, a campaign against Hurrian Namar is attested by a royal relief carved in the rock at Pir Hussain, near Diarbakr, and a royal residence was built at Tell Brak, a key position in the heart of the Khabur basin, which controlled all the roads of Jazirah.[22] In the extreme south, Magan (Oman?) probably revolted, for Narâm-Sin 'marched against Magan and personally caught Mandannu, its king'. But the main campaign was directed against the powerful Lullubi. The Akkadian victory over them is commemorated by another rock sculpture at Darband-i-Gawr, near Sar-i-Pul (Iran) and by a masterpiece of Mesopotamian sculpture: the famous stele found at Susa and now the pride of the Louvre museum.[23] There Narâm-Sin, armed with the bow and the horned tiara of the gods on his head, is shown climbing a steep mountain and treading upon the corpses of his enemies; his infantry, pictured on a smaller scale, follows. The gods, who dwarfed the humans in Early Dynastic Sumerian sculpture, are now, significantly, reduced to discrete symbols: two stars in the sky.

Did the reign end in semi-disaster? A document known as 'the Cuthean Legend of Narâm-Sin' shows the King of Akkad 'bewildered, confused, sunk in gloom, sorrowful, exhausted' from an overwhelming invasion by the Lullubi and other enemies, but finally victorious.[24] But, here again, the mixture of facts and fancy calls for extreme caution. There is no doubt, however, that Narâm-Sin was the last great monarch of the Akkadian dynasty. No sooner was he dead than the pressure at the frontiers of the empire became formidable. Throughout his reign, Elam and Mesopotamia had lived on friendly terms: the king had bestowed his favours upon Susa, and the energetic governor of Elam, Puzur-Inshushinak, had subdued on his behalf the tribes of the southern Zagros. But under Narâm-Sin's successor, Shar-kali-sharri, Puzur-Inshushinak declared himself independent, abandoned the Akkadian language for his own tongue, Elamite, and dared take the supreme title 'King of the Universe'. The 'King of Agade', whose name, ironically, meant 'King of all Kings', was powerless to intervene, so busy was he with the repression of revolts in Sumer and with wars against the Lullubi, the Guti and the nomads of Syria.

Shar-kali-sharri, like Rimush and Manishtusu, disappeared in a palace revolution (2230 BC), and the Akkadian empire collapsed as rapidly as it had been built up. The state of anarchy in the capital was such that the Sumerian King List simply says:

> 'Who was king? Who was not king?
> Was Igigi king?
> Was Nanum king?
> Was Imi king?
> Was Elulu king?
> Their tetrad was king, and reigned 3 years!'[25]

Several Sumerian cities became independent, following the example set by Uruk where a local dynasty (Uruk IV, five kings, 30 years) reigned from the last days of Narâm-Sin. From Elam, Puzur-Inshushinak conducted a raid into Mesopotamia and reached the neighbourhood of Agade. In Kurdistan, Annubanini, King of the Lullubi, carved his image on the rock with an inscription in Akkadian boasting of widespread conquests.[26] Yet it was neither the Elamites nor the Lullubi, but the Guti who won the decisive battle, although we do not know how, where and when. Under the last puppet kings of Akkad, they were already installed in Mesopotamia, and for about a century the Sumerians and Akkadians were to obey sovereigns who responded to such strange names as Inimagabesh or Jarlagab.

The rise and fall of the Akkadian empire offers a perfect illustration of the rise and fall of all subsequent Mesopotamian empires: rapid expansion followed by ceaseless rebellions, palace revolutions, constant wars on the frontiers and, in the end, the *coup de grâce* given by the highlanders: Guti now, Elamites, Kassites, Medes or Persians tomorrow. A civilization based on agriculture and metal-work in a country like Iraq required, to be viable, two conditions: perfect co-operation between the various ethnic and socio-political units within the country itself, and a friendly, or at least a neutral attitude from its neighbours. Unfortunately, neither one nor the other ever lasted for any length of time. The narrow nationalism of the Sumerians, inherited from a distant past and founded on the attachment to local gods, could not accommodate itself to obedience to a common ruler, always necessarily 'foreign'. On the other hand, the treasures accumulated in the prosperous cities of the plain attracted the poor shepherds of the hills no less than the shepherds of the steppe, and they were bent upon pillage. It was not enough for the Mesopotamians to keep them at a respectful distance: they had to conquer them, to subdue them if they wished to keep open the vital arteries of their trade. In this endless guerrilla war on two fronts, the kings of Akkad, as later the kings of Ur, Babylon and Assyria, used up their strength and, sooner or later, their empires collapsed.

The death of Shar-kali-sharri in 2230 practically marks the end of the 'Akkadian period' as it is often called. But, short as it was, this period exerted a deep and lasting influence on Mesopotamian history. The geographical horizon of Sumer was considerably enlarged. The Semitic language of the Akkadians found a wider audience, and the first two historical populations of Iraq were intimately blended for future destinies. The Sumero-Akkadian culture and its support, the cuneiform writing, were adopted not only by the people of northern Mesopotamia, but by the Hurrians, the Lullubi and the Elamites. Conversely, Mesopotamia was immensely enriched by the introduction of bronze, silver, wood and stone in large quantities, while numerous prisoners of war, used as slaves, provided cheap and abundant labour. Bahrain (Dilmun), Oman (?Magan), and the whole Persian Gulf came under Mesopotamian influence, while Proto-Indian seals, vases and ornaments found in Iraq testify to commercial relations with the Indus valley (perhaps the Meluhha of our texts) where flourished the brilliant civilization of Harappa and Mohenjo-Daro.[27] In art, the new tendencies were towards realism, and true portraits replaced the more or less conventional figures of Early Dynastic times. Politically, the period rings the knell of the small city-states and heralds the advent of large, centralized kingdoms. In the social and economic fields, the Akkadian preference for private property and the constitution of large royal estates[28] tended to 'unsettle the fundamental principles of the Sumerian city-temple'.[29] Even the Sumerian reaction which succeeded the Akkadian interlude could not entirely revert to old-fashioned ideas and customs and, in many respects, the kings of Ur followed the pattern laid down by Sargon and his dynasty.

CHAPTER X

SUMERIAN RENAISSANCE

ABOUT the Guti who overthrew the Akkadian empire and ruled over Mesopotamia for almost a hundred years, we know next to nothing.[1] The Sumerian King List gives 'the hordes of Gutium' twenty-one kings, but only five of them have left us inscriptions and this, coupled with silence from other sources, points to a period of political unrest and cultural regression. The invaders were certainly not very numerous; they ravaged the country, probably destroyed Agade, and occupied Nippur and a few strategic points, yet many cities must have enjoyed almost complete freedom, keeping alive a spirit of national resistance which, eventually, culminated in the liberation of Sumer and Akkad. When, about 2120 B C, Utu-hegal, ensi of Uruk, mustered an army and rose against 'the stinging serpent of the hills', several princes in southern Iraq followed him. The hated foreigners were defeated; Tiriqan, their king, tried to escape, was captured, and handed over to the Sumerian leader:

'Utu-hegal sat down; Tiriqan lay at his feet. Upon his neck he set his foot, and the sovereignty of Sumer he restored into his (own) hands.'[2]

Nippur was no doubt recovered, and Uruk, the city which, since the days of Gilgamesh had given Sumer no less than four dynasties, could stand once again at the head of the city-states. But its fifth dynasty was short-lived: after seven years of reign, Utu-hegal was evicted by one of his own officials, Ur-Nammu,* governor of Ur, who took the titles 'King of Ur, King of Sumer and Akkad'. Thus was founded the Third Dynasty of Ur (*circa* 2113–2006 B C)

* The name means 'servant (literally: dog) of the goddess Nammu' and has nothing to do with the city of Ur.

which represents one of the most brilliant periods in the history of ancient Iraq, for not only did Ur-Nammu and his successors restore the Akkadian empire throughout its length and breadth, but they gave Mesopotamia a century of relative peace and prosperity, and sponsored an extraordinary renaissance in all branches of Sumerian art and literature.

UR-NAMMU AND GUDEA

Compared with the Sargonic period, the time of the Third Dynasty of Ur—the 'Ur III' or 'Neo-Sumerian' period, as it is sometimes called—is conspicuously poor in historical inscriptions and, much as we should like to, we cannot follow Ur-Nammu in the battles which served to enlarge his kingdom. The collapse of the Guti followed by the violent death of Utu-hegal ('his body was carried off by the river') must have resulted in complete political vacuum, and we can assume that the whole of Mesopotamia fell into the hands of the King of Ur in a comparatively short time. The rest of the reign (2113–2096) was devoted to the fulfilment of more domestic, but nonetheless urgent and important tasks: the restoration of order and prosperity, and the care of the gods.3 Ur-Nammu 'freed the land from thieves, robbers and rebels' and promulgated what is considered to be the most ancient collection of laws in the world. Found at Nippur more than 50 years ago though only recently published,4 the tablet bearing this 'code' is badly damaged. What remains of the laws, however, is of considerable interest, for it appears that at least some crimes (such as physical injury) were not punished by death or mutilation, as later in the Code of Hammurabi or the Hebraic law, but the offender was obliged to pay compensation in silver, the weight of which varied according to the gravity of the crime. This, of course, is the sign of a society far more polished and civilized than is usually imagined. Ur-Nammu also revived agriculture and improved communications by digging a number of canals; commerce with Magan, suspended during the Guti domination, was resumed; towns were fortified against future wars and an enormous amount of rebuilding was carried out. But in the minds of archaeologists, the name of Ur-Nammu will be for ever associated with the *ziqqurats*, or stage-towers which he erected in

Ur, Uruk, Eridu, Nippur and various other cities and which are still the most impressive monuments of these sites.

The best preserved of these stage-towers, the ziqqurat of Ur, can be taken as an example.5 Built of mud bricks but covered with an 8 foot thick 'skin' of baked bricks set in bitumen, the stage-tower of Ur measures, at its base, 200 × 150 feet. It had at least three storeys, and though only the first and part of the second storeys have survived, its present height is about 60 feet. Yet, this enormous mass gives an astonishing impression of lightness due partly to its perfect proportions and partly to the fact that all its lines are slightly curved, a trick long thought to have been invented by the Greek architects who built the Parthenon of Athens, nearly two thousand years later. Against the north-eastern face of the tower, three long flights of steps converge towards a landing half-way between the first and the second platforms, and from this point, other steps once led to the second and third storeys and, finally, to the shrine crowning the whole structure. The ziqqurat stood on a large terrace in the heart of the 'sacred city'—the walled area reserved for gods and kings which occupied most of the northern half of the town. It cast its shadow over the great courtyard of Nanna—a low-lying open space surrounded by stores and lodgings for the priests—the temples of the moon-god and of his consort the goddess Ningal, the royal palace and other less important buildings. Towering above the walls of the capital-city, it mirrored itself in the Euphrates which flowed along its western side. Even now, the rounded red-brown pyramid topping the enormous greyish mound of the ruins forms a landmark visible from many miles away. The ziqqurats of other cities are not so well preserved and differ from that of Ur in several details, but their shape, their orientation and their position in relation to the main temples remain essentially the same. What then, it may be asked, was the purpose of these monuments?

The pioneers of Mesopotamian archaeology naïvely thought that the ziqqurats were observatories for 'Chaldaean' astronomers or even towers 'where the priests of Bêl could spend the night away from the heat and mosquitoes', but this, of course, is foolish. Comparison with Egypt comes immediately to mind and, indeed, Egyptian influence on Sumerian architects cannot be entirely ruled out; but it must be emphasized that the ziqqurats, contrary to the pyramids, do not contain tombs or chambers;[6] as a rule, they were built upon older, more modest structures erected during the Early Dynastic period, and these low, one-storeyed, primitive ziqqurats derived, it is now generally believed, from the platforms that supported the temples of the Ubaid, Uruk, and Proto-Literate periods.[7] However, the knowledge that the majestic towers of Ur-Nammu represent the last stage in a continuous architectural development offers no clue as to their exact religious significance. Why these platforms? Why these towers? Philology throws no light on the problem, since the word *ziqqurat* (sometimes transcribed ziggurat or zikkurat) comes from a verb *zaqâru* which simply means 'to build high', and we have the choice of several theories.[8] Some authors believe that the Sumerians were originally highlanders who worshipped their gods upon the mountain-tops and so built these towers to serve as artificial mountains in the flat Mesopotamian plain. Others, rejecting this over-simplified and somewhat questionable explanation, think that the purpose of the temple platform (and therefore of the ziqqurat) was to raise the main god of the city above the other gods and to protect him from the promiscuity of laymen. Yet another group of scholars sees in the monument a colossal staircase, a bridge between the lower temples where the routine ceremonies of the cult were performed and the upper sanctuary, half-way between heaven and earth, where men and gods could meet on certain occasions, and this, we believe, is nearer the truth. All considered, perhaps the best definition of the ziqqurat is given by the Bible (Genesis xi. 4) where it is said that the 'Tower of Babel' (i.e. the ziqqurat of Babylon) was meant 'to reach unto heaven'. In the deeply religious mind of the Sumerians, these enormous, yet curiously light constructions were 'prayers of bricks' as our Gothic cathedrals are 'prayers of stone'. They extended to the gods a permanent invitation to descend on earth at the same time as they expressed one of man's most remarkable efforts to rise above his miserable condition and to establish closer contacts with the divinity.

Judging from the dispersion throughout southern Iraq of bricks stamped with Ur-Nammu's name, it would appear that the building of temples was the king's privilege. Yet we know of a city not far from the capital where a grandiose building programme was carried out by the local ruler with truly royal magnificence: this was Lagash under its famous ensi Gudea.

We have seen (Chapter VIII) that Lugal-zagge-si of Umma had put an end to the protracted conflict between his city and Lagash by setting fire to the monuments of the latter and turning it into a mass of ruins. But in the ancient Orient towns were rarely as completely destroyed as the texts would have us believe, and somehow Lagash survived. Towards the end of the Gutian period, it was in the hands of energetic princes who apparently managed to remain independent and set themselves the task of reinvigorating the faded glory of their city. One of them was Gudea, a contemporary of Ur-Nammu, whose numerous statues and inscriptions provide the most admirable examples of Sumerian achievements in art and literature.[9]

Gudea built—or rather rebuilt—at least fifteen temples in Lagash, but on none of them was he so lavish as on the E-ninnu, the temple of Ningirsu, the city-god. On two large clay cylinders and on some of his statue inscriptions,[10] he explains at length why and how he built it, giving us, incidentally, invaluable details on the complicated rites essential to the foundation of sanctuaries in ancient Mesopotamia. It is typical of Sumerian thinking that the decision to erect a temple is given, not as an act of will of the ruler, but as the fulfilment of a wish of the god expressed in the form of a mysterious dream:

'In the heart of a dream, here was a man: his height equalled the sky, his height equalled the earth . . . To his right and to his left, lions were crouching . . . He told me to build him a temple, but I did not understand his heart (= his desire) . . .

'Here was a woman. Who was she not, who was she? . . . She was holding in her hand a stylus of flaming metal; she was holding the tablet of good writing of heaven; she was immersed in her thoughts . . .'

Troubled and perplexed, Gudea first sought comfort from his 'mother', the goddess Gatumdug, and then proceeded by boat to the temple of the goddess Nanshe 'interpreter of dreams'. Nanshe explained that the man was Ningirsu and the woman Nisaba, the goddess of science; she advised Gudea to offer Ningirsu a chariot 'adorned with shining metal and lapis-lazuli'.

'Then, inscrutable as the sky, the wisdom of the Lord, of Ningirsu, the son of Enlil, will soothe thee. He will reveal to thee the plan of His temple, and the Warrior whose decrees are great will build it for thee.'

Gudea obeyed. Having united the citizens of Lagash 'as the sons of the same mother' and made peace reign in every house, he desecrated the old temple and purified the city:

'He purified the holy city and encircled it with fires . . . He collected clay in a very pure place; in a pure place he made with it the brick and put the brick into the mould. He followed the rites in all their splendour: he purified the foundations of the temple, surrounded it with fires, anointed the platform with an aromatic balm . . .'

When this was done, craftsmen were brought from afar:

'From Elam came the Elamites, from Susa the Susians. Magan and Meluhha collected timber from their mountains . . . and Gudea brought them together in his town Girsu.

'Gudea, the great *en*-priest of Ningirsu, made a path into the Cedar mountains which nobody had entered before; he cut its cedars with great axes . . . Like giant snakes, cedars were floating down the water (of the river) . . .

'In the quarries which nobody had entered before, Gudea, the great *en*-priest of Ningirsu, made a path and then the stones were delivered in large blocks . . . Many other precious metals were carried to the ensi. From the Copper mountain of Kimash . . . its copper was mined in clusters; gold was delivered from its mountains as dust . . . For Gudea, they mined silver from its mountains, delivered red stone from Meluhha in great amount . . .'

Finally, the construction work proper was started and within one year the sanctuary was completed, beautifully appointed and ready for the god's ceremonial entry:

'Respect for the temple—says Gudea proudly—pervades the country; the fear of it fills the strangers; the brilliance of the Eninnu enfolds the universe like a mantle!'

Alas, of this magnificent temple, practically nothing remains, and we would be tempted to tax Gudea with gross exaggeration were it not for the seventeen odd statues of the ensi that have come to us, mostly as the result of illicit digging.9 Carved out of hard, polished black diorite from Magan, they are executed with a simplicity of line, an economy of detail, a sensitivity of expression which give them a prominent place in the gallery of world sculpture. If such masterpieces were displayed in the sanctuaries of Lagash, we can well believe that the rest of the decoration and the buildings themselves were of no inferior quality.

This young man sitting calmly, a faint smile upon his lips, his hands clasped in front of his chest, the plan of a temple or a foot rule across his knees, is the finest example of a figure unfortunately soon to disappear: the perfect Sumerian ruler, pious, just, cultured, faithful to the old traditions, devoted to his people, filled with love and pride for his city, and above all pacific—in all the inscriptions of Gudea, only one military campaign in Anshan (East of Elam) is mentioned. There is therefore no doubt that the timber, metal and stone used in his buildings were acquired by trade and not by territorial conquests. What was given in exchange is not disclosed, but the widespread commercial undertakings of the ensi of Lagash testify to the almost unbelievable prosperity of a Sumerian city after two hundred years of Akkadian government and a century of foreign occupation.

SHULGI, AMAR-SIN AND THE SUMERIAN EMPIRE

'Abandoned on the battlefield like a crushed vessel',[11] Ur-Nammu died in an untold war and was succeeded by his son Shulgi* who reigned forty-seven years (2095–2048 BC). The first half of this long reign was spent in peaceful activities: the temples and ziqqurats started by Ur-Nammu were completed and new buildings erected; the gods were reinstated in their shrines under the care of high-priests appointed by the king; the calendar was reformed and a new measure of grain, the royal *gur* (about 7 bushels) superseded the local measures formerly in use; in all probability, the political, economic and administrative reorganization of the kingdom took place during this period. On the

* This name, which probably means 'strong young man', was formerly read *Dungi*.

24th year, however, started a long series of annual military campaigns in the plains north of the Diyala and in the hills of Kurdistan. The reasons for these campaigns are by no means evident, and that so many of them were necessary to break down the resistance of relatively unimportant towns and countries is somewhat baffling. But the paucity of historical texts for the whole period must again be emphasized: almost our only source of information consists of the date-lists with their concise and stereotyped sentences: 'Year when Urbillum was devastated', 'year when Simurrum and Lullubum were devastated for the ninth time', etc.[12] In other regions, however, Shulgi pursued a more diplomatic policy: he married his own daughters to the governors of Marhashi and Anshan (S.W. Iran) and in Susa—now completely under Sumerian control—he built temples for the national gods of Elam.[13] Following the example set by Narâm-Sin, Shulgi called himself 'King of the Four Quarters (of the World)' and was worshipped as a god during and after his lifetime. Twice monthly, offerings were made to his statues throughout the empire and the name of 'divine Shulgi' was given to a month of the Sumerian calendar.

Amar-Sin,* son of Shulgi, reigned only nine years (2047–2039). Like his father, he divided his time between the building of temples and the conduct of wars in the same north-easterly districts. Like his father, he was deified and, with complete lack of modesty, referred to himself as 'the god who gives life to the country' or 'the god sun (i.e. judge) of the Land'. According to a late omen-text, Amar-Sin died of an infection caused by a shoe-bite.[14] He was buried, side by side with Shulgi and probably Ur-Nammu, in a vast and remarkable underground mausoleum found intact but plundered, in the sacred city of Ur, next to the famous 'Royal Cemetery'.[15]

Shulgi and Amar-Sin ruled over an empire at least as large as the Akkadian empire but considerably more coherent. While the Kings of Agade had relied upon their troops and put their faith in dubious vassal kings, the monarchs of Ur extended to a vast territory the political system traditional in Sumer. In Elam, Syria and Lebanon as well as in Mesopotamia, the administrative unit was the city-state governed by an *ensi* (*ishakku* in Akkadian) and,

* The name, formerly read Bur-Sin, is sometimes transcribed *Amar-Su'en*.

in theory, the king was just another ensi, *primus inter pares*, elected by Enlil in Nippur to lead the destinies of so many different peoples. If in some cities—such as Mari and Assur—the ensis enjoyed almost complete independence, in other places they had lost their former privileges: appointed or confirmed by the sovereign, transferable from one city to another, visited regularly by royal inspectors, or even subjected to the authority of province governors, they were little more than prefects responsible for their own districts. In the peripheral regions, the ensis were usually locally born, while in Mesopotamia, government officials were chosen among Sumerians and Akkadians alike. This wise policy cemented together the various ethnic groups, encouraged economic and cultural progress in the more distant provinces, and ensured internal peace for the best part of a century. The centralization of government and the eccentric position of the capital city obliged the Kings of Ur to improve the system of land communications. Fortresses staffed by police forces were built along the main roads, and there were fixed halting-places, such as Lagash, where royal couriers received a double ration of food: one 'for their stay in the town', the other 'for the road'.[16] As the merchants and their caravans followed the same routes, the material and spiritual products of the Sumero-Akkadian civilization could travel easily and safely from one end of the empire to the other. Close commercial relations existed between Elam and Sumer, and comparatively backward countries, such as northern Syria, received from Mesopotamia the impulse which triggered off the development of their own culture.

Despite the immense number of texts available, the economic structure of the Sumerian empire is still imperfectly known. For various reasons, no one has yet undertaken the formidable task of analysing the 16,000 odd contracts, vouchers, payrolls, accounts, etc., already published with a view to drawing detailed and accurate conclusions, so that, at present, we cannot see the wood for the trees.[17] Two points, however, emerge from even a brief survey of this copious literature: the growing importance of private property and private business, and the ever-increasing part played by the secular authority (as opposed to the temples) in the economic life of the country. Just how large was the private sector of the economy, we do not know, but in Sumer at least—and presumably in other parts of the empire—a number of individuals owned land, houses, chattels, slaves and animals which they could sell by contract. Prices varied according to quality, place and time, and were expressed in silver or in grain. On an average, fields and date-palm groves at Nippur were worth about one shekel of silver (about one-quarter of an ounce) per *sar* (116 square feet); a healthy male slave cost about eleven shekels, an ass, five *gur* of barley, a pig, two *gur* and a kid, one-fifth of a *gur*.[18] Grain for sowing could be borrowed from the palace or from the temples at 20 per cent interest, but private money-lenders made fortunes from short-term loans at $33\frac{1}{2}$ per cent. As for land on lease-hold, the normal return expected from the tenant was one-third of the crop.[19] It is therefore small wonder that the poorer people were engulfed in debt to the point of selling their children as slaves, and that a large proportion of the population preferred to work for the local temples or for the king against regular wages paid in grain, food and clothing. Throughout Mesopotamia the temples were still the most important owners of land, precious metals, cattle and labour; but they no longer possessed the quasi-totality of the country as in Early Dynastic times. The royal government had its own estates, its own stores and workshops, its own scribes, merchants, artisans, labourers and slaves; it had at its disposal great numbers of men for large-scale public works and an army of civil servants to enforce its authority. Yet, the Crown and the Temple were by no means rival institutions. The king was traditionally the supreme chief of the clergy, and in Sumer proper it was he, and not the ensis, who built the temples, presented them with rich donations, appointed the high-priests and conducted the main religious ceremonies. In return, the temples paid regular taxes to the palace and, in a serious financial crisis, put their wealth at the service of the king. To a great extent the temple economy was subjected to the royal authority, and in practice the revenues of the temple and the state are often indistinguishable. Thus at Puzurish-Dagan (modern Drehem), a few miles south of Nippur, Shulgi founded a vast storehouse where converged cattle, sheep, goats, grain, beer and other goods from the four corners of the empire. These were either 'presents' or regular tributes, payments in kind made by the ensis of many cities according to a strict annual rotation system, the *bala*.[20] Highly specialized scribes registered the in-coming and out-going goods with typical Sumerian thoroughness, and their records show that most issues went to the various temples of Nippur, the great religious metropolis. But there is strong reason to believe that a large part of the stocks accumulated in Drehem was directed to Ur for use in the royal palace.[21]

The concentration of political and economic powers in the hands of the kings of Ur resulted in a largely state-controlled society within a vast territory administratively unified. Private enterprise was still restricted and hazardous, and the greater part of the population regimented and practically enslaved, but the state-sponsored trade, industry and agriculture flourished. The government was rich and strong. Apart from a small mountainous district in north-eastern Iraq, the king was obeyed from Byblos[22] to Susa apparently without the slightest resistance. There were no civil wars and no palace revolutions. The population of Mesopotamia was on the increase, and everywhere new temples were built, new towns and villages founded. The brilliant civilization of Sumer permeated the entire Fertile Crescent, and to the gods responsible for their victory and prosperity, the Sumerians expressed their gratitude in remarkable works of art and literature. To the contemporaries of Shulgi and Amar-Sin, the empire must have looked like a large, well-kept, almost indestructible edifice. But the soldiers keeping watch along the dusty roads of the desert knew that the nomads were already on the move. Across the Euphrates and the Khabur, they trickled towards the green valley now in harmless little streams; in a not too distant future, their bellicose tribes would form a rushing torrent which no power could stem.

THE FALL OF UR

The first indication that things were not as quiet as they had been on the western frontier occurs during the reign of Shu-Sin* (2038–2030 BC), the brother and successor of Amar-Sin. Like the previous kings of Ur, 'divine' Shu-Sin restored a number of temples and campaigned in the Zagros mountains where he defeated a coalition of several Iranian rulers.[23] But the formula for his fourth year strikes an unfamiliar note, for in that year, we

* Or Shu-Su'en. The former reading *Gimil-Sin* is now abandoned.

are told, the king 'built the fortress of MAR.TU (called) which keeps away *Tidnum*'. Now, we know from other sources that MAR.TU in Sumerian and Tidnum (or, more usually, Amurrum) in Akkadian were different names for the country west of the Euphrates and its inhabitants. This vast region corresponds to present-day Syria, including the desert around Palmyra, the Orontes valley and the mountains which border the Mediterranean Sea. Part of its population lived in town and villages, but when the Sumerians or Akkadians spoke of the MAR.TU or *Amurrû*—the 'Amorites' as we call them—they had in mind those with whom they were in particularly close contact: the nomadic tribes who roamed the Syrian desert and often crossed the rivers to graze their flocks in the steppes of Mesopotamia.[24] Since Early-Dynastic times, these wandering Amorites were well known to the Sumerians, either as individuals who had abandoned their tribe to live and work in the cities, or as bedouins whose uncouth way of life was considered with disgust and contempt:

'The MAR.TU who know no grain . . . The MAR.TU who know no house nor town, the boors of the mountains . . . The MAR.TU who digs up truffles . . . who does not bend his knees (to cultivate the land), who eats raw meat, who has no house during his lifetime, who is not buried after his death . . .'[25]

Or again:

'They have prepared wheat and *gú-nunuz* (grain) as a confection, but an Amorite will eat it without even recognizing what it contains!'[26]

Against these savages who raided villages and attacked the caravans, frequent police operations were directed and, on occasion, a full-scale campaign was launched. Thus, one of the years of Shar-kali-sharri, the last great king of Agade, was named, after his victory over the MAR.TU 'in mount Basar', i.e. Jabal Bishri, between Palmyra and Deir-ez-Zor, and there are references to Amorite prisoners of war in texts of Shulgi and Amar-Sin. But now, the situation was reversed: the Sumerians were on the defensive; somewhere between Mari and Ur, they had to build a fortress in order to keep the nomads at bay.

For a time, this measure must have proved effective, since we do not hear about the Amorites during the next 10 years. Meanwhile, Shu-Sin died and was succeeded in 2029 by his son, Ibbi-Sin. What happened during the change of reign, we shall probably never know, but no sooner was the new king enthroned than the empire literally disintegrated.[27] One by one, the eastern provinces and city-states—starting with Eshnunna in the second year of Ibbi-Sin and Susa in his third year—declared themselves independent and broke away from Ur. At the same time, the Amorites were exerting an ever-increasing pressure on the borders of the kingdom. In the fifth year, they broke through the defences and penetrated deep into the heart of Sumer. How critical the situation had become is shown by two letters exchanged between the king and one of his generals, Ishbi-Irra, a native from Mari, who had been ordered to buy a large quantity of grain in Nippur and nearby Isin and to convey it to Ur. Ishbi-Irra declares himself unable to carry out his mission because the MAR.TU have ravaged the country and cut off all roads leading to the capital city, and are ready to attack Isin and Nippur; he asks to be formally entrusted with the defence of the two cities. In his reply, the king agrees, advises his officer to seek the help of other ensis, and offers to buy the grain at double its normal price. Soon afterwards, Ibbi-Sin succeeded in defeating the MAR.TU, but his subjects were starving and his authority was challenged by his own officials. In the eleventh year (2017), Ishbi-Irra proclaimed himself king in Isin—the very city he had pledged to protect on behalf of his lord—and a few years before, an Amorite sheikh called Nablânum had been crowned in Larsa, only 25 miles from Ur. To make matters worse, the Elamites took advantage of the situation to invade Sumer, as they had done so often in the past. Abandoned by the gods, beset with famine, attacked on two fronts, practically reduced to the capital city and its immediate neighbourhood, the great Sumerian empire was by now only the shadow of a kingdom. Ibbi-Sin fought to the last and apparently attempted to secure the alliance of the Amorites against the Elamites and the troops of his rival, Ishbi-Irra.[28] But this plan also failed. In 2006 BC, the Elamites were at the walls of Ur—those walls which Ur-Nammu had built 'as high as a shining mountain'. They attacked the great city, took it, sacked it, burned it down and withdrew, leaving behind a small garrison. The unfortunate

Ibbi-Sin was taken prisoner to Iran, 'to the end of Anshan whose cities he himself, like a bird, had devastated',[29] and died there. Years later, when Ur was again a flourishing city, its destruction was still remembered and lamented by the Sumerians as a national catastrophy:

> 'O Father Nanna, that city into ruins was made . . .
> Its people, not potsherds, filled its sides;
> Its walls were breached; the people groan.
> In its lofty gates, where they were wont to promenade, dead
>   bodies were lying about;
> In its boulevards, where the feasts were celebrated,
>   scattered they lay.
> In all its streets, where they were wont to promenade,
>   dead bodies were lying about;
> In its places, where the festivities of the land took place,
>   the people lay in heaps . . .
> Ur—its weak and its strong perished through hunger;
> Mothers and fathers who did not leave their houses
>   were overcome by fire;
> The young lying on their mothers' laps,
>   like fish were carried off by the waters;
> In the city, the wife was abandoned, the son was abandoned,
>   the possessions were scattered about.
> O Nanna, Ur has been destroyed, its people have been
>   dispersed!'[30]

CHAPTER XI

THE AMORITES

THE fall of Ur at the close of the third millennium BC is one of the major turning points in the history of ancient Iraq: it does not only ring the knell of a dynasty and of an empire, it marks the end of the Sumerians as a ruling nation. Intervening at the last moment, the Elamites had taken the capital city, but the secession of entire provinces, the revolt of Ibbi-Sin's officials, and the Amorite invasion were the real causes of the Sumerian defeat. The Elamites were soon expelled from Iraq; the Semites remained. From then on, they were to hold the reins of government for nearly fifteen hundred years.

Even before Ur was captured, the Sumerian empire had collapsed. Syria and Elam had recovered their freedom, and Mesopotamia had been shattered into a mosaic of large or small kingdoms, the most important being those of Isin and Larsa in the south, Assur and Eshnunna in the north. For about two centuries (*circa* 2000–1800 BC), these kingdoms coexisted, though by no means peacefully: those of the south fought each other for the possession of Ur and the sovereignty over Sumer and Akkad; those of the north, for the control of the great trade-routes which crossed Upper Mesopotamia. Meanwhile, the nomadic Semites continued to enter Iraq from the west, pitching their tents up to the foot of the Zagros or founding new kingdoms around the towns they occupied. The rulers of one of these towns, Babylon, soon became powerful enough to compete with their neighbours, and during the first half of the eighteenth century BC, Hammurabi succeeded in eliminating his rivals and subdued the whole of Mesopotamia. The empire he built alone—the 'Old Babylonian Empire' as it may be called—was short-lived, but even after its fall, Babylon remained, together with its rival Assur, one of the two poles of Mesopotamian history and civilization.

The rulers who replaced the Sumerians on the political stage were either Akkadians from Iraq, or Western Semites—'Amorites' in the broad sense of the term—from Syria and the western desert. The former were highly civilized; the latter, presumably uncouth bedouins, assimilated the Sumero-Akkadian culture with remarkable ease and rapidity, partly because they came from regions long submitted to its influence and partly because the language presented them with no major difficulty. As they spoke Semitic dialects, they adopted in writing the Akkadian language, and slowly in the south, rapidly in the north, the latter prevailed over Sumerian in private and official inscriptions. But this linguistic revolution hardly affected the religious, ethical and artistic concepts current in Mesopotamia since proto-historic times. The new-comers worshipped the Sumerian gods under their Semitic names, and the old Sumerian myths and epic tales were piously copied, translated or adapted with, in general, only minor alterations. As for the scarce artistic production of the period, there is practically nothing to distinguish it from that of the preceding Ur III period.[1] Generally speaking, the civilization created by the Sumerians outlived them and survived these years of turmoil as it had survived the Akkadian domination and the Gutian conquest.

The advent of the Western Semites, however, had deep and lasting repercussions on the political, social and economic structure of ancient Mesopotamia. The division of the country into kingdoms erased all traces of city-states, and with the city-states disappeared most of the principles upon which they were founded. Men, land and cattle ceased to belong physically to the gods, as in Early Dynastic times, or to the temples and the king, as under the Third Dynasty of Ur. The new monarchs gave or let out for an indefinite period numerous parcels of royal or sacerdotal land, freed the inhabitants of several cities from taxes and forced labour and, in general, encouraged by all possible means the development of private property. Soon, a new society emerged, a society of small farmers, free citizens and enterprising merchants which was to last throughout the ages. Deprived from their privileges, the temples became 'land-owners among other land-owners, tax-payers among other tax-payers'.[2] The priests assumed the service of the gods and cared for the spiritual needs of the people, while the king governed and cared for the welfare of his subjects, but the economic life of the country was no longer exclusively—or almost exclusively—in their hands. If, as in the past, each kingdom identified itself with its chief-god, if each sovereign claimed to owe his sceptre to divine favour, the traditional view according to which no prince could rule over Sumer and Akkad unless he had been elected by Enlil in Nippur became obsolete. The Sumerian *lugals* had invoked Enlil's blessings to justify their conquests; to the ruthless sheikhs who had seized the power by the sword and knew no other law than that of razzia, the investiture of the local god appeared sufficient. Thus, Nippur lost its importance and Enlil, his royal prerogative. When Babylon became the only capital-city of Mesopotamia, the name of its god Marduk was substituted to that of Enlil in the Epic of Creation. Nothing could better symbolize the end of the Sumerian supremacy.

The period which opens with the fall of Ur and ends with the reign of Hammurabi—the so-called 'Isin-Larsa period'—is extremely rich in events. For greater clarity, we must consider separately northern and southern Mesopotamia, starting with the latter.

ISIN, LARSA AND BABYLON

The kingdoms of Isin and Larsa3 were founded within eight years of each other but, for almost a century, Isin overshadowed Larsa. While the Amorite prince of Larsa, Nablânum, had to content himself with hardly more than the town he had conquered, Ishbi-Irra of Isin possessed the three important centres of Nippur, Uruk and Eridu. Towards the end of his reign, he captured the Elamite garrison of Ur and recovered the ruined, but still prestigious city. The occupation of Sippar by his grandson, Idin-Dagan, brought the frontiers of the kingdom from the Persian Gulf to the latitude of Baghdad; it extended now along the whole course of the Lower Euphrates, the vital artery of Sumer.

Ishbi-Irra was, it will be recalled, an Akkadian from Mari, and in the names of two of his descendants appears the great god of that city, the wheat-god Dagan. Yet, these Semites considered themselves as the true successors of the Sumerian kings of Ur. Most of them were deified, like Shulgi and Amar-Sin, and hymns were composed in their honour.4 They took the titles 'King of

Ur, King of Sumer and Akkad', restored and embellished the former capital-city, renewed active commercial relations with Dilmun5 and, ironically, were obliged to defend their kingdom against those to whom they owed it, fighting the Elamites, building fortresses against the MAR.TU and imposing tribute upon their nomadic tribes. In the official inscriptions from Isin, the Sumerian language is used exclusively, and it must be emphasized that practically all the great pieces of Sumerian literature found in the famous 'library' of Nippur were composed or copied during that period at the request of monarchs craving for Sumerian culture. Sumer in those days was like the declining Roman empire where everything was Latin, save the emperors.

The supremacy of Isin went on unhindered until the reign of Lipit-Ishtar, the author of a 'Code' of Law of which some forty-three articles and parts of the prologue and epilogue have survived.6 As it happens, these laws deal mostly with succession, real estates, hire contracts and the condition of privately owned slaves, and therefore give us a limited but interesting insight into the society which was then taking shape. Unfortunately, this peaceful legislator entered into conflict with a formidable warrior whose name sounds like the beat of a battle-drum, Gungunum, King of Larsa. Gungunum had already campaigned in the Zagros when, in his eighth year (1924 BC), he attacked the kingdom of Isin and occupied Ur, claiming sovereignty over Sumer and Akkad. A few years later, Lagash, Susa and perhaps Uruk fell into his hands. Larsa possessed now one-half of southern Iraq and a door on the 'Lower Sea'.

The loss of its main town and sea-port was for Isin a severe setback further aggravated by the extinction of the ruling family. Lipit-Ishtar—who died the year he lost Ur—was replaced by an usurper who, in turn, was defeated and killed by Abi-sarê of Larsa. About 20 years later, another usurper called Irra-imitti lost Nippur to his rival Sumu-El and soon the kingdom was reduced to Isin and its immediate neighbourhood. The story of Irra-imitti's death and succession deserves to be told, since it illustrates a rare and strange Mesopotamian institution: on occasions, when omens were exceptionally sombre and the king feared the wrath of the gods, a commoner was placed upon the throne as 'substitute king', reigned for a hundred days, and was then put to death. This is how a Babylonian chronicle describes what happened in Isin:7

'That the dynasty might not end, King Irra-imitti made the gardener Enlil-bâni take his place upon his throne and put the royal crown upon his head. Irra-imitti died in his palace because he had swallowed boiling broth. Enlil-bâni who was upon the throne did not relinquish it and was installed as king.'

We must add that the lucky gardener was deified and managed for twenty years to govern what little remained of the kingdom of Isin, while Nûr-Adad and Sin-idinnam of Larsa, pushing their troops northwards, conquered city after city. By now, however, the two rivals had in that region a common enemy, Babylon.

The first kings of Isin had kept the Amorites at bay but, after their downfall, the latter once again crossed the Euphrates in large numbers and poured into Iraq. In Kish, Uruk, Sippar, Marad8 and other towns, their chiefs proclaimed themselves kings, adding to the political confusion. In the first year of Sumu-El of Larsa (1894 BC), one of these sheikhs, Sumu-abum, chose for his capital a city a few miles to the west of Kish, on the left bank of the Euphrates, in that 'waist' of Mesopotamia the historical importance of which has already been stressed. This city had been governed by an *ensi* at least under the Third Dynasty of Ur, but had never played a part in Sumerian politics. Its name in Sumerian was KÁ.DINGIR.RA, in Akkadian *Bâb-ilim*, both meaning 'The Gate of God'; we call it, after the Greeks, Babylon. It was clear from the start that the energetic and clever rulers of Babylon were strongly determined to make it, not only a great and rich city, but the capital of the whole country. The war waging between Isin and Larsa and the multiplicity of small Amorite kingdoms gave them all the pretexts they needed. It took them nearly 60 years but, with infinite patience, using sometimes diplomacy and sometimes brute force, the first five kings of the First Dynasty of Babylon conquered, piece by piece, the whole country of Akkad. They were approaching Nippur, key of Sumer, when they met with the strongest resistance from the foreign princes who now held the sceptre in Larsa.

The Elamites, as we well know, never missed an opportunity to interfere in Mesopotamian affairs. In 1834 BC, the throne of

Larsa was vacant, Silli-Adad having been killed in the war with
Babylon after a brief reign. An Elamite official, Kudur-Mabuk,
who controlled the Amorite tribes established between Tigris and
Zagros, occupied Larsa and appointed one of his sons king in that
city, contenting himself with the title 'Father (i.e. protector) of
Amurru'. It is remarkable that the two sons of Kudur-Mabuk,
Warad-Sin ('slave of Sin') and Rîm-Sin ('bull of Sin') who reigned
successively in Larsa bear Semitic and not Elamite names. Even
more remarkable is the fact that these freshly imported foreigners
behaved in every respect like genuine Mesopotamian monarchs,
building no less than nine temples and a dozen important monuments in the city of Ur alone. In other times, they would have
been great pacific rulers like Ur-Nammu, but as long as Isin was
still alive and Babylon active, there could be no peace in Sumer.
Rîm-Sin defeated a dangerous coalition led by his Babylonian
rival and, in 1794 BC, succeeded in taking Isin, overthrowing at
last Larsa's oldest enemy. Two years later, Hammurabi ascended
the throne of Babylon.

At this point, we must leave the south for a while and turn our
attention towards the northern half of Iraq. There again we meet
with 'warring kingdoms' in fierce competition, but the cultural
setting, the political and economic motives of the conflict are
markedly different.

ESHNUNNA, ASSUR AND MARI

Situated between the Tigris and the Zagros mountains, ten miles
to the east of the Diyala, Eshnunna (Tell Asmar) was a relay on
the road from Upper Mesopotamia to Elam and, as such, was
subjected to a triple current of influences: it lay within the sphere
of Sumero-Akkadian civilization, had close contact with the northern countries—its god, Tishpak, was identical with the Hurrian
god Teshup—and was linked with Elam by strong economic,
political and cultural ties.[9] It was therefore perhaps not mere
coincidence if Eshnunna was, with Susa, the first city-state to break
away from Ur in the second year of Ibbi-Sin (2028 BC). As far as
we know, the passage to freedom was swift and smooth: the
rulers of Eshnunna called themselves 'servant of the god Tishpak'
instead of 'servant of the King of Ur' and replaced by local names

the names of months and years in use throughout the Sumerian empire; in the capital-city the temple once built for the deified King of Ur Shu-Sin was secularized and a large palace was erected beside it; in official inscriptions, Akkadian replaced the Sumerian language. These early rulers, who responded to Semitic or Elamite names, immediately enlarged their kingdom far beyond its original boundaries: with the help of Amorite bands, they occupied the entire valley of the lower Diyala, including the important centre of Tutub (Khafaje), and perhaps dominated as far north as the region of Kirkuk. One of them, Bilalama—a contemporary of the second king of Isin—is credited by some scholars with a 'Code' of Law, written in Akkadian, which antedates by about two centuries the Code of Hammurabi, and has with it many points in common.[10] The 'Laws of Eshnunna', incidentally, were not found at Tell Asmar, but at Tell Harmal, a small mound at the outskirts of Baghdad excavated by the Iraqis between 1945 and 1949.[11] Tell Harmal (ancient *Shaduppum*) was the administrative centre of an agricultural district of the kingdom of Eshnunna, and a copy of the royal laws was kept in the 'town-hall' for easy reference. The same site has also yielded a number of interesting tablets, in particular date-lists and mathematical problems.

The reign of Bilalama was followed by a period of repeated setbacks during which Eshnunna was sacked by the King of Dêr (modern Badrah, about 65 miles east of Tell Asmar), defeated in war by the ruler of Kish and deprived of most of its possessions. But the fortune of the kingdom was eventually restored, and about 1850 BC, with 'the enlarger of Eshnunna', as Ipiq-Adad II calls himself, starts a new period of expansion marked by the occupation of Rapiqum on the Euphrates (somewhere near Ramâdi), of Assur on the Tigris, of Qabra in the plain of Erbil, and of Ashnakkum on the Khabur. The situation of these towns clearly indicates that the kings of Eshnunna aimed at conquering the whole Tigris valley, Upper Jazirah, and the foothills of Kurdistan, and at establishing a bridgehead on the Euphrates, for only thus could they effectively control the great trade route, which, from the north and west, converged towards their capital in the general direction of Susa. But the capture of these cities was only temporary, and the patient efforts made by the last rulers of Eshnunna to recover the territories formerly gained and lost met with failure. Four powerful kingdoms—Babylon and Larsa in the south, Assur to the north and Mari to the west—now encircled Eshnunna and opposed to its ambitions an insuperable barrier.

The foundation of the Assyrian kingdom and its promotion to the rank of a great political and military power are capital events in a period particularly rich in new developments. The city which gave its name to this kingdom, Assur[12] (or, more exactly, *Ash-shur*) lay in a strong strategic position: built on a hill overlooking the Tigris just north of the point where it enters the Fat-ha gorge through Jabal Hamrîn, protected on one side by the great river, on the other by a canal, and on the third side by the desert, it commanded the road which, from Sumer or Akkad, went up the Tigris valley either to Kurdistan or to Upper Jazirah. Successively Sargon, Narâm-Sin and the kings of Ur had occupied this key-place, the origins of which went back to the Early Dynastic period and probably earlier, and there is no evidence that Assur was independent before the second millennium B C. Yet the northern equivalent of the Sumerian King List, the great Assyrian King List found at Khorsabad and published by A. Poebel in 1942[13] gives a series of seventeen kings of Assur who, if we were to take the list at its face value, would have lived in Early Dynastic times. But here, as in the Sumerian list, dynasties recorded as successive may have been, in fact, parallel; in addition, our document states that these kings 'lived in tents', which may mean that they did not actually govern the city of Assur but some important tribe in the neighbourhood; and finally, it must be noted that the names of several early Assyrian monarchs—such as Tudia, Ushpia, Sulili or Kikkia—are neither Semitic nor Sumerian, but belong to some other ethnic stratum, possibly Hurrian.

After the fall of the Sumerian Empire, Assur, like many other cities, became independent. Puzur-Ashur I, who must have reigned about 2000 B C, opens a new line of kings bearing such genuine Akkadian names as Sargon or Narâm-Sin.[14] Two of them, Ilushuma and Erishum I, have left us inscriptions mentioning the building of temples for Ashur, Adad and Ishtar in the city.[15] Moreover, Ilushuma is known to have raided deep into southern Iraq during the reign of Ishme-Dagan of Isin (1953–

1935 BC),[16] and it was probably during this period that the new kingdom was enlarged to include Nineveh, 60 miles to the north of Assur. But the true founders of Assyrian might were the Western Semites who, during the first centuries of the second millennium, flooded northern Iraq as they flooded the southern regions. Halê, the chief of an Amorite tribe, pitched his tent somewhere between the Khabur and the Tigris, and his successors ruled in the orbit of the 'Akkadian' kings of Assur until one of them called Ilâ-kabkabû succeeded in taking the city and ascended the throne. About the same time, another Amorite became King of Mari on the Euphrates, and from then on, the destinies of the two great northern kingdoms were intimately blended.

Mari is already well known to the reader, and no detailed account of its long past is needed here. Let us simply recall that, during the Early Dynastic period, a dynasty from Mari is said to have ruled over Sumer for over a century, that the town was captured and sacked by Sargon of Akkad on his way to northern Syria, and that it was an important provincial city of the kingdom of Ur, governed by very active *shakkanakû*. Thereafter, there is a regrettable gap in our information until about 1900 BC, when Western Semites—probably from the region of Aleppo—occupied Mari and made it the capital of a kingdom extending along the Euphrates from the Khabur to the vicinity of 'Anah. The first king of the Amorite dynasty of Mari, Iaggid-Lim, was a contemporary of Ilâ-kabkabû with whom he exchanged, we are told, 'solemn oaths'.[17] But this friendship was eventually broken, Iaggid-Lim's 'fortress' was destroyed, and his son Iahdun-Lim had to reconquer the kingdom. Soon, however, the ruler of Mari embarked upon ambitious military ventures and even reached the Mediterranean:

'He conquered the country on the shore of the "Ocean", made it obey his orders and obliged it to follow him. He imposed upon it a perpetual tribute which was delivered regularly.'[18]

This remarkable success must have excited the jealousy of the Assyrians. Whether they were responsible for the murder of Iahdun-Lim, who was massacred by his servants, remains doubtful, but they seized the occasion to lay their hand on Mari.

SHAMSHI-ADAD I AND HIS SONS

The man who annexed Mari and built up what is often referred to as 'the first Assyrian Empire', Shamshi-Adad or -Addu (1814–1782 BC) began his career as an outlaw.[19] When his brother Amînu succeeded Ilâ-kabkabû, Shamshi-Adad fled to the South, gathered a troop of mercenaries, took Ekallâtum—an as yet unidentified city on the Middle Tigris, which formerly belonged to Eshnunna—marched against Assur and snatched the sceptre from Amînu's hands. Once enthroned, he led his armies to the West, to the forest-covered mountains of Lebanon and to that sea which marked the boundaries of the world and fascinated all Mesopotamian conquerors, the Mediterranean:

'A stela inscribed with my great name I set up in the country of Labân (Lebanon), on the shore of the Great Sea.'[20]

Then, after Iahdun-Lim had been murdered, Shamshi-Addu occupied Mari, put it in the hands of his son Iasmah-Adad, and appointed another of his sons, Ishme-Dagan, viceroy of Ekallâtum. The Assyrians now held both the Tigris and the Euphrates and governed nearly all northern Mesopotamia.

In the whole history of ancient Iraq, few periods are as well documented as the reign of Shamshi-Adad and his sons. Moreover, our information is derived, not from the usual official inscriptions, but from the most accurate and reliable documents that an historian can expect: the letters exchanged between the three princes, and between Iasmah-Adad and other rulers, and the reports from various officials to their masters; in all, more than three hundred tablets forming part of the royal archives found in the palace of Mari.[21] While these letters are generally undated and therefore difficult to arrange in chronological order, they throw an invaluable light on the daily routine of the court and on the relationship between the governments of Assur, Mari and Ekallâtim and the various peoples, kingdoms and tribes surrounding them. Besides—and this is not the least of their interest—they offer a first-hand moral portrait of the three rulers. For the first time we are in the presence, not of mere names, but of living persons with their qualities and defects: Ishme-Dagan, a born warrior like his father, always ready to go to battle and proud to announce his victories to his brother—'At Shimanahe, we fought and I have taken the entire country. Be glad!'[22]—but, on occasion, taking him under his wing:

'Do not write to the king. The country where I stay is nearer the capital city. The things you want to write to the king, write them to me, so that I can advise you . . .'[23]

Iasmah-Adad of Mari, on the contrary, docile, obedient, but lazy, negligent, cowardly:

'You remain a child, writes his father, there is no beard on your chin, and even now, in the ripeness of age, you have not built up a "house" . . .'[24]

Or again:

'While your brother here is "killing the *dâwîdum*", you, over there, you lie about amidst women. So now, when you go to Qatanum with the army, be a man! As your brother is making a great name for himself, you too, in your country, make a great name for yourself!'[25]

And finally, Shamshi-Adad the father, wise, cunning, meticulous, sometimes humorous, who advises, reprimands or congratulates his sons and keeps Mari under very close control, a control which would have been found unbearable by a more mature prince.

A constant source of worry for the three rulers were the nomads, particularly numerous in the region of Mari.[26] In and around that kingdom were three large groups of tribes: the Hanaeans, the Bene-Iamina and the Sutaeans. Established for a long time on the Euphrates, the Hanaeans (*Hanû*) formed, with the Akkadians, the bulk of the local population, partly settled, living in camps or villages under their own sheikhs and notables. Periodically, they were subjected to census and their young men were incorporated in the royal army where their military quali-ties—'their only idea is to make use of their weapons and defeat the enemy'[27]—were highly appreciated. Although these hardened troopers, on at least one occasion, misbehaved and looted the palace they were given to guard, the Hanaeans were not much of a problem. But with the 'Sons of the South', the *Bene-Iamina*,[28] it was another matter. Extremely numerous and mobile, always

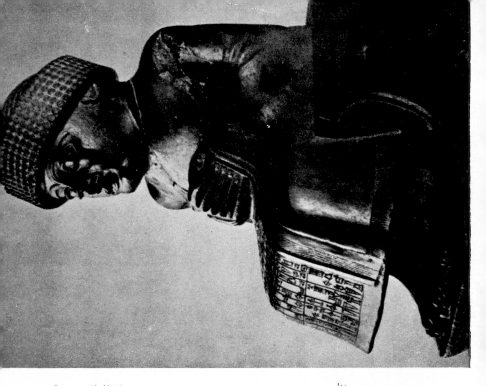

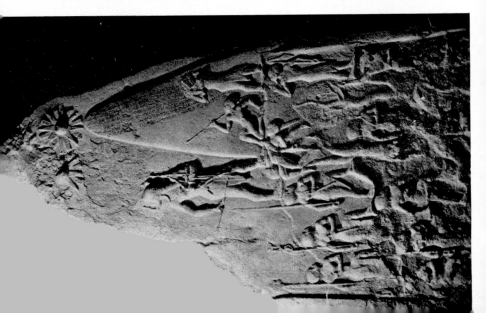

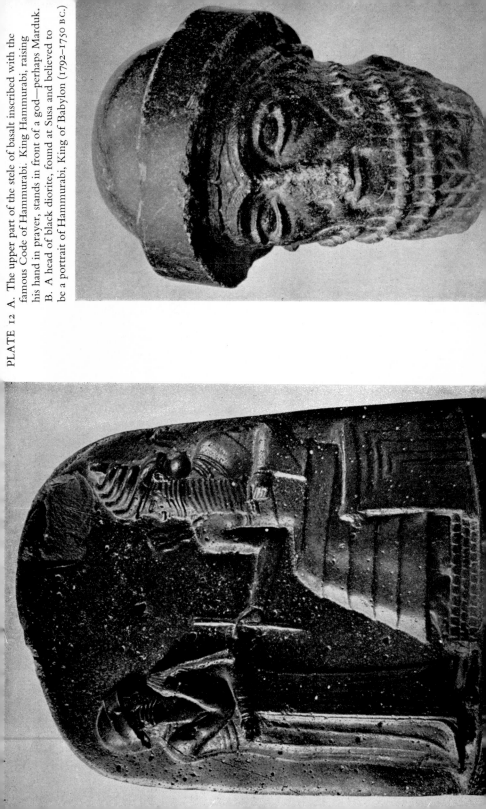

PLATE 12   A. The upper part of the stele of basalt inscribed with the famous Code of Hammurabi. King Hammurabi, raising his hand in prayer, stands in front of a god—perhaps Marduk. B. A head of black diorite, found at Susa and believed to be a portrait of Hammurabi, King of Babylon (1792–1750 B.C.)

on the move along the Khabur or across the Euphrates, always ready for razzia, they escaped control, dodged royal census and recruitment, and eventually lent assistance to the King of Eshnunna and other enemies of the Assyrians. Iasmah-Adad, however, handled them gently, gave them land and ploughs and grain in time of famine, and remained on fairly good terms with them. As for the Sutaeans (*Sutû*), numerically perhaps the most important, they appear as inveterate bandits who attacked caravans, raided towns and ravaged entire districts and against whom the use of force was almost always necessary.

The relations between the Assyrian kingdom and the small kingdoms around it varied from place to place and often, we may say, from day to day. With the West (Syria), they were as a rule excellent. We learn, for instance, that Aplahanda, King of Karkemish (Jerablus), sent 'excellent wine', food, ornaments and fine clothing to his 'brother' Iasmah-Addu, granted him the monopoly over certain copper mines in his territory and offered to give him 'whatever he desired'.[29] We also read that Iasmah-Adad gave boats for the sheep-rearing nomads from Iamhad (Aleppo) to cross the Euphrates, married the daughter of the ruler of Qatanum (or Qatna) and sent troops to his aid.[30] In return, the ruler of Qatna put his pastures at the disposal of Iasmah-Addu's shepherds and proposed to pay him a visit. But the peoples and tribes to the north and east of Assyria proper were far less friendly. Throughout the twenty odd years covered by the royal correspondence, we see Shamshi-Adad intervening in the 'Upper Country' (Balikh and Khabur valleys) and leading campaign after campaign along the Zab and around Kirkuk, while the impetuous Ishme-Dagan was fighting the Turukkû tribe and the petty kings established at the foot of the Zagros.

In most of these wars, we see the hand of a monarch whom our letters never call otherwise than 'the man of Eshnunna', but who must have been Dadusha. As it has already been suggested, the kings of Eshnunna had once conquered most of 'Subartu' (Assyria) and part of the 'Upper Country' (Jazirah), but the Assyrian expansion under Shamshi-Adad had deprived them of their northern provinces and cut their routes of supplies. Dadusha was not a man to accept this situation. Patient, determined, good war-leader and, no doubt, good diplomatist, he battled and intrigued throughout his reign. To Ishme-Dagan in particular, his immediate neighbour, the 'man of Eshnunna' was a constant menace, and hostilities were almost permanent: armies of several thousand men from both sides crossed the uncertain frontier between the two states and swiftly moved up and down the broad 'corridor' between the Tigris and the Zagros. Thus for a time the Assyrians occupied Malgum (probably near Kut-el-Imara) deep in enemy territory, while troops from Eshnunna joined forces with the Turukkû in Kurdistan and appeared around Kirkuk. Even Mari was threatened, and the news that the enemy was advancing along the Euphrates caused a great deal of panic in the western capital; 'Promptly send me numerous troops', writes Iasmah-Addu to his brother, 'the distance is great!'[31] But 'the smoke did not turn into fire' as was feared, and Mari was saved. On the Euphrates as on the Tigris, the Assyrians were strong and Eshnunna was held in check.

Finally, we come to Babylon, the second powerful neighbour of Assyria. With Babylon, the relations were cold but polite, since neither Sin-muballiṭ (1812–1793 BC) nor Hammurabi (1792–1750 BC)—both contemporaries of Shamshi-Adad—had yet turned their ambition towards the north. Thus, Shamshi-Adad dispatched to Hammurabi tablets copied at his request, and Iasmah-Adad returned to Babylon a caravan which had been delayed in Mari and a Turruku captive who had escaped and sought refuge in that city.[32] In only one letter do we feel a shadow of anxiety: apparently, Iasmah-Adad had been informed of certain unfriendly projects of 'the man of Babylon', but one of his officials, after enquiry, reassures him:

'Now, may my lord's heart be at ease, for the man of Babylon will never do harm to my lord.'[33]

Some thirty years later, however, Hammurabi was to take and destroy Mari.

CHAPTER XII

HAMMURABI

THE victory over four powerful princes and the unification of Mesopotamia are in themselves remarkable achievements sufficient to single out Hammurabi* as one of the greatest Mesopotamian monarchs. But the King of Babylon was not merely a successful war-leader: his handling of his opponents reveals the qualities of a skilful diplomat; his Code of Law displays a passion for justice, which, to a great extent, balances the repulsive cruelty of punishments; his inscriptions show a genuine concern for the welfare of his subjects and a deep respect for the traditions of a country which was, after all, foreign to his race; his letters[1] prove that the descendant of an Amorite sheikh could administer a vast kingdom with the same care and attention to detail as the ruler of a Sumerian city-state. Hammurabi's long and glorious reign brought, once again, peace and unity to the country, raised Babylon to the rank of a major capital city and sanctioned the supremacy of the Semites in Mesopotamia. The impression of serene strength conveyed by the works of art,[2] the elegant perfection attained by the Akkadian language,[3] even the artificial but grandiose reorganization of the Sumero-Akkadian pantheon to fit the royal prerogatives attributed to Marduk, all these further contribute to make these forty-three years (1792–1750 BC)[4] a decisive period in the history of ancient Iraq. Without any doubt, the great figure of King Hammurabi, statesman and lawgiver, deserves special attention.

THE STATESMAN

When Hammurabi ascended the throne, he inherited from his

* The name—sometimes written *Hammurapi*—seems to mean 'the god *Hammu* (a western Semitic god) is great'.

father, Sin-muballiṭ, a comparatively small kingdom, some 80 miles long and 20 miles wide, extending from Sippar to Marad or, in terms of modern topography, from Fallujah to Diwaniyah. All around were larger states and more powerful kings: the south was entirely dominated by Rîm-Sin of Larsa, who, two years before, had taken Isin and put an end to the rival dynasty (1794 BC); to the north, the horizon was barred by the three kingdoms of Mari, Ekallâtum and Assur in the hands of Shamshi-Adad and his sons; and to the east, just across the Tigris, Dadusha, allied to the Elamites, still reigned in Eshnunna. The new King of Babylon was no less determined than his ancestors to enlarge his domain, but he waited patiently for five years before making the first move. Then, when he felt secure enough on the throne, he attacked in three directions: he captured Isin and advanced along the Euphrates as far south as Uruk (sixth year), campaigned in Emutbal, between Tigris and Zagros, and occupied the key to that district, Malgum (seventh and ninth years), and finally took Rapiqum, upstream of Sippar (tenth year). Thereafter, it would seem from his date-formulae that for twenty successive years he devoted his time solely to the embellishment of temples and the fortification of towns.5

This short series of military operations infringed on the territories of Larsa and Eshnunna and no doubt aroused considerable hostility from Rîm-Sin and from Ibal-pî-El II, who, in 1790 BC, had succeeded Dadusha, but we have no means of knowing if and how they retaliated. As for the Assyrians, they would have rejoiced at the humiliation of 'the man of Eshnunna' had they not been occupied with more serious problems. In the seventh year of Hammurabi (1786), Shamshi-Adad had died, leaving the sceptre to the more energetic of his two sons, Ishme-Dagan. The weak Iasmah-Adad was still viceroy of Mari and we possess a letter from the new king to his brother assuring him that his position would not be altered and that he, Ishme-Dagan, would protect him:

'Have no fear. Your throne is definitely your throne and I hold in my hand (the gods) Adad and Shamash. The people of Elam and the man of Eshnunna, I have them on a leash. Have no fear. As long as we live, I and you, for ever you will sit on your throne.

Let us swear together a solemn oath of the gods, then I and you, let us meet and establish fraternity between us for always.'6

But, a few months later, Iasmah-Adad was overthrown by a prince of the 'national' dynasty of Mari, Zimri-Lim, son of Iahdun-Lim, who, with the help of the King of Aleppo, succeeded in 'ascending the throne of his father's house'.7

The royal archives of Mari, so useful for the period of Assyrian interregnum, are again our main source of information on the reign of Zimri-Lim and, indeed, on almost the entire reign of Hammurabi.8 Despite the hatred he must have conceived for the Assyrian usurper, Zimri-Lim was wise enough to preserve his correspondence, and on comparison it is remarkable, though not surprising, that he followed essentially the same policy. Having in a few campaigns ascertained his authority over the 'Upper Country' (Khabur and Balikh valleys), he handled the nomads with a firmer hand than his predecessor and crushed the turbulent Bene-Iamina.9 Relations with the West were more cordial than ever: ambassadors and messengers from Syrian kingdoms were constantly calling at Mari, and Zimri-Lim himself visited Aleppo and dedicated a statue to Adad, the patron-god of that city.10 While we can hardly expect friendly relations between Mari and Assur, there is no evidence that Ishme-Dagan attempted to overthrow Zimri-Lim. Hostilities were limited to attacks on one or two cities on the border between the two kingdoms, and as troops from Eshnunna co-operated with the Assyrians on these occasions,11 we may suspect that Ishme-Dagan had turned an old enemy into an ally. In any case, 'the man of Eshnunna', who plotted in the Upper Country and even launched a full-scale expedition in the region of Harran,12 remained for Zimri-Lim the most dangerous of his two eastern neighbours.

The movements of the ruler of Eshnunna and his Elamite allies were watched with equal anxiety by Zimri-Lim's best friend, Hammurabi. Since Babylon and Mari commanded the entire course of the Euphrates, they had everything to gain in joining hands together. Zimri-Lim's ambassador at the court of Babylon kept him fully posted on 'all the important affairs' of that kingdom and, reciprocally, Babylonian messengers reported to Hammurabi all the news they heard in Mari, this bilateral 'intelligence service' functioning, it seems, with the full knowledge and approbation of the two sovereigns. The two kings lent each other troops—even soldiers from Aleppo were called to the rescue of Babylon by Zimri-Lim[13]—and rendered each other the minor or major services expected from good neighbours. But the attitude of Hammurabi, in the light of later events, was perhaps less disinterested than it appears, and he may have used his ally merely to consolidate his power. Piece by piece emerges from these undated and therefore unclassifiable archives the figure of a patient and cunning politician who tries various combinations—he is now the ally, now the enemy of Eshnunna; now he fights Rîm-Sin and now negotiates with him[14]—observes more than he acts and waits for the right time to strike with the certainty of winning.

At long last, in the twenty-ninth year of his reign, this time arrived—sooner perhaps than Hammurabi had expected since, according to his own version of the events, Babylon was attacked by a coalition of Elamites, Guti, 'Subarians' (Assyrians) and people from Eshnunna:

'The leader beloved of Marduk, after having defeated the army which Elam ... Subartu, Gutium, Eshnunna and Malgium had raised in masses, through the mighty power of the great gods consolidated the foundations of Sumer and Akkad.' (Year-formula 30.)

The following year (1763 BC), Hammurabi took the offensive and, 'encouraged by an oracle', attacked Larsa. Rîm-Sin—whom he contemptuously calls 'the King of Emutbal', Emutbal being the homeland of Rîm-Sin's family—was overthrown after a reign of sixty years, the longest in Mesopotamian annals.

In the thirty-first year, a new coalition comprising the same enemies as before was formed. This time, the 'hero' not only 'overthrew their army', but advanced 'along the bank of the Tigris' as far as 'the frontier of Subartu'. Implicitly, this was the end of Eshnunna.

Now the master of southern and central Mesopotamia, Hammurabi was not a man to stop there. The great empires of Akkad and Ur must have been in his mind when he decided to attack his old friend Zimri-Lim:

'Mari and Malgum he overthrew in battle and made Mari and . . .
also several other cities of Subartu by a friendly agreement
(listen) to his orders.' (Year-formula 32).

These last words seem to indicate that Zimri-Lim did not lose
his throne but was made a vassal of Hammurabi. Two years later,
however, the Babylonian troops were again sent to Mari, perhaps
to quell a rebellion. This time, the city wall was dismantled, the
beautiful palace of Zimri-Lim was sacked and burnt down, and
the great metropolis of the Middle Euphrates turned into ruins
for ever (1759 BC).

Finally, in the thirty-sixth and thirty-eighth years of his reign,
Hammurabi 'overthrew the army of the country Subartu (Assy-
ria)' and 'defeated all his enemies as far as the country of Subartu'.
What treatment was reserved for Assur, we do not know.
Somehow, the Assyrian dynasty managed to survive, but the
Assyrian domination in northern Iraq had come to an end.

Thus, in ten years, all but one of the five Mesopotamian kingdoms had successively disappeared and Mesopotamia now formed
one single nation under Babylonian rule. How far Hammurabi's
power extended is difficult to say. A stele with his inscription was
found near Diarbakr, at the foot of the Taurus, but Elam and
Syria remained independent. In those days they were stronger
countries than in the days of Ur-Nammu, and to subdue them
would have required more time and forces than were at Hammurabi's disposal. The Babylonian monarch called himself
'mighty King, King of Babylon, King of the whole country of
Amurru, King of Sumer and Akkad, King of the Four Quarters
of the World' but, wisely no doubt, he did not attempt to gain
effective control over 'the Universe'.

THE LAWGIVER

While achieving by arms the unity of Mesopotamia, Hammurabi
carried out a series of administrative, social and religious measures
which aimed at concentrating in his hands and in those of his
successors the government of a nation made up of several ethnic
groups and conspicuous for the multiplicity of its laws and customs,
the complexity of its pantheon and the persistence of local

traditions and particularism. Domestic affairs were handled by the king with the same mixture of ruthless energy and astute moderation as he so successfully used in his foreign policy. Thus, provincial governors were subjected to tight royal control and had, it seems, little initiative, but in every city, matters of local interest, petty court cases and the collection of taxes were left to an Assembly of Elders, so that Hammurabi's subjects had at least the illusion of self-government. In order to legalize his dynasty and to curtail any future claim to the kingship over Sumer and Akkad, Hammurabi put the god of Babylon, Marduk—hitherto a third-rank deity[15]—at the head of the pantheon; but he tactfully proclaimed that the divine lordship had been conferred to Marduk by Anu and Enlil and that he, Hammurabi, had been 'called' by the same great gods 'to promote the welfare of the people'.[16] Docile to royal instructions, the priests rearranged divine genealogies, endowed Marduk with the qualities of other gods and rewrote the Epic of Creation to give him the leading rôle. Yet the old Sumero-Akkadian beliefs were not fundamentally altered. Everywhere, including Nippur, the temples were rebuilt, repaired or embellished in the true Mesopotamian royal tradition, and any steps that might have hurt the religious feelings of the population were carefully avoided.

The famous Code of Law issued by Hammurabi

'To cause justice to prevail in the country
To destroy the wicked and the evil,
That the strong may not oppress the weak',[17]

can no longer be considered as 'the most ancient in the world'—we possess now similar documents from the reigns of Ur-Nammu, Lipit-Ishtar and Bilalama—but it is still the most complete and, as such, deserves more than a few words.[18] It should be stressed, however, that the word 'Code' is somewhat misleading, since we are not confronted here with a thorough legislative reform, nor with an exhaustive corpus of logically arranged legal dispositions, such as Justinian's *Institutes* or Napoleon's *Code Civil*. Indeed, the Mesopotamians were never ruled by any other system than a 'common law', handed down from reign to reign and occasionally modified to fit the social and economic conditions prevalent at a given period. One of the first acts of every ruler, at least since

Urukagina, was to 'ordain *mêsharum*', a word which can be translated by 'justice', but which, in this context, covered a number of other things, such as remitting certain debts and obligations and fixing the prices of certain commodities—an efficient way of regulating the economy of the country. This is what is meant, for instance, by the formula of the second year of Hammurabi: 'he established justice in the country', and a good example of a *mêsharum*-act has survived in the 'edict' of King Ammiṣaduqa, one of Hammurabi's successors, published a few years ago (see below, Chapter XV). In all other matters, the new king simply applied the laws of his predecessors, thereby ensuring a continuity in tradition which, in this domain as in others, was one of the main features of the Mesopotamian civilization.[19] In the course of the reign, however, social and economic changes occurred which required the laws to be adjusted, and the king pronounced sentences on a number of isolated cases for which no precedent could be found. These royal decisions (*dînat sharrim*), duly recorded and eventually collected together to be used for reference by the judges of future generations, formed the so-called 'Codes of Law', and we possess several such copies of the Code of Hammurabi on clay tablets, ranging from the Old Babylonian period to the time of the Chaldaean dynasty (sixth century BC).

Towards the end of his reign, Hammurabi ordered his royal decisions to be carved on steles which were placed in temples, bearing witness that the king had performed his important functions of 'king of justice' satisfactorily and had acted according to the gods' hearts. One of these steles, found in an excellent state of preservation, is in itself a remarkable work of art. Erected originally in the temple of Shamash at Sippar, it was taken to Susa as war booty by the Elamites in the twelfth century BC, discovered there in 1901 by the French and transported to the Louvre Museum. It is an 8 foot high stele of polished basalt, roughly conical in shape, on top of which is carved a scene representing Hammurabi in the attitude of prayer facing either Marduk or Shamash, the sun-god and god of justice, seated on his throne. The rest of the stele, front and back, is covered with vertical columns of text beautifully engraved and written in the purest Babylonian language. After a long prologue enumerating the religious deeds of the king, come at least 282 laws[20] dealing with various offences, with trade and commerce, marriage, family and property, the fees and responsibilities of professional men, legal problems connected with agriculture, wages and rates of hire, and the sale and purchase of slaves. Finally, a long epilogue calls for divine punishments against whoever would deface the monument or alter 'the just laws which Hammurabi, the efficient king, set up'.

It appears from the Code and various other documents that the Babylonian society was divided into three classes: free men (*awêlu*), *mushkênu* and slaves (*wardu*). The term *mushkênum*, here left untranslated, has been rendered by 'plebeian', 'commoner', 'villein' or 'poor' (cf. Arabic *meskín*) but it seems to indicate, in fact, some sort of military or civilian 'state's dependant' who submitted to certain obligations and restrictions in return for certain privileges.[21] The slaves were recruited partly among prisoners of war and their descendants, partly among impoverished free men who sold themselves or their children to their creditors. Shaven and branded with a distinctive mark, they were considered as belonging to their masters, and severe penalties were pronounced against those who assisted or harboured fugitive slaves. Yet their condition was not as hopeless as one would imagine: they could be set free or adopted by their masters, and we learn with surprise that at least some of them could marry the daughters of free men (§§ 175–6). Fees and punishments varied according to the social condition. For instance, the cost of a life-saving operation was fixed at 10 shekels of silver for an *awêlum*, 5 shekels for a *mushkênum* and 2 shekels for a slave (§§ 215–17). Similarly, 'if a man has pierced the eye of an *awêlum*, they shall pierce his eye', but 'if he has pierced the eye or broken the bone of a *mushkênum*, he shall pay one mina of silver', and, in the case of a slave, one-half of his value (§§ 196, 198, 199). Compensation in kind or money, which formed the basis of the Sumerian penal system, was now partly replaced by death, mutilation or corporal punishment, and when the victim or plaintiff was a free man, the terrible Law of Retaliation was usually applied, even if the offence was not intentional. Thus:

'If a surgeon performed a major operation on an *awêlum* with a bronze lancet and has caused the death of this man . . . they shall cut off his hand (§ 218).

'If an architect built a house for an *awêlum* but did not make his work strong, and if the house that he built collapsed and has caused the death of its owner, that architect shall be put to death (§ 229).

'If it has caused the death of a slave of the owner, he shall give slave for slave to the owner of the house (§ 231).'

Cruel as it appears to civilized minds, the Code of Hammurabi, in many of its laws, is surprisingly close to our modern ideas of justice. The laws concerned with family and property, in particular, represent a remarkable effort to protect women and children from arbitrary treatment, poverty and neglect, and if penalties, in this section also, are exceedingly severe, their application is mitigated by the admission of forgiveness and of extenuating circumstances. The wife's adultery is punished by death, but the husband may pardon his spouse and the king her lover, thus saving them from being 'bound together and thrown into the river' (§ 129). The prisoner's wife who, in her husband's absence, has 'entered the house of another man' incurs no punishment if she has done so because 'there was nothing to eat in her house' (§ 134). A man may divorce his wife without giving her anything if she misbehaved (§ 141), but if he divorces her because she has not borne him sons, 'he shall give her money to the value of her bridal gift and shall make good to her the dowry which she has brought from her father's house'²² (§ 138). The husband of a diseased woman may marry another woman, but he must keep his wife in his house and maintain her 'so long as she lives' (§ 148). When a man dies, his property is divided between his sons, but his widow has the usufruct of this property (§ 171) and may dispose freely of any 'field, plantation, house or chattel' he may have given her (§ 150). When a woman dies, her dowry does not return to her father, but goes to her sons (§ 162). Similar measures protect the sons of the 'first wife' against those of the 'slave-girl' or concubine and guarantee the children's rights against undeserved disherison (§ 168).

Another point of general interest in the Code is the frequent reference to the institution called *ilkum* (§§ 26–41). Apparently, persons of certain professions, such as the *rêdum* ('gendarme'), the *ba'irum* (? fisherman) or the *nash biltim* (literally 'tribute-bearer') received from the king corn, land, sheep and cattle in return for certain duties, the most explicit of which is military service. The fief (*ilkum*) thus acquired remained the personal property of the fief-holder throughout his life and was divided between his heirs after his death. It could not be sold nor assigned by the holder to his wife or daughters, though it could be used to pay his ransom if he was captured in the service of the king, or forfeited to a substitute if he refused to fulfil his military duties or deserted. Clearly, then, the granting of an *ilkum* was not a simple reward for services rendered to the crown, but a measure probably introduced by Hammurabi himself,²³ to attach firmly to the land a number of his subjects and to create between them and the king a bond comparable to the feudal bond which, in medieval Europe, attached lord and liegeman.

Such are, very briefly, some of the main features of this famous Code. Less original perhaps than it was thought, it remains unique by its length, by the elegance and precision of its style and by the light it throws on the rough, yet highly civilized society of the period. Written in the last years of Hammurabi, it crowns his long and successful reign. Looking back on his achievement, the King of Babylon could proudly proclaim:

'I rooted out the enemy above and below;
I made an end of war;
I promoted the welfare of the land;
I made the people rest in friendly habitations;
I did not let them have anyone to terrorize them.
The great gods called me,
So I become the beneficent shepherd whose sceptre is righteous;
My benign shadow is spread over my city.
In my bosom I carried the people of the land of Sumer and Akkad;
They prospered under my protection;
I have governed them in peace;
I have sheltered them in my strength.'²⁴

CHAPTER XIII

IN THE DAYS OF HAMMURABI

No matter how fascinating the ever changing spectacle of political and economic situations, there are times which call for a pause; there are periods so richly documented that the historian feels compelled to leave aside monarchs and dynasties, kingdoms and empires, wars and diplomacy, and to study the society in a static condition as it were. How did people live? What did they do in everyday life? These are questions which come naturally to mind and deserve an answer.

In Mesopotamia, the days of Hammurabi—or, more exactly, the century which begins sixty years before his reign (1850–1750 BC, in round figures)—is one of these periods. Here our sources, both archaeological and epigraphic, are particularly copious. It is true that we know very little about the capital cities of southern Iraq: Isin and Larsa remain practically unexplored, and eighteen years of excavations at Babylon have barely scratched the surface of the huge site, the height of the water-table having prevented the German archaeologists from digging much below the Neo-Babylonian level (609–539 BC). In the small area where deep soundings were possible, only a few tablets and fragments of walls pertaining to the First Dynasty were found, some 40 feet below the surface. But on other sites, other archaeologists have been more fortunate. The monuments they have unearthed—the royal palace of Mari, the palace of the rulers at Tell Asmar, the temples and private houses of Ur, to mention only the most important—are perhaps not very numerous, but they are of outstanding quality. As regards written documents, we are even better provided, for not only do we have the Code of Hammurabi, but his correspondence, the royal archives of Mari, and many legal, economic, administrative, religious and scientific texts from

Mari, Larsa, Sippar, Nippur, Ur, Tell Harmal and various other sites: in all, perhaps thirty or forty thousand tablets. Indeed, it can be said without exaggeration that Mesopotamia 1800 years before Christ is much better known to us than any European country a thousand years ago, and it would be in theory possible for historians to draw a fairly complete picture of the Mesopotamian society in the eighteenth and nineteenth centuries BC. As this would go far beyond the limits of the present work, we shall limit ourselves to the sketching of the three main aspects of this society: the god in his temple, the king in his palace, the citizen in his house.

THE GOD IN HIS TEMPLE

The advent of the Western Semites brought surprisingly little change in the Sumero-Akkadian pantheon. Amurru, the eponymous god of the Amorites, had his own sanctuaries but never attained celebrity, and though many proper names in Old Babylonian times were formed with such typically Syro-Palestinian gods as El, Erah, Lim or Hammu, there is no evidence that they were the object of an organized cult in Mesopotamia. All things considered, the only major innovation was the promotion of Marduk to the supreme rank and his endowment with the powers and prerogatives of Enlil. But the cult of Marduk remained for a long time a purely official affair, a state cult lacking emotional resonance. The subjects of Hammurabi—as indeed the king himself—continued to worship Anu, Enlil, Ea, Sin, Shamash, Ishtar and the thousand odd deities who, from time immemorial, had 'turned a smiling face' on the people of Iraq. In all the cities of Sumer and Akkad, the Sumerian gods (now generally called by their Semitic names) remained in their shrines, and the fervour of their worshippers, far from withering under the wind of political change, seems to have been enhanced. The diffusion of terra-cotta figurines of gods, the existence of 'domestic chapels', the predominance of 'presentation scenes' on the cylinder-seals of the period[1] testify to the close, personal relationship that existed now between man and divinity.

The temples—the 'houses' (*bîtu*) of the gods as they were called —varied in size and layout. Some were small wayside chapels which were part of a block of houses and consisted of hardly more than an open courtyard with an altar and a pedestal for the divine statue;[2] others were larger detached or semi-detached buildings, comprising several courts and rooms;[3] and finally, there were the enormous temple-complexes of the greater gods, which often included several shrines for the minor deities of their household and retinue.[4] These temples no longer retained the admirable simplicity of the early Sumerian sanctuaries (see above, Chapter IV). Throughout the ages they had increased in complexity to incorporate the numerous services of a strongly organized religious community. Moreover, their plan reflects a high degree of specialization in the performance of the cult, and it appears that a distinction was made between the parts of the temple open to the public and those reserved for the priests, or perhaps for certain categories of priests only. Whether the concept that the great gods could only be approached by degrees was developed by the Sumerians or introduced by the Semites is a much debated problem which cannot be discussed here.[5]

All the main Mesopotamian temples had in common certain features.[6] They all comprised a large courtyard (*kisalmahhu*) surrounded by small rooms which served as lodgings, libraries and schools for the priests, offices, workshops, stores, cellars and stables. During the great feasts, the statues of the gods brought from other temples were solemnly gathered in this courtyard, but on ordinary days it was open to all, and we must imagine it, not as an empty and silent space, but as a compromise half-way between a cloister and a market-place, full of noise and movement, crowded with people and animals, unceasingly crossed by the personnel of the temple, the merchants who did business with it and the men and women who brought offerings and asked for help and advice. Beyond the *kisalmahhu* was another courtyard, usually smaller, with an altar in its middle, and finally, the temple proper (*ashirtu*), the building to which none but the priests called *erib bîti*, 'those who enter the temple', had access. The temple was divided by partitions into three rooms, one behind the other: vestibule, ante-cella and cella (holy of holies). The cella contained the statue of the god or goddess to whom the temple was dedicated. Usually made of wood covered with gold leaves, it stood on a pedestal in a niche cut in the back-wall of the cella. When all doors were open, the statue could be seen shining faintly in the semi-darkness of the shrine from the small courtyard but not from the large one, as it was at a right angle with the temple doorway. At the god's feet, flower pots and incense burners were arranged, and low brick benches around the cella and ante-cella supported the statues of other gods and of worshippers, together with royal steles and various *ex-votos*. A two-steps altar, a table for the sacred meals, basins of lustral water, stands for insignia and dedicated weapons made up the rest of the temple furniture. Rare and expensive materials were used in the construction of the building: cedar beams supported its roof and its doors were made of precious wood, often lined with copper or bronze sheets. Lions, bulls, griffins or genii made of stone, clay or wood guarded the entrances. At the corners of the temple precinct and buried under the pavement were brick boxes containing bronze or clay 'nails', royal inscriptions and the statuettes of the kings who had founded or restored the sanctuary. These 'foundation deposits' (*temenu*) authenticated the sacred ground, marked its limits and repelled the netherworld demons.

Every day throughout the year, religious ceremonies were performed in the temples: the air vibrated with music, hymns and prayers; bread, cakes, honey, butter, fruit were laid on the god's table; libations of water, wine or beer were poured out into vases; blood flowed on the altar and the smoke of roasting flesh mixed with the fumes of cedar-wood, cyprus-wood or incense filled the sanctuary. The main object of the cult was the service of the gods, the *dullu*. The gods were supposed to live a physical life and had daily to be washed, anointed, perfumed, dressed, attired and fed, the regular supply of food being ensured by 'fixed offerings' established once and for all by the king as supreme chief of the clergy, and by pious foundations. In addition, certain days of the month considered as sacred or propitious—the days when the moon appeared or disappeared, for instance—were devoted to special celebrations. There were also occasional ceremonies of purification and consecration, and, of course, the great New Year Festival celebrated in some cities in the spring and the autumn. But the priests also served as intermediates between men and gods. More than anyone else, they knew the proper way of approaching the great gods; on behalf of the sick, the sorrowful, the repentant sinner, they would offer

PLATE 13. The ziggurat of Ur is the best preserved of all the stage-towers of Mesopotamia. Built by the kings of the Third Dynasty of Ur (2113–2006 BC), it was restored by successive Babylonian rulers down to Nabonidus (556–539 BC)

PLATE 14

A. The 'Goddess with the Flowing Vase'. Statue found in the Royal Place of Mari.

B. A votive dog dedicated to the goddess Nin-Sin by a high official of Lagash, 'for the life of Sumu-El', King of Larsa (1894–1866 BC.)

PLATE 15

A. Stone head of Iarim–Lim,
King of Aleppo, a contemporary
of Hammurabi, King of
Babylon. From Alalah, near
Antioch (Turkey.)

B. From the archives of
Assyrian merchants established
in Anatolia: envelope of a clay
tablet with summary of the
content and seal impressions.

PLATE 16

A. Believed to be the work of a Hurrian artist: the head of an unknown god found at Jabbul, near Aleppo.

B. Impression of a cylinder-seal. 'Presentation scene' typical of the Old Babylonian period.

sacrifices, recite prayers and lamentations, sing hymns of grace and psalms of contrition; and as they alone could read into the mysterious future, there was no king nor commoner who, on frequent occasions, would not consult them and ask for an omen. For each of these acts of cult, a strict and complicated ritual was laid down.7 Originally prayers and incantations were in Sumerian, but under the First Dynasty of Babylon, the Akkadian language was allowed into the Temple, and we possess, for instance, a 'Ritual for the Covering of the Temple Kettle-Drum' where it is said that a certain prayer should be whispered 'through a reed tube' in Sumerian into the right ear of a bull, and in Akkadian into its left ear.8

A large number of priests were attached to the main temples. Sons and grandsons of priests, they were brought up in the sanctuary and received a thorough education in the temple school, or *bît mummi* (literally 'House of Knowledge'). At their head was the high-priest, the *enu* (Akkadian form of the Sumerian word *en*, 'lord') and the *urigallu*, originally the guardian of the gates, but now the main officiant. Among the specialized members of the clergy, the *mashmashshu* who recited incantations, the *pashîshu* who anointed the gods and laid their table, the *kâlû* who chanted lamentations, the *âshipu* or exorcist and the *bârû* who interpreted dreams and foretold the future were the most important. But there were other categories of priests as well as singers, musicians, artisans, servants and slaves. The personnel at the service of female deities was no less numerous and varied. The high-priestess (*entu*) was often of royal blood9 and the *nadîtu*-priestesses who could marry but were not allowed to bear children,10 usually came from the best families. Side by side with these respectable ladies were various categories of women who had devoted themselves to what was then considered not a shameful profession, but a particular form of contact between man and the divinity: sacred prostitution. All these people formed a closed society which had its own rules, traditions and rights, lived partly from the revenues of the temple land, partly from banking and commerce, and partly 'from the altar',11 and played an important part in the affairs of the state and in the private life of every Mesopotamian. But the days when the temple controlled the entire social and economic life of the country were over. The vital centre, the heart and brain of the state was now the royal palace.

The importance given to the royal palace (Sum. *é-gal*, Akkad. *ekallum*, 'great house') is a striking feature of the Old Babylonian period. The concentration of authority in the hands of the monarch, the requirements of a centralized administration, the costly exigency of prestige had concurred to transform the king's residence—hitherto a relatively modest building[12]—into a vast compound of apartments, reception rooms, offices, workshops and stores surrounded, for safety reasons, by strong defensive walls. Mansion, castle and serai, the palace had become a city within the city.

Of such royal abodes, there is no finer example than the palace of Mari.[13] Found in an excellent state of preservation, it is remarkable not only for its size—it measures some 650 by 450 feet and covered an area of about seven acres—but for its intelligent and harmonious layout, the beauty of its decoration and the quality of its construction. Archaeologists have called it 'the jewel of archaic Oriental architecture',[14] and such was its fame in antiquity that the King of Ugarit, on the Syrian coast, did not hesitate to send his son 350 miles inland for the sole purpose of visiting 'the house of Zimri-Lim'.[15]

The enormous wall of the palace (40 feet thick in places), laid on stone foundations and reinforced by towers, was pierced with only one gate on its northern side. Passing through a guarded vestibule, a first courtyard and a dark corridor, one would enter the great courtyard of the palace, a truly majestic open space (4,500 square feet) flooded with sunlight and paved with gypsum slabs except in its middle where palm-trees may have been planted. On the side opposite the entrance, three elegantly curved steps led to a high, oblong 'audience room' used in all probability by the King of Mari when he addressed his subjects. Through a door in the western wall of the 'courtyard of honour' and an L-shaped passage, royal personages, ambassadors, high officials of the kingdom and other visitors of importance were introduced into another courtyard, smaller but particularly neat and attractive with its floor of hard, white plaster and its walls covered with frescoes, some of them sheltered from rain and excessive heat by a light canopy resting on wooden poles. The brightly coloured paintings, which have in part survived and are now the pride of the Louvre and Aleppo museums, represent religious state ceremonies: a bull brought to sacrifice, the King of Mari 'touching the hand' of Ishtar (a ritual of investiture performed during the New Year festival), offerings and libations to a goddess and other fragmentary scenes. Beyond this courtyard were two long rooms, one behind the other. The first room contained a plastered and painted *podium* which once supported a statue—perhaps the 'goddess with the flowing vase' found nearby, beheaded and thrown down on the ground. The other room was the throne-room. At one end, against the wall, was a low stone pedestal, probably marking the place for high-ranking visitors, while at the other end, a long, magnificent flight of steps led to a raised platform where, we would imagine, sat the monarch in stately splendour.[16]

Audience-room and throne-room with their annexes formed the heart of the palace. Around them were various quarters. On either side of the gate were lodgings for guests and for the palace garrison. Near the north-western corner of the building, a group of nicely decorated rooms and bathrooms—one with two terra-cotta baths still in place—are considered as forming the royal apartments. Nearby lived the palace superintendent and various officials. Farther south was a two-roomed school, with rows of clay benches and school-exercise tablets scattered on the floor. From the courtyard of honour a long series of corridors gave access to a double chapel—presumably dedicated to the goddesses Anunit and Ishtar—for the king's private devotions. The remainder of the three hundred odd rooms and courtyards of the palace was occupied by kitchens, stores, servants' quarters, smithies and potters' kilns.

Not less remarkable than its plan was the construction of the building. The walls, extremely thick as a rule and rising in places to a height of 16 feet, were made of large mud-bricks covered with several layers of clay and plaster. In many rooms—especially the bathrooms and lavatories—a coating of bitumen protected the floor and the lower part of the walls. No window was found, and it is likely that the rooms were lighted, either through their wide and high doors opening on to courtyards, or through round apertures in the ceiling, which could be blocked with mushroom-shaped clay 'plugs'. The existence of a second storey, at least in certain parts of the palace, is suggested by the remains of stair-cases. As for the drainage, it was effected by means of brick gutters laid under the pavement, and of bitumen-lined clay pipes going down 30 feet underground. The whole system had been so skilfully planned and installed, that the waters of a violent rainstorm which burst one day during the excavations were evacuated within a few hours, the drains having worked again, most efficiently, after forty centuries of disuse![17]

As the palace of Mari illustrates the surroundings in which lived the Mesopotamian kings, so do the tablets discovered in various rooms of the palace—together with Hammurabi's letters discovered on other sites—give us a clear picture of their routine occupations. Perhaps the most striking fact emerging from these documents is the interest taken by the king himself in the affairs of the kingdom. Provincial governors, army chiefs, ambassadors to foreign courts, officials of all ranks and even simple individuals constantly wrote to their sovereign, keeping him informed of what was happening in their particular field of activities and ask-ing for advice. In return the king gave orders, encouraged, blamed, punished, or asked for more information. A steady flow of letters carried by escorted messengers came in and out of the palace. Military and diplomatic matters, justice and public works formed, of course, the bulk of the state correspondence and we see, for instance, Hammurabi intervening in Larsa, now the capital city of his southern provinces, to pronounce legal deci-sions, appoint officials, summon civil servants to his court, and order the digging or clearing-out of canals. Similarly, Ismah-Adad and Zimri-Lim give instructions for the census of nomads and the mobilization of troops and exchange presents and ideas with their royal 'brothers'. But more trivial subjects were also touched upon, as will be shown from a few examples taken at random. The daughters of Iahdun-Lim, held captive in Mari by the Assyrian usurper Iasmah-Adad, are now grown up; Shamshi-Adad writes to his son suggesting that they be sent to his palace at Shubat-Enlil where they will be taught music. The chariots made in Mari are of much better quality than those made in

Ekallâtum; Ishme-Dagan asks his brother to send him a few, together with good carpenters.[18] In Terqa,[19] locusts have appeared, and the governor of that city sends basket-loads of the insects to his master Zimri-Lim who, like the modern Arabs, appreciates this delicacy.[20] In Terqa again, a man has had a strange, ominous dream which is the talk of the town; the king will be interested to hear it.[21] A certain Iaqqim-Addu, governor of Sagaratim[22] has captured a lion; he has put it in a wooden cage and is shipping it to Zimri-Lim. Near Mari, the mutilated body of a child has been found; Bahdi-Lim, the palace superintendent, assures the king that an inquest will be made at once. A female servant of the royal palace has escaped and fled from Assur to Mari; Shamshi-Adad requests his son to return her under escort. A woman exiled to Nahur, near Harran, is unhappy and begs Zimri-Lim: 'Could my Lord write so that they take me back and that I see again the face of my Lord whom I miss?'[23] And so it goes, tablet after tablet, in a simple, matter-of-fact style contrasting sharply with the pompous tone of the official inscriptions: 'To My Lord, say this: thus speaks XXX, your servant.'[24] This is the rare occasion when we really live with these people, when we understand their problems and share their worries. At the same time, we realize how widespread was already the art of writing, how numerous the scribes, how efficient the royal chancellery, how busy and conscientious the kings and their officials. Nothing conveys a stronger impression of travelling back into time than a visit to the royal palace of Mari and a glimpse at the contents of its archives.

THE CITIZEN IN HIS HOUSE

It now remains for us to examine how the ordinary citizens of Mesopotamian towns, the *awêlum*, lived almost four thousand years ago. For this, we must travel six hundred miles down the Euphrates, from Mari to the great city of Ur. There again, architectural remains combined with texts give us nearly all the information wanted. So well preserved were the 10,000 square yards of streets and private houses excavated in 1930–31 by Sir Leonard Woolley, that even today, after thirty years of exposure to wind and rain, they conjure up the past with a vividness such as can be found only in the ruins of Pompeii and Herculanum.[25]

Muddy in winter, dusty in summer, soiled by the rubbish thrown out of the houses and never collected, the streets are all but attractive. They wind without much planning between compact blocks of houses, blank, windowless façades pierced by occasional small doors. Here and there, however, little shops grouped in bazaars or set among the houses throw a note of gaiety in the austere scenery. Like the shops of a modern Oriental *suq*, they consist of a showroom opening widely on to the street, and of one or several back-rooms for the storage of goods. Food, clothes, rugs, pots, spices and perfumes are sold in disorderly, colourful and aromatic displays. At intervals, the red glow of a furnace in the smithy's dark workshop, the brick counter of a 'restaurant' where one can purchase and eat from clay bowls onions, cucumbers, fried fish or tasty slices of grilled meat, or a small chapel advertised by terra-cotta figurines hung on either side of the doorway. To enter the courtyard, drop a handful of dates or flour on the altar and address a short prayer to the god smiling in his niche takes only a few minutes and confers long-lasting blessings.

Very little traffic in the streets: they are too narrow for carts and even a donkey carrying a bulky load would obstruct most of them. Servants who go shopping, water-carriers, peddlars avoid the sun and hug the shadows of the walls, but in the early morning or late afternoon, a public writer, or a story-teller reciting 'Gilgamesh' would gather small crowds around him at the crossroads, while two or three times a day, flocks of noisy children invade the streets on their way to or from one of the schools.

If we push one of the doors and enter a house, a pleasant surprise awaits us, for it is cool, comfortable and much larger than it appears from outside. Having washed our feet in a small lobby, we pass into the central courtyard and notice that it is paved and that a vertical drain opens in its middle, so that it can be rinsed clean and will not be flooded during the rainy season. All around us is the building. The walls are uniformly plastered and white-washed, but we know that their upper part is made of mud bricks, their lower part of burnt-bricks carefully laid and jointed with clay mortar. A 3 foot wide gallery supported by wooden poles runs around the courtyard, dividing the building into two storeys: on the first floor live the owner of the house and his family, while the ground floor is reserved for servants and visitors. We recognize the kitchen, the workshop and store-room, the ablution room and lavatories, and that constant feature of all Oriental residences: the long, oblong chamber where the guests are entertained and eventually spend the night, the 'diwan'. The house furniture, now of course vanished, would consist of a few tables, chairs, and chests and of quantities of rugs and cushions.

The above description, valid for most houses of the Isin-Larsa and Old Babylonian periods at Ur, will sound familiar to those who have visited the Near East. It would apply word for word to any Arab house of the old style such as can still be seen today in some parts of Aleppo, Damascus or Baghdad. Kingdoms and empires have vanished, languages and religions have changed, many customs have fallen into disuse, yet this type of house has remained the same for thousands of years merely because it is best suited to the climate of that part of the world and to the living habits of its population. But our Babylonian houses had something which no longer exists: behind the building was a long and narrow courtyard, partly open to the sky and partly covered with a pent-house roof. The roof protected a brick altar and a grooved pillar upon which stood the statuettes of the household gods, the 'personal gods' so dear to the Babylonians. In the open part of the courtyard, under the brick pavement, was a vaulted tomb where all the members of the family were buried in turn, except for the small children who were buried in vases in or around the domestic chapel. Thus, the cult of the tutelary gods and the cult of the ancestors were closely associated within the house precincts. The deceased were no longer interred in cemeteries distant from the town as in earlier days,[26] but continued to take part in the life of the family.

The objects and tablets found in the houses throw precious light on the occupations of their owners. We know, for instance, that the headmaster of a private school was called Igmil-Sin, and that he taught writing, religion, history and mathematics. Although we can hardly believe that the Sumero-Akkadian grammar found in the factory of Gimil-Ningishzida, the bronze-smith, was for his own use, we perfectly understand how Ea-nâṣir, the copper merchant and unlucky speculator of 'No. 1, Old Street' came to sell part of his house to a neighbour.[27] All these people were modest, middle-class citizens and it would appear from the size, construction and comfort of their houses that their standard of living was fairly high. Yet, if some of them were prosperous, others were half-ruined. The transfer of power and wealth from the southern to the central part of Iraq under Hammurabi combined with the restriction of maritime trade in the Persian Gulf must have seriously affected the rich merchants of Ur.[28] Their city, however, was no longer passing from hand to hand as it had done so often during the struggle between Isin and Larsa. Mesopotamia was now united under a powerful and respected monarch, and for many of Hammurabi's subjects, the future may have appeared full of promise. But this period of peace and stability was short: ten, twenty years at most. The next generation would have to face new wars and witness the beginning of formidable changes affecting, not only Mesopotamia, but the entire Near East.

CHAPTER XIV

NEW PEOPLES

A T the dawn of the second millennium BC, while the princes of Isin and Larsa were fighting each other in Sumer, important events took place beyond the Taurus and the Zagros mountains. Peoples coming from faraway regions entered Asia Minor and founded in the heart of Anatolia what would be known later as the Hittite Kingdom. About the same time, in Armenia and in Iran, other foreigners settled among the Hurrian and Kassite tribes as a ruling aristocracy. Three or four hundred years later, the Hittites raided Babylon, the Kassites overthrew the great kingdom painstakingly built by Hammurabi, and the Hurrians, under their 'Mitannian' leaders, firmly occupied the northern districts of Mesopotamia.

Hittites, Mitannians and the ruling class of the Kassites belonged to a very large ethno-linguistic group called 'Indo-European', and their migrations were but part of wider ethnic movements which affected Europe and India as well as Western Asia. Directly or in-directly, the Indo-Europeans brought civilization into regions still lingering in the Chancolithic Age (Anatolia, Greece) threatened civilization in regions where it had reached the highest levels and, directly or indirectly altered the ethnic, political, cultural and economic set-up of the Old World. In the Near East, their intrusion had multiple and far-reaching effects, the most obvious being the emergence of young and ambitious nations with which both Egypt and Mesopotamia would have to reckon. From 1600 BC onwards, political issues in the Orient are raised to truly international scale, and it is no longer possible to treat Iraq as though it were isolated—or almost isolated—from the rest of the world. Mesopotamian history will have to be drawn against an increasingly wider background including now Egypt and Anato-lia, tomorrow Iran with the Medes and Persians, and finally

Europe with the Greco-Macedonian conquerors. If we want to understand the next sequence of events, we must therefore at this stage broaden our horizon considerably. The present chapter will give a bird's-eye view of Indo-European migrations followed by an outline of Hittite, Hurrian, Syrian and Egyptian history from the twentieth to the sixteenth century BC in round figures.

THE INDO-EUROPEANS

The adjective Indo-European applies to a vast linguistic family comprising languages now spoken in countries as far apart as America and India, Scandinavia and Spain. All modern European languages (with the exception of Basque, Finnish and Hungarian) as well as Armenian, Persian and several Hindu dialects, belong to this group as belonged to it in antiquity Hittite, Sanskrit, Greek, Latin and many other tongues. In spite of obvious differences, it is easy to demonstrate that these languages are closely interrelated, and it is generally believed that they all derive from a 'Common Indo-European Language' which has left no written trace.[1] Moreover, a comparative study of vocabularies has led certain scholars to the conclusion that all Indo-European speaking peoples had originally similar ways of life and institutions: essentially herdsmen and skilled in horse-breeding, they practised intermittent agriculture, knew the wheel, the boat and metal techniques, were organized in families and tribes and worshipped anthropomorphic gods. Finally, from the distribution of linguistic provinces in early historical times, it has been inferred that the homeland of the Indo-Europeans before they divided into several branches lay somewhere between the Baltic and the Black Sea, probably in the plains of Southern Russia. But difficulties arise when one tries to correlate the various chalcolithic cultures which have left traces in Eastern Europe with the Indo-European-speaking peoples, since writing does not appear in those regions until a very late date and precise identifications are impossible. All these 'Pontic' cultures, however, have a common feature: the presence of stone or copper battle-axes in tumulus-graves, and most historians agree that the "Battle-Axe Warriors' have more claim than anyone else to represent the 'original' Indo-Europeans. These considerations should make it clear that the following reconstruction of Indo-European movements lies, to a great extent, in the realm of speculation, and should be taken with due caution.

The first Indo-European migrations took various forms, reached different countries at different times and were certainly very slow, covering decades and even centuries. As far as can be ascertained, they started about the end of the third millennium BC and spread in all directions from the South Russian 'homeland'. In Europe,[2] the Battle-Axe folk moved northwards along the Volga and westwards across the open plains of Poland and Germany. By 1600 BC they had reached Denmark and the Rhine valley where they mingled with another ethnic group, the 'Beaker Folk' (so called because of their large, bell-shaped drinking vessels), who probably originated in Spain, and the resulting culture is taken by some scholars as the prototype of the great Celtic (and therefore linguistically Indo-European) civilization which flourished in Central Europe towards the end of the second millennium BC. But the Battle-Axe warriors cannot be credited with the introduction of metal in Europe, although they certainly hastened its diffusion. Before their arrival, copper had already been brought from the Caucasus and from Anatolia by peaceful tradesmen and artisans who followed the Danube valley or crossed the Mediterranean Sea, so that there were, in the middle of a still Neolithic continent, old islands of metal cultures, notably in Rumania, Hungary, Spain, Greece and Crete. The last two countries are of special interest to us, owing to the close relationship which has always existed between the Aegean countries, Egypt and Western Asia.

The first Bronze Age culture in Greece,[3] the Early Helladic culture, seems to have been founded, at the beginning of the third millennium, by immigrants from Anatolia and benefited from intensive commercial intercourse with Asia Minor, the Cyclades and Crete. But about 1800 BC, the Greek peninsula was the setting for a large-scale invasion followed by radical changes in architecture, burial customs and ceramic. Sizeable towns were built on the ruins of humble villages; a grey wheel-made pottery replaced the dark hand-made ware of the preceding period, and as the new settlers were buried with numerous bronze weapons, including occasional battle-axes, it has been suggested that the Middle Helladic culture was introduced by the Indo-Europeans. Now, the following Late Helladic or Mycenean culture appears, in many respects, to result from the internal development of Middle Helladic, and the Myceneans spoke an Indo-European (Greek) dialect and were, in fact, Greeks, as recently proved by Ventries' genial decipherment of their 'Linear B' writing.4 We may therefore conclude that Indo-European migrations reached continental Greece at the beginning of the eighteenth century BC, i.e. about the time Hammurabi reigned in Babylon. Whilst Greece was thus conquered and organized, the brilliant Minoan civilization flourished in the island of Crete.5 Crete was the meeting point of Egyptian and Asiatic influences, and indeed, the development of its civilization had been triggered off by early contacts with Egypt, while the local bronze industry was certainly of Anatolian origin, and the *tholoi* tombs and double-axe amulets of the Early Minoan culture (? 2500–1850 BC) recall similar though much older monuments and objects found in proto-historic Mesopotamia (see page 61). Yet, the final product of this mixture was extremely original and surprisingly 'Western European' in character. If the palaces erected at Cnossos, Mallia and Phaistos resemble in their layout the contemporary palace of Mari, their architecture and decoration owed no more to foreign arts than did the egg-shell 'Kamares' pottery, nor were the Minoan hieroglyphic and 'Linear A' writings on clay tablets—both as yet undeciphered—of foreign origin. During this Middle Minoan period (1850–1550 BC), which corresponds to the Middle Egyptian Kingdom and to the First Dynasty of Babylon, Crete gave more than it received: it exported its products throughout the Aegean and eastern Mediterranean countries, and aided the young Mycenean civilization of continental Greece to mature. In 1450 BC, however, the Myceneans landed in the island, in turn impressed their mark on its culture and built an insular Empire which spanned the Aegean: the Indo-Europeans had conquered the sea.

If we now turn from Europe to Asia, we find another group of Indo-European-speaking peoples—the Aryans or Indo-Aryans—moving southwards from Russia at the end of the third millennium. In the course of a long peregrination, two branches detached themselves from a common stem: through Iran or the Caucasus, the first branch penetrated into the massif of Armenia, and hence to the Taurus foothill region, where it mingled with the very old

'Asianic' people, the Hurrians; the second branch seized control over other Asianic tribes established further south in the Zagros and on the Iranian plateau: the Kassites. The bulk of the Aryans continued their course in a south-easterly direction and eventually reached the former Indian provinces of Sind and Punjab, now in Pakistan. Fourteen years of excavations at two sites of the Indus valley, Mohenjo-Daro and Harappa, have shown that this region was, during the third millennium BC, the centre of a flourishing civilization known as the Indus Civilization or Harappa culture.[6] With its well-planned towns and comfortable brick houses, its attractive painted pottery and its delicately carved and inscribed seals, the Harappa culture is strangely reminiscent of and can favourably compare with the Sumerian civilization, and indeed there is some evidence of commercial contacts between the 'Proto-Indians' and the inhabitants of Mesopotamia during the Early Dynastic and Akkadian periods (see page 135). But the Aryans came with their horse-driven chariots, and swept all this away, if we believe that the sudden catastrophe which destroyed Mohenjo-Daro and Harappa some time before 1500 BC and plunged India into darkness for twelve centuries was the result of their arrival in the Indus valley.

Such is the general background against which we must now examine more closely two peoples which, by their geographical position, had intimate contacts with Mesopotamia, and exerted a considerable influence on its history: the Hittites and the Hurrians.

ASIA MINOR AND THE HITTITES

Despite the considerable amount of field work done in Turkey during the last few years, the archaeology and early history of Asia Minor are still imperfectly known.[7] The sequence of prehistoric cultures is established only in broad outline, and although the first historical events in that region took place at the beginning of the second millennium BC, they are only known to us from occasional references in texts of a much later date. This accounts for the somewhat patchy character of the description which follows.

The earliest settlements (Mersin, Tarsus, Sakje-Gözü) date back to Neolithic times, possibly in the fifth millennium BC. They are situated in Cilicia, geographically an extension of the great Syro-Mesopotamian 'Fertile Crescent', which explains the strong affinities between the material they have yielded and that from Hassuna and from the 'Amuq plain (see above, page 57). But in the Chalcolithic Age (*circa* 3800–2600 BC), other districts became inhabited and other sites, such as Troy (founded about 3000 BC), Yortan, Alishar and Dündartepe, can be put on the map. Significantly, all these sites lie on a line running from east to west across the peninsula, and seem to mark the 'copper route' from the Caucasus to the Aegean. Also in the same general area are the main cities of the Early Bronze Age (2600–1900 BC): Troy again Polatli and Alaja. Thus, while a rather brilliant civilization, gradually blossomed in the western part of Turkey, fertilizing Greece, Crete and the Cyclades, and while traces of advanced cultures can be found along its northern and southern borders, the Armenian highland in the extreme east lagged behind, and the central plateau of Anatolia was still sparingly inhabited. Chalcolithic and Bronze cultures vary in detail from region to region, but a number of features give the whole of prehistoric Asia Minor a certain unity: the pottery is predominantly monochrome, 'burnished', dark in colour and attractive; the houses are built of stone and mud bricks, their walls being strengthened by wooden beams, and metal-work reaches a high degree of perfection as illustrated by the so-called 'Priam treasure' of Troy II (*circa* 2600 BC) and by the lavish furniture of the 'Royal Cemetery' at Alaja (*circa* 2400 BC).

The first written documents appear in Asia Minor about 2000 BC, but they are of foreign origin. Asia Minor was one of the main metallurgic centres of the Near East and as such had always maintained active commercial relations with ancient Iraq. It is therefore not surprising to find colonies of Assyrian merchants installed on this side of the Taurus at least since the reign of Ibbi-Sin of Ur (2029–2006 BC). One of these colonies —perhaps the most important—was discovered at Kültepe (ancient *Kanesh*), near the town of Kayseri in Cappadocia.[8] There, Czech and Turkish excavations carried out over a number of years have unearthed the traders' houses together with hundreds of their 'business letters'. These are, of course, clay tablets often contained in a sealed clay-envelope, and are written in a dialectal variety of Akkadian called 'Old Assyrian'. Since they cover at least six generations, they tell us a great deal about the merchants and their trade. We learn, for instance, that they exported to Assyria copper, gold and semi-precious stones and imported lead and woven materials, and that payments were made in silver. The goods were transported by caravans of donkeys, and we can trace back the long track they followed. The activities of the community depended from an organization, the *karum*, which functioned as Chamber of Commerce, tribunal and consulate under an annually appointed chairman or *limmu*. But perhaps the main interest of this correspondence is that it is our only source of information on Anatolia itself at the dawn of its history. The Assyrian merchants were on very good terms with the natives, the local chieftains enriching themselves with taxes levied on imported goods. The country was divided into about ten small kingdoms which seemed to obey one ruler called 'prince of princes'. Most of the local names belong to the old, 'Asianic' layer of population (*Hattians*), but the presence of Indo-European names in small numbers indicates that the 'Hittites' had already crossed the Bosphorus and crept into Asia Minor.

Taken in its broader sense, the word 'Hittite' covers the totality of the intruders, three peoples which spoke different though closely related Indo-European languages: Luwian, Palaite and Nesite. The Luwians seem to have arrived first, the others later. Soon, they were scattered over the peninsula. The Luwians whose language was later written in hieroglyphs settled to the west of Cilicia, along the coast, the Palaites probably in the hilly region of Sivas, and the so-called Nesites in Cappadocia—indeed, the city of Nesa or Nesha has been tentatively identified with Kanesh-Kültepe. Centuries later, those Nesite-speaking invaders conquered the centre of the Anatolian plateau, just east of Ankara, the country called *Hatti* by its indigenous population, and took their name from it. They became the *Hittites* proper who played such an important part in Near Eastern history during the second millennium BC.[9]

From the nearest civilized country, Mesopotamia, the Hittites borrowed the cuneiform script and adapted it to their own Indo-European language. Most of the Hittite texts in our possession are not older than the fourteenth or thirteenth centuries BC, but they sometimes refer to events which took place in what was already the remote past. One text, for instance, speaks of Pitkhanas, King of Kussara, and his son Anittas, who subdued five neighbouring kingdoms (including Hatti) and transferred his residence to Nesa. As the names of these rulers also appear in the tablets from Kültepe, and as Anitta's campaigns seem to have put an end to the Assyrian colonies in Cappadocia, it is possible to date these events to *circa* 1900 BC. A gap of nearly two centuries follows. Then, about 1740 BC, another King of Kussara, Tudkhaliyas I, opened a new dynasty and his grandson, Labarnas I, (1680–1650 BC), is said to have 'made the seas his frontiers' and divided 'the land' between his children. Labarnas was considered by the Hittite monarchs as their true ancestor, and must be credited with having laid the foundation of what we call the Old Hittite Kingdom, a period of brief but considerable glory for the Hittites, as will be seen in the next chapter.

Leaving, for the time being, the Hittites, we must now turn to one of their most interesting neighbours: the Hurrians.

HURRIANS AND MITANNIANS

Known 60 years ago from one single cuneiform text (a letter found at el-Amarna in Egypt) and from a reference in the Bible (the '*Horites*' of Genesis xxxvi. 20–30), the Hurrians have recently become a subject of considerable interest for historians and archaeologists. Unlike the Hittites, they played no part in Near Eastern politics until the fifteenth century BC, and then only for a short period, but there is now ample evidence that they formed an important and active element in the population of Mesopotamia and Syria during the second millennium BC. Yet, they still remain in many respects an elusive people, and what we know of them can be told in a few words.[10]

Their language, written in cuneiform script, is neither Semitic nor Indo-European, but belongs to the vague so-called 'Asianic' group, its nearest relative being Urartian, the language spoken in the country of Urarṭu (Armenia) in the first millennium BC. Their national gods were Teshup, a storm-god of the mountains, and his consort Hepa, a form of mother-goddess. Whether the Hurrians had an art of their own is open to discussion, but the ceramic

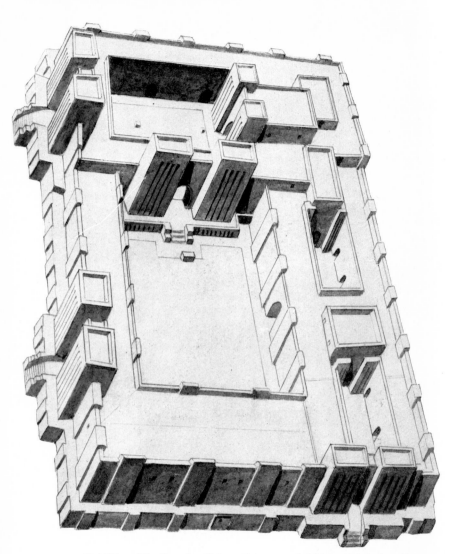

PLATE 17. The Temple of Ishtar-Kititum at Ishchâli, in the Diyala valley.
Old Babylonian period. Reconstruction by Harold D. Hill.

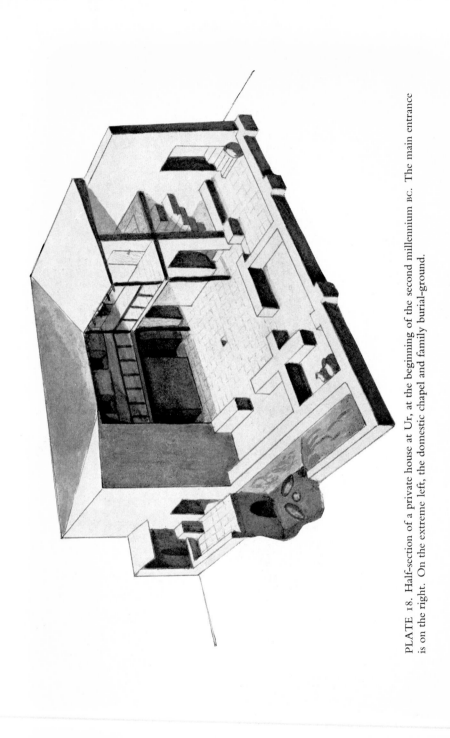

PLATE 18. Half-section of a private house at Ur, at the beginning of the second millennium BC. The main entrance is on the right. On the extreme left, the domestic chapel and family burial-ground.

associated with their presence in certain sites is most characteristic. These elegant goblets decorated with flowers, birds and geometrical designs painted in buff colour on a dark-grey background contrast with the plain Mesopotamian pottery of the time and date a level as surely as did the Halaf or Ubaid painted wares in proto-historic ages.

Language and religion point to the mountainous North, more precisely to Armenia, as the original homeland of the Hurrians, but they were never strictly confined to that region. We have already seen (page 131) Hurrian kingdoms established on the upper Tigris and on the upper Euphrates during the Akkadian period. Under the Third Dynasty of Ur, isolated personal names in the economic records from Drehem, near Nippur, suggest that the Hurrians formed in Sumer small groups of immigrants comparable to Armenians in modern Iraq. During the first quarter of the second millennium, Hurrian infiltrations in the 'Fertile Crescent' amounted, at least in some regions, to a peaceful invasion. In the Syrian town of Alalah, between Aleppo and Antioch, the Hurrians formed the majority of the population as early as 1800 BC.[11] At the same time, Hurrian personal names and religious texts in Hurrian are found in the archives of Mari and Chagar Bazar. A century or so later, the Hurrians practically possess northern Iraq. They occupy the city of Gasur, near Kirkuk, change its name into Nuzi, adopt the language and customs of its former Semitic inhabitants, and build up a very prosperous Hurrian community.[12] Tepe Gawra and Tell Billa,[13] near Mosul, fall equally under their influence. After 1600 BC, the Hurrian ceramic replaces the crudely painted pottery peculiar to the Khabur valley, and the Hurrian element dominates in northern Syria, northern Iraq, and Jazirah. We should not be surprised, therefore, to find in those regions, at the beginning of the fifteenth century BC, a Hurrian kingdom powerful enough to hold in check the Assyrians in the east, the Hittites and Egyptians in the west. The heart of this kingdom lay in the Balikh-Khabur district, in the region called *Hanigalbat* by the Assyrians and *Naharim* ('the Rivers') by the Western Semites, and it is probable that the name of our 'Hurrians' (*Hurri*) survived in Orrhoe, the Greek name for modern Urfa.

In a number of texts, the Hurrian kingdom of Jazirah is called

Mitanni and from this word derives the appellation 'Mitannian', applied to the Indo-European element discernible in the Hurrian society at a certain period. We do not know when and how the Indo-Aryans came to be mixed with the Hurrians and took control over them, but there is little doubt that, at least during the fifteenth and fourteenth centuries BC, they were settled among them as a leading aristocracy. The names of several Mitannian kings, such as Mattiwaza and Tushratta, and the term *mariannu*, which designates a category of warriors, are most probably of Indo-European origin, and in a treaty between Mitannians and Hittites, the gods Mitrasil, Arunasil, Indar and Nasattyana—which are, of course, the well-known Aryan gods Mithra, Varuna, Indra and the Nasatyas—are invoked side by side with Teshup and Hepa. It was, no doubt, those ancient nomads of the Russian plains who taught the Hurrians the art of horse-training—a Hurrian living in Boghazköy wrote a complete treatise on this subject, using Indo-European technical terms—and in this way, introduced or rather popularized the horse in the Near East.

If the contribution of the Hurrians to the civilization of Meso-potamia was negligible,[14] their impact on the less advanced cultures of Syria, though difficult to define, must have been considerable. In any case, their large-scale intrusion in the latter country seems to have started a series of political disturbances and ethnic movements the effects of which were felt as far away as Egypt.

SYRIA AND EGYPT

In prehistoric times, Syria* shared with Iraq and southern Turkey the Neolithic and Chalcolithic cultures of the 'Fertile Crescent'.[15] The first settlement of Jericho resembles and perhaps antedates Jarmo, and sherds of the Hassuna, Halaf and Ubaid pottery have been found as far south as the Jordan valley (see above, Chapters III and IV). But Syria did not offer geographical conditions as favourable to the formation of vast agricultural societies as the Tigris-Euphrates plain or the Nile valley, and it remained at a comparatively primitive stage when civilization crystallized in Sumer and in Egypt. It would appear from the place names

---

* The term *Syria* is taken here in its broadest sense and includes Syria proper, Lebanon, Palestine and Transjordan.

attested in early cuneiform texts that the population of *northern* Syria, in the third millennium BC, was not Semitic but belonged to an ethnic stratum of unknown affiliation—possibly the unnamed people or peoples responsible for its proto-historic cultures. On the Lebanese coast and in Palestine, on the contrary, the Western Semites seem to have been at home at a very early date. The distinction here made between the north and the south—the dividing line passing just north of Byblos—is capital, since it reflects on the economic, cultural and political development of the country. During the Akkadian and Ur III periods, northern Syria was attracted within the Mesopotamian sphere of influence, while Lebanon and Palestine turned their backs to the east and looked towards Egypt.[16]

Relations between Syria and Egypt, already attested in Pre-Dynastic times, are well documented under the Old Egyptian Kingdom (*circa* 2800–2400 BC). This was the time of the great pyramids and Egypt looked like its monuments: lofty, massive, apparently indestructible. Docile to the orders of Pharaoh—the incarnate god who sat in Memphis—and of his innumerable officials, toiled a hard-working people and an army of slaves. But if the Nile valley was rich, it lacked an essential material: wood. The mountains of Lebanon, within easy reach, were thick with pine, cypress and cedar forests. Thus, a very active trade was established between the two countries to their mutual profit. Byblos (Sem. *Gubla*, Eg. *Kepen*), the great emporium of timber, became strongly 'Egyptianized', and from Byblos, Egyptian cultural influence spread along the coast. But the relations between the Egyptians and the populations of the Palestinian hinterland were far less friendly. The nomads who haunted the Negeb, in particular, repeatedly attacked the Egyptian copper mines in the Sinai peninsula and on occasions raided the Nile delta, obliging the Pharaohs to retaliate and even to fortify their eastern border. The downfall of the Old Kingdom left Egypt unprotected, and we know of the large part played by the 'desert folk', the 'Asiatics', in the three hundred years of semi-anarchy which followed.

The first centuries of the second millennium witnessed the expansion of the Western Semites in Syria as well as in Mesopotamia. While Amorite dynasties rose to power in many Mesopotamian towns, northern Syria was divided into several Amorite kingdoms, the most important being those of Iamhad (Aleppo), Karkemish and Qatna. Prepared by long years of Sumero-Akkadian influence, the country made enormous strides towards civilization. Around the palaces of local rulers, large fortified cities were built, and the objects and sculptures discovered in the palace of Iarim-Lim, King of Alalah, for instance, are by no means inferior in quality to those found in the contemporary palace of Zimri-Lim, King of Mari.[17] We have already seen that the Mari archives offer ample proof of intimate and friendly contacts between Mesopotamia and Syria and, indeed, one cannot escape the impression of a vast community of Amorite states stretching from the Mediterranean to the Persian Gulf. At the same time, commercial relations between Syria and Crete were intensified. A colony of Minoan traders established itself in the port of Ugarit (Ras Shamra)[18] and the exquisite Kamares crockery found its way to the tables of Syrian monarchs. Egypt, then in the full revival of its Middle Kingdom (2160–1660 BC) renewed and consolidated the ties which attached it to the Lebanese coast and endeavoured to counter the growing Hurrian influence in northern Syria by lavishing presents on the Amorite courts. This, at any rate, is a possible explanation for the vases, jewels and royal statues sent to Byblos, Beirut, Ugarit, Qatna and Neirab (near Aleppo) by the Pharaohs of the Twelfth Dynasty.[19]

The region to the south of the Lebanon, however, presents us with a very different picture, Much poorer than northern Syria and less open to foreign influences, Palestine in the Middle Bronze Age (2000–1600 BC) was a politically divided and unstable country, 'in the throes of tribal upheaval',[20] where the Egyptians themselves had no authority and apparently little desire to extend their political and economic ascendancy. The arrival among those restless tribes of Abraham and his family—an event whose after-effects are still acutely felt in the Near East—must have passed almost unnoticed. Small clans or large tribes constantly travelled in antiquity from one side to the other of the Syrian desert, and there is no reason to doubt the reality of Abraham's migration from Ur to Hebron *via* Harran as described in Genesis xi, 31. A comparison between the biblical account and the archaeological and textual material in our possession suggests that it must have taken place 'about 1850 BC, or a little later',[21] perhaps as the result of the difficult conditions which prevailed then in southern Iraq, torn apart between Isin and Larsa. The historical character of the Patriarchal period was further reinforced—and so it was thought some years ago—by the mention in cuneiform and hieroglyphic texts dating mostly from the fifteenth and fourteenth centuries BC, of a category of people, generally grouped in bellicose bands, called *Habirû* (or *'Apiru* in Egyptian) a name which sounded remarkably like biblical *'Ibri*, the Hebrews. There was, at last, the long awaited appearance in non-hebraical sources of Abraham's kin! Unfortunately, recent and thorough reappraisals of these sources have shown beyond any doubt that the Habiru have nothing in common with the Hebrews but a similitude of name. They were neither a people nor a tribe, but a class of society made up of refugees, of 'displaced persons' as we would say today, who frequently turned into outlaws.[22]

About 1660 BC, the Palestinian chieftains, whose turbulence and hostile attitude had already worried the last Pharaohs of the Twelfth Dynasty, succeeded in invading Egypt. They are known as Hyksôs, the Greek form of the Egyptian name *hiq-khase*, 'chieftain of a foreign hill-country'.[23] Although they governed Egypt for less than a hundred years and never occupied more than the Nile delta, their influence on the warfare, the arts and even the language of that country was considerable. In the end, however, the kings of the Eighteenth Dynasty overthrew the Hyksôs, chasing them up to the gates of Gaza, and with this exploit opens what we call the New Empire (1580–1100 BC), undoubtedly the most glorious period in the history of ancient Egypt. By contrast, Mesopotamia, at about the same time (1595 BC), fell into the hands of other foreigners, the Kassites, and entered into a long period of political lethargy.

CHAPTER XV

THE KASSITES

A FTER this large, if sketchy, survey of the Near East, we must now return to Mesopotamia which we left, it will be remembered, at the end of Hammurabi's reign, in the middle of the eighteenth century B C.

The ethnic movements just described were then about to bear fruit: the Hittites were enforcing their rule upon the indigenous populations of Anatolia; the Hurrians were peacefully invading northern Syria and northern Iraq; and behind the Zagros range, an Aryan aristocracy was organizing the Kassites into a nation of warriors. If the Babylonian court was aware of these changes, it probably saw in them little cause for alarm, since none of these peoples yet appeared to constitute an immediate danger to Iraq, and indeed, the first cracks in the edifice erected by Hammurabi resulted, not from foreign aggression, but from its own intrinsic weakness. The empire of Babylon was the work of one man and rested almost entirely upon his strong personality. Built up in a few years through the aggregation of five sovereign states, each of them with a long tradition of independence, it had been force-fully and prematurely centralized. The efforts made by the king to concentrate in Babylon the political, economic and spiritual life of the country might, in the long run, have benefited Meso-potamia as a whole, but their immediate effect was to ruin the provinces and to create a considerable amount of discontentment, particularly in the once prosperous cities of Sumer and in Assyria where the memory of Shamshi-Adad's great deeds was still alive. Small wonder, then, that the death of Hammurabi (1750 B C) was followed by an outburst of revolts leading to the rapid disintegra-tion of his kingdom. When, a century and a half later, the Hittites came and captured Babylon, it had fallen to the rank of a minor capital city. What little power and glory it subsequently regained was, ironically, the work of other foreigners, the Kassites, who ascended the throne left vacant by Hammurabi's successors and occupied it for more than four hundred years.

HAMMURABI'S SUCCESSORS

Hammurabi's son and heir, Samsu-iluna (1749–1712 BC) was apparently endowed with some of his father's qualities, for he fought with remarkable endurance against the various enemies of Babylon.[1] But it was like mending a ragged cloak: for every rent patched, a new one appeared, and the final result was an enormous loss of territory. Thus, in the early years of the reign, an adventurer calling himself Rîm-Sin, like the last king of Larsa, led a revolt in the districts bordering Elam and kept afield for at least two years before he was caught and slain. Later, a certain Iluma-ilu—pretendedly a descendant of Damiq-ilishu, the last king of Isin—raised the flag of independence in Sumer, became the master of the entire country south of Nippur, and founded the so-called 'Second Dynasty of Babylon' or Dynasty of the Sea-Land (*circa* 1740 BC). A long and bloody war followed in the course of which several Sumerian cities, including Ur, were sacked, dismantled and burnt down by one or other of the two enemies. At about the same time, the north-eastern districts, under Babylonian obedience as a result of Hammurabi's last campaign, also recovered their freedom—probably through the rebellion of one of Shamshi-Adad's obscure successors, Adasi, who remained famous in Assyrian annals for having 'ended the servitude of Assur'.[2] In addition to facing this series of domestic disasters, Samsu-iluna had to protect his kingdom against the threat of foreign invasion: we learn from year-names that he defeated a Kassite army in his eighth year and an Amorite army in his thirty-fifth year—not to mention the frequent incursions of Sutaean raiders who captured men and women and sold them as slaves to the Mesopotamians themselves.[3] At the end of this disastrous reign, Babylon was safe, but the kingdom, amputated of its northern and southern provinces, had shrunk back to its original boundaries: those of the country of Akkad.

Samsu-iluna's four successors, however, managed to preserve their reduced heritage for about a century. Abi-eshuh (1711–

1684 BC) repelled a second Kassite attack, tolerated or perhaps encouraged the settling of Kassite individuals in Babylonia as agricultural workers, but was unable to prevent the Kassite chief Kashtiliash I from establishing himself in Hana (modern 'Anah), on the Euphrates, only two hundred miles from Babylon.4 In a grandiose effort to dislodge Iluma-ilu from the swamps where he had taken refuge, he dammed the Tigris but failed to catch his rival who continued to reign unchallenged over Sumer. As for Ammi-ditana, Ammi-saduqa and Samsu-ditana who reigned after Abi-eshuh, they seem to have made little effort to recover the territories lost to the crown. As far as we can gather from the scanty material at our disposal, the war with the Sea-Land continued with alternating victories and defeats on both sides. Fortified towns were built in various parts of Babylonia and behind these defences, the descendants of Hammurabi restored temples, dug canals, legislated and administered their kingdom with diligence and care.5 It is doubtful whether these keen and capable and pious monarchs who, year after year, offered to the gods their own statues, ever suspected that the storm which was to sweep away their throne was gathering in the distant north-west, far beyond the snow-capped Taurus mountains.

We have said in the last chapter that Tudkhaliyas and his son Labarnas were considered by the Hittites to be their first national rulers. These kings resided in Kussara (possibly to be identified with Alaja Höyük6) and were perhaps not as powerful as their descendants liked to believe. But when Labarnas II (1650-1620 BC), the son of Labarnas I, added to the royal domain the important pre-Hittite principality of Hatti, took for residence its capital-city, Hattusas (modern Boghazköy) and from then on called himself Hattusilis, he was laying down solid foundations for the Hittite kingdom. The young and ambitious nation soon found its frontiers too narrow and looked for other lands to conquer, but the fierce Gasgas tribes in the north, the Troyans and Luwians in the west and the Hurrians in the east firmly occupied the rest of Asia Minor and opposed to its expansion an insuperable barrier. Only to the south was the road relatively free and it led beyond the Taurus to Syria and beyond Syria, to either Egypt or Mesopotamia, fertile countries where two thousand years of civilization had accumulated an enormous amount of alluring wealth. The

Hittites, therefore, marched southwards. The first large city they encountered was Aleppo (*Halpa* in their language), then the capital of the important Amorite kingdom of Iamhad. Unable to conquer Aleppo, Hattusilis negotiated and signed with its king a treaty of friendship. But his son, Mursilis I (1620–1590 BC) adopted a more energetic policy:

'He destroyed the city of Halpa,' says a Hittite text, 'and took to Hattusas prisoners from Halpa and its treasures.'7

After Aleppo, Karkemish succumbed. From Karkemish, the Hittite army followed the Euphrates downstream and suddenly appeared at the gates of Babylon. Just what happened then we do not know. Babylonian writers are naturally reticent about this painful affair, and only in a chronicle of much later date8 do we find the laconic entry:

'Against Samsu-ditana the men of Hatti marched, against the land of Akkad.'

But the Hittite text already quoted is more explicit:

'Thereafter he (Mursilis) went to Babylon and occupied Babylon; he also attacked the Hurrians and kept the prisoners and possessions from Babylon at Hattusas.'

Thus, Babylon was taken and plundered. We know from other sources that the statues of Marduk and his consort, the goddess Sarpanitum, were taken away as booty and, for some obscure reason, left behind at Hana when the Hittites retreated. As for Samsu-ditana, he lost his sceptre as well, probably, as his life. Thus disappeared in one day and presumably without much resistance, the dynasty which an obscure Amorite sheikh had founded, and which Hammurabi had made famous. It had lasted for exactly three hundred years (1894–1595 BC).

IRAQ UNDER KASSITE RULE

The Hittite campaign, if it had been followed by the permanent occupation of Babylon, might have changed the course of oriental history. It proved, however, to be no more than a daring razzia. Soon after his victory, Mursilis returned to Hattusas, where dangerous palace intrigues required his presence, and never came back. After the withdrawal of the Hittite army the fate of Babylon is not known with certainty. It would appear, however, that the Kassite ruler of those days—most probably the eighth king of the dynasty, Agum II (Kakrime)—sat on the throne left vacant by the death of Samsu-ditana. From then on, a long line of Kassite monarchs was to govern Mesopotamia or, as they called it, *Kar-Duniash*, for no less than four hundred and twenty-four years (1595–1171 BC).

Established in Iran from time immemorial, the Kassites (Akk. *kashshû*) originally occupied the central part of the Zagros range known today as Luristan, immediately to the south of Hamadan. Unlike their northern neighbours, the Guti and the Lullubi, they played no part in the Near Eastern politics during the third millennium. Their sudden aggressiveness, in the middle of the eighteenth century, seems to have been stimulated by the Indo-European warriors who had come from the east a century or two before, taught them the art of horse-rearing and taken control of their tribes. Since we possess no text entirely written in Kassite, but only Akkadian texts containing Kassite words and expressions, a short bilingual list of gods and a list of personal names, all we can say about the Kassite language is that it was agglutinative, belonged to the vast 'Asianic' group and was perhaps distantly related to Elamite.[9] The Indo-European element is attested by the presence in the Kassite pantheon of Aryan gods such as Shuriash (Ind. Surya), Maruttash (Ind. Marut) and Buriash (perhaps identical with Boreas, the Greek god of the north wind), side by side with Sumero-Akkadian deities and with Kassite gods proper (Kashshu, Shipak, Harbe, Shumalia, Shuqamuna). On such scanty evidence rests our knowledge of the ethnic and cultural background of these highlanders.

Unfortunately, we are not much better off as regards the period of Kassite domination in Iraq. As archaeological excavations progress, no doubt more documents will come to light, but all we have at present is less than two hundred royal inscriptions[10]—most of them short and of little historical value—a few letters and a number of economic texts, which is very little indeed for four hundred years—the length of time separating us from Elizabeth I! The bulk of our information derives, in fact, from sources foreign to the kingdom of Babylon, such as the el-Amarna correspondence found in Egypt (see below Chapter XVI) or the 'Synchronous History', a chronicle written by an Assyrian scribe in the seventh century BC.[11] This silence makes the Kassite period one of the most obscure in Mesopotamian history, and the words 'dark age' and 'decadence' come easily to mind. Yet, if we make full use of our sources and if we take into account the monuments erected by the Kassite kings, these long years of political stagnation appear, compared with the last years of the First Dynasty of Babylon, as an epoch of revival and even of progress, at least in some fields. There is no doubt, for instance, that the Kassites restored order, peace and unity in a country devastated by half a millennium of war, kept up with Meso-potamian traditions and behaved in every way like good, sensible Mesopotamian monarchs. Thus, one of the first acts of Agum Kakrime (1602–1585 BC) after he became King of Babylon was to bring back from Hana the statues of Marduk and Sarpanitum and to reinstate them in their temples, lavishly furnished for the occasion.[12] This gesture was calculated to win him the heart of his subjects, but it had a deeper significance: it meant that the foreigner recognized Marduk as the master of his new kingdom and in-tended to pose as the legitimate successor of the extinct dynasty. Some eighty years later, Ulamburiash defeated Ea-gâmil, King of the Sea-Land, thereby recovering for Babylon the entire country of Sumer (1517 BC). Whether he was less fortunate in an unrecorded war with Assyria, or whether he gave up all hopes of imposing his authority upon that country, we do not know; but he signed with the Assyrian prince Puzur-Ashur III an agreement concerning the frontier which, somewhere around Samarra, separated the two kingdoms.[13] Thus was consecrated the division of Mesopotamia into two parts: Assyria and Babylonia, a dicho-tomy whose effects were to be felt for nearly a thousand years. In their own domain, the Kassite kings undertook to rebuild and embellish the old and famous sanctuaries of Nippur, Larsa, Ur, and Uruk. One of them, Kara-Indash (*circa* 1445–27 BC) has left us in E-Anna, at Uruk, a very interesting piece of work: a temple the façade of which was made of bricks moulded in such a way that, when put together, they made up the figures of divine beings in low relief.[14] This ingenious technique—perhaps a substitute for rock carving—was then new in Mesopotamia; it was used later by the Chaldean dynasty in Babylon and by the Achaemenians in Susa and Persepolis. The most enthusiastic of Kassite builders, however, was Kurigalzu II (*circa* 1345–24 BC) who not only restored the sacred city of Ur, destroyed under Samsu-iluna, but founded a new and important town, now represented by the ruins of 'Aqar Quf.

The 170 foot high tower of 'Aqar Quf casting its shadow over the plain and standing a conspicuous landmark twenty miles due west of Baghdad is the core of a huge ziqqurat which once rose in the middle of Dûr-Kurigalzu, the fortified city (*dûru*) and royal residence of King Kurilgalzu. Iraqi excavations carried out at 'Aqar Quf between 1943 and 1945 have unearthed the base of the ziqqurat with its monumental staircase, three temples and part of a palace.[15] The palace was decorated with frescoes and comprised an ambulatory with square pillars, another architectural novelty. The temples were dedicated to the divine family: Enlil, Ninlil and their son Ninurta. The presence of these Sumerian gods in a city founded by a Kassite king proves the degree to which the foreigners had been assimilated. Various objects of interest were found in the temples, including a more than life-size statue of Kurigalzu engraved with a long Sumerian inscription[16] and painted terra-cotta figurines modelled with considerable skill.

The Kassites are sometimes credited with the introduction of the horse into Mesopotamia. This is not strictly correct. The 'ass from foreign countries' (*anshu-kur-ra*), as the Sumerians called it, appears sporadically in texts of the Ur III period, and horses are mentioned under their Akkadian name *sîsû* in the royal correspondence from Mari.[17] But the use of the horse as a draft animal was certainly made more common during the Kassite period by the Hurrians and by the Kassites themselves. The appearance on Near Eastern battlefields of fast horse-driven chariots created, of course, a revolution in warfare, while the replacement of load-carrying donkeys by horse-driven wagons made commercial transport easier and faster. Several other major or minor changes were wrought by the Kassites or, at least, took place during their reign. They range from the way of measuring fields to the fashion of dressing, but cannot be described here in detail. Two of them, however, are for the historian of particular interest. One is the

substitution for the old dating system of year-names of a simpler
system whereby the years of each reign, counting from the first
New Year following coronation, were expressed in figures, e.g.
'first, second, etc., year of King N.' The other novelty is the
kudurru. The Akkadian word *kudurru* means 'frontier, boundary',
and these little steles are often called 'boundary stones' although
they were, in reality, donation charts, records of royal grants of
land written on stone and kept in temples, while copies on clay
were given to the land-owners.[18] A kudurru was usually divided
into two parts: on the *recto* or on top of the stele were sculpted
the images of the gods—often replaced by their symbols: a sun-
disc for Shamash, a moon-crescent for Sin, a hoe for Marduk,
etc.—under whose guarantee was placed the donation made by
the king; on the *verso* or under the sculptures, was engraved a
long inscription giving the name of the person who benefited
from the grant, the exact location and measurements of the
estate, the various exemptions and privileges attached to it, a list
of witnesses and, finally, multiple and colourful maledictions
against 'whosoever in the future should deface, alter or destroy'
the kudurru.

These small monuments are, with cylinder-seals,[19] about the
only works of art of the Kassite period that have survived, and
few of them are attractive. The workmanship is mediocre, the
subjects stereotyped and lifeless. On the seals—now almost entirely covered with an inscription—as well as on the kudurrus,
the designs are predominantly symbolic and static. Sterile since
the days of Hammurabi, the plastic arts were passing through a
phase of stagnation which was to end only in the seventh and
sixth centuries BC, with the flowering of Assyrian sculpture. In
literature, the Kassite period was marked by considerable efforts
to salvage the cultural heritage handed down from more creative
ages, and by a new, typically priestly approach to ethical problems. Scientific works, such as medical and astronomical observations, compiled during the Isin-Larsa and Old Babylonian
periods were copied and grouped into collections; dictionaries
and lists of cuneiform signs were composed. Under the First
Dynasty of Babylon, most of the great Sumero-Akkadian myths
and legends had been rethought, recast into a simple, clear,
elegant language and rejuvenated; under the Kassite rule, they

were edited by generations of temple scribes and couched in a rather sophisticated dialect, 'Standard Babylonian'—markedly different from the vernacular 'Middle Babylonian'. The religious and philosophical concepts traditional in Mesopotamia were preserved, but in the relationship between men and gods, the stress was put on resignation rather than on confidence, on superstition rather than on faith. Pieces of wisdom literature, such as *Ludlul bêl nemêqi* (see above, page 91) are highly representative of the new spirit,[20] while the current bigotry is reflected in 'hemerologies' (i.e. calendars of propitious and ill-fated days) and in collections of incantations against demons. All this was perhaps not very original, but at least the erudite priests of Babylon saved the Mesopotamian culture from oblivion, just as the European monks in the Middle Ages saved the Greco-Roman culture. Such was the prestige of Mesopotamian culture in the ancient Near East that it was adopted from Anatolia to Egypt: the Epic of Gilgamesh, for instance, was translated into Hittite and Hurrian, and copies of Babylonian legends were found on the banks of the Nile. Moreover, the Babylonian language was a *lingua franca* in all oriental courts and diplomatic circles throughout the second half of the second millennium, at a time when Babylonia was, politically speaking, almost inactive. Thus, if in the new international concert Mesopotamia played only third or fourth fiddle, she still ranked very high in the field of civilization.

CHAPTER XVI

KASSITES, ASSYRIANS AND THE ORIENTAL POWERS

THREE out of the four centuries covered by the Kassite period were occupied by violent conflicts between the great nations of the Near East. The reasons for these conflicts were: the conquest of Syria by the Egyptians, the renewed claims of the Hittites over that country, and the formation of a large Hurri-Mitannian kingdom extending from the Mediterranean to the Zagros and acting as an obstacle to Egyptian, Hittite and, later, Assyrian ambitions. But while the territories disputed—Syria and Jazirah—lay within a short distance of Babylon, the Kassite monarchs were either too weak or too wise to allow themselves to become involved in the conflagration, and it was not until the middle of the fourteenth century that Assyrian pressure forced them into war. Thus, from 1600 to 1350 BC in round figures, the Babylonians enjoyed almost complete peace, with the exception of their victorious war against the Sea-Land and of skirmishes along their northern frontier; and when the whole Orient, after 1480 BC, went up in flames, they alone sat back, watching what has been aptly described as 'a scrum of empires'. Because of the comparatively minor rôle played by Babylonia and, for a long time, Assyria in the great political turmoil of the second millennium, we need not give here more than a summary of these intricate events, the details of which can be found in any history dealing with the wider aspects of the ancient Near East. Some emphasis, however, will be placed on those events which took place in Mesopotamia proper and influenced the destinies of that country.[1]

EGYPT VERSUS MITANNI

The effects of the new political situation arising from the invasion of Egypt by the Hyksôs (1660 BC) and from the fall of the First

Dynasty of Babylon (1595 BC) were not felt immediately. In the light of the little data available, the sixteenth century appears as a relatively stable period during which the nations whose armies were later to stand face to face on the battlefields of Syria were dressing their wounds or furbishing their weapons. As early as 1580 BC, the Hyksôs were driven out of the Nile delta, but the first Pharaohs of the Eighteenth Dynasty were too busy enforcing their authority within their own country to engage in foreign adventures, and even the famous campaign of Tuthmosis I across Syria up to the Euphrates (*circa* 1520 BC) was a raid without lasting consequences. In Anatolia, the Old Hittite Kingdom was slowly crumbling, undermined by palace revolutions no less than by foreign attacks. The king who had taken Aleppo and Babylon, Mursilis I, was assassinated in 1590 BC, and his successors surrendered all claims over the territories south of the Taurus mountains. In Assur reigned the dynasty of Adasi, the prince who had shaken off the Babylonian yoke; but for a few building inscriptions[2] and for a reference to Puzur-Ashur III in the Synchronous History, these princes would remain for us mere names on a list. As for Babylonia, she was being reunited and reorganized by the Kassites, obviously unwilling or unable to indulge in dreams of expansion, Perhaps the most active of all Oriental nations during that period were the Hurrians and their Mitannian war lords. While the complete absence of textual evidence precludes any positive statement, we may at least surmise, on the basis of subsequent events, that the Hurri-Mitannians were taking advantage of the vacuum created in northern Syria and northern Iraq by the collapse of the Hammurabian empire and the withdrawal of the Hittites to build themselves a great kingdom in those regions.

Then, suddenly, at the dawn of the fifteenth century, trouble broke out in the Near East, coming from an unexpected direction. Sheltered by the deserts which border the Nile valley, Egypt had lived for two thousand years isolated politically, though not commercially, from the rest of the Orient. Its north-eastern frontier, it is true, was vulnerable, and on several occasions, the 'vile 'Amu', the 'Sand-farers', the hated Asiatics had crossed the isthmus of Suez, made armed incursions into the delta and given cause for serious concern; they had, however, never managed to gain full control of the country. But the long and humiliating Hyksôs episode had taught the Egyptians a lesson: in order to avoid a similar invasion, they must fight the Asiatics in their country of origin and reduce them to servitude. It was with this idea in mind that Tuthmosis III, in 1480 BC, undertook the conquest of Syria, opening new fields to Egyptian ambitions and setting a pattern of Egyptian politics which can be followed throughout history down to the present day. The fact that it took him seventeen years to become the master of Palestine and of the coastal strip of Lebanon and Syria proves that he was up against forces far superior to those of the Syro-Palestinian princelings, or that his opponents received all the support in men, horses and weapons that only a powerful state could afford. The true enemies of Egypt in Syria were neither the Canaanites nor the Amorites, but the Hurri-Mitannians, long entrenched in those regions and now strongly organized. The kingdom of Mitanni occupied the region called *Hanigalbat* by the Assyrians,3 that is the steppe between the Euphrates and the Tigris, to the south of the Taurus range, and somewhere in this area—possibly near the head of the Khabur river—lay its capital Washukkanni, the exact location of which has not yet been determined.4 Its northern and southern frontiers were probably as ill-defined for the Hurri-Mitannians as they are for us, though we know from Hittite sources that the Hurrians were established in Armenia, threatening the Hittite kingdom. During the fifteenth century, northern Syria to the west and Assyria to the east were under Mitannian allegiance. The first king of Mitanni whose name has survived, Paratarna (*circa* 1480 BC) is mentioned in the statue inscription of Idrimi, King of Alalah, who refers to him as his overlord, as well as in a tablet found at Nuzi, near Kirkuk.5 Also found in this city was the seal of Paratarna's successor, Shaushatar.6 In addition there is ample evidence for a Hurri-Mitannian political influence in Ugarit, in Qatna and, indirectly, in Palestine. An even greater influence can be detected in northern Iraq, and there is every reason to believe that all the Kings of Assur who reigned between 1500 and 1360 BC were the vassals of the King of Mitanni: when one of them dared to revolt, Shaushatar, we are told, plundered Assur and took to Washukkanni 'a door of silver and gold'.7

The victories of Tuthmosis III put only part of this vast

kingdom under Egyptian domination. In Syria the Mitannians kept Alalah and Karkemish, whence they were able to foster in the districts they had lost rebellions serious enough to justify several Egyptian campaigns under Amenophis II. Under Tuthmosis IV (1420–1405 BC), this state of permanent though indirect hostility came to an end, and the most friendly relations were established between the courts of Thebes and Washukkanni: 'seven times' the pharaoh asked Artatama I of Mitanni for the hand of his daughter,[8] and Amenophis III (1405–1367 BC) married Shutarna's daughter, Kilu-Hepa.[9] The fear of the Hittites is often given as the reason for this sudden and complete change in politics, but this is by no means certain. About 1467 BC, Tudkhaliyas I in Anatolia had founded a new dynasty and immediately reasserted Hittite rights upon the districts south of the Taurus by taking Aleppo—possibly acting in collusion with Tuthmosis III.[10] His immediate successors, however, entangled as they were in Anatolian wars, could hardly be considered so dangerous for both Egypt and Mitanni as to provoke a *rapprochement* between the two countries. The truth, in all probability, is that the Egyptians realized their inability to occupy the whole of Syria, and the Mitannians their inability to regain ground in Palestine and on the Syrian coast; both accepted the *status quo* and turned an old enmity into a friendly alliance.

THE TIME OF SUPPILULIUMAS

After the time of Shamshi-Adad and Hammurabi, the fourteenth century BC is the most copiously documented period in the second millennium. Hittite annals and treaties, Assyrian inscriptions, Assyrian and Babylonian chronicles and, above all, the 300-odd letters written by the kings of Western Asia, great or small, to Amenophis III and IV and found at el-Amarna in Egypt[11] throw on these years of armed conflicts and subtle diplomatic moves the most welcome light. Moreover, these documents bring out with particular clarity some of the most powerful or fascinating personalities of the ancient Orient: Amenophis IV, the mystic pharaoh more interested in religion than in politics; Kurigalzu II, the only Kassite king who could pose as a conqueror; Ashur-uballit, the shrewd prince who liberated Assyria and turned it again into a great nation; and, transcending them all in merit, the energetic Hittite monarch who imposed his mark upon the whole period: Suppiluliumas.[12]

During the first quarter of the century, the diplomatic and matrimonial ties already existing between Egypt and Mitanni were reinforced and extended to other nations, giving the entire Near East the appearance of a happy family in which Egypt played the part of the wealthy relative. Tushratta having succeeded his father Shutarna on the Mitannian throne (*circa* 1385 BC) gave his daughter Tadu-Hepa to Amenophis III as spouse, and when the old Pharaoh fell ill, sent him the image of Ishtar of Nineveh who was reputed to cure the most intractable diseases. Similarly, the Kassite Kadashman-Enlil I added his sister and his daughter to Amenophis' opulent harem and received from him large quantities of gold.[13] Even the Assyrians, no doubt with the consent of their Mitannian overlord, sent ambassadors to the court of Thebes. But in 1375 BC, a man of obscure origin, Suppiluliumas, became king in Boghazköy and a few years later led the Hittite army into Syria. A direct attack against Aleppo—now once more in Mitannian hands—having failed, in a second campaign he crossed the Euphrates near Malatiya, entered the land of Mitanni from the north plundering Washukkanni on his way, turned westward, crossed the Euphrates again near Karkemish, took Aleppo, subdued the region called Nuhashshe to the south of that city, ravaged Qatna and captured the stronghold of Qadesh (Tell Nebi Mend, south of Homs) which marked the northern limit of Egyptian dominion in central Syria. At the same time, he skilfully played on the rivalry between Syrian princelings and managed to put under Hittite suzerainty the kingdoms which did not lie directly across his path, including Ugarit and Alalah. Finally, leaving behind him a number of ardent supporters, he returned to the Anatolian homeland where important and difficult tasks were to absorb his activities for about 20 years.

This brilliant military and diplomatic exploit was a severe blow to the Egyptians and a near disaster for the Mitannians who found themselves deprived of all their possessions west of the Euphrates. In Syria, some of the most enterprising local rulers, backed by the Hittites, fell upon their neighbours who cried to Egypt for help, and their clamour—mingled with the clamour of Palestinian chieftains continuously attacked by bands of *Habirû*—fill the el-Amarna archives. But most of these letters remained un-answered. Amenophis III, too old and too ill to intervene, died soon after the Hittite campaign, leaving the throne to the weak, effeminate and theologically minded Amenophis IV (1367–1350 BC), himself for a long time under the influence of the queen-mother Teye. For various reasons, Amenophis IV refused to be involved in the Syrian imbroglio, but otherwise pursued the foreign policy of his predecessor, marrying the youngest of his father's Mitannian wives, Tadu-Hepa—perhaps the same person as the charming 'Nefertiti'—and remaining on the best possible terms with his contemporary, the Kassite Burnaburiash II (1375–1347 BC). Details of the good relations between the pharaoh and the king of 'Kar-Duniash' can be read in the el-Amarna corre-spondence. The two monarchs, the two 'brothers' as they call each other, exchange presents, the Kassite offering horses, lapis-lazuli and other precious stones, the Egyptian, ivory, ebony and, above all, gold. Occasionally the quantity of gold received did not quite tally with the quantity announced, and the King of Babylon complained bitterly:

'The former gold which my brother sent—because my brother did not look to it himself, but an officer of my brother sealed and sent it—the forty minas of gold which they brought, when I put them in the furnace did not come out full weight.'[14]

But these were only passing clouds. In spite of the distance—'the road is very long, the water supply cut off and the weather hot'[15] —messengers went to and fro between the two countries at the risk of being attacked by Canaanite bandits or by bedouins. We also learn that Amenophis IV married one of Burnaburiash's daughters and that, on this occasion, the pharaoh sent to Babylon an enormous number of bridal gifts, the list of which makes up more than 307 lines of text in four columns![16]

If the Egyptians closed their ears to the appeals of their Syrian vassals, why, it may be asked, did the Mitannians remain passive before the Hittite aggression and did not even attempt to recover their former dominion? The answer is that they were themselves in the throes of civil war. Tushratta owed his crown to the murder of his elder brother, and his authority was challenged by several members of the royal family. As he ascended the throne of Mitanni, another of his brothers, Artatama, declared himself 'King of Hurri' and founded a separate dynasty, though it is by no means certain that the kingdom was divided between the two rivals as some historians believe. The Kings of Hurri—Artatama and his son Shutarna II—sought assistance outside their own country and engaged in friendly relations with the Assyrian princes still under Mitannian obedience. Soon there was a strong pro-Hurrian and pro-Assyrian party in Washukkanni itself. Palace intrigues, no doubt fomented by the two allies, culminated, about 1360 BC, in the death of Tushratta, murdered by one of his sons. Unable to preserve his throne, the legitimate heir, Mattiwaza, fled to Babylon where Burnaburiash, faithful to his neutral policy, refused to grant him asylum, and finally took refuge at the Hittite court, while Assyria and another small state of the Upper Tigris valley, Alshe, 'divided the land of Mitanni between themselves'.[17] Thus, without shooting an arrow, Ashur-uballit I of Assyria (1365–1330 BC) not only freed his country from Mitannian domination, but brought about the downfall of the kingdom to which his fathers paid tribute. Encouraged by this success, he took the titles 'Great King' and 'King of the Universe', corresponded directly with his 'brother', Amenophis IV,[18] and gave his daughter in marriage to Burnaburiash in the hope that his grandson would one day reign over Babylonia.

All this happened shortly after Suppiluliumas departed from Syria. When he returned, twenty years later, the political situation in the Near East had changed to his advantage. In Egypt, Amenophis IV had died in 1350 BC and his successors—including the famous Tut-ankh-Amôn—were too busy repairing the disastrous results of his religious policy to pay much attention to Syrian affairs. In northern Mesopotamia, the Mitannian kingdom had disintegrated and Ashur-uballit was building up his Assyrian forces. In Babylonia, after a short civil war provoked by the murder of Ashur-uballit's grandson,[19] Kurigalzu II had ascended the throne in 1345 BC; but the eyes of this great builder and warrior were turned, not towards the west but towards the east: he attacked and defeated Hurpatila, King of Elam, and governed that country for at least part of his reign.[20] The main objective of Suppiluliumas was therefore to liquidate any remaining pocket of resistance and to organize the territories conquered. He signed treaties with obedient Syrian princes, gave Aleppo to one of his sons and to another, Karkemish, with the mission of helping Mattiwaza to recover his throne. In the ensuing war, Mattiwaza was successful for a while but was finally defeated, and the Assyrians advanced as far as the Euphrates, erasing all traces of the Mitannian kingdom. When Suppiluliumas died (1335 BC), the whole of Syria up to the region of Damascus was firmly in Hittite hands, but Assyria was the second great power in the Near East.

ASSUR AND SUSA VERSUS BABYLON

For the Hittites, to whom the Achaeans and other warlike people established along the coasts of Asia Minor denied access to the Mediterranean, the possession of active and prosperous ports such as Ugarit and Sumur[21] was undoubtedly an asset. Moreover, Syria itself was fertile and could also be used as a starting point for eventual military operations in Mesopotamia or in Egypt. But these advantages were, to a great extent, upset by the duplicity and unruly behaviour of the local chieftains: rebellions soon followed Suppiluliumas' death, obliging his second and successor, Mursilis II (1334–1306 BC) to intervene in person, and it might have been of some comfort for him to know that, at the same time, the King of Egypt, Seti I, had to bear a similar burden in his Palestinian dominion. Probably fomented by the Hittites in Palestine and by the Egyptians in Syria, these revolts were but the symptoms of a deeper conflict between the two great nations, a conflict which reached its acme when the young and ambitious Ramesses II (1290–1224 BC) decided to repeat Tuthmosis' exploits and to bring the frontier of his kingdom up to the Euphrates. The war he waged against the Hittites ended in one of the most famous battles of antiquity: Qadesh (1285 BC), but no decisive result was obtained. Both enemies claimed victory and retained their respective positions. Sixteen years later, however, Ramesses signed with Hattusilis III of Hatti a peace treaty of which we possess by chance the Egyptian as well as the Hittite version[22]— the latter, incidentally, in Akkadian language—and even married a Hittite princess. Were the two champions tired of fighting, or did the growing strength of Assyria reconcile them as the Hittite menace had reconciled Egyptians and Mitannians? The importance given in the treaty to clauses of mutual assistance in case of war, together with the overtures made at about the same time by Hattusilis to the Kassites,[23] seem to give weight to the second theory.

Ever since Assyria had become a nation, its fortune had been written on the map. To the north and east, the narrow strip of Tigris valley belonging to the god Ashur was surrounded by high, almost inaccessible mountains haunted by predatory peoples, such as the Guti and Lullubi, which could only be kept at bay by frequent and difficult police operations. To the west, the steppe of Jazirah extended for hundreds of miles, wide open to the armies of hostile states or to nomadic raiders; the possession of that steppe spelled safety for the Assyrians, but it also meant the control of important trade-routes and, eventually, of northern Syria, with a window on the Mediterranean. Finally, to the south and within short distance lay the rich plain and opulent cities of the Mesopotamian delta, a constant source of temptation but also of worry, since Akkadians, Sumerians, and Babylonians had always claimed lordship over the northern half of Mesopotamia. During the second millennium, the frontier in this area was heavily fortified, and when Babylon was strong all the Assyrians could expect to gain was a few villages; when she was weak, however, all hopes were permissible, including that of access to the Persian Gulf. These geographical considerations account for the triple series of wars which fill Assyrian annals from the thirteenth century onwards: guerrilla wars in the mountains, wars of movement in Jazirah, and wars of position on the middle Tigris. These were the price Assyria had to pay, not only for her expansion, but also for her freedom.

As soon as Ashur-uballiṭ had delivered his country from Mitannian domination, hostilities opened on these three fronts. His son, Enlil-nirâri, attacked Babylon, defeated Kurigalzu and, we are told, 'they divided the fields, they divided the district, they fixed (anew) the boundaries'.[24] The fragmentary annals of Arik-dên-ilu speak of campaigns in the Zagros, while we learn from those of his successor, Adad-nirâri I, that he threw his armies across Jazirah and conquered—at least momentarily—that region 'as far as Karkemish which is on the bank of the Euphrates';[25] another text shows him forcing the Kassites into a new frontier agreement.[26] But the greatest warrior of the dynasty was undoubtedly Shalmaneser I (1274–1245 B C) who, having subdued 'the mighty mountain fastnesses' of Uruadri (Uraṛṭu, Armenia) and 'the land of the Guti who know how to plunder', turned against Assyria's former allies, the Hurrians, attacked Shattuara, 'King of Hanigalbat' and his Hittite and Ahlamû mercenaries and defeated them:

'I fought a battle and accomplished their defeat. I killed countless numbers of his defeated and widespreading hosts . . . Nine of his strongholds and his capital city I captured. One hundred and eighty of his cities I turned into tells and ruins . . . Their lands I brought under my sway, and the rest of their cities I burned with fire.'[27]

It was perhaps this exploit, performed a few years after the battle of Qadesh, which brought together Egyptians and Hittites, for the Hurrians had now lost their last stronghold, and the Assyrians in Karkemish were at the gates of Syria.

In the middle of the thirteenth century the critical situation of Babylon, already threatened by its powerful neighbour, was aggravated by the sudden reappearance of Elam on the political stage after an absence of about 400 years. The new dynasty which occupied the throne in Susa was made of energetic princes determined, among other things, to assure their authority over the Kassites of Iraq as well as over those who had remained in Iran. Shortly after 1250 B C, the unfortunate Kashtiliash IV found himself caught between two enemies: Untash-GAL—the Elamite ruler who built the magnificent ziqqurat and temples of Chogha-Zambil, near Susa—and the Assyrian Tukulti-Ninurta I (1244–1208 B C). The Elamite won a battle, but Tukulti-Ninurta occupied the capital city. This exploit filled the Assyrians with considerable pride and forms the subject of the only Assyrian epic tale that has come to us: a poetic and, naturally, strongly biased, narrative known as the 'Tukulti-Ninurta Epic'.[28] In this, the blame is put entirely on Kashtiliash, who is accused of having broken his oath and plotted against Assyria, thus deserving to be abandoned by the gods of his country and defeated. Yet the shorter account of the war in a building inscription found in Assur gives the impression that Tukulti-Ninurta acted without being provoked:

'I forced Kashtiliash, King of Kar-Duniash, to give battle; I brought about the defeat of his armies, his warriors I overthrew. In the midst of that battle my hand captured Kashtiliash, the Kassite king. His royal neck I trod on with my feet, like a *galtappu* (kind of lamb). Stripped and bound, before Ashur my lord I brought him. Sumer and Akkad to its farthest border I brought under my sway. On the lower sea of the rising sun, I established the frontier of my land.'29

Three princes, puppets of the Assyrian, sat in quick succession on the throne of Babylon and were in turn attacked by the Elamites who advanced as far as Nippur. But after seven years of servitude, the Babylonians themselves restored their national dynasty. Says a Babylonian chronicle:

'The nobles of Akkad and Kar-Duniash revolted, and they sat Adad-shum-uṣur on the throne of his father.'30

As for the Assyrian monarch who had been the first to reach the Persian Gulf, he died ignominiously several years later, no doubt in punishment for his crimes:

'As for Tukulti-Ninurta who had brought evil upon Babylon, Ashur-nadin-apli, his son, and the nobles of Assyria revolted, and they cast him from his throne. In Kâr-Tukulti-Ninurta, they besieged him in his palace and slew him with the sword.'31

Weakened by family dissensions and internecine warfare, his successors launched only small-scale offensives against Babylonia, and it was the Elamites and not the Assyrians, who, in 1174 BC, delivered the mighty blow which brought the Kassite dynasty to its knees. That year, Shutruk-nahhunte left Susa at the head of a vast army, invaded southern Iraq and plundered it as it had never before been plundered. Famous monuments, masterpieces of Mesopotamian sculpture such as the stele of Narâm-Sin, the Code of Hammurabi and the Obelisk of Manishtusu were carried away to Susa for ever. Babylon was captured and given to Shutruk-nahhunte's son. A Kassite prince with the Babylonian name of Enlil-nadin-ahhê ('Enlil gives brothers') resisted for three years, but was finally overthrown (1171 BC).[32] Supreme humiliation: the god Marduk was taken in captivity by the Elamites as he had been taken by the Hittites 424 years before. Thus ended the longest dynasty in the history of Babylon.

The fall of the Kassite dynasty may be used as a convenient landmark in the history of ancient Iraq, but it was insignificant compared with the events which took place in the Near East during the twelfth century BC. When the Elamites invaded Babylonia, the Hittite kingdom of Boghazköy had already disappeared; Egypt, which had just escaped another invasion from the east, was greatly weakened by internal divisions; the Philistines were established in Canaan, Moses was leading his people into the Promised Land, the nomadic Aramaeans were threatening both the Syrian princes and the Assyrian monarchs, and far away in the west, the Dorian Greeks were invading the Hellenic peninsula. Once again the Indo-Europeans had moved into Western Asia, spreading the use of iron as their forebears had spread the use of the horse, and opening a new age in the history of humanity, but also starting a chain reaction of ethnic movements accompanied by political convulsions which rapidly changed the face of the Orient.

CHAPTER XVII

THE TIME OF CONFUSION

THE mass-movements of Indo-European population which took place in south-eastern Europe during the thirteenth century BC escape analysis and can only be deduced from the profound repercussions they had upon Greece and Western Asia. It was probably the arrival in the Balkans of prolific and pugnacious tribes, the Illyrians, which thrust out the Thraco-Phrygians into Anatolia where they overthrew the Hittite kingdom shortly after 1200 BC, and drove the Dorians, Aeolians and Ionians into the Hellenic peninsula, the Aegean islands and the western districts of Asia Minor, where they destroyed the Mycenaean (or Achaean) Empire (Trojan war, *circa* 1270 BC). Dislodged by this double current of invaders, the inhabitants of the Aegean shores and isles, the 'Peoples of the Sea' as the Egyptians called them, fled southward along the coasts of Asia Minor and Syria and arrived, threatening, at the gate of Egypt. Ramesses III defeated them both at sea and on land (1174 BC); but some of the warriors went into the Pharaoh's service, while others settled on the maritime fringe of Canaan. Among the latter were the *Peleset*, or Philistines, who eventually gave their name to the whole country, Palestine. At about the same time, another less known but equally important ethnic movement started somewhere around the Caspian Sea. The Indo-European-speaking peoples which we call 'Iranians' entered Iran from the north, following approximately the same route as the earlier Indo-Aryan emigrants. The *Parthava* (Parthians) and the *Haraiva* remained on the borders of Turkestan and Afghanistan, while the *Madai* (Medes), *Parsua* (Persians) and *Zikirtu* marched farther west and occupied the plateau from lake Urmiah to Isfahan, rapidly gaining control over the poorly equipped indigenous population.[1]

This cascade of migrations, involving as they did the Mediterranean area and the central parts of Anatolia and Iran, left Iraq unaffected. But it coincided with a period of increased activity among the nomadic Semites who roamed the Syrian desert: Sutû, Ahlamû and, above all, the vast confederation of Aramaean tribes. The vacuum created in Syria by the collapse of the Hittite empire and the relative weakness of Assyria and Babylonia encouraged the Aramaeans to invade the Syrian hinterland, to cross the Euphrates and to penetrate deeper and deeper into Mesopotamia, settling as they advanced and forming, throughout the Fertile Crescent, a network of kingdoms, large or small, which enclosed Assur and Babylon in an ever narrowing circle and nearly submerged them. Simultaneously, other Semites, the Israelites, coming from the Sinai desert and taking advantage of the confusion which reigned in Canaan after Egypt had withdrawn from Asia, conquered a large band of territory on either side of the Jordan and made it their homeland. Up to a point, the progress of the Aramaeans in Iraq can be followed through the Assyrian royal inscriptions, and the conquest of Canaan by the Israelites through the biblical narrative; but the rest of the Near East between 1200 and 1000 BC is plunged in profound darkness. The Hittite archives from Boghazköy come abruptly to an end about 1190 BC, and there is just enough information from Egypt for us to perceive the decadence of that great country under the last Ramessides and its separation into two rival kingdoms at the dawn of the eleventh century. With the coming of the light again, about 900 BC, the political geography of Western Asia has once again changed: Aramaean principalities flourish from the Lebanon to the Zagros; the remnants of the 'Peoples of the Sea', Philistines and Zakkalas, share Canaan with the Israelites; along the Lebanese coast, the 'Phoenicians' enter a period of extreme prosperity, while the extreme north of Syria and the Taurus massif are the seats of several 'Neo-Hittite' kingdoms; Egypt is divided and weak; the kings who ascend the throne of Babylon in quick succession have little real power, but in Assyria a line of energetic princes is busy loosening the Aramaean grip and rebuilding an Empire; and behind the Zagros, the Medes and Persians are firmly established though not yet ready to play their historical rôle. These are the peoples which the Assyrians are going to meet, fight and conquer in their great movement of expansion during the first millennium BC, and with which the reader should now become acquainted.

ISRAELITES AND PHOENICIANS

So familiar are we with the Bible that, for most of us, no more than a brief outline of early Hebraic history is needed here. We have already seen (page 196) that Abraham and his family came from Ur in Sumer, to Hebron in Canaan, probably about 1850 BC, and there are many good reasons for placing Joseph's migration to Egypt during the Hyksôs period (1660–1580 BC). For at least four centuries, those who now called themselves 'Israelites' lived, multiplied and prospered in the Nile delta, until they were driven out by a Pharaoh 'whose heart the Lord had hardened'— more probably Ramesses II (1290–1224 BC) than his successor Mernephtah.[2] A man of supreme intelligence and powerful personality, the first great religious reformer in the history of humanity, Moses united the Israelites around the cult of a unique and universal God, led their long march across the Sinai peninsula and died when they reached the threshold of the 'Promised Land'. Joshua was their next leader, but the conquest of Canaan was in fact achieved by each of the twelve tribes fighting for its own territory under elected chiefs or 'Judges', and must have taken at least a hundred years. The formation of an Israelite kingdom under Saul and the victories won by David (1010–955 BC) over the Philistines, the Canaanites and the states lying east of the Jordan (Amon, Edom and Moab) consecrated the supremacy in Palestine of Abraham's progeny. Allowances being made for oriental emphasis, the reign of Solomon was a period of considerable glory for the young nation.[3] For the first time in history, Palestine obeyed one ruler whose authority extended 'from Dan (at the foot of mount Hermon) to Beersheba (on the border of Negeb)'. Jerusalem, formerly a small, unimportant town, took rank of capital city, and nearly 200,000 workmen—so we are told—took part in the building of its temple. The Israelite army was armed with weapons of iron and well provided with horses and chariots. From Ezion-Geber, near Akaba, Solomon's ships sailed down the Red Sea and returned from Arabia loaded with gold. The king himself, though credited with proverbial wisdom, lived in a sumptuous palace among 'seven hundred wives and three hundred concubines'. Such extravagance was more than this small and austere nation could stand financially and morally. The glorious reign ended in revolts and, after Solomon's death (935 BC) the kingdom was divided by plebiscite into two parts: Israel in the north, with Samaria for capital city, Judah in the south, still commanded from Jerusalem. The period of united monarchy had lasted a bare century.

To the north-west of Israel, the Canaanites of Lebanon and of the Syrian coast—the 'Phoenicians' as the Greeks were later to call them—were among the first victims of the great turmoil of the twelfth century. The richest of their cities, Ugarit, was for ever destroyed by the Peoples of the Sea,[4] while the great emporium of timber, Byblos, already ravaged by local wars during the el-Amarna period, was ruined by the decadence of its traditional client, Egypt, under the successors of Ramesses III. But by 1000 BC the situation in that area had taken a turn for the better. Because of their position at the points where the roads crossing the Lebanon mountains reach the sea, Arvad (Ruâd island), Sidunu (Sidon, modern Saida) and Ṣûri (Tyre, modern Sûr) had become the ports of the powerful Aramaean kingdoms of central Syria, and the southernmost of these towns, Tyre, benefited from the proximity of the Israelites whom it supplied with timber, expert craftsmen and sailors.[5] The three cities soon grew rich on this trade and formed the new political and economic centres of Phoenicia.

The Syro-Lebanese coast has always been the meeting point of Europe and Asia. At the dawn of the first millennium BC, two thousand years of intimate contact with the Cretans, Mycenaeans and Cypriots on the one hand, and with all the nations of the Near East on the other, had resulted in the development of a composite but brilliant Phoenician civilization.[6] The main contribution of the Phoenicians to the cultural treasure of humanity was, undoubtedly, the invention of the alphabet and its diffusion *via* the Greeks throughout Europe and *via* the Aramaeans throughout Western Asia where it eventually superseded all previous syllabic and ideographic writing systems. The exact date and place of the invention are thorny problems which need not be touched upon here, however briefly,[7] but we should at least mention that, of the three alphabets simultaneously in use on the Mediterranean coast during the last quarter of the second millennium—the 'classical' and the 'pseudo-hieroglyphic' alphabets of Byblos and the 'cuneiform' alphabet of Ras-Shamra (Ugarit)—the last named served as a support for a copious and extremely interesting literature, the discovery of which has considerably enlarged and modified our ideas on ancient Canaanite religion and mythology.[8] In the domain of the arts the Phoenicians were perhaps not so creatively minded, but proved excellent pupils. Inspired by Aegean and Egyptian artists, their craftsmen were unrivalled in the Near East, at least during the first millennium BC. They wove beautiful clothes, which they embroidered or dyed with the famous Sidonian purple, made vials of translucent glass, chiselled delicate jewels, carved exquisite ivories and were masters in wood- and metal-work. Their own country produced, besides timber, well-reputed wine and oil. All this formed a light but valuable cargo which the Phoenicians, sailors at heart, could now carry around the world themselves, the Dorian invasion of Greece having liberated the sea from its former masters, the Mycenaeans. Soon, Tyrians, Sidonians and Arvadites became the leaders of an astonishing movement of maritime and colonial expansion which reached its peak between the ninth and the sixth centuries BC with the foundation of Carthage (814 BC), the creation of numerous warehouses in Malta, Sicily and Spain, and the exploration of the Atlantic coasts of Europe and Africa.

THE NEO-HITTITES

Proceeding northward along the Mediterranean shore we reach, in the extreme north of Syria, the realm of the people called 'Hieroglyphic Hittites' or, more simply, 'Neo-Hittites'.[9] These terms require some explanation. We know that the Hittites who had Hattusas (Boghazköy) for capital city used a cuneiform script, borrowed from the Assyrians, to write on clay tablets their Indo-European language. But, at the same time, another kind of script was used in Asia Minor to write, on rock or stone, official or religious inscriptions. This script consisted of drawings or hieroglyphs bearing no relation to the archaic Sumerian pictograms nor to the Egyptian or Cretan hieroglyphs. Many more such inscriptions also appear in various sites of the Taurus mountains and of northern Syria, in association with monuments which can be dated from the first centuries of the first millennium BC, i.e. after the fall of the Hittite empire. The deciphering of hieroglyphic Hittite by various scholars—now confirmed and completed by the discovery, in 1947, of bilingual Phoenician-Hittite inscriptions at Kara Tepe, in Cilicia[10]—has shown that the language of these inscriptions was a dialectal variety of Luwian, the Luwians being one of the more or less closely related Indo-European-speaking peoples which entered Asia Minor at the beginning of the second millennium. It looks, therefore, as though, in the great reshuffling of population which took place in the twelfth century, the Luwians, who originally occupied the south-western part of Asia Minor, had moved, or been pushed, southward and eastward, and had established themselves in the southern provinces of the former Hittite empire, provinces which had been spared by the Phrygians and bypassed by the Peoples of the Sea. But this, of course, is highly conjectural. Moreover, it is important to emphasize that there was no break in the transmission of Hittite culture in those regions, and that the term 'Neo-Hittite' is no more than a convenient appellation. The Hittite influence brought into Syria by Suppiluliumas and his predecessors outlived them by nearly five hundred years.

From the tenth century onwards, a compact mosaic of Neo-Hittite kingdoms covered the territory comprised between the Taurus range and the Orontes river, forming what the Assyrians called *Hatti* or *Great Hatti*—(the province of Antioch is still called 'Hatay' by the Turks). Starting from the north, we find, in the heart of the Taurus mountains, about twelve city-states forming the confederation of Tabal (the *Tubal* of the Bible) and along the upper Euphrates, the kingdom of Kummanu with Milid (modern Malatiya) for capital city. Then come Kummuhu, the classical Commagene, and Gurgum, around the town of Marqasi (Marash). Farther west, the rich plain of Cilicia is occupied by the Danuna-folk who obey the King of Ataniya (Adana) and hold sway over the surrounding highlanders. To the north of Aleppo lie Ya'diya (capital Sam'al, modern Zenjirli), in the Amanus mountains, and Karkemish and Til-Barsip (Tell Ahmar) which command the passage of the Euphrates. Aleppo itself, so often taken and lost by the Mitannians and the Hittites, had lost much of its importance to Arpad,[11] while Alalah, in the 'Amuq plain (*Hattina*), was governed first from 'Azaz, then from the as yet unidentified city of Kunalua. Finally, hieroglyphic inscriptions found at Hama testify to periodical occupation of the city by the Neo-Hittites.

Excavations at Zenjirli, Sakje-Gözü, Karkemish, Tell Tayanat and, more recently, Kara Tepe (ancient Azitawandas) have shed considerable light on the art and architecture of the Neo-Hittites and enable us to understand the resistance encountered by the Assyrians when they tried to overthrow these small but very strong kingdoms. The towns, roughly circular in plan, were protected by a double, massive wall: an outer wall around the lower town and an inner wall around the acropolis. The royal palace, in the centre of the city, often had its entrance preceded by a portico of wooden columns resting on stone bases sculptured with crouching lions and sphinxes. Its plan was usually of the type called by the Assyrians *bît hilâni:* a series of oblong rooms, one behind the other, the long sides of which ran parallel with the front of the building. The 'processional way' leading to the acropolis and the façade of the palace were decorated with sculptured slabs of basalt or limestone lining the lower part of the walls. The subjects most commonly represented on these 'orthostats' are hunting scenes, royal banquets and marching soldiers, frequently intermingled with hieroglyphic inscriptions. The sculptures, too often crude and unskilled, are not, however, devoid of movement and life, and some indeed attain a high standard of barbaric beauty. Undoubtedly, we meet here with a provincial version of Hittite art tempered with Assyrian, Egyptian and even Aegean influences.

The Neo-Hittite kingdoms flourished from the tenth to the eighth centuries BC and their full history will be revealed when all the hieroglyphic Hittite inscriptions are accurately translated and published. Between 745 and 708 BC they fell, one by one, into Assyrian hands and disappeared as independent states, but long before that date some of them had already yielded to their immediate neighbours, the Aramaeans.

THE ARAMAEANS

The problem of Aramaean origin is, as usual in such matters, a very difficult one.[12] The Aramaean language, or Aramaic, belongs, like Canaanite and Hebrew, to the north-western group of Semitic dialects but on many points shows strong affinities with Arabic, which might perhaps suggest that the Aramaeans originated or had lived in Arabia. On the other hand, there are several reasons to suppose that their homeland was the Syrian desert and the Fertile Crescent, and it must be recalled that the memory of a close, though unspecified, ethnic relationship between Aramaeans and Hebrews has been preserved in the Bible, where Jacob (Israel) himself is once qualified as a 'wandering Aramaean'.[13] At what period the Aramaeans made their first appearance in cuneiform texts is another debatable point. In texts of the Akkadian, Ur III and Old Babylonian periods occasional mention is made of a city *Arami* and of individuals by the name of *Aramu*, but since this may be no more than a phonetic resemblance, two dates only must be considered: the fourteenth or the twelfth century, depending upon whether the identity, or at least some kind of relationship between the Aramaeans and the Ahlamû is accepted or not. The Ahlamû are first mentioned in a mutilated letter from el-Amarna alluding to the King of Babylon; during the same period their presence is attested in, or near, Assyria, at Nippur and even at Dilmun (Bahrain), and we have seen (page 216) that Shalmaneser I defeated the Hurrians and their Hittite and Ahlamû allies. In the following century they cut the road from Babylon to Hattusas, and Tukulti-Ninurta I (1244–1208 BC) claims that he conquered Mari, Hana and Rapiqu on the Euphrates and 'the mountains of the Ahlamû'.[14] We are thus confronted with a confederation of troublesome tribes active in the Syrian desert, along the Euphrates and about the Persian Gulf, at least from the fourteenth century BC. But an inscription of Tiglathpileser I (1115–1077 BC) refers for the first time to the 'Ahlamû-Aramaeans' (*Ahlamê Armaia*)[15] and from then on the Ahlamû rapidly disappear from Assyrian annals to be replaced by the Aramaeans (*Aramû, Arimi*). In the text just quoted, the word *Armaia* is 'gentilic' (adjective), and the expression could be translated: '(Those of) the Ahlamû (who are) Aramaean', in which case we might be entitled to consider the Aramaeans as an important and, in time, dominant fraction of the Ahlamû tribes. It is possible, however, that the two peoples had nothing in common, but, operating in the same area, were regarded by the sedentary Mesopotamians as one and the same detestable desert folk.[16]

In any case there can be no doubt that the Aramaeans were established in Syria as early as the eleventh century BC. We read in the Bible that Saul; David and Solomon fought against the Aramaean kingdoms which lay across the northern frontier of Israel: Aram-Sôbah in the Beqʻa, Aram-Bêt-Rehob and Aram-Maʻakah around mount Hermon, Geshur in the Hauran and the state which was soon to govern them all: Damascus (*Dimashqa, Dammesheq*). Farther north the Aramaeans were in possession of Hama, on the Orontes, and were soon to become strong enough to dissociate the Neo-Hittite block. During the tenth or the ninth century they conquered Samʻal (Zenjirli), the region of Aleppo which they renamed Bît-Agushi, and Til-Barsip which became the chief town of Bît-Adini. Only the plain of Antioch (Hattina) and Karkemish remained Hittite in Syrian land. At the same time, the Aramaeans invaded the steppe to the east of the Euphrates, where they settled in such numbers that the whole region became known as *Aram Naharaim*, 'Aram of the Rivers'. One of their earliest kingdoms in Mesopotamia was Bît-Bahiâni, which had for capital city the very ancient site of Tell Halaf, abandoned since proto-historic times (see above, page 58 ss.) and now called Guzana. The Aramaean progression in Mesopotamia will be described later. Now we would simply draw attention to the names of the Aramaean kingdoms, usually formed with the word *bît(u)*, 'house', followed by the name of an ancestor. Despite the apparent similarity with our 'House of Hanover', 'House of Windsor', etc., we have here a typically tribal way of expressing land ownership: the state, the 'kingdom' is both the territory around the tent (or house) of the chief and all the chief's relatives, or 'the clan'.

The Aramaeans, whether merchants, peasants, shepherds, soldiers or bandits, were originally uncouth bedouins and contributed nothing to the civilizations of the Near East. Whatever their ancestral religion, it appears from their inscriptions as well as from their own names that they worshipped Sumero-Akkadian and Canaanite gods, such as Hadad (Adad), the storm-god, El, the supreme deity of Canaan, Sin, Ishtar (whom they called 'Attar), the Phoenician goddess 'Anat ('Atta), etc. Nor was there originality in the field of the arts, the Aramaeans following the traditions of the countries where they settled. The Kings of Damascus, for instance, employed Phoenician sculptors and ivory-carvers, and Sam'al under its new masters retained all the features of a Neo-Hittite city. Archaeological excavations at Tell Halaf-Guzana have brought to light the palace of Kapara, an Aramaean ruler who probably lived at the beginning of the ninth century BC:[17] it was a building of the *bîthilâni* type, decorated with orthostats, perhaps cruder than the contemporary sculptures of northern Syria, and with strange-looking, almost morbid statues which, on analysis, display a mixture of Mesopotamian, Hittite and Hurrian influences, as would be expected in a region—the Khabur valley—where the three cultures converged.

Yet to these barbaric Aramaeans befell the unique privilege of imposing their language upon the whole Near East. They owed it partly to the sheer weight of their number and partly to the fact that they adopted, instead of the cumbersome cuneiform writing, the Phoenician alphabet slightly modified, and carried everywhere with them the simple, practical script of the future. As early as the eighth century BC, Aramaic language and writing competed with the Akkadian language and script in Assyria, and thereafter gradually spread throughout the Orient. About 500 BC, when the Achaemenian monarchs looked for a tongue which could be understood by all their subjects, they chose Aramaic which became the *lingua franca* of their vast empire. At the close of the pre-Christian era, Sumerian and even Hebrew were already dead languages, Akkadian was dying and Greek, introduced by the Macedonian conquerors, was mostly used for official purposes, but Aramaic—the language spoken by Jesus—reigned unchallenged as the common dialect of all the peoples of the Near East, and was to remain so until the Arab invasion (seventh century AD). The Arabic script itself derives from a cursive form of Aramaic, as do all present and past alphabets used in Asia. Moreover, during the sixth century AD, the Aramaic language gave birth, in northern Mesopotamia, to the extremely rich Syriac literature which the Nestorian missionaries carried as far as Mongolia, and Syriac has survived as the liturgic tongue of several Oriental Churches. Indeed, Aramaic dialects are still spoken in some parts of the Near East, in particular among the Christian communities of northern Iraq. Few languages in the world can claim such a long and continuous tradition.

But it is time for us to return to our subject, Iraq, which we have left at the end of the Kassite dynasty, nearly twelve hundred years before Christ.

THE DARK AGE OF MESOPOTAMIA

After their victory over the Kassites, the Elamites did not occupy Babylonia for long, either because the conquest of vast territories in western Iran absorbed all their energy, or because they already felt the presence of the newly arrived Medes and Persians as a dagger in their back. However this may be, the Elamite garrisons withdrew or were expelled, and princes, native of Isin, founded the Fourth Dynasty of Babylon, also called 'Second Dynasty of Isin'.[18] Soon the new kings were powerful enough to interfere in Assyrian domestic affairs, and when Elam sank into anarchy after the brilliant reign of Shilak-Inshushinak, the Babylonian Nebuchadrezzar I* (circa 1124–1103 BC) attacked it. A first campaign met with failure—'the Elamite followed and I fled before him; I sat down on the bed of weeping and sighing'[19]—but the defection of one of the Elamite lords, Ritti-Marduk, who fought on the Babylonian side, made the second campaign a glowing success. The account of the war, written on a *kudurru* granting privileges to Ritti-Marduk as a reward for his assistance, is one of the most poetic military records of antiquity:[20]

'From Dêr, the holy city of Anu, he (the King of Babylon) made a leap of thirty double-leagues. In the month of Tammuz (July–August) he took the road. The blades of the picks burn like fire; the stones of the track blaze like furnaces; there is no water (in the wadis) and the wells are dry; stop the strongest of the horses and stagger the young heroes. Yet, he goes, the elected king supported by the gods; he marches on, Nebuchadrezzar who has no rival. . . .'

---

* *Nabû-Kudurri-uṣur:* 'the god Nabû protects the frontiers'.

The battle was fought on the banks of the river Ulaia (Kerkha):

'At the command of Ishtar and Adad, the gods of the battle, Hulteludish, King of Elam, fled and disappeared for ever, and King Nebuchadrezzar stood up in victory: he took Elam and plundered its treasures.'

But the victory had no lasting results. Elam was not truly conquered, and Nebuchadrezzar's successors had to fight, not for the possession of foreign lands, but for the protection of their own kingdom against the eternal rival: Assyria.

Despite a serious crisis of succession and the temporary loss of their eastern provinces to Shilak-Inshushinak, the eleventh century as a whole was for the Assyrians an epoch of prosperity. Ashur-dân I, 'who attained to grey hair and a ripe old age'[21] and Ashur-rêsh-ishi, both contemporaries of the first kings of the Fourth Dynasty of Babylon, received tribute from the Sutû, kept the Ahlamû at bay, won a few battles over the Babylonians and did a considerable amount of repair work on the palace and temples of their capital city. But at the end of the century, storms gathered at the four points of the compass, which could have destroyed Assyria had it not been for the restless energy of one of the two or three great Assyrian monarchs since the days of Shamshi-Adad: Tiglathpileser I (1115–1077 BC).* To the north the Mushki—perhaps identical with the Phrygians—had crossed the Taurus with 20,000 men and were marching down the Tigris valley in the direction of Nineveh; to the east the Zagros tribes were hostile; to the west the Aramaeans—now mentioned for the first time—were established in force along the Euphrates and had started crossing the river; and to the south one of the Kings of Babylon had captured Ekallâtê, bringing his frontier up to the Lower Zab, 20 miles only from the city of Assur. Tiglathpileser first marched against the Mushki and massacred them and their allies. Then, anxious to secure his northern frontier, he went up 'to the heights of the lofty hills and to the top of the steep mountains' of the land of Nairi, penetrated into Armenia and set up his 'image' at Malazgird, far beyond lake Van, while one of his armies chastized the lands of Musri and Qummani, in the

---

* Tiglathpileser is the Hebraic form of *Tukulti-apal-esharra*, '(By the) protection of the son of Esharra' (i.e. Enlil's son, Ninurta).

Zagros range. The Aramaeans were forced beyond the Euphrates and pursued to their stronghold Jabal Bishri, west of Deir-ez-Zor, but the Syrian desert was swarming with this new, tough enemy:

'Twenty-eight times', says the king, 'I fought the Ahlamû-Aramaeans, (once) I even crossed the Euphrates twice in a year. I defeated them from Tadmar (Palmyra), which lies in the country Amurru, Anat, which lies in the country Suhu, as far as Rapiqu, which lies in Kar-Duniash (Babylonia). I brought their possessions as spoils to my town Assur.'[22]

It was probably in the course of these campaigns that Tiglath-pileser 'conquered' Syria and reached the Phoenician coast where he received tribute from Arvad, Byblos and Sidon.[23] Finally, came the victorious war against Babylon:

'I marched against Kar-Duniash . . . I captured the palaces of Babylon belonging to Marduk-nadin-ahhê, King of Kar-Duniash. I burned them with fire. The possessions of his palace I carried off. The second time, I drew up a line of battle chariots against Marduk-nadin-ahhê, King of Kar-Duniash, and I smote him.'[24]

To these military exploits, the King of Assyria added hunting activities, and he was out for big game: four wild bulls 'which were mighty and of monstrous size' killed in the country of Mitanni, ten 'mighty bull elephants in the country of Harran and in the district of the river Khabur', 120 lions slain on foot, 800 lions laid low from the royal chariot, and even a narwhal 'which they call sea-horse' killed in Mediterranean waters, near Arvad.[25]

The murder of Tiglathpileser, however, put an end to this glorious period. The mounting tide of Aramaean invasion, the desperate efforts made by the Assyrians to dam it up, the irremediable decadence of Babylon, Sumer and Akkad wide open to the Sutû and the Aramaeans, foreign wars, civil wars, floods, famine, such is the pitiful picture offered by Iraq during the tenth and ninth centuries BC. If ever there was a time of 'troubles and disorders',[26] of confusion and hardship, a dark age rendered even darker by the paucity of our sources, it was the 166 years which elapsed between the death of Tiglathpileser I (1077 BC) and the advent of Adad-nirâri II (911 BC).

Through the fragmentary annals of the Assyrian kings, we can follow the Aramaean progression in northern Mesopotamia in broad outline.[27] Under Ashur-bêl-kala (1074–1057 BC), they were still on the right bank of the Euphrates, but fifty years later, they had crossed the river and advanced as far as the Khabur. A few decades later, during the reign of Tiglathpileser II (966–935 BC), we find them around Nisibin, between the Khabur and the Tigris. Ashur-dân II (934–912 BC) tried to push them back and claimed great success, but it appears clearly from the annals of Adad-nirâri II and of his successors (see next chapter) that, at the dawn of the ninth century, the Aramaeans had settled *en masse* all over the steppe of Jazirah: there were Aramaean kingdoms on the Euphrates (Bît-Adini) and on the Khabur (Bît-Bahiâni, Bît-Hadipê), and powerful Aramaean tribes occupied the mountain Tûr 'Abdîn, north of Nisibin, and the banks of the Tigris. Caught between the nomads and the highlanders, Asssyria was threatened with asphyxia.

In Babylonia the situation was even worse, as shown by the ancient chronicles.[28] Nebuchadrezzar's fifth successor, Adad-apal-iddina (1067–1046 BC) was an Aramaean raised to the throne of Babylon by the Assyrians, perhaps in the vain hope of diverting the Aramaean influx toward southern Iraq. Under his reign, the Sutû plundered and ruined one of the greatest sanctuaries of Akkad: the temple of Shamash in Sippar. Between 1050 and 1000 BC, Babylon had seven kings divided between three dynasties. The first of these dynasties (Babylon V) was founded by a Kassite born in the Sea-Land; the second (Bît-Bazi), probably by an Aramaean; the third, by an Elamite. Under Nabû-mukin-apli (990–955 BC), the first King of Babylon VIII, all kinds of bad omens were observed and 'the Aramaeans became hostile'. They cut off the capital city from its suburbs with the result that, for several years in succession, the New Year Festival (which required the free movement of divine statues to and from Babylon) could not be celebrated: 'Bêl (Marduk) went not forth and Nabû went not (from Barsippa to Babylon).'[29] The following monarchs are no more for us than mere names on a list, but in all probability, it was during this obscure period that a number of Aramaean tribes, known from later Assyrian inscriptions—the Litaû, Puqudû, Gambulû—settled between the lower Tigris and the frontier of

Elam, and that the Kaldû (Chaldeans) invaded the land of Sumer. No one could have imagined then that, three hundred years later, the Kaldû would give Babylon one of its greatest monarchs, the second Nebuchadrezzar. But in that short interval, the Assyrian empire had grown, reached its peak and collapsed.

CHAPTER XVIII

THE RISE OF ASSYRIA

Towards the end of the tenth century BC, Assyria was at her lowest ebb. The lack of unity among her enemies had saved her from rapid destruction, but economic collapse was impending. She had lost all her possessions west of the Tigris and her vital arteries, the great trade routes that ran across Jazirah and through the mountain passes, were in foreign hands. Hostile highlanders occupied not only the heights of the Zagros, but the foothills down to the edge of the Tigris valley, while Aramaean tribes pitched their tents almost at the gates of Assur. Her territory consisted of no more than a narrow strip of land, hardly a hundred miles long and fifty miles wide alongside the river, mostly on its left bank. Yet, reduced, cornered and exposed as she was, Assyria was still a compact, solid and tough nation. Her main cities were free; she had chariots, horses and weapons; her men, trained by years of almost constant fighting, were the best warriors in the world; above all, her dynastic line remained unbroken, the crown having passed from head to head in the same family for more than two centuries.[1] In the fragmented and chaotic Near East of the time, no other kingdom could claim such privileges: Babylonia was half-ruined and partly occupied by the Aramaeans; Egypt, ruled by Lybian princes, was divided and almost powerless; the latest invaders—the Phrygians in Anatolia, the Medes and Persians in Iran—were still remote and relatively harmless competitors, and in Armenia, the great rival kingdom of tomorrow, Urarṭu, was not yet fully grown. Of all these nations, Assyria, despite appearances, was undoubtedly the strongest, and many must have thought that if only she could awake and fight back, she would be second to none.[2]

GENESIS OF AN EMPIRE

Assyria awoke in 911 BC. The prince who ascended the throne that year, Adad-nirâri II (911–891 BC), does not rank among the illustrious, and his name did not go down to posterity, as did those of Sargon and Ashurbanipal. But it is he who loosened the grip of Assyria's enemies and unknowingly opened the last and most brilliant chapter in the history of the northern kingdom. The war he waged and won was, in his own eyes, a war of national liberation.3 The Aramaeans were driven out of the Tigris valley and dislodged from the Kashiari mountains (Tûr 'Abdîn, a rugged volcanic massif lying to the east of Mardin) from which they threatened Nineveh. Several cities in eastern Jazirah, which had been 'torn away from Assur' were recovered and their walls either dismantled or fortified against possible counter-attacks. Other campaigns saw the Assyrian army in Kurdistan whose inhabitants were 'cut down in heaps' and pushed back to the mountains. Finally, the King of Babylon—who was then Shamash-mudam-miq, of the eighth dynasty—was twice attacked, twice defeated and lost a large piece of land to the north of the Diyala river.4 Tukulti-Ninurta II (890–884 BC), apparently as energetic as his father, did not live long enough substantially to enlarge the royal domain, but he rebuilt the wall of Assur 'from its foundation to its top', and a circular expedition in the south-western districts reconquered by Adad-nirâri won him the respect of the Aramaeans settled therein.5 When he died, the frontier of Assyria encompassed the whole of northern Iraq from the Khabur to the Zagros and from Nisibin to perhaps Tekrit or even Samarra. His son, the young Ashurnaṣirpal II, inherited this already large and powerful kingdom and took the first steps towards transforming it into what we should call an empire.

It would be a mistake, however, to think of the Assyrian empire as a planned enterprise, an organized body formed by the deliberate addition of land after land, province after province to the original nucleus. The wars which the Assyrian monarchs waged year after year and which eventually resulted in the conquest of the greater part of the Near East, these wars which fill their annals and make us almost forget their other achievements, had three different, though closely interwoven motives. As we have already shown, they were fundamentally defensive, or rather preventive wars aiming at protecting 'the land of the god Assur' from its hostile neighbours. Then, since a victorious campaign meant the capture of men and booty, and since a vanquished country could be persuaded to pay regular tribute, they were predatory wars. The Assyrians indulged in razzias; what they desired above all was a vast hunting ground, 'a geographical area through which they could raid without encountering effective opposition'.[6] As long as foreign countries could be plundered and were willing to pay the ransom of their independence, there was no need to annex and govern them. Last but not least, there was behind these armed expeditions a religious, almost a moral motive. In Mesopotamian philosophy, the divine hierarchy in heaven had its counterpart on earth, and since the god Ashur stood well above the other gods, it was imperative that his vicar and representative, the King of Assyria, should hold sway over all other princes. This, in general, could only be achieved by force and, if necessary, by recourse to terrorism. What to us seems simply massacre and robbery was therefore religiously justifiable. The king's enemies were the god's enemies: they were 'wicked devils' deserving punishment. Thus each Assyrian campaign was a measure of self defence, an act of brigandry, but also a crusade. The booty collected and the tribute levied on foreign countries were a source of income and a means of weakening possible aggressors, as well as a token of submission to the supreme deity of Assyria.

Almost every year, usually in the spring, the King of Assyria mustered his troops 'at the command of Ashur' and led them on the dusty tracks of the Mesopotamian plain or on the perilous paths of the Taurus and of the Zagros. In the early days, his opponents in those regions were merely chiefs of tribes or local princelings. Some fought bravely, though rarely with success; others fled to the desert or hid on inaccessible mountain peaks; others 'embraced the feet' of the Assyrian war-lord, brought presents, promised to pay regular tribute and were spared. But woe to those who failed to keep their promise! In the course of another campaign, a punitive expedition was directed against them and a storm swept over their country: the rebels were tortured, the population massacred or enslaved, the towns and villages set on fire, the crops burned, the trees uprooted. Terror-stricken, the neighbouring chieftains hastened to offer gifts and to swear allegiance. Then, its duty accomplished, loaded with spoil, trailing behind it human captives, flocks and herds, the army returned home and disbanded. As an example of what Assyria gained from these wars, here is a list of the booty taken by Ashurnaṣirpal in one single, small district of the mountainous North:

40 chariots 'equipped with the trappings of men and horses',
460 horses 'broken to the yoke',
2 talents of silver, 2 talents of gold,
100 talents of lead, 100 talents of copper,
300 talents of iron,
1,000 vessels of copper,
2,000 pans of copper,
bowls and cauldrons of copper,
1,000 brightly coloured garments of wool and linen,
tables of *sha*-wood and 'couches made of ivory and overlaid with
    gold' from the ruler's palace,
2,000 head of cattle,
5,000 sheep,

not counting the ruler's sister, the 'daughters of his nobles with their rich dowries' and his 15,000 Ahlamû-Aramaean subjects 'snatched away and brought to Assyria'. The local prince was put to death, and an annual tribute was imposed on his successor, consisting of 1,000 sheep, 2,000 *gur* of grain, 2 minas of gold and 13 minas of silver.7 In the same campaign, Ashurnaṣirpal gathered presents and spoil from no less than five countries and nine major cities.

As years went by, the boundaries of the Assyrian hunting ground were pushed further and further afield. Behind the petty states of their immediate neighbourhood, the kings of Assur found larger and more powerful kingdoms: Urartu in Armenia, the Medes in Iran, Elam and Egypt. The raids of rapine became wars of conquest. Assyria had grown stronger, but her opponents were bigger and tougher. The increased distances rendered more difficult the collection of tribute and the suppression of revolts. It became necessary, in most places, to replace the native rulers and their courts by Assyrian governors and civil-servants and to

extend to these far-away regions the division into provinces which
had prevailed in Assyria proper since very early days. In this way
an empire took shape with its huge, complex and perfectly
organized administrative machinery. But the original objectives
were never forgotten, and the extortion of taxes remained the
foundation of Assyrian government. It is certain that the Aramaean
merchants and the Phoenician sailors and craftsmen benefited, to
a certain extent, from the facility and security of communications
throughout this vast territory and from the ever increasing
demands of the Assyrian palaces for luxury goods. It is probable
that some of the more backward districts received a thin varnish
of civilization.[8] But, outside Assyria proper—which included now
the entire steppe between the Euphrates and the Tigris—there is
no evidence that the conquerors made much effort to diffuse their
highly advanced culture, to care for the economic development
of the distant provinces and satellite states, to improve, even
indirectly, the welfare of their populations. The silence of the
royal correspondence found at Nineveh and at Nimrud on this
subject, the almost complete absence of Assyrian texts in Syria,
Palestine, Armenia and Iran, the generally poor character of the
Assyrian level in excavated sites of these countries, the constant
references to spoil, massacres and destruction in the royal annals
(however exaggerated they may be), everything points to im-
poverishment or, at least, stagnation. The men, horses, cattle and
sheep brought into Assyria by the thousand, the enormous yearly
income in silver, gold, copper, iron, grain and other commodities
so accurately registered by the palace scribes, all this was generally
not purchased but taken by force. Wealth was constantly being
transferred from the periphery to the centre, from the depend-
ences and 'protectorates' to the Mesopotamian homeland. The
Assyrians took much and gave very little, with the result that if
the state was rich, its distant subjects were destitute and in almost
constant rebellion. The system upon which the empire was
founded had in itself the germs of its own destruction.

ASHURNAṢIRPAL

With Tukulti-Ninurta's son, we meet the first great Assyrian
monarch of the new period. Ambition, energy, courage, vanity,

cruelty, magnificence, Ashurnaṣirpal II* (884–859 BC) possessed
to the extreme all the qualities and defects of his successors, the
ruthless, indefatigable empire-builders. There is no smile, no piety,
almost no humanity in the statue of him found at Nimrud and
now in the British Museum, but the rigid attitude of a conceited
despot, the aquiline nose of a bird of prey, the straight-looking
eyes of a chief who demands absolute obedience, and in his hands,
the mace and the spear.9

No sooner was he upon the throne than, without the shadow
of a pretext, he went forth to ransack the hilly countries to the
north of Mesopotamia.10 This took him as far as the land of
Kutmuhu, in the upper Tigris valley, where he received tribute
from several local princes and presents from the Mushki, or
Phrygians, who held outposts on the southern slopes of the
Taurus mountains. While he was there, he received news that a
vassal Aramaean city on the lower Khabur had revolted, and he
immediately proceeded to punish the rebels—a march of at least
two hundred miles, in the middle of the summer:

'To the city of Sûru of Bît Halupê I drew near, and the terror of
the splendour of Ashur, my lord, overwhelmed them. The chief
and the elders of the city, to save their lives, came forth into my
presence and embraced my feet, saying: "If it is thy pleasure, slay!
If it is thy pleasure, let live! That which thy heart desireth, do!"
. . . In the valour of my heart and with the fury of my weapons
I stormed the city. All the rebels they seized and delivered them
up.'11

Further campaigns in the course of the reign were directed against
other rebels in the Kashiari mountains, in the land of Zamua (the
region around modern Suleimaniyah) and on the middle
Euphrates. Then, when the kingdom was pacified, the first stride
was made towards reaching Syria and the Mediterranean, a goal
which Shamshi-Adad I once had set and which no Assyrian
monarch of value could overlook. Beyond the Khabur and the
Balikh, within the great bend of the Euphrates, lay the important
Aramaean kingdom of Bît-Adini. Ashurnaṣirpal invaded it and,
'with mines, battering rams and siege engines', took Kaprabi

* The exact spelling of the name is *Ashshur-nâṣir-aplu*, meaning 'the god Assur
is guardian of the heir'.

(possibly Urfa), a city which 'was exceedingly strong and hung like a cloud from heaven'. The ruler of Bît-Adini, Ahuni, brought tribute and left hostages in Assyrian hands: the way was clear for the great Syrian expedition of the following year (877 BC). The annals go into considerable detail over this campaign, and we can follow the king and his army step by step, by daily marches of about twenty miles, from Karkemish to the plain of Antioch, across the Orontes and finally, 'along the side of mount Lebanon and to the Great Sea of the land of Amurru'. There, Ashurnaṣirpal repeated the gesture of his predecessors:

'I cleaned my weapons in the deep sea and performed sheep-offerings to the gods. The tribute of the sea-coast—from the inhabitants of Tyre, Sidon, Byblos, Mahallata, Maiza, Kaiza, Amurru, and (of) Arvad which is (an island) in the sea: gold silver, tin, copper, copper containers, linen garments with multi-coloured trimmings, large and small monkeys, ebony, boxwood, ivory from walrus tusk—(thus ivory) a product of the sea—(this) their tribute I received and they embraced my feet.[12]

The Assyrians returned home *via* the Amanus mountains where trees were cut down and sent to Assur, and a royal stele set up. Taken by surprise, the Neo-Hittite and Aramaean princes of northern Syria had offered no resistance. Contrary to the claims made by the king, however, this triumphal campaign was not a conquest but another razzia, the first long-range Assyrian razzia since the days of Tiglathpileser I, two hundred years before. Even in Mesopotamia, the territory gained by Ashurnaṣirpal was comparatively small, and the main result of the reign was to pave the way for the following kings. Fortresses such as Tushhan on the upper Tigris, Kâr-Ashurnaṣirpal and Nibarti-Ashur on the middle Euphrates, were founded and staffed with garrisons.[13] The position of Assyria in northern Iraq was consolidated, its nearest neighbours in the mountainous half-circle counted as vassals. The entire Near East learnt that the Assyrians were, once again, on the move and trembled with fear.

They had every reason to tremble, for Ashurnaṣirpal was preceded by a well deserved reputation for cruelty. Humanitarian concepts in warfare were unknown in those days and a few spectacular examples, duly recorded and displayed in writing and

PLATE 19

A. The ziqqurat of 'Aqar Quf during the excavations.

B. Façade of the temple built by the Kassite King Kara-Indash at Uruk.

PLATE 20

A. Painted terra-cotta head, from 'Aqar-Quf.

B. Terra-cotta lioness, from 'Aqar-Quf.

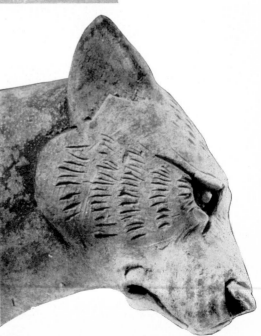

PLATE 21. From the palace of
Kapara, the Aramaean ruler of
Guzana-Tell Halaf:

A. One of the reliefs decorating the
palace walls.

B. A grotesque stone bird which,
together with other animals, kept
watch at the palace gate.

PLATE 22

A. Kudurru of Nebuchadrezzar I
(1124–1103 BC) recording the king's
victorious campaign against the Elamites.

B. A colossal Assyrian statue emerges
from the earth at Nimrud.

pictures in various places, were, no doubt, necessary to inspire respect and enforce obedience. All conquerors in antiquity practised a policy of terror, and the Assyrians were no exception. But Ashurnasirpal surpassed them all. Not only were the rebellious or recalcitrant rulers put to death, flayed and their skin 'spread over the walls of their city', but unarmed prisoners, innocent civilians, men, women and children alike, were tortured with sadistic refinements:

'I built a pillar over against his city gate and I flayed all the chiefs who had revolted, and I covered the pillar with their skin. Some I walled up within the pillar, some I impaled upon the pillar on stakes, and others I bound to stakes round about the pillar.... And I cut the limbs of the officers, of the royal officers who had rebelled...'

Many captives from among them I burned with fire, and many I took as living captives. From some I cut off their noses, their ears and their fingers, of many I put out the eyes. I made one pillar of the living and another of heads, and I bound their heads to tree trunks round about the city. Their young men and maidens I burned in the fire.

Twenty men I captured alive and I immured them in the wall of his palace...

The rest of their warriors I consumed with thirst in the desert of the Euphrates...'[14]

And so it continues in too many parts of the royal inscriptions, and indeed, it is difficult to say which is the more shocking: the atrocities themselves, or the detailed, methodical, self-gratifying way in which the chief executioner describes them.

It is only fair to add that the memory of Ashurnasirpal must be credited with other, more commendable achievements. Part of his thirst for blood was quenched by the hunting prowesses which his sculptors have immortalized. He had a taste for zoology and botany and brought back 'from the lands in which he had travelled and the mountains he had passed' all kinds of beasts, trees and seeds to be acclimatized in Assyria. Above all, he was possessed with that passion for building which is the mark of all great Mesopotamian monarchs. Without neglecting the traditional restoration of temples in Assur and Nineveh, he decided, early in his reign, to build himself a new 'royal residence' away from the old capital city. Had the Aramaean invasion shown that Assur, on the right bank of the Tigris, was dangerously exposed to attacks coming from the west, or was the move prompted by pride alone? We do not know, but if safety was sought, the site selected by Ashurnaṣirpal, Kalhu (biblical Calah, modern Nimrud, 22 miles south of Mosul) was strategically excellent, protected as it was by the Tigris to the west and by the upper Zab flowing at some distance to the south. Shalmaneser I, in the thirteenth century BC, had founded a town there, but it had long fallen into ruins. Thousands of men were put to work: the ruin-mound, the 'tell' was levelled, and the building site extended; a massive wall reinforced with towers was erected, enclosing a rectangle about five miles in perimeter, and a partly natural, partly artificial hill in a corner of this rectangle became the acropolis supporting the ziqqurat, several temples, and the royal palace:

'A palace of cedar, cypress, juniper, boxwood, mulberry, pistachio-wood and tamarisk, for my royal dwelling and for my lordly pleasure for all time I founded therein. Beasts of the mountains and of the seas of white limestone and alabaster I fashioned and set them up in its gates ... Door-leaves of cedar, cypress, juniper and mulberry I hung in the gates thereof; and silver, gold, lead, copper and iron, the spoil of my hand from the lands which I had brought under my sway, in great quantities I took and placed therein.'[15]

At the same time, a canal called *Patti-hegalli* ('which opens abundance') was dug from the Zab with the double purpose of sheltering the town further and of watering the surrounding plain. Prisoners from the subdued lands were settled in the new capital city whose tutelary god, significantly, was the war-god Ninurta.

Ashurnasirpal's palace at Nimrud was one of the first monuments ever excavated in Mesopotamia. Between 1845 and 1851, Layard worked on its central part and—much to the awe and wonder of his labourers—dug up a number of colossal winged bull-men, lions, genii, and slabs covered with reliefs and inscriptions.[16] Some of these treasures were sent to England, and are now the pride of the British Museum; others, too heavy to be removed, were reinterred to be unearthed again just over a century later by other British archaeologists. Since 1949, the team of the British School of Archaeology in Iraq, headed by Professor Mallowan, has been able to excavate the whole building, making each year sensational discoveries.[17] We now possess the complete plan of the palace. It covered an area of more than six acres and was divided into three parts: the administrative quarters (a series of rooms around a large courtyard), the ceremonial block with its spacious reception-hall and throne-room, and finally, the domestic wing, including the royal apartments, the harem, stores and ablution-rooms. In the ceremonial block, the main gates were flanked by huge *lamassû*, or protective genii, the mud-brick walls decorated with frescoes and with carved and inscribed orthostats, the floors paved with burnt bricks stamped with the name of the king. An interesting feature of the domestic wing was the presence of an 'air conditioning' system in the form of broad air-vents cut in the thickness of the walls to admit fresh air from above. The door-leaves of precious wood have perished in the fire which destroyed Nimrud, like other Assyrian cities, in 612 B C, but a number of objects have survived, in particular beautifully incised or carved panels of ivory, often covered with gold, which once decorated the royal furniture. There were also weapons and tools of bronze or iron, clay jars and a number of tablets. As it now stands, Ashurnasirpal's palace is the best preserved of Assyrian royal dwellings, and the visitor who wanders through this maze of rooms and courtyards, who walks along these narrow corridors lined with huge slabs to be suddenly confronted, in the dim light of a doorway, with some terrifying monster of stone, can well imagine the emotion which must have seized those who entered the building to approach 'the wonderful shepherd who fears not the battle'.

Among the finds made in the palace was a very large stele bearing the figure of the king and a long inscription from which we learn of the festivities that accompanied the opening ceremony, in 879 B C.[18] An enormous banquet—the menu of which is given in detail—was offered by Ashurnasirpal to the entire population of the town as well as to foreign ambassadors, in all no less than 69,574 guests for ten days. And the final sentence makes us for a moment forget the other, unsavoury aspects of this great monarch:

'The happy people of all the lands together with the people of Kalhu for ten days I feasted, wined, bathed, anointed and honoured and sent them back to their lands in peace and joy.'

SHALMANESER III

Constantly on the battlefield, starting his campaigns from Nineveh or from one of his provincial palaces, Ashurnaṣirpal's son, Shalmaneser III* (858–824 BC) appears to have spent only the last years of his life in Kalhu. Yet, it is from that city and its neighbourhood that come his most famous monuments. One of them is the 'Black Obelisk', found by Layard in the temple of Ninurta over a century ago and now in the British Museum.[19] It is a six-foot high block of black alabaster ending in steps, like a miniature ziqqurat. A long inscription giving the summary of the king's wars runs around the monolith, while five sculptured panels on each side depict the payment of tribute by various foreign countries, including Israel whose king, Jehu, is shown prostrate at the feet of the Assyrian monarch. The recent excavations at Nimrud have brought to light a statue of the king in the attitude of prayer, and a huge building situated in a corner of the town wall, which was founded by him and used by his successors down to the fall of the empire. This building, nicknamed by the archaeologists 'Fort Shalmaneser', was in fact the *ekal masharti* of the inscriptions, the 'great store-house' erected 'for the ordinance of the camp, the maintenance of stallions, chariots, weapons, equipment of war, and the spoil of the foe of every kind'.[20] In three vast courtyards the troops were assembled, equipped and inspected before the annual campaigns, while the surrounding rooms served as armouries, stores, stables, and lodgings for the officers. Finally, we have the remarkable objects known as 'the bronze gates of Balawat'. They were discovered in 1878 by Layard's assistant, Rassam, not at Nimrud, but at Balawat (ancient Imgur-Enlil), a small tell a few miles to the north-east of the great city. There, Ashurnaṣirpal had built a country palace later occupied by Shalmaneser, and the main gates of this palace were covered with long strips of bronze, about ten inches wide, worked in 'repoussé' technique, representing some of Shalmaneser's armed

---

* *Shulmanu-asharedu*, 'the god Shulmanu is the chief'.

expeditions. A brief legend accompanies the pictures.[21] Besides their considerable artistic or architectural interest, all these monuments are priceless for the information they provide concerning Assyrian warfare during the ninth century BC.

In the number and scope of his military campaigns, Shalmaneser surpasses his father.[22] Out of his thirty-five years of reign, thirty-one were devoted to war. The Assyrian soldiers were taken further abroad than ever before: they set foot in Armenia, in Cilicia, in Palestine, in the heart of the Taurus and of the Zagros, on the shores of the Persian Gulf. They ravaged new lands, besieged new cities, measured themselves against new enemies. But because these enemies were much stronger than the Aramaeans of Jazirah or the small tribes of Iraqi Kurdistan, the victories of Shalmaneser were attenuated with failures, and the whole reign gives the impression of a task left unfinished, of a gigantic effort for a very small result. In the north, for instance, Shalmaneser went beyond 'the sea of Nairi' (lake Van) and entered the territory of Urartu, a kingdom which had been recently formed amidst the high mountains of Armenia. The Assyrian claims, as always, complete success and describes the sack of several towns belonging to the King of Urartu, Arame. Yet he confesses that Arame escaped, and we know that, during the next century, Urartu grew to be Assyria's main rival. Similarly, a series of campaigns in the east, towards the end of the reign, brought Shalmaneser or his commander-in-chief, the *turtanu* Daiân-Ashur, in contact with the Medes and Persians who then dwelt around lake Urmiah. There again the clash was brief and the 'victory' without lasting consequences: Medes and Persians were, in fact, left free to consolidate their position in Iran.

The repeated efforts made by Shalmaneser to conquer Syria met with the same failure. The Neo-Hittite and Aramaean princes whom Ashurnaṣirpal had caught by surprise had had time to strengthen themselves, and the main effect of the renewed Assyrian attacks was to unite them against Assyria. Three campaigns were necessary to wipe out the state of Bît-Adini and to establish a bridgehead on the Euphrates. In 856 BC, Til-Barsip (modern Tell Ahmar), the capital city of Bît-Adini, was taken, populated with Assyrians and renamed Kâr-Shulmanashared, 'the Quay of Shalmaneser'. On top of the mound overlooking the Euphrates a palace was built, which served as a base for operations on the western front.[23] But whether the Assyrians marched towards Cilicia through the Amanus or towards Damascus *via* Aleppo, they invariably found themselves face to face with coalitions of local rulers. Thus, when Shalmaneser, in 853 BC, entered the plains of central Syria, his opponents, Irhuleni of Hama and Adad-idri of Damascus (Ben-Hadad II of the Bible), met him with contingents supplied by 'twelve kings of the sea-coast'. To the invaders they could oppose 62,900 infantry-men, 1,900 horsemen, 3,900 chariots and 1,000 camels sent by 'Gindibu, from Arabia'. The battle took place at Karkara (Qarqar) on the Orontes, not far from Hama. Says Shalmaneser:

'I slew 14,000 of their warriors with the sword. Like Adad, I rained destruction upon them ... The plain was too small to let their bodies fall, the wide countryside was used up in burying them. With their corpses, I spanned the Orontes as with a bridge.'[24]

Yet neither Hama nor Damascus were taken, and the campaign ended prosaically with a little cruise on the Mediterranean. Four, five and eight years later respectively, other expeditions were directed against Hama with the same partial success. Numerous towns and villages were captured, looted and burned down, but not the main cities. In 841 BC, Damascus was again attacked. The occasion was propitious, Adad-idri having been murdered and replaced by Hazael, 'the son of a nobody'.[25] Hazael was defeated in battle on mount Sanir (Hermon), but locked himself in his capital city. All that Shalmaneser could do was to ravage the orchards and gardens which then surrounded Damascus as they surround it today, and to plunder the rich plain of Hauran. He then took the road to the coast and, on mount Carmel, received the tribute of Tyre, Sidon and *Iaua mâr Humri* (Jehu, son of Omri), King of Israel, the first biblical figure to appear in cuneiform inscriptions. After a last attempt to conquer Damascus in 838 BC, the Assyrian confessed his failure by leaving Syria alone for the rest of his reign.

In Babylonia Shalmaneser was luckier, though here again he failed to exploit his success and missed the chance which was offered to him. Too weak to attack the Assyrians and too strong to be attacked by them, the kings of the Eighth Dynasty of Babylon had hitherto managed to remain free. Even Ashurnaṣirpal had spared the southern kingdom, giving his contemporary, Nabû-apal-iddina (885–852 BC), time to repair some of the damage caused by the Aramaeans and the Sutû during 'the time of confusion'.[26] But in 851 BC, hostilities broke out between king Marduk-zakir-shumi and his own brother, backed by the Aramaeans. The Assyrians were called to the rescue. Shalmaneser defeated the rebels, entered Babylon, 'the bond of heaven and earth, the abode of life', offered sacrifices in Marduk's temple, Esagila, as well as in the sanctuaries of Kutha and Barsippa, and treated the inhabitants of that holy land with extreme kindness:

'For the people of Babylon and Barsippa, the protégés, the free-men of the great gods, he prepared a feast, he gave them food and wine, he clothed them in brightly coloured garments and presented them with gifts.'[27]

Then, advancing further south into the ancient country of Sumer, now occupied by the Chaldaeans (Kaldû), he stormed it and chased the enemies of Babylon 'unto the shores of the sea they call Bitter River (nâr marratu)', i.e. the Persian Gulf. The whole affair, however, was but a police operation. Marduk-zakir-shumi swore allegiance to his protector but remained on his throne. The unity of Mesopotamia under Assyrian rule could perhaps have been achieved without much difficulty. For some untold reason—probably because he was too deeply engaged in the north and in the west—Shalmaneser did not claim more than nominal suzerainty, and all that Assyria gained was some territory and a couple of towns on its southern border. The Diyala to the south, the Euphrates to the west, the mountain ranges to the north and east now marked its limits. It was still a purely northern Mesopotamian kingdom and the empire had yet to be conquered.

The end of Shalmaneser's long reign was darkened by extremely serious internal disorders. One of his sons, Ashur-danin-aplu, revolted and, with him, twenty-seven cities, including Assur, Nineveh, Erbil and Arrapha (Kirkuk). The old king, who by then hardly left his palace in Nimrud, entrusted another of his sons,

Shamshi-Adad, with the task of repressing the revolt, and for four years Assyria was in the throes of civil war. The war was still raging when Shalmaneser died and Shamshi-Adad V ascended the throne (824 BC). With the new king, begins a period of Assyrian stagnation which lasted for nearly a century.

CHAPTER XIX

THE ASSYRIAN EMPIRE

THE great revolt of 827 BC was not a dynastic crisis in the usual sense of the term; it was an uprising of the rural nobility and of the free citizens of Assyria against the great barons of the kingdom: the rich and insolent provincial governors to whom Ashurnaṣirpal and his successor had entrusted the lands they had conquered, and the high officials of the court, such as the *turtanu* Daiân Ashur, who, in the last years of Shalmaneser, had assumed powers out of proportion to the real nature of their duties. What the insurgents wanted was a king who really governed and a more even distribution of authority among his subordinates. They were fighting for a good cause, with the crown prince himself at their head, but a thorough administrative reform at this stage would have shaken the foundations of the still fragile kingdom. Shalmaneser judged that the revolt had to be crushed and no one was better qualified to crush it than his energetic younger son. It took Shamshi-Adad V five years to subdue the twenty-seven cities wherein his brother had 'brought about sedition, rebellion and wicked plotting', and the remainder of his reign (823–811 BC) to assert his authority over the Babylonians and the vassal rulers of the mountainous North and East who had taken advantage of the civil war to shake off the Assyrian 'protection' and to withold their tribute.¹ In the end, peace and order were restored, but no drastic changes were made in the central and provincial governments and the malaise persisted, giving rise, in the course of the following years, to other major or minor outbreaks of violence. This permanent instability affecting the infrastructure of the State, combined with other factors such as the youth and slackness of some of Shamshi-Adad's successors and the ever growing part taken by the rival kingdom of Urarṭu in Near Eastern politics, accounts for the temporary weakness of Assyria during the first half of the eighth century B C.

Shamshi-Adad's son, Adad-nirâri III (810–783 B C) was very young when his father died, and for five years the government of Assyria was in the hands of his mother Sammuramat—the legendary Semiramis. How this queen, whose reign has left hardly a trace in Assyrian records,[2] acquired the reputation of being 'the most beautiful, most cruel, most powerful and most lustful of Oriental queens'[3] is at first sight a most baffling problem. A possible explanation[4] is that Herodotus, who invented the legend of Semiramis in the fourth century B C, drew his information from the priests of Babylon. If Sammuramat was Babylonian by birth, she must have contributed actively to the propagation in her kingdom of Babylonian religious ideas and practices, to the 'Babylonization' of Assyria which, in the cultural field, is one of the salient features of the period. The Babylonian clergy was naturally proud of its queen, and we may assume that whatever stories were told about her were artfully embroidered. The imagination of the gullible traveller, inflamed by the personality of this extraordinary woman, did the rest, and subsequent Greek authors further enlarged upon the qualities and defects of Semiramis. She was eventually credited with such fantastic achievements as the building of Babylon and the conquest of Egypt and India; she epitomized all the deeds and prowess of the kings who reigned before and after her, and in the course of time her name became the symbol of Mesopotamia's vanished glory. By an ironic trick of fate, the memory of the virile Assyrian empire builders passed to the ancient Greeks under the guise of a woman.

As soon as he was of age to perform his royal duties, Adad-nirâri displayed the qualities of a capable and enterprising monarch.[5] In his first year of effective reign he invaded Syria, and imposed tax and tribute upon the Neo-Hittites, Phoenicians, Philistines, Israelites and Edomites. Succeeding where his grandfather had failed, he entered Damascus and received from Ben-Hadad III 'his property and his goods in immeasurable quantity'. Similarly, the Medes and Persians in Iran were, in the emphatic style of his royal inscriptions, 'brought in submission to his feet', while 'the kings of the Kaldû, all of them' were counted as vassals. But these were mere raids and not conquests. The spasmodic efforts of this true offspring of Shalmaneser III bore no fruit, and his premature death marks the beginning of a long period of Assyrian decline.

Adad-nirâri had four sons who reigned in succession. Of the first, Shalmaneser IV (782–772 BC) very little is known, but his authority seems to have been singularly limited, for his commander-in-chief, Shamshi-ilu, in an inscription found at Til-Barsip (Tell Ahmar), boasts of his victories over the Urartians without even mentioning the name of his master, the king—a fact unprecedented in Assyrian records.[6] The reign of the second son, Ashur-dân III (771–754 BC) was marked by unsuccessful campaigns in central Syria, an epidemic of plague, and revolts in Assur, Arrapha (Kirkuk) and Guzana (Tell Halaf)—not to mention an ominous eclipse of the sun. As for the third son, Ashur-nirâri V (753–746 BC), he hardly dared leave his palace and was probably killed in a revolution which broke out in Kalhu and put upon the throne his younger brother, Tiglathpileser III.[7]

Thus, for thirty-six years (781–745 BC), Assyria was practically paralysed, and during that time the political geography of the Near East underwent several major or minor changes. Babylonia, twice defeated on the battlefield by Shamshi-Adad V but still independent, fell into a state of quasi-anarchy recalling the worst decades of the tenth century. About 790 BC, for several years 'there was no king in the country', confessed a chronicle, while Eriba-Marduk (782–763 BC) claimed as a great success a simple police operation against the Aramaeans who had taken some 'fields and gardens' belonging to the inhabitants of Babylonia and Barsippa.[8] In Syria, the Aramaean princes were too absorbed in their traditional quarrels to achieve anything like unity. Attacked on two fronts, humiliated by the Assyrians of Adad-nirâri and defeated by the Israelites of Ahab, the kings of Damascus lost their political ascendency to the benefit of Hama first, then of Arpad (Tell Rifa'at, near Aleppo), the capital city of Bît-Agushi. In Iran, the Persians started migrating from the north to the south, towards the Bakhtiari mountains, and the Medes were left free to extend their control over the whole plateau.

Around lake Urmiah, the Mannaeans (*Mannai*), a non-Indo-European people which excavations have shown to be far more civilized than one would have thought,[9] organized themselves into a small but solid nation. But the main development took place in Armenia where, in the course of the ninth and eighth centuries, Urarṭu grew from a small principality on the shores of lake Van to a kingdom as large and powerful as Assyria itself. Under Argistis I (*circa* 778–750 BC), it extended approximately from lake Sevan, in Russian Armenia, to the present northern frontier of Iraq and from lake Urmiah to the upper course of the Euphrates in Turkey. Outside the national boundaries were vassal states or tribes which paid tribute to Urarṭu, acknowledged its suzerainty, or were tied to it by military agreements. Such were the Cimmerians in the Caucasus, all the Neo-Hittite kingdoms of the Taurus (Tabal, Milid, Gurgum, Kummuhu) and the Mannai in Iran. Argistis' successor, Sardur III (*circa* 749–734 BC) also succeeded in detaching Mati'-ilu, King of Arpad, from the alliance he had just signed with Adad-nirâri III[10] and, through Arpad, the political influence of Urarṭu was rapidly spreading among the Aramaean kingdoms of northern Syria.

Old and recent excavations in Turkish and Russian Armenia—in particular at Toprak Kale (ancient Rusahina), near Van, and at Karmir Blur (ancient Teisbaini), near Erivan—have supplied us with copious information on the history and archaeology of the kingdom of Urarṭu.[11] Its main cities were built of stone or of mud bricks resting on stone foundations; they were enclosed in massive walls and dominated by enormous citadels, where food, oil, wine and weapons were stored in anticipation of war. Urartian artisans were experts in metallurgy and they have left us some very fine works of art displaying a strong Assyrian influence. All over Armenia, numerous steles and rock inscriptions in cuneiform script and in 'Vannic' language—an offspring of Hurrian—bear witness to the heroism and piety of Urartian kings, while hundreds of tablets give us an insight to the social and economic organization of the kingdom, essentially based on vast royal estates worked by warriors, prisoners of war, or slaves. The pastures of the Ararat massif and the fertile valley of the Arax river made Urarṭu a fairly rich cattle-breeding and agricultural country, but most of its wealth came from the copper and iron mines of Armenia, Georgia, Commagene and Azerbaijan which it possessed or controlled.

The emergence of such a large, prosperous and powerful nation had a decisive influence on the history of Assyria. The ever growing part assumed by Urartu in Near Eastern economics and politics, no less than its presence at the gates of Iraq was, for the Assyrians, a source of constant worry, but also a challenge. A series of unfortunate experiences under Shalmaneser IV had taught them that any attempt to strike a direct blow at Urartu, in the present state of affairs, would meet with failure. Before they could stand face to face with their mighty rivals, they had to strengthen their own position in Mesopotamia and conquer and firmly hold Syria and western Iran, those two pillars to Urartian dominion outside Armenia. The time of quick, easy, fruitful razzias was over. Assyria had no choice but to become an empire or perish.

TIGLATHPILESER III

Fortunately, Assyria found in Tiglathpileser III (745–727 BC) an intelligent and vigorous sovereign who took a clear view of the situation and applied the necessary remedies. Not only did he 'smash like pots'—to use his own expression—the Syrian allies of Urartu and the Medes, but he turned the subdued lands into Assyrian possessions, reorganized the army and carried out the long-awaited administrative reform which gave Assyria the internal peace it needed. From every point of view, Tiglathpileser must be considered as the founder of the Assyrian empire.

The administrative reform, gradually enforced after 738 BC,[12] aimed at strengthening the royal authority and at reducing the excessive powers of the great lords. In Assyria proper, the existing districts were multiplied and made smaller. Outside Assyria, the countries which the king's victorious campaigns brought under his sway were, whenever possible or suitable, deprived of their local rulers and transformed into provinces. Each province was treated like an Assyrian district and entrusted to a 'district lord' (bêl pihâti) or to a 'governor' (shaknu, literally: 'appointed') responsible to the king. The countries and peoples who could not be incorporated in the empire were left with their own government but placed under the supervision of an 'overseer' (*qêpu*). A very efficient system of communications was established between the royal court and the provinces. Ordinary messengers or special runners constantly carried reports and letters sent by the governors and district chiefs or their subordinates to the king and the court officials, and the orders (*amât sharri*, 'king's word') issued by the monarch. In some cases the king sent his personal representative, the *qurbutu*-official, who reported on confidential affairs and often acted on his own initiative. District-chiefs and province governors had large military, judicial, administrative and financial powers, though their authority was limited by the small size of their charge and by the constant interference of the central government in almost every matter. Their main task was to ensure the regular payment of the tribute (*madattu*) and of the various taxes and duties to which Assyrians and foreigners alike were subjected, but they were also responsible for the enforcement of law and order, the execution of public works and the raising of troops in their own district. The last mentioned function was of considerable importance for the motherland. Formerly the Assyrian army was made of peasants and slaves supplied by the landlords of Assyria and put at the king's disposal for the duration of the annual campaign. Under Tiglathpileser III, the army of conscription was replaced by a permanent army (*kisir sharruti*, 'bond of kingship'), formed mainly of contingents levied in the dependencies of the kingdom. The military strength of Assyria was immediately increased several fold and the blood of her own sons was spared, but in the long run, this army made up of ill-assorted and often untrustworthy foreign elements proved more difficult to command and inferior in endurance and courage to the sturdy peasants of northern Iraq.

Another of Tiglathpileser's initiatives was the practice of mass-deportation. He must have thought that the best way of preventing revolts was to uproot what we would now call 'national feeling'—the fidelity to local gods and traditions—by mixing together the populations of the empire. Whole towns and districts were emptied of their inhabitants, who were resettled in distant regions and replaced by people brought by force from other countries. In 742 and 741 BC, for instance, 30,000 Syrians from the region of Hama were sent to the Zagros mountains, while 18,000 Aramaeans from the left bank of the Tigris were transferred to northern Syria. In Iran, in 744 BC, 65,000 persons were displaced in one single campaign and another year the exodus affected no less than 154,000 people in southern Mesopotamia.[13] Such pitiful scenes are occasionally depicted on Assyrian bas-reliefs: with little bags on their shoulders, holding their emaciated children by the hand, long files of men walk with the troops, whilst their wives follow in carts. Many must have died on the endless, sun-scorched tracks. Those who survived were not badly treated; they found a home in the ruins of burnt-down villages or in fortresses founded by the king, a field to plough and a reason to live; but their spirit of resistance—so their masters liked to believe—was broken for ever. This cruel policy was followed by Tiglathpileser's successors, but failed to bring the results expected: it did not prevent rebellions from breaking out with increasing frequency and, together with the devastations of war, contributed to the dislike of the Assyrians general in the ancient Near East. As a Babylonian civil servant from Nippur once dared write to King Esarhaddon: 'The king knows that all lands hate us on account of Assyria.'[14]

The campaigns of Tiglathpileser III bear the imprint of his methodical mind.[15] First, an expedition in southern Iraq 'as far as the Uknû river (Karûn)' relieved Babylon from the pressure of the Aramaeans and reminded Nabû-nâsir who, three years before, had founded the short-lived IXth Dynasty, that the King of Assyria was still his protector. As usual, 'pure sacrifices' were offered to the gods in the sacred cities of Sumer and Akkad, from Sippar to Uruk. Then, Tiglathpileser attacked Syria or, more precisely, the league of Neo-Hittite and Aramaean princes led by Mati'-ilu of Arpad, who obeyed Sardur III, the powerful King of Urarṭu. Sardur rushed to help his allies, but he was defeated near Samsat, on the Euphrates, and, fleeing ignominiously on a mare, 'escaped at night and was seen no more'. Arpad, besieged, resisted for three years, finally succumbed and became the chief town of an Assyrian province (741 BC). In the meantime, a victorious campaign against Azriyau, King of Ya'diya (Sam'al), and his allies of the Syrian coast resulted in the annexation of north-western Syria, and, probably, Phoenicia (742 BC). Numerous princes of the neighbourhood took fright and brought presents and tribute. Among them were Rasunu (Rezin), King of Damascus, Menahem, King of Israel,[16] and a certain Zabibê, 'Queen of the Arabs'. In all probability, the starting point of the Syrian campaigns was Hadâtu (modern Arslan Tash), between Karkemish and Harran, where archaeological excavations have unearthed one of Tiglathpileser's provincial palaces, an elaborate building strikingly similar in layout to Ashurnaṣirpal's palace in Nimrud, though smaller. Near the palace, a temple dedicated to Ishtar has yielded interesting pieces of sculpture, and in another building were found sculptured panels of ivory which once decorated the royal furniture of Hazael, King of Damascus, taken as booty by Adad-nirâri III.[17]

Having thus disposed of the Syrian vassals of Urartu, Tiglathpileser turned his weapons towards the east (campaigns of 744, 739 and 737 BC). Most of the central Zagros was 'brought within the borders of Assyria' and an expedition was launched across the Iranian plateau, in the heart of the land occupied by 'the powerful Medes', as far as mount Biknî (Demavend) and the 'salt desert', to the south-west of Teheran. Never before had an Assyrian army been taken so far away in that direction. The scanty remains of another of Tiglathpileser's provincial palaces found at Tepe Giyan, near Nihavend, testify to the reality of the campaigns and to the interest taken by the king in Iranian countries.[18] Later (probably in 735 BC) an attack was organized directly against Urartu, and Sardur's capital, Tushpa (Van), was besieged, though without success.

In 734 BC, Tiglathpileser returned to the Mediterranean coast where the situation was anything but peaceful. Tyre and Sidon were restless because of the restrictions imposed by the Assyrians on the export of timber to Philistia and Egypt; the troops had to intervene and make 'the people jump around'.[19] Still worse, an anti-Assyrian coalition comprising all the kingdoms of Palestine and Trans-Jordania had been organized by the Philistine rulers of Ascalon and Gaza. Tiglathpileser himself crushed the rebels. The Prince of Ascalon was killed in action; the 'man of Gaza' fled 'like a bird to Egypt'; Amon, Edom, Moab and Judah, as well as another queen of the Arabs called Shamshi paid tribute. Two years later, Ahaz, King of Judah, pressed by Damascus and Israel, called the Assyrians to the rescue. Tiglathpileser took Damascus,

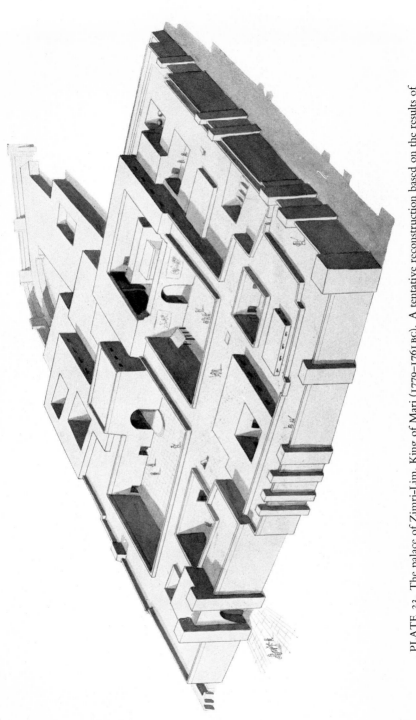

PLATE 23. The palace of Zimri-Lim, King of Mari (1779–1761 BC). A tentative reconstruction based on the results of archaeological excavations.

PLATE 24

A. From the palace of Kapara, an Aramaean prince who reigned in Guzana (Tell Halaf), in the ninth century BC, this crude, though impressive statue of an anonymous 'sitting goddess'.

B. *Kudurru* of the time of Marduk-nadin-ahhê (*circa* 1100 BC), King of Babylon. Note the high cylindrical tiara adorned with feathers and the embroidered dress, both of Kassite origin. Above the king, various divine symbols.

annexed half of Israel and established Hoshea as King in Samaria.[20]

Meanwhile, a series of *coups d'état* had taken place in southern Iraq, following the death of Nabû-nâsir in 734 BC. When the Aramaean chieftain Ukîn-zêr claimed the Babylonian throne (731 BC), the Assyrians tried to persuade the citizens of Babylon to rise against him and promised tax-exemption to any Aramaean who would desert from his chief.[21] But after diplomacy had proved useless, Tiglathpileser defeated the usurper, ravaged the territory of his tribe and decided to govern Babylonia himself. In 729 BC, he 'took the hand of Bêl (Marduk)' during the New Year Festival and was proclaimed King of Babylon under the name of Pulû. Two years later he died or, to use the Babylonian expression, 'he went to his destiny'.

SARGON II

The short reign of Tiglathpileser's son, Shalmaneser V (726–722 BC), is obscure. All we know for certain is that Hoshea, the puppet King of Israel, revolted and that Shalmaneser besieged Samaria for three years; but whether it was he who captured the city or the next king of Assyria is still a debated question.[22] Equally obscure are the circumstances which brought his successor to the throne, and no one can say whether he was an usurper or another of Tiglathpileser's sons. In any case, his name was in itself a promise of glory, for he was called Sharru-kîn (Sargon), like one of the earliest kings of Assur and like the illustrious founder of the Dynasty of Akkad.[23]

Shortly before Sargon was enthroned, two events of capital importance, which were to influence Assyrian strategy and diplomacy for a hundred years, took place in the Near East: the interference of Egypt in Palestine and of Elam in Babylonia. Both were the consequences of Tiglathpileser's victory, since it is obvious that his advance on the Iranian plateau had cut across the only trade routes left open to Elam, whilst his conquest of Phoenicia had wrested Egypt from one of her main clients. Thus, Elamites and Egyptians joined the Urartians as Assyria's avowed enemies, but since neither of them were yet capable of attacking a nation at the peak of its power, they had recourse to slower but safer methods: they fostered revolts among the vassals of Assyria, and whenever the Aramaean sheikhs of southern Iraq or the princelings of Palestine, threatened by the invincible Assyrian army, begged for help, they lent them all the support they could in men and weapons. The political history of Sargon's reign is, in fact, nothing but a long struggle against such rebellions.

Trouble, however, began at home and for a year Sargon had his hands tied by domestic disorders, which ended after he had freed the citizens of Assur from 'the call to arms of the land and the summons of the tax-collector' imposed upon them by Shal-maneser V.[24] Only then could he deal with the critical situation which had arisen in Babylonia and Syria during the change of reign. In Babylonia—now the second jewel of the Assyrian crown—a Chaldean ruler from Bît-Iakin, on the shores of the Persian Gulf, Marduk-apal-iddina* (Merodach-Baladan of the Old Testament) had ascended the throne in the same year as Sargon and was actively supported by Humbanigash, King of Elam. In 720 BC, Sargon marched against him and met his enemies at Dêr (Badrah), between the Tigris and the Zagros. His inscriptions claim complete victory, but the impartial 'Babylonian Chronicle' states clearly that the Assyrians were defeated by the Elamites alone, while Merodach-Baladan, in a text recently published, proudly declares that 'he smote to overthrow the widespread host of Subartu (Assyria) and smashed their weapons'.[25] Amusing detail: Merodach-Baladan's inscription was found at Nimrud, where Sargon had taken it from Uruk after 710 BC, replacing it in that city with a clay cylinder bearing his own and, of course, radically different version of the event. This shows that political propaganda and 'cold war' methods are not the privilege of our epoch. There can be no doubt, however, that the Assyrians met with a check, for we know that Marduk-apal-iddina reigned over Babylonia for eleven years (721–711 BC), behaving not as a barbarian chieftain, but as a great Mesopotamian monarch and leaving traces of his building activities in various cities.

Not less dangerous for Assyria was the coalition of revolted Syrian provinces headed by Ilu-bi'di, King of Hama, and the rebellion of Hanuna, King of Gaza, assisted by an Egyptian army. But here, Sargon had better luck. Ilu-bi'di and his allies were

* 'The god Marduk has given an heir.'

defeated at Qarqar and Hanunu was captured and flayed. As for the Egyptian general Sib'e, he 'fled alone and disappeared like a shepherd whose flock has been stolen' (720 BC).[26] Eight years later, the Egyptians fomented another revolt in Palestine. This time the leader was Iamani, King of Ashdod, followed by Judah, Edom, and Moab and supported by 'Pi'ru of Musru', i.e. Pharaoh of Egypt (probably Bocchoris). Again, Sargon was victorious: Iamani fled to Egypt, but he was soon extradited by the Nubian king who then held sway over the Nile valley:

'He threw him in fetters, shackles and iron bands, and they brought him to Assyria, a long journey.'[27]

The friendly attitude of the new ruler of Egypt (Piankhi?) towards Assyria accounts for the calm which reigned in Palestine during the rest of Sargon's reign.

We do not know for sure whether the Elamites had a hand in the dissensions which broke out among the ruling families of the central Zagros and gave Sargon in 713 BC the opportunity of conquering various principalities and towns in the regions of Kermanshah and Hamadan and to receive tribute from the Medes, but there can be no doubt as to who fomented troubles among the Mannaeans, the Zikirtu and other tribes of Azerbaijan, for Urartu remained in the north the main enemy of Assyria. A glance at Sargon's correspondence shows at once the care with which the Assyrian officials posted in those mountainous districts 'kept the watch of the king' and informed him of every move made by the Urartian monarch or his generals, of every change in the political loyalties of the surrounding peoples.[28] Yet, despite repeated interventions by Sargon, Rusas I of Urartu managed, between 719 BC and 715 BC, to replace the Mannaean rulers friendly to Assyria by his own creatures. In 714 BC the Assyrians launched a large-scale counter-offensive. The great campaign of Sargon's eighth year is recorded in his Annals, but a more detailed account of it has reached us in the form of a letter curiously addressed by the king to 'Ashur, father of the gods, the gods and goddesses of Destiny, the city and its inhabitants and the palace in its midst'—most certainly a document written to be read in public at the end of the annual campaign, with the view of creating a strong impression.[29] The march through the

mountains of Kurdistan was exceptionally difficult, owing to the
geography of the region no less than the resistance of the enemy,
and our text abounds in poetic passages like this:

'Mount Simirria, a great peak which stands like the blade of a
lance, lifting its head above the mountains, abode of Bêlit-ilâni;
whose summit on high upholds the heavens and whose roots
below reach the centre of the netherworld; which, like the spine
of a fish, has no passage from side to side and whose ascent from
back to front is difficult; on whose flanks gorges and precipices
yawn, whose sight inspires fear . . . with the wide understanding
and the inner spirit endowed to me by Ea and Bêlit-ilâni, who
opened my legs to overthrow the enemy countries, with picks of
bronze I armed my pioneers. The crags of high mountains they
caused to fly in splinters; they improved the passage. I took the
head of my troops. The chariots, the cavalry, the fighters who
went beside me, I made fly over this mountain like valiant
eagles . . .'[30]

Sargon crossed rivers and mountains, fought his way around
lake Urmiah and lake Van and finally conquered Urarṭu's most
sacred city, Muṣaṣir (south of lake Van), taking away the national
god Haldia. Urarṭu was not destroyed, but it had suffered a
crushing defeat. At the news of the fall of Muṣaṣir, Ursâ (Rusas)
was overwhelmed with shame: 'With his own dagger he stabbed
himself through the heart like a pig and ended his life.'

But the Urartians had already had time to rouse anti-Assyrian
feelings in other countries. In 717 BC, the still independent ruler
of Karkemish plotted against Sargon and saw his kingdom invaded and turned into an Assyrian province. During the next
five years, the same fate befell Quê (Cilicia), Gurgum, Milid,
Kummuhu and part of Tabal, in other words, all the Neo-
Hittite kingdoms of the Taurus. Behind these plots and 'revolts'
were not only 'the man of Urarṭu', but also Mitâ of Mushki (i.e.
Midas, King of Phrygia), whom Rusas had managed to attract
into his sphere of influence.

At the beginning of 710 BC, Sargon was everywhere victorious.
The whole of Syria-Palestine (with the notable exception of
Judah) and most of the Zagros range were firmly in Assyrian
hands; the Medes were considered as vassals; Urarṭu was dressing

its wounds; the Egyptians were friendly, the Elamites and Phrygians hostile but peaceful. Yet Babylon, under Merodach-Baladan, remained as a thorn in the side of Assyria, and in that same year, Sargon attacked it for the second time in his reign. The Chaldean had enlisted the help of all the tribes dwelling in the ancient country of Sumer, and for two years he offered strong resistance to the Assyrian army. Finally, encircled in Dûr-Iakîn (Tell Lahm) and wounded in the hand, he 'slipped in through the gate of his city like mice through holes' and took refuge in Elam.[31] Sargon entered Babylon and, like Tiglathpileser III, 'took the hand of Bêl'. The repercussions of his victory were enormous. Midas the Phrygian offered him his friendship. Upêri, King of Dilmun (Bahrain) 'heard of the might of Assur and sent his gifts.' Seven Kings of Iatnana (Cyprus) 'whose distant abodes are situated a seven days' journey in the sea of the setting sun' sent presents and swore allegiance to the mighty monarch whose stele has actually been found at Larnaka.[32] The repeated efforts made by its enemies to undermine the Assyrian empire had been of no avail; at the end of the reign it was larger and apparently stronger than ever.

As a war chief, Sargon liked to live in Kalhu (Nimrud), the military capital of the empire, where he occupied, restored and modified Ashurnaṣirpal's palace. But moved by incommensurable pride, he soon decided to have his own palace in his own city. In 717 BC were laid the foundations of 'Sargon's fortress', *Dûr-Sharrukîn*, a hitherto virgin site 15 miles to the north-east of Nineveh, near the modern village of Khorsabad.[33] The town was square in plan, each side measuring about one mile, and its wall was pierced by seven fortified gates. In its northern part, an inner wall enclosed the citadel, which contained the royal palace, a temple dedicated to Nabû, and the sumptuous houses of high-ranking officials, such as Sin-ah-uṣur, the vizier and king's brother. The palace itself stood on a fifty-foot high platform overriding the city wall and comprised more than two hundred rooms and thirty courtyards. Part of it, erroneously called 'harem' by the early excavators, was later found to be made of six sanctuaries, and nearby rose a ziqqurat whose seven storeys were painted with different colours and connected a by spiral ramp. A beautiful viaduct of stone linked the palace with the temple of

Nabû, for in Assyria the religious and public functions of the king were closely interwoven. As expected, the royal abode was lavishly decorated. Its gates and main doors—as, indeed, the gates of the town and of the citadel—were guarded by colossal bull-men; blue glazed bricks showing divine symbols were used in the sanctuaries, and in most rooms the walls were adorned with frescoes and lined with sculptured and inscribed orthostats, a mile and a half of reliefs long. Thousands of prisoners of war and hundreds of artists and artisans must have worked at Dûr-Sharrukîn, since the whole city was built in ten years. Yet there is ample evidence that it was scarcely inhabited and almost immediately abandoned. In one of his so-called 'Display Inscriptions', Sargon says:

'For me, Sargon, who dwells in this palace, may he (Ashur) decree as my destiny long life, health of body, joy of heart, brightness of soul.'34

But the god hearkened not to his prayer. One year after Dûr-Sharrukîn was officially inaugurated Sargon 'went against Tabal and was killed in the war' (705 BC). His successors preferred Nineveh to the Mesopotamian Brazilia, and Khorsabad, deserted, fell slowly into ruins.

CHAPTER XX

THE HOUSE OF SARGON

SARGON'S descendants—the Sargonids, as they are sometimes called—governed Assyria in unbroken succession for almost a century (704–609 BC), bringing the Assyrian empire to its farthest limits and the Assyrian civilization to its zenith. Yet the wars of Sennacherib, Esarhaddon and Ashurbanipal, which through the inflated language of the royal inscriptions look like glorious wars of conquest were, at their best, nothing but successful counter-attacks. At the end of Sargon's reign, the Assyrians ruled, directly or indirectly, over the entire 'Fertile Crescent' and over parts of Iran and Asia Minor. They had a window on the Mediterranean and a window on the Persian Gulf; they controlled the entire course of the Tigris and the Euphrates as well as the great trade routes crossing the Syrian desert, the Taurus and the Zagros. Supplied with all kinds of goods and commodities by their subjects, vassals and allies, they lived in prosperity and could have lived in peace, had it not been for the increasingly frequent revolts provoked by their oppressive policy and encouraged—at least in Palestine and Babylonia—by Egypt and Elam. The conquest of Egypt by Esarhaddon and the destruction of Elam at the hands of Ashurbanipal were, therefore, neither long-range razzias in the traditional style, nor the fruits of a planned strategy: they were defensive measures taken by these monarchs to put an end to an unbearable situation; they represent the final outcome of long and bitter conflicts more imposed upon Assyria by her enemies than desired by her. In this endless struggle, the Assyrians used up their strength, ruined their own possessions and failed to pay sufficient attention to the capital event which was taking place, during that time, behind the screen of the Zagros: the formation of a powerful Median kingdom, the future instrument of their downfall. About 640 BC, when total victory seemed at last achieved, when Ashurbanipal rose in triumph over all the foes of Assyria, it suddenly became apparent that the colossus had feet of clay.

SENNACHERIB

As implied by his name, Sennacherib—*Sin-ahhê-eriba*, 'the God Sin has increased the (number of) brothers'—was not Sargon's first-born son, but, for some untold reason, he was chosen as his legitimate heir, brought up in the 'House of Succession' and entrusted early with high administrative and military functions, especially on the northern frontier. He was thus well prepared for his royal duties when, in 705 BC, he ascended the throne of Assyria.[1]

Throughout his reign, the northern and eastern frontiers, once the theatre of so many of his father's wars, were comparatively calm. Sargon's victories in Kurdistan, in Armenia and in the Taurus had struck such damaging blows at Urarțu and Phrygia that they were no longer to be feared as potential aggressors. Moreover, these two nations were under attack by a new enemy: the Cimmerians (Assyr. *Gimirrai*), a warlike people from southern Russia who, at the end of the eighth century, had crossed the Caucasus and entered Western Asia. Already during the last years of Sargon's reign, the Cimmerians, established in what is at present the Soviet Republic of Georgia, had risen in revolt against their Urartian suzerain and inflicted upon him a crushing defeat.[2] Now they were pushing forward along the southern shore of the Black Sea, in the folds of the Pontic range, harassing both Phrygia and her western neighbour, the young and fabulously rich kingdom of Lydia. At the same time, other Cimmerians were penetrating the north-western corner of Iran, making alliance with the Mannai and the Medes. Sennacherib was, no doubt, informed of these events, but he either failed to foresee their remote consequences, or was unable to intervene in these far-away regions. The four campaigns he launched to the north and the west were of medium scale and medium range; they were directed, not against the Cimmerians or the Medes, but against restive vassals: princes of the central Zagros, city-chiefs of Kurdistan, rulers of Cilicia—probably supported by Greek troops[3] —and one of the kings of Tabal.

In reality, the attention of Sennacherib was almost entirely absorbed by the extremely serious rebellions which had broken out in the Mediterranean districts and in Babylonia as soon as the news of Sargon's death was made public. In Phoenicia and Palestine, Egyptian propaganda had persuaded Lulê, King of Sidon, Sidka, King of Ascalon, Ezekiah, King of Judah and the inhabitants of Ekron to sever their links with Nineveh. In his fourth year of reign (701 BC), Sennacherib went forth to chastise the rebels. Lulê fled to Cyprus, Sidka was carried away to Assyria, an Egyptian army sent to the rescue of Ekron was defeated, and in all these cities more friendly rulers were put upon the throne. Then Sennacherib attacked Judah, besieged and captured the strongly fortified town of Lachish4 and sent an army against Jerusalem. Here must be placed the dramatic scene described in the Second Book of Kings:5 over the wall of the sacred city, three of Ezekiah's officials parley 'in the Jews' language' with three dignitaries of the Assyrian court—the *turtanu*, the *rab-shaqê* and the *rab-sharish*. The Assyrians mock the Jews who trust 'upon the staff of this bruised reed, Egypt', promise 'two thousand horses' if they submit, and finally resort to threats. But Ezekiah, encouraged by Isaiah the prophet, stubbornly refuses to open the gates of Jerusalem. A compromise is reached, the Assyrians withdraw and the city is spared, but at what price! Ezekiah has to give 30 talents of gold, 800 talents of silver, 'all kind of valuable treasures as well as his daughters, his harem, his male and female musicians', not counting several cities cut off from his land and given to the Philistines.6 At the end of this memorable campaign, Sennacherib planned to invade Egypt. He had already reached Pelusium (Tell el Farama, 30 miles east of the Suez canal), when his camp was ravaged 'by the angel of the Lord who went out at night and smote one hundred four-score and five thousand', says the Bible, 'by a legion of rats gnawing everything in the weapons that was made of rope or leather', says Herodotus, or, as Berossus tells us, 'by a pestilential sickness' killing '185,000 men with their commanders and officers'.7 The Assyrian inscriptions are, of course, silent on this inglorious episode.

In Babylonia the situation was far worse than in Palestine, and the war against the Aramaeans and their Elamite allies went on during most of Sennacherib's reign. The year he ascended the throne, Sargon's old rival, Marduk-apal-iddina (Merodach-Baladan) left Elam where, it will be remembered, he had taken refuge and, assisted by Elamite officers and troops, raised the entire Aramaean population of southern Iraq against the Assyrians, entered the capital city and proclaimed himself King of Babylon. In 703 BC, the King of Assyria led his armies against him. Defeated under the walls of Kish, the Chaldaean escaped and hid 'in the midst of the swamps and marshes' where he could not be found. Sennacherib plundered his palace, captured innumerable prisoners, deported 208,000 persons to Assyria and gave Babylon a king of his choice, Bêl-ibni, 'the son of a master-builder' who had grown up in Nineveh 'like a young hound'. But, three years later, Merodach-Baladan reappeared in Bît-Iakin, his native country, and stirred up enough trouble to provoke a second Assyrian intervention. Bêl-ibni, more than suspect of collusion with the rebels, was taken away and replaced by Sennacherib's own son, Ashur-nadin-shumi. As for Merodach-Baladan, he refused to offer battle:

'He gathered together the gods of his whole land in their shrines, and loaded them into ships and fled like a bird to the (Elamite) swampland of Nagite, which is in the midst of the sea.'[8]

Six relatively peaceful years elapsed. Then, in 695 BC, under pretext of capturing the Elamite cities 'on the other side of the Bitter River, whither the people of Bît-Iakin had scattered before the mighty weapons of Ashur', Sennacherib organized a formidable combined land and sea operation aimed at securing for the Assyrians an access to the Persian Gulf through the hostile Sea-Land.[9] A fleet of ships, built at Nineveh by Syrian craftsmen and manned by Phoenician and Cypriot sailors, was sent down the Tigris as far as Upâ (Opis).[10] There it was necessary to change rivers probably because the Tigris, in those days, emptied its waters into extensive swamps and its lower course was not navigable. The ships were therefore carried overland to the Arahtu canal which linked the Twin Rivers and continued their course on the Euphrates, while the army advanced on dry land. The meeting point was at Bab-Salimeti, near the mouth of the river. The Assyrian troops embarked, crossed the head of the Persian Gulf, landed in Elamite territory, conquered a few cities and returned loaded with spoil.

Of Marduk-apal-iddina, there is no longer question and we know that he died in exile. But the Elamites immediately retaliated. Hallushu, their king, invaded Mesopotamia, took Sippar, captured Ashur-nadin-shumi and put one of his followers on the throne of Babylon. Thus started a series of direct conflicts between Elam and Assyria, which lasted seven years with alternating victories and defeats on either side.[11] In 689 BC, the Babylonians—now again under a pro-Assyrian viceroy—revolted and bought the support of Umman-menanu, King of Elam. A great battle took place at Hallulê, on the Tigris. Described as a victory in the Assyrian records, it was, in fact, a near-defeat.[12] Blind with rage, Sennacherib avenged himself on Babylon and dared to accomplish the unthinkable: he destroyed the illustrious and sacred city, the second metropolis of the empire, the 'bond of heaven and earth' which his forebears had always treated with infinite patience and respect:

'As a hurricane proceeds, I attacked it and, like a storm, I overthrew it ... Its inhabitants, young and old, I did not spare and with their corpses I filled the streets of the city ... The town itself and its houses, from their foundations to their roofs I devastated, I destroyed, by fire I overthrew ... In order that, in future, even the soil of its temples be forgotten, by water I ravaged it, I turned it into pastures.

To quiet the heart of Ashur, my lord, that peoples should bow in submission before his exalted might, I removed the dust of Babylon for presents to the (most) distant peoples, and in that Temple of the New Year Festival (in Assur), I stored up (some) in a covered jar.[13]

The great gods of Sumer and Akkad could not leave such a crime unpunished. Eight years later, in Nineveh, on the twentieth day of Tebet (January 681 BC), whilst praying in a temple, Sennacherib met with the death he deserved: he was 'smashed with statues of protective deities' by one of his own sons.[14]

Brutal and cowardly—most of his wars were fought by his generals—Sennacherib has been severely judged. Yet let us give him his due: the king who destroyed Babylon did an enormous amount of constructive work in Assyria. Not only were temples and public buildings erected or restored in several towns and colossal hydraulic works undertaken throughout the country, giving a new start to agriculture, but the very old city of Nineveh (*Ninua*), hitherto a simple 'royal residence', was enlarged, fortified, embellished and made into a capital city worthy of the vast empire it commanded. Within a few years, its circumference passed from about 2 miles to nearly 8 miles, embracing two separate boroughs, now represented by the mounds of Kuyunjik and Nebi Yunus, opposite Mosul, on the left bank of the Tigris.[15] The outer wall, made of great limestone blocks, was 'raised mountain high', while the inner wall was pierced with fifteen gates leading in all directions. The squares of the town were widened; its avenues and streets were paved and 'caused to shine like the day'. In the northern part of the city (Kuyunjik), stood the old palace, but it had been neglected, and an affluent of the Tigris, the Tebiltu river, had ruined its foundations. The monument was torn down, and on a large terrace thrown over the Tebiltu was built Sennacherib's magnificent abode, the 'Palace without a Rival':

'Beams of cedar, the product of mount Amanus, which they dragged with difficulty out of (these) distant mountains, I stretched across their roofs. Great door-leaves of cypress, whose odour is pleasant as they are opened and closed, I bound with a band of shining copper and set them up in their doors. A portico patterned after a Hittite palace, which they call in the Amorite tongue *bîthilâni*, I constructed inside for my lordly pleasure.'[16]

Enormous copper pillars resting on lions of bronze were cast in moulds 'like half-shekel coins'—a technique which Sennacherib boasts of having invented—and adorned the palace gates. Protective genii of silver, copper and stone were set 'towards the four winds'. Huge slabs of limestone, sculptured with war scenes, were dragged through the doors and made to line the walls. Finally, at the side of the palace, was opened 'a great park like unto mount Amanus, wherein were planted all kinds of herbs and fruit–trees'. To increase the vegetation in and around the town, water was brought from far-away districts by means of a canal cut 'through mountain and lowland', and the remains of a remarkable aqueduct visible near the village of Jerwan testify to the veracity of the royal annals as well as to the ability of the king's engineers.[17]

Proud of himself and of his work, Sennacherib liked to be portrayed on the hills of his own country, of this 'land of Assur' to which he was fanatically devoted. At Bavian, near Jerwan, at Maltai, near Dohuk and on the Judi Dagh, on the Turkish–Iraqi frontier,[18] can still be seen, carved in the rock, the gigantic image of the 'mighty king, ruler of widespread peoples', standing in front of the gods whom he had so gravely offended.

ESARHADDON

The murder of Sennacherib plunged Assyria into a violent, though fortunately short dynastic crisis, and Esarhaddon* had to conquer by the sword the throne he had legally inherited.[19] He was Sennacherib's youngest son, and the fact that he had been chosen as the crown prince aroused the jealousy of his brothers. In the opening chapter of his annals, Esarhaddon tells how their slanderous accusations turned his father's heart against him, to the point where he was obliged to leave his own country and seek refuge 'in a hiding place'—possibly Cilicia or Tabal. The parricide is not mentioned, but it is clear that Sennacherib was dead when his sons 'butted each other like kids to take over kingship', thereby losing popular support among the Assyrians themselves. Encouraged by the gods, the exile hastened towards Nineveh, determined to claim his rights to the throne. The usurpers had deployed their army in the steppe to the west of the Tigris, blocking the road to the capital city; but no sooner did Esarhaddon attack than their soldiers deserted to him, while the people of Assyria came to meet him and kissed his feet. Making his own army 'jump over the Tigris as if it be a small ditch', he entered Nineveh and, in March 681 BC, 'sat down happily on the throne of his father'. The wicked brothers had fled 'to an unknown country', but the officers who had assisted them were put to death, together with their progeny.[20]

The first act of the new monarch was to atone for Sennacherib's sin by rebuilding Babylon. The gods, in their anger, had decreed that the town should lie in ruins for 70 years, but the priests found an easy way of overcoming this difficulty: 'The merciful Marduk turned the Book of Fate upside down and ordered the

* *Ashur-aha-iddin*, 'The god Ashur has given a brother'.

restoration of the city in the eleventh year', for, in the cuneiform script, the figure 70 becomes 11 when reversed, just as our figure 9 becomes 6. All the people of Kar-Duniash could then be summoned to 'carry the basket', and, in due course, Babylon was not only rebuilt, but 'enlarged, raised aloft and made magnificent'.[21] Although the great city was probably not as thoroughly destroyed as Sennacherib would have us believe, the work of restoration occupied the whole reign, and it was not until the accession year of Ashurbanipal (669 BC), that Marduk and the other gods of Akkad could return from Assur, where they were held captive, to be reinstated in their temples.[22] This act of justice won Esarhaddon the friendship of many of his Babylonian subjects: with the exception of an abortive attempt made by Merodach-Baladan's son, in 680 BC, to capture Ur, there was no serious trouble in southern Iraq during the rest of the reign, and indeed the Babylonians themselves repulsed the Elamite Humba-haldash, when, in 675 BC, he invaded their country. In that other troublesome area of the empire, Phoenicia, Esarhaddon proved that if he could forgive, he could also punish. Abdi-Milkuti, King of Sidon, who revolted in 677 BC, was caught and beheaded; Sidon was 'torn up and cast into the midst of the sea', its inhabitants deported to Assyria and its territory given to the rival city of Tyre.[23] These drastic measures ensured—at least for a while—peace on the Mediterranean coast, and left Esarhaddon free to deal with the serious problems that had arisen along the northern and eastern borders.[24]

About the beginning of his reign, another nomadic people from southern Russia, the Scythians (Assyr. *Ishkuzai*), had crossed the Caucasus and joined the Cimmerians already established in Asia Minor, Armenia and Iran. The arrival of these warlike tribes, with which they were closely related, gave a new impetus to the predatory activities of the Cimmerians. In 679 BC, they suddenly broke through the Taurus mountains, threatening the Assyrian garrisons in Tabal and causing some unrest among the vassal rulers of Cilicia. Esarhaddon swiftly counter-attacked, 'tramped upon the neck' of the Cilician rebels and 'cut with the sword' Teushpa and his hordes, forcing them to retreat beyond the Kizil-Irmak river. Cimmerians and Scythians then fell upon the kingdom of Phrygia which they overthrew 3 years later with the help of the Urartians. Happy to see this human flood diverted from his own kingdom, Esarhaddon made peace with the Cimmerians, gave an Assyrian princess in marriage to the Scythian chief Bartatua (the 'Protothyes' of Herodotus) and even kept on friendly terms with Rusas II of Urarṭu. On the eastern side of the Armenian massif, however, the repeated efforts made by the Assyrians to obtain tribute from the Mannai—now under strong Cimmerian and Scythian influence—met with failure, despite claims to the contrary in the royal inscriptions. To the south-east of lake Urmiah, the vast Iranian plateau was occupied by the Medes, in theory under Assyrian control but in fact independent, and this was the time (*circa* 680 BC) when Khshathrita ('Phraortes'), son of Daiakku ('Deioces'), was uniting their numerous tribes under his authority. Esarhaddon did all he could to prevent the development of a situation whose immediate effect was to cut down the supply of Median horses to the Assyrian army and whose remote consequences were perhaps dimly foreseen. Several raids of cavalry were launched across the plateau as far as the desert to the east of Teheran, and three important princes of the Medes, who had begged Esarhaddon's help against their own vassals, were placed under Assyrian protection and imposed regular tribute. Further south, a series of successful operations in the central Zagros and an alliance sealed with the Gambulû—an Aramaean tribe settled on the left bank of the lower Tigris—aimed at forming a barrier of buffer states between Elam and Mesopotamia; but Esarhaddon struck an even greater victory when, after the death of Humba-haldash, he plotted and succeeded in putting on the Elamite throne a prince friendly to Assyria: Urtaki (675 BC).

While obtaining, by a remarkable combination of force and diplomacy, a precarious peace in Babylonia, in Phoenicia and along the 1,200 miles of his northern and eastern frontiers, Esarhaddon was preparing for his great project: the conquest of Egypt. Already, in 679 BC, he had captured the city of Arzani 'on the border of the Brook of Egypt' (Wadi al 'Arish, in the Negeb). Then he had endeavoured to win the friendship of the Arabs, by now settled in large numbers in the Syrian desert, since without their co-operation no large-scale military campaign in the south-western regions of the empire could be undertaken. For example, he had given back to its former ruler, Hazail, the stronghold of Adumatu (al Jauf), which Sennacherib had conquered, together with its gods, and when a certain Uabu (Wahab) revolted against Hazail's son, the latter received full military support from the Assyrians.25 Finally, in the spring of 671 BC, when he felt all the frontiers secure and the Arabs friendly or neutral, Esarhaddon led his army into Syria, the first step on the road to Egypt. An attempt was made to besiege Tyre whose king had revolted, but the city resisted and no time was wasted in trying to capture it. Marching southwards, the Assyrians reached Rapihu (Tell Rifah, south of Gaza) and crossed the Sinai desert where they saw, among other dreadful things, 'two-headed serpents whose attack spelled death' and 'green animals whose wings were batting'. After fifteen days of considerable hardship, they entered the green land of Egypt.

Despite the strong resistance offered by the pharaoh Taharqa and his army, the conquest of this vast country took surprisingly little time:

'From the town of Ishhupri as far as Memphis (*Mempi*), his royal residence, a distance of fifteen days (march), I fought daily, without interruption, very bloody battles against Tahraqa (*Tarqú*), King of Egypt and Ethiopia, the one accursed by all the great gods. Five times I hit him with the point of (my) arrows (inflicting) wounds (from which he should) not recover, and then, I laid siege to Memphis, his royal residence, and conquered it in half a day by means of mines, breaches and assault ladders. His queen, the women of his palace, Ushanahuru, his "heir apparent", his other children, his possessions, horses large and small cattle beyond counting I carried away as booty to Assyria. All Ethiopians I deported from Egypt—leaving not even one to do homage (to me). Everywhere in Egypt, I appointed new (local) kings, governors, officers, harbour overseers, officials and administrative personnel. I installed regular sacrificial dues for Assur and the (other) great gods, my lords, for all times. I imposed upon them tribute due to me (as their) overlords, (to be paid annually) without ceasing.'26

But Egypt was not to be an easy prey. Two years later, Taharqa came back from the South where he had fled, recovered Memphis

PLATE 25

A. Sennacherib worshipping the Gods. Rock sculpture of Bavian, near Mosul.

B. Tablet from Nimrud showing archaic, pictographic signs, together with their Neo-Assyrian equivalents. About 2,500 years separate the two scripts.

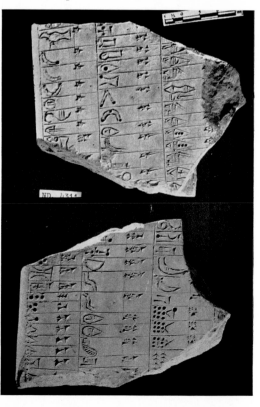

PLATE 26

Ashurbanipal in his gala chariot. Relief from Nineveh.

PLATE 27

A. Specimen of
Assyrian writing on
stone (Nimrud).

B. Scene of deporta-
tion. Relief from
Khorsabad.

and fomented a rebellion against the Assyrians in the Nile Delta. Esarhaddon was, once again, on his way to Egypt when he fell sick in Harran and died (669 BC).

Three years before, in May, 672, in the presence of the army and nobles of Assyria, foreign ambassadors and representatives from subject countries, he had solemnly proclaimed his son, Ashurbanipal, the legitimate heir to the throne and appointed another of his sons, Shamash-shum-ukîn, viceroy in Babylonia. That same day, the vassal princes had signed a long and detailed treaty of loyalty to the crown prince, copies of which have recently been found at Nimrud.²⁴ Even Esarhaddon's mother, the Aramaean-born Naqi'a-Zakutu, had thrown the weight of her influence into the balance and obtained from the Babylonians and their future viceroy an oath of allegiance to the future ruler of Assyria.²⁷ Esarhaddon, the brave and wise king who left nothing to chance, had ensured that no dynastic crisis would follow his death.

ASHURBANIPAL

The change of reign took place smoothly and, on the same day, the two princes sat upon their respective thrones: Ashurbanipal in Nineveh, Shamash-shum-ukîn in Babylon. The empire, however, was not divided. In all probability, the purpose of the arrangements made by Esarhaddon was to satisfy his Babylonian subjects by granting them sovereignty, but it had been made clear to all concerned that Ashurbanipal took precedence over his brother. The latter had full authority within his own kingdom; the former held sway over Assyria proper, the distant provinces and the vassal rulers, and was responsible for the conduct of war and the foreign policy of the empire as a whole. It was perhaps an awkward solution, but it worked perfectly well for 17 years.

With the crown of Assyria, Ashurbanipal★ (668–631 BC)²⁸ inherited the task, interrupted by his father's death, of repressing the Egyptian revolt. The commander-in-chief was therefore at once despatched to Syria, where he gathered auxiliary troops supplied by 'twenty-two kings of the sea-coast, of the midst of the sea and of the mainland', and took the road to Egypt. An army sent by Taharqa to stop the invasion was routed, and the unfor-

★ *Ashur-ban-aplu*, 'The god Ashur is the creator of the son'.

tunate pharaoh left Memphis by boat and fled to Thebes (Assyr. Ni'). This time the Assyrians pursued him and finally entered the capital city of Upper Egypt, obliging Taharqa to seek refuge 'on the other side of the river'. It was, no doubt, a brilliant feat of arms, but the Assyrians were now about 1,300 miles from their homeland, in the midst of a strange and hostile country, the language, religion and customs of which were utterly foreign to them. Three hundred years later, Alexander the Great, in a similar position, put on his head the double crown of the pharaohs and was proclaimed the son of Amen-Rê, the great god of Egypt; but Ashurbanipal, deputy and instrument of the god Ashur, could not even think of doing this. Besides, to govern this vast country directly would have required more troops and civil servants than were at his disposal. The King of Assyria had therefore no choice but to follow his father's policy: twenty native 'kings, governors and regents' of the Delta and of the Nile valley appointed by Esarhaddon, 'who had left their offices in the face of the uprising of Taharqa and scattered into the open country', were reinstalled, the Assyrian garrisons were made stronger and the regulations more severe. It was an invitation to revolt. No sooner had the expeditionary corps withdrawn than:

'All the kings . . . talked about rebellion and came, among themselves, to the unholy decision: "Taharqa has been driven out of Egypt, how can we, ourselves, stay?" And they sent their mounted messengers to Taharqa, King of Nubia, to establish a sworn agreement: "Let there be peace between us and let us come to mutual understanding; we will divide the country between us, no foreigner shall be ruler among us!" '29

The Assyrian officers, however, got wind of the plot. They arrested the rebels and sent them to Nineveh. There they were put to death, with the exception of Necho (*Nikku*), who must have given such signs of repentance that he was forgiven, 'clad in brilliant garments' and, the ring of investiture on his finger, sent back to Sais, his city. For a while calm reigned in Egypt, but in 655 BC, Taharqa died in exile and was succeeded by his son-in-law Tanuatamûn, whom the Assyrians call *Tandamane*. Boldly the young prince came forth from the South, 'made a great slaughter among the Children of Rebellion'30 and occupied Memphis, which, however, he forsook for Thebes when he heard that Ashurbanipal himself was on his way to Egypt at the head of a strong army. Entering Thebes for the second time, the Assyrians ransacked and destroyed it 'as if by a floodstorm', and carried away 'booty heavy and beyond counting', including two tall obelisks coated with bronze. The great city never recovered from the devastation.

The fluctuations of Assyrian fortune on the banks of the Nile had, as could be expected, repercussions in Phoenicia where Ba'alu, King of Tyre, and Iakinlu, King of Arvad (Ruâd Island), faithful vassals in 669, refused to obey Ashurbanipal's orders in 665 B C. Tyre—then an impregnable island off the Lebanese coast —was 'strangled' from the mainland, reduced to famine and forced to surrender. Similar tactics were probably used against Arvad, bringing the same result. Yet the rulers of these two cities were treated with astonishing leniency, no doubt because Ashurbanipal, whose army was fully engaged in the Egyptian venture, could neither afford to lose his Phoenician allies, nor spare troops for other fronts. For the same reason, he refused to answer the calls for help from Gyges (*Gugu*), King of Lydia—'a distant place, whose name the kings, my fathers, had not heard'—harassed by the Cimmerians.

The victory over Tanuatamûn and the Phoenicians gave Ashurbanipal a few years of respite during which he was able to devote his attention to the northern and eastern frontiers. The chronology of the reign is extremely uncertain, but it is probably between 665 and 655 B C, that must be placed the campaign against the Mannai described in the royal records, the repulse of a Cimmerian attack announced by an omen,[31] the alliance with Madyes, chief of the Scythians, which was to prove so useful a few years later, and the war against Urtaki, king of Elam, 'who gave no thought to the good done to him' by Esarhaddon and 'overran Akkad like a dense swarm of grasshoppers.'[32] There is hardly any mention of the Medes, but we learn from other sources that they were then temporarily dominated by the Scythians. The relations with Urarṭu appear to have been as good as during the reign of Esarhaddon.

Shortly before the middle of the seventh century, the gods, who had always stood at Ashurbanipal's side, suddenly seemed to abandon him. About 655 BC, Psamtik (*Psammetichus I*)—possibly a son of Necho—raised the flag of independence in the Nile Delta and, with the help of Ionian and Carian mercenaries, expelled the Assyrians from Egypt, pursuing them as far as Ashdod, in Palestine. We owe this information to Herodotus,33 for there is naturally no mention of this disaster in the cuneiform records, except for a passage in the 'Rassam cylinder' where Ashurbanipal states that Gyges 'sent his force to the aid of Tushamilki, King of Egypt, who had thrown off the yoke of his (Ashurbanipal's) sovereignty'.34 In other times, an army would have been sent against Psammetichus, and Egypt would not have slipped so easily out of Assyrian hands. But it so happened that the bulk of the Assyrian army was engaged in a fierce struggle with the Elamites, and Ashurbanipal had to give up Egypt in order to save Mesopotamia. The King of Elam was then Tept-Humban (the *Teumman* of Assyrian inscriptions), an usurper who, six or seven years before, had seized the throne, obliging the sons of Urtaki to take refuge in Nineveh. War broke out when Teumman demanded their extradition, which Ashurbanipal refused. The Elamites attacked, aided by the unfaithful Gambulû. Driven back into their own country, they were defeated at Tulliz, on the Kerkha river. Teumman was killed in the battle; his head was cut off and triumphantly taken to Nineveh where—as shown in a famous bas-relief35—it was hung on a tree in the garden of the royal palace. The Gambulû were punished and Elam was divided between two members of the Urtaki family: Humbanigash and Tammaritu. There, as in Egypt, the Assyrians would not or could not put the vanquished country directly under their rule, and the half-measures they adopted left ultimately no choice but abandonment or utter destruction.

This episode of the Elamite war was hardly concluded when Babylonia revolted. For 17 years, Shamash-shum-ukîn had behaved as a faithful brother, but gradually the virus of Babylonian nationalism overtook him and he came to think that, after all, Babylon was as much entitled to world domination as Nineveh. In 651 BC, he closed the gates of Sippar, Babylon and Barsippa to the Assyrians and contrived a huge coalition comprising Phoenicia, the Philistines, Judah, the Arabs of the Syrian desert, the Chaldaeans of southern Iraq, the Elamites and even

Lydia and Egypt. Had all these peoples attacked simultaneously, Assyria would have been overwhelmed. Fortunately, the plot was discovered in time. In a strongly worded proclamation, Ashurbanipal warned the people of Babylon:

'Regarding the empty words which this false brother told you, I have heard all that he has said. They are nothing but wind. Do not believe him . . . Do not, for a moment, listen to his lies. Do not contaminate your good name, which is unsullied before me and before the whole world, nor make yourselves sinners against the divinity.'[36]

But the Babylonians refused to listen, and the King of Assyria marched against his brother. For three years, says a Babylonian chronicle, 'the war went on and there were perpetual battles'.[37] In the end, Shamash-shum-ukîn lost hope, set fire to his own palace and perished in the flames (648 BC). Sumer and Akkad were pacified and a Chaldaean noble, Kandalanu, was appointed viceroy of Babylon. At the same time, Ashurbanipal proceeded to punish the other rebels and became at once entangled in a war against the Arabs who had not only lent their support to Shamash-shum-ukîn, but were continuously raiding the western vassal-states. It was a difficult war, waged against elusive enemies fighting bravely and vanishing in a dreadful desert 'where parching thirst is at home, where there are not even birds in the sky'. Yet, here again, the Assyrian army accomplished marvels: Uate' and his allies, the Nabataeans—who already dwelt around the Dead Sea—were defeated; Abiate' and his Qedar tribe were surrounded, cut off from water wells and forced 'to cut open their camels and drink blood and filthy water against their thirst'. Another Uate', son of Hazail, was caught and, a ring in his jaw and a collar around his neck, was 'made to guard the bar at the east gate at Nineveh'. The booty taken in this campaign was such, says Ashurbanipal, that:

'Camels were bought within my country for less than one shekel of silver on the market place. The *sutammu*-workers received camels and (even) slaves as a present, the brewer as baksheesh, the gardener as an additional payment!'[38]

The Arabs subdued, Ashurbanipal sent his troops against his former protégé, the King of Elam, who had accepted bribes from the rebellious King of Babylon and given him assistance. The vicissitudes of this long Elamite war, the plots and revolutions which brought three princes in succession to the throne in Susa, are wearisome details that have no place here. Suffice it to say that in 639 BC, the Assyrians won the last battle. The land of Elam was devastated entirely and its capital city thoroughly plundered. This, incidentally, was mere retaliation, for among the spoil were found 'the silver, gold, property and goods of Sumer and Akkad and of the whole of Babylonia, which the former Kings of Elam had carried off in some seven raids'. The ziqqurat of Susa was destroyed, its sanctuaries violated, its gods taken captive or 'thrown to the winds'. The vanquished Elamites were even chased beyond the grave, and their country, symbolically, erased from the map:

The sepulchre of their earlier and later kings who did not fear Assur and Ishtar, my lords, and who had plagued the kings, my fathers, I destroyed, I devastated, I exposed to the sun. Their bones, I carried off to Assyria. I laid restlessness upon their shades. I deprived them of food-offerings and libations of water.

For a distance of a month and twenty-five days' journey I devastated the provinces of Elam. Salt and *sihlu* (a prickly plant) I scattered over them ... The dust of Susa, Madaktu, Haltcmash and the rest of their cities, I gathered together and took to Assyria ... The noise of people, the tread of cattle and sheep, the glad shouts of rejoicing, I banished from its fields. Wild asses, gazelles and all kinds of beasts of the plain, I caused to lie down among them, as if at home.'39

Thus were avenged countless insults and thus settled a three-thousand-year-old quarrel between Elamites and Mesopotamians.

Shortly after the sack of Susa, Ashurbanipal celebrated his triumph. From his sumptuous palace of Nineveh, this learned, magnificent and ruthless monarch could contemplate 'the whole world' prostrate at his feet. Three Elamite princes and a 'king of Arabia' were, literally, harnessed to his chariot. His treacherous brother had met with a death appropriate to his crimes and a puppet king governed the Babylonians. The proud merchants of Tyre and Arvad, the stiff-necked Jews,40 the restive Aramaeans, had been subjugated. The Mannai had been 'smashed' and the Cimmerians kept at bay. The rulers of Tabal and Cilicia, at first hostile, had brought their daughters to the royal couch. For having aided Psammetichus, Gyges of Lydia had seen his country set afire by the wild warriors of the North and lost his life, but now Ardys, his son, was asking as a favour to bear the Assyrian yoke. Nineveh was overflowing with the booty taken in Memphis, Thebes, Susa and countless other cities, and the 'great name of Ashur' was respected and feared from the green shores of the Aegean to the burning sands of Arabia. Never had the Assyrian empire looked so strong, the Assyrian might so invincible. And yet, how many shadows were there to this dazzling picture! The rich land of Egypt lost for ever; Elam conquered but turned into ruins; Babylonia devastated and inflamed with hatred for the Assyrians; the Phoenicians enslaved and losing their maritime and colonial empire to their Greek rivals; the vassal princes unreliable; the Assyrian army tired and depleted by a century of hard and bloody wars; the frontiers brought back from the Nile to the Dead Sea, from Mount Ararat to the first folds of the Taurus, from the Caspian Sea to the Zagros range; and beyond the Zagros, doubtful allies—the Scythians—and redoubtable foes—the Medes. The Assyrian empire, despite appearances, was weaker than it had ever been, and many must have thought secretly what the Israelite prophets dared to proclaim:

> 'And it shall come to pass
> that all they that look upon thee
>   shall flee from thee,
> and say: 'Nineveh is laid waste:
>   who will bemoan her? . . .
> There shall the fire devour thee;
> the sword shall cut thee off,
> it shall eat thee up like a cankerworm. . . .
> There is no healing of thy bruise;
> thy wound is grievous:
> all that hear the bruit of thee
>   shall clap the hands over thee:
> for upon whom hath not thy wickedness
>   passed continually?'[41]

CHAPTER XXI

THE GLORY OF ASSYRIA

THE reign of Ashurbanipal, like the reign of Hammurabi, is a momentous period in the history of ancient Iraq and calls for a pause. Having described at length how the Assyrian empire was formed, to be logical we should now examine what went on behind the façade of wars and diplomatic moves. What was, for instance, the social and economic structure of this vast political unit, embracing the entire Fertile Crescent and stretching—at least for a while—from the Caspian Sea to the Nile valley? What were the materials, the routes and the volume of its internal and external trades? What ties linked, in time of peace, Nineveh with the vassal-states? What influence did the Assyrian domination have on the material and spiritual life of the Babylonians, Syrians, Iranians and other subject peoples and on the life of the Assyrians themselves? In short, what *was* the Assyrian empire?

The answer to this question can only be found in the comparative study of a very large number of administrative, legal and economic texts from various parts of the empire, but unfortunately these texts are not yet available in sufficient quantity. At the present time, most of our information is obtained from business documents and contracts found in the ruins of Assur, Nineveh and Kalhu and belonging to the archives of palaces and temples.[1] But because of their relatively small number and limited scope these documents do not reflect the economic conditions prevalent throughout the whole Assyrian empire any more than the spacious houses of the rich citizens of Assur and Khorsabad[2] reflect the standard of living of the average Assyrian. Much is to be expected from the excavations of secondary cities and villages, and it must be mentioned that one of our main sources for the study of land ownership and tenure is a census carried out by the local authorities of Harran. Outside Assyria proper there is little to be gleaned. For a variety of reasons, the period of Assyrian rule in Babylonia is far from being as copiously documented as the following Neo-Babylonian and Achaemenian periods, so that little can be learned from a survey of the economic texts dispersed in several publications. As for the peripheral areas of the empire—such as Syria, Phoenicia, Palestine or the provinces situated in the Taurus or the Zagros—they have, up to now, remained silent, partly because very few of the main administrative centres have been excavated or even located on the map, and partly because most business transactions, from the eighth century onwards, were couched in Aramaic on parchment or papyrus and have completely disappeared.

It will therefore be many years before the social and economic history of the Near East under Assyrian rule can be written—if indeed it can ever be written—and rather than embark upon an impossible synthesis of elements which simply do not exist, we shall confine ourselves to a brief survey of the best known aspects of the Assyrian civilization, starting with the three factors of Assyria's vanished might and everlasting glory: the state, the army, the arts. In a second chapter, we shall take advantage of Ashurbanipal's famous library to describe the stage reached by the various Mesopotamian sciences in the seventh century BC. By so doing we hope to dispel an impression which is all too readily gained from the reading of endless war-records: it would be utterly wrong to regard as a nation of bloodthirsty ruffians led by megalomaniac tyrants what was, in fact, a great people and the most civilized of its time.

THE ASSYRIAN STATE

'Great king, mighty king, king of the Universe, king of the country of Assur', the man who sat on the throne in Nineveh embodied all the overwhelming power of a preying nation and assumed the highest religious and governmental responsibilities. The officials who assisted him, the provincial governors who obeyed his orders, the ambassadors who conveyed his messages were not his ministers but merely his 'servants'. In many ways, the king was the state. Yet the difference between an Ashurbanipal, absolute master of millions of people, and the *ensi* of an early Sumerian city state, who ruled over a few acres of land, lay in the extent of their authority, not in its nature. The original principle of kingship by divine election had been carried on through twenty-three centuries, and in theory the King of Assyria was only a human being selected amongst others to act on behalf of the gods for the benefit of the community.[3] He was the earthly representative and instrument of Ashur, just as Gudea was the representative and instrument of Ningirsu. Indeed, before Shamshi-Adad I, in the eighteenth century BC, took the title of 'king' (*sharrum*), all the early rulers of Assyria called themselves *ishakkum* (=*ensi*) of the god Ashur, and this appellation remained for a long time in the long list of Assyrian royal titles.

The principle of divine election would have opened the door to endless dynastic crises had it not been tempered by the strong hereditary character of the Assyrian monarchy. The reigning sovereign chose his successor from among his sons and had him accepted by the other members of the royal family, the court officials, the nobles and the vassal-princes. Admittedly, the god Ashur was supposed to have inspired his choice, and the gods Sin and Shamash, consulted by means of an oracle, proclaimed: 'Verily, he is your replacement!'; but we know that this was a mere formality. To be the son of a king conferred a right to kingship, and in their inscriptions, several Assyrian monarchs take great pride in their long line of royal ancestors going back, in some cases, to the mythical hero Adapa.

Once chosen, the crown prince left his father's palace and entered the *bît redûti*, or 'House of Succession', situated in Tarbisu (modern Sherif Khan), on the Tigris, a few miles upstream of Nineveh. There he was prepared for his royal functions and gradually entrusted with important military and administrative duties, which included replacing the king as head of the state in time of war. Some princes received a very complete education. Ashurbanipal, for instance, describes his scholarly and military training as follows:

'The art of the Master Adapa I acquired: the hidden treasure of all scribal knowledge, the signs of heaven and earth . . . and I have studied the heavens with the learned masters of oil divination; I have solved the laborious problems of division and multiplication, which were not clear; I have read the artistic script of Sumer and the obscure Akkadian, which is hard to master, taking pleasure in the reading of the stones from before the flood . . . This is what was done of all my days: I mounted my steed, I rode joyfully, I went up to the hunting lodge (?). I held the bow, I let fly the arrow, the sign of my valour. I hurled heavy lances like a javelin. Holding the reins like a driver, I made the wheels go round. I learned to handle the *arîtu* and the *kababu* shields like a heavy-armed bowman . . . At the same time, I was learning royal decorum, walking in the kingly ways. I stood before the king, my begetter, giving commands to the nobles. Without my consent, no governor was appointed; no prefect was installed in my absence.'4

Eventually, the prince's father died, mourned by all Assyrians. He was buried, not in Nineveh or Kalhu, but in the oldest capital city of the kingdom, Assur, where five heavy sarcophagi of stone, which once contained the bodies of Ashur-bêl-kala, Ashurnasirpal, Shamshi-Adad V and, perhaps, Sennacherib and Esarhaddon's wife, Esharhamat, but which had been plundered in antiquity, were found in vaulted chambers underneath the Old Palace.5 The coronation followed the royal funeral after a short interval and took place in the same city. It was a simple ceremony. Carried on a portable throne and preceded by a priest who called out: 'Ashur is king! Ashur is king!' the crown prince went to Ekur, the temple of the national god. He entered the sanctuary, offered a gold bowl full of oil, a *mana* of silver and a richly embroidered garment. Prostrate before the deity, he was anointed by the high-priest and given the insignia of kingship: 'the crown of Ashur and the sceptre of Ninlil',* whilst these words were pronounced:

'The diadem on thy head—may Ashur and Ninlil, the lords of
    the diadem, put it upon thee for a hundred years.
Thy foot in Ekur and thy hands stretched towards Ashur, thy
    god—may they be favoured.

* The goddess Ninlil, originally the female counterpart of Enlil, was the spouse of the god Ashur.

Before Ashur, thy god, may thy priesthood and the priesthood of
  thy sons find favour.
With thy straight sceptre make thy land wide.
May Ashur grant thee quick satisfaction, justice and peace'!6

The new king then proceeded to the palace, where the nobles
and officials did homage to him and relinquished their badges of
office. The gesture, however, was purely symbolic: as they had
been appointed beforehand, they were immediately reinstated.
We may safely assume that the ceremony was followed by public
rejoicing.

The King of Assyria governed in much the same way as all
his predecessors, although the state letters suggest that more
initiative was left to local authorities than, for instance, in the
days of Hammurabi. Day by day, the king was kept informed of
all matters of importance arising within the empire and in the
foreign countries; he gave orders and advice, appointed adminis-
trators, dealt with complaints, received and entertained high
officials and foreign ambassadors, and carried on a voluminous
correspondence with the aid of an army of scribes. As the supreme
chief of the army, he drew up plans for military campaigns,
inspected the troops and often personally conducted the operations. Off the battlefield, he displayed his courage and skill by
shooting wild game with the bow from his chariot, or by fighting
lions with the spear in the palace grounds. Office work, receptions,
hunting, these activities would be comparable to those of a
modern head of state but for the fact that the king of Assyria was
also a priest and, as such, was the slave of a complicated system
of magico-religious practices which took much of his time and
added to the already heavy burden of his daily tasks. As the first
servant of the gods and head of the clergy, he saw that temples
were built or maintained, appointed some of the priests, and took
an active part in the main religious ceremonies of Assyria and
Babylonia, such as the feast of the New Moon or the New Year
Festival, and in certain rituals which seem to have been designed
especially for him, in particular the *tâkultu* ('eating') ritual—a
banquet offered to all the gods in exchange for their protection—
and the *bît rimki* ('bath-house') ritual—a royal bath during which
prayers were addressed to various deities.7 As the representative

of his people, the king was 'manipulated like a talisman—or he became the scapegoat charged before the gods with all the sins of the community'.[8] He had to submit to occasional fasting, ritual shaving and other humiliations, and when the omens were desperately bad for Assyria, he escaped death only through the subterfuge of a 'substitute king'. We have already seen (page 153) an example of this strange Mesopotamian institution in the Isin-Larsa period. A letter written during the reign of Ashurbanipal alludes to a similar situation:[9] it appears that a certain Damqi, the son of the superintendent of Akkad, had been chosen by a prophetess in a trance, given a lady of the court in marriage and put to death with his wife after a short 'reign'. This was but an extreme and exceedingly rare application of a widespread belief. The Mesopotamians believed that the gods expressed their will in many ways and were constantly on the watch for signs and portents. Whether it was based on the movements of stars and planets, the interpretation of dreams and of natural phenomena, the configuration of the liver of sacrificed sheep, the flight of birds, the birth of monsters, the behaviour of drops of oil thrown on water, or the aspect of flames, divination was, in Assyria, a highly developed and official 'science'.[10] The king was duly warned, verbally or by letter, of favourable and unfavourable omens, and no decision of importance was taken without first consulting the barû-priests (or diviners), or the royal astrologers. Here are two examples taken from the royal correspondence:

Bêl-ushezib writes to Esarhaddon:

'When a star shines forth like a torch from the sunrise and in the sunset fades away, the army of the enemy will attack in force.

'When the south wind rises suddenly and having risen continues, and as it continues, becomes a gale, and from a gale increases to a tempest—a day of destruction—the prince, on whatever expedition he goes, will obtain wealth.'[11]

From Zakir to Ashurbanipal:

'On the 15th day of the month of Tebet, in the middle watch, there was an eclipse of the moon. It began on the east (side) and turned to the west. The evil disturbance which is in the land of Amurru and its territory is its own harm. The disturbance is the fault of the King of Amurru and his land, for allowing the enemy of the king, my lord, to be in the land of Amurru. Let the king, my lord, do as he wishes. The hand of the king, my lord, shall capture him. The king shall accomplish his defeat . . .'[12]

And here are the conclusions of an observation made on a sheep's liver at the king's request (the obscure technical terms refer to details on the surface of the liver):

'Summarising: the "path" is double; the left one crosses over the right one; there is no KAL; one "digit" on the side of the "station"; the posterior part of the liver is damaged on the right side; there is a SA.TI on the "crown".
Total: five unfavourable signs;
            not one single favourable sign;
                  (the result) is unfavourable.'[13]

It would be a mistake, however, to think that the home and foreign policy of Assyria was ruled by superstition, when all we know of her history bears the print of realism. Astrologers and diviners gave the king a general set of circumstances, within which he felt free to 'do as he wished', and there were even cases when he asked for several omens in succession until he obtained one that fitted his plans.

In theory an absolute monarch, the king could neither reign nor govern without the consent and support of the Assyrian aristocracy, the *mâr banûti* ('sons of creation'). To them the monarch presented the heir of his choice and on whether they accepted him or not depended the domestic peace of the kingdom. The revolutions which followed the reigns of Shalmaneser III and Sennacherib, for instance, were essentially due to some of the nobles supporting a candidate other than the crown prince. The generals, high priests and provincial governors appointed by the king came exclusively from the upper class of society, and on their loyalty to the throne depended the cohesion of the empire and the regular functioning of its government. Little is known of the central administration because the titles borne by the high officials do not always correspond to their functions and because these functions were far from being strictly defined. There were no ministers in the modern sense of the term, but a group of advisers among whom the four or five highest officials of the kingdom: the *turtanu* (commander-in-chief), the *rab shaqê* (chief cup-bearer), the *nâgir ekalli* (palace superintendent), the *abarakku* and the *shaknu*. With the exception of the turtanu, none of these officials appears to have specialized in a particular task. Appointed for 30 years—which, in antiquity, was equivalent to a lifetime—and granted vast territories for their sustenance, they were dignitaries rather than civil servants. Their order of precedence is given by the lists of *limmu* (eponyms), since each of them in turn gave his name to the first five years of the reign, the accession year bearing the name of the king and the other years the names of provincial governors. The great dignitaries possessed large houses in the centre of the capital city and, like the queen mother and the king's sons and daughters, they had their own court, a replica in miniature of the huge royal court housed in the royal palace, which employed hundreds of men and women. All these people lived on their own lands or on the vast estates belonging to the crown and received their share of war booty and of the multiple taxes levied in Assyria and in the vassal-countries.[14] As the empire grew in size, so did the courts of Nineveh. There is no doubt that, under the Sargonids, they were swollen beyond measure and utterly corrupt; they had become parasites of the State and the centres of constant intrigue.

Immediately after the nobles came the *ummanê* ('experts'), a term covering all free men with a definite profession, such as bankers, merchants, physicians, scribes, artisans, etc. Organized in guilds similar to those of our Middle Ages, they practised in separate quarters of the town, trained apprentices and handed down their business to their sons. Since the prosperity of the kingdom rested upon them, their importance was almost equal to that of the nobles and, although of mixed blood—like all large capital cities, Nineveh had many foreigners—they were treated by the king with considerable respect. The 'people of Assyria' who sided with Esarhaddon in his struggle for the throne, the 'City and its inhabitants' to which Sargon addressed the account of his campaign in Kurdistan were this Assyrian 'bourgeoisie'. The *mushkênû* of the Old Babylonian period had disappeared as a social class, though the term remained with the meaning 'under-privileged', 'miserable', as in Arabic *meskin*. Very low in the scale of society were the *hupshi*, an ill-defined class apparently made up of non-professional men working as agricultural labourers or regular soldiers, and the slaves (*ardê*), recruited as a rule amongst the prisoners of war and, therefore, increasingly numerous. The word 'slave' has detestable connotations, but, even in Assyria, slavery was not such a terrible condition as is commonly believed. If slaves could be bought and sold (their price ranged from 10 shekels to more than one *mana* of silver under the reign of Ashurbanipal), it appears from legal documents that some of them at least could learn a profession, acquire property, borrow grain or money, bear witness in court and even possess their own slaves. A few of them occasionally succeeded in reaching fairly high administrative posts.[15]

Widely different in wealth, culture and social standing, the various classes of Assyrian society shared a common duty: they were at the king's disposal for the execution of the great public works and for the 'national industry' of Assyria, war.

THE ASSYRIAN ARMY

Called-up almost every year during three centuries, driven from the snow-capped mountains of Armenia and Iran to the swamps of the Sea-Land and the burning sands of Egypt, indefatigable and nearly always victorious, the army was the unrivalled instrument of Assyrian might.[16] Like the Macedonian phalanx and the Roman legion, the secret of its success lay in the quality of its troops, the superiority of its weapons and, as we may well imagine, the rigidity of its discipline.

Originally, the Assyrian army was recruited among the peasants of northern Iraq, a mixed race of born warriors who combined the boldness of the bedouin with the tenacity of the farmer and the toughness of the highlander. As the theatre of operations grew wider and the enemy stronger, this army of conscription became numerically insufficient and we have seen (page 254) that Tiglath-pileser III created a permanent army made up mostly of troops levied in the peripheral districts of the empire by the provincial governors: horsemen from Iran and the Aramaean settlements of Babylonia, camel-drivers from Arabia, infantrymen from Anatolia and Syria-Palestine. In addition, certain tribes, such as the

PLATE 28

A. Statue of Ashurnasirpal, King of Assyria (884–859 B C). This impressive alabaster statue, 40 inches high, was found intact by Layard, just over a century ago, in the temple of Ninurta at Nimrud (ancient *Kalhu*.)

B. The 'Black Obelisk' of Shalmaneser III, King of Assyria (858–824 B C). Tributes are brought to the Assyrian monarch, and submissive princes fall prostrate at his feet.

PLATE 29. Fragment of the Bronze Gates from the palace of Shalmaneser III at Imgur-Enlil (Balawat). The Assyrian army has reached the sources of the Tigris. Animals are being brought to sacrifice. At the point where the river emerges, a sculptor chisels a royal stele.

Ituai, were exempted from taxes in return for regular service. The free men of Assyria could still be called upon when necessary, but many of them could send a slave as a substitute, or could afford the pay of a *hupshi*. Later, the vassal-countries contributed important contingents, and groups of Medes, Cimmerians and Scythians, attracted by the prospect of booty, joined the Assyrian army as mercenaries in ever increasing numbers. Under Esarhaddon and Ashurbanipal, it had become 'une cohue à la Xerxes'[17] and had lost a great deal of its cohesion and dash. This may explain to some extent the rapidity and apparent ease with which it was finally defeated.

Despite the wealth of war-records that have survived, we know surprisingly little about the size, organization and tactical methods of the army. The number of soldiers engaged in action is very rarely given—Ashurnasirpal once speaks of 50,000 men; at the battle of Qarqar, Shalmaneser III fielded 120,000 men to the enemy's 70,000 troops—and, if the enemy losses are grossly inflated, the casualties suffered by the Assyrians are practically never mentioned. There are several gaps in our knowledge of the military hierarchy: from the *turtanu* and the *rab shaqê* (who often acted as his lieutenant), we pass almost immediately to the 'captains of seventy' and the 'captains of fifty'. We learn, however, that there were various grades among the cavalry officers, for instance, and that the king's bodyguard, the 'dagger-men' and other units had their own 'colonels'. The battles are invariably described in vague, though colourful terms, so that we are left in the dark as to the tactics applied, and only on rare occasions do we find references to ambushes and surprise attacks.[18] All considered, our main source of information remains the innumerable scenes of war sculptured on slabs in the palaces of Nimrud, Khorsabad and Nineveh or carved in 'repoussé' in the bronze gates of Balawat. The infantrymen depicted fall into two categories: light infantry (bowmen and slingers) and heavy infantry (lancers). The light infantrymen were clad in a short tunic and had no defensive weapon, whereas the lancers were protected by a coat-of-mail and by a round or oblong shield, sometimes taller than themselves. Slingers were, as a rule, bare-headed, but archers and lancers wore a tall conical helmet, or, more rarely, a crested helmet resembling the later Greek one. Besides their distinctive weapons,[19] most infantrymen carried a short sword, a dagger or a mace. All of them, at least since Tiglathpileser III, had half-boots, laced in front. Cavalrymen wore a similar 'uniform' and were armed with a small bow or a long lance. They rode without saddle or stirrups but, in late Sargonid times, horses were protected by armour, so that both riders and mounts strangely resemble our Medieaval knights. A third category of soldiers fought on light, two-wheeled chariots drawn by two or three horses, each chariot carrying three or four men: a driver, one or two bowmen and two shield-bearers. Male and female servants and wagons loaded with supplies and baggage followed the army in campaign. Rivers were crossed either in ordinary boats, or in reed boats sealed with bitumen (the *qûfa* of the Arabs, still in use on the upper Tigris), or on inflated goatskins.

One of the major assets of the Assyrian army was its equipment in efficient siege-weapons. Many towns, particularly in Armenia and Syria, were strongly fortified and to capture them was no mean task. But the army included an important corps of pioneers who filled in the moats, threw earthworks against the ramparts and dug tunnels, whilst the assailants shot arrows from towers, battered weak points, doors or walls with enormous rams and progressed under cover of large shields. The besieged enemy tried to resist by hurling oil fire and lighted torches on the war engines or by entwining the rams with chains. The final assault was made through breaches or from ladders. Once the town had been taken and looted and its inhabitants massacred or captured, it was either set on fire, dismantled and razed, or fortified anew, depending on its strategic interest.

War being an object of immense pride to the Assyrian monarchs, the official sculptors have depicted it in all its multiple aspects and with a profusion of detail. Scores of reliefs, obviously intended to illustrate the written descriptions that ran endlessly on orthostats, on steles, on monoliths, on mountain rocks and around statues, represent soldiers parading, fighting, killing, plundering, pulling down city-walls and escorting prisoners. In this series of pictorial war-records without equivalent in any country, among this almost monotonous display of horrors, must be set apart some reliefs which have no parallel in the inscriptions: those that show soldiers at rest in their camps and under their tents, grooming horses, slaughtering cattle, cooking food, eating, drinking, playing games and dancing. These little scenes, teeming with life, give the tragedy of war a refreshing human touch. Through the ruthless killer of yore emerges a familiar and congenial figure: the humble, simple, light-hearted, eternal 'rank-and-file'.

ASSYRIAN ARTS

The Assyrian army has vanished long ago, routed and destroyed in the great disaster of the years 614–609 BC, but the monuments of Assyrian art have mercifully survived, no less impressive by their quality than by their number.

Ever since the colossi of stone 'whose icy eyes had contemplated Nineveh' reached Europe for the first time, over a hundred years ago, the words 'Assyrian arts' are suggestive of sculpture and, particularly, of reliefs. Sculpture in the round is poorly represented on the banks of the Tigris during the first millennium BC. For some unknown reason, the capital cities of Assyria have yielded very few statues and the best ones—such as the statue of Ashurnasirpal in the British Museum—are conventional, lifeless and inferior in many respects to the works of the great Neo-Sumerian masters. Reliefs, on the contrary, are always interesting, often attain to real beauty and undoubtedly represent 'the greatest and most original achievement of the Assyrians'.[20]

The technique of relief is almost as old as Mesopotamia itself, but it was for a long time confined to steles set up in temples. It found its first expression in the 'hunting stele' of Warka (Uruk or Proto-Literate period) and was carried on, through such masterpieces as the 'Stele of the Vultures' of Eannatum and the 'Stele of Victory' of Narâm-Sin, down to the Kassite and Middle Babylonian kudurrus. The Assyrians followed the tradition with a few religious subjects (e.g. the god Ashur as a vegetation-god in the Berlin Museum[21]), then broke away from it with representations of the king. The imperial steles, usually erected in conquered countries to commemorate Assyrian victories, are, at the best, honest works of art, more remarkable perhaps for their historical value than for the quality of their execution. Reliefs carved on slabs, on the other hand, are probably of foreign origin. The idea of applying sculptured decoration to architectural elements seems to have originated in Anatolia, among the Hittites who, as early as the second millennium B C, adorned the walls of their palaces with 'orthostats'. In the hills of their own country, the Assyrians found in abundance a calcareous rock, rather porous and brittle but sufficient for most purposes, or they imported better materials from abroad. They had unlimited labour to quarry and transport the blocks, excellent artists to draw the subjects, skilful artisans to handle the chisel. They adopted the Hittite invention and raised it to an extraordinary degree of perfection. The colossal, yet lively winged bull-men and lion-men who guarded the gates of their palaces and seemed to emerge from them are treated with a harmonious sobriety in their mass and a wealth of precision in their detail which are probably unique. The slabs carved in low relief which lined rooms and corridors and were made to be looked at more closely are striking for the perfect balance of their composition, the sharpness of observation they reveal— especially where animals are concerned—and the sense of move- ment which pervades them. This is really 'grand art', superior to all that the world had already produced in this domain and second only to the sculpture of classical Greece.

It is obviously impossible for us to give here even a brief analysis of Assyrian reliefs.[22] We would like, however, to under- line a peculiarity of this form of art which sets it apart from similar productions of the ancient Near East. All the monuments of Mesopotamia had hitherto possessed a religious significance and revolved, in one way or other, around the divinity. In Assyrian sculpture, however, the central subject is usually the king—not a king supernatural in heroism and in size as the god-king of Egyptian reliefs, but a human, albeit dominating and exceedingly valorous, monarch. Moreover, whilst the king is portrayed parading, hunting, resting, receiving homage or tribute, or lead- ing his armies in war, he is practically never shown performing his priestly functions. Genii, demi-gods, heroes are also repre- sented, but the gods are conspicuously absent—except on rock sculptures—or reduced to their symbols: a spear stuck in an altar or a winged disc in the sky. Since kingship in Assyria was just as immersed in religion as in Sumer and Babylonia, there is only one possible explanation: the sculptured slabs which adorned the royal palaces were a form of political propaganda; narrative as much as decorative, they were there not to please or placate the gods, but to inspire respect, admiration and fear in the human race. From a general point of view, the work of the Assyrian sculptors appears as one of the first attempts ever made to 'humanize' the arts and to deprive them of magical or religious meaning inherited from prehistoric times.

It was known for a long time that some statues and reliefs were painted. On the other hand, brightly coloured glazed bricks bearing ornamental or representative motifs were used in temples and palaces and formed, as it were, a transition between reliefs and frescoes.[23] On the basis of recent excavations, we may now assume that mural paintings adorned the walls of most, if not all, official buildings and of many private residences. Because the paint was laid on fragile plaster, it has generally disappeared, but at Khorsabad, Nimrud and Tell Ahmar (Til-Barsip), large fragments have been copied in situ or removed to museums. Mural paintings, like reliefs, had deep roots in the country[24] and, at least in Assyria, favoured profane subjects. These varied according to the size and function of the room. They ranged from simple friezes of geometrical designs to elaborate panels covering the the greater part of the walls and combining floral motifs, animals, scenes of war and hunting and royal effigies, arranged in horizontal bands. From the examples recovered, Assyrian painting appears as being by no means inferior to Assyrian sculpture, and the frescoes of Tell Ahmar, recently published in colour for the first time,[25] display a great freedom of expression as well as high qualities of craftsmanship.

The Assyrians were, or perhaps we should say employed, experts in metal-work and have left us some very fine pieces of bronze, gold and silver plates, vessels and ornaments of various kinds. Their female slaves, working in royal factories, wove carpets of elaborate design and embroidered with fairy hands, as can be seen from the robes worn by the kings and their courtiers and reproduced in stone in the most minute detail. Their stone-cutters, contrary to their sculptors, preferred the traditional religious and mythological motifs to profane subjects, and the Neo-Assyrian cylinder-seals, engraved with extreme skill and

care, exhibit a cold, though often fascinating beauty. But among
the so-called 'minor arts', a place of honour must be given to the
ivories found in Assyria.

Known in Mesopotamia in Early Dynastic times,[26] ivory-work
fell into disuse to reappear in the middle of the second millennium
in countries under Egyptian influence: Palestine (Lachish, Megiddo) and the Mediterranean coast (Ugarit). The prosperity of the
Phoenician cities, of the Israelite kingdom and of the Aramaean
states of Syria and their intensive commercial relations with
Egypt (which supplied the raw material) account for the extraordinary development of this form of art not only in Syria-
Palestine (Samaria, Hama), but also in Assyria, Iran (Ziwiyeh)
and Armenia (Toprak Kale) at the beginning of the first millennium BC. There is no doubt that the majority of the ivories discovered at Assur, Khorsabad, Arslan Tash (Hadâtu) and particularly
at Nimrud—the richest site of all[27]—had been received as tribute
or taken as booty from the western districts of the empire. But
a number of pieces, purely Assyrian in style and inspiration, must
have been made in Assyrian workshops, though it is impossible
to decide whether they were executed by imported Syro-Phoeni-
cian artists or by the Mesopotamians themselves. Applied to the
decoration of chairs, thrones, beds, screens and doors, or shaped
into boxes, bowls, vases, spoons, pins, combs and handles, ivory
was worked in many different ways: engraved, sculptured in
relief, in the round or in open-work, inlaid with semi-precious
stones, plain, painted or gold-plated. Not less remarkable was the
variety of the subjects treated. Beside the purely Egyptian motifs,
such as the birth of Horus or the goddess Hathor, there are
'women at the window', cows, deer and griffins which are more
specifically Phoenician in style, and animals fighting together,
heroes struggling with wild beasts, nude women or goddesses,
hunting scenes and processions which are regarded by the best
experts as partly Syrian and partly Mesopotamian. These subjects,
it is worth noticing, are emphatically peaceful. A few pieces
portray the stiff figure of 'the mighty King of Assur' alone or
accompanied by his soldiers, but those smiling women—the
admirable 'Mona Lisa' from Nimrud, for instance—those gay
musicians and dancers, those calm, enigmatic sphinxes, those
cows suckling their calves and, in a graceful, loving movement,

turning their heads to lick them, are pleasantly relaxing. Whether they were made in Assyria or not, the ivories throw a new light on the mentality of their owners. They bear witness that the Assyrians were sensitive to charm and delicacy just as their libraries testify to their taste for erudition.

CHAPTER XXII

THE SCRIBES OF NINEVEH

IN 1849, Sir Henry Layard, the pioneer of British archaeology
in Iraq, was excavating Sennacherib's palace in Nineveh
when he opened 'two large chambers of which the whole
area was piled a foot or more deep in tablets'.[1] Three years
later, Layard's assistant, Hormuz Rassam, made a similar discovery
on the same mound of Kuyunjik, in the palace of Sennacherib's
grandson, Ashurbanipal. In all, more than 25,000 tablets and
fragments were amassed and sent to the British Museum where
they form the richest collection of their kind in the world.[2]
On examination, it was found that 'Ashurbanipal's library'*
could be divided into two parts: on the one hand, 'archive
documents', such as letters, contracts, economic and historical
inscriptions; on the other hand, 'library documents' proper,
consisting of literary, religious and scientific compositions.
These form the most important part of the royal collection,
and their interest is further enhanced by the fact that many of
them are copies of ancient Sumerian and Babylonian tablets made
in Nineveh at the king's request. Several letters preserved in the
royal correspondence also afford evidence that the Kings of
Assyria were craving for culture and had organized a widespread
search for old inscriptions, particularly in the highly civilized
countries of Sumer and Akkad:

'When you receive this letter,' writes Ashurbanipal to a certain
Shaduna, 'take with you these three men (their names follow) and
the learned men of the city of Barsippa, and seek out all the
tablets, all those that are in their houses and all those that are
deposited in the temple Ezida. . . .

* Most tablets found in Sennacherib's palace belonged, in fact, to Ashurbanipal, this monarch having used his grandfather's residence in his earlier years.

'Hunt for the valuable tablets which are in your archives and which do not exist in Assyria and send them to me. I have written to the officials and overseers . . . and no one shall withhold a tablet from you; and when you see any tablet or ritual about which I have not written to you, but which you perceive may be profitable for my palace, seek it out, pick it up, and send it to me.'3

Royal palaces were not the only places in which valuable tablets were kept. All the capital cities and the main provincial towns of Assyria had temple libraries and even perhaps private libraries. There were important libraries at Assur and Nimrud, and recent Anglo-Turkish excavations at Sultan Tepe, near Harran, have brought to light a rich collection of literary and religious texts belonging to a priest of the moon-god Sin called Qurdi-Nergal and including, besides such well-known pieces as the Gilgamesh Epic, the Legend of Narâm-Sin and the 'Tale of the Righteous Sufferer', masterpieces of literature—like the beautiful 'Tale of the Poor Man of Nippur'—which were formerly unknown.4

Once the ancient tablets had been brought to Assyria, they were either kept as they were, or copied in the small, neat cuneiform script characteristic of the period. Many texts were partly or entirely rewritten and adapted to the fashion of the day, but others were copied to the letter, and it often happened in such cases that the scribe left in blank words or sentences which had been destroyed on the original, added his own commentary, or wrote in the margin *ul idi*, 'I do not understand', or *hepu labiru*, 'old break'. Sometimes the scribe did not impress his style into clay but into wax spread over ivory or wooden boards, several boards being bound together by means of metal hinges like a miniature folding screen. In 1953, a number of such writing boards, some of them still bearing traces of an astronomical composition, were discovered at Nimrud in a well where they had been thrown during the sack of the city.5 While administrative and commercial documents were usually stored in jars or baskets, library tablets seem to have been stored on shelves, but since they were invariably found scattered on the floors of ruined buildings, it is extremely difficult to understand the method of classification followed. We know, however, that tablets belonging to the same series were numbered, or ended with a catch-line announcing the first sentence of the next tablet. For instance, tablet III of *Enuma elish* (the Epic of Creation) ends with the sentence:

'They founded for him a princely chamber'

which opens the narrative in tablet IV. Tablet XI of the Assyrian version of 'Gilgamesh' has, at the end, the following 'colophon':

'Tablet XI of "He Who Saw Everything" (of the series of) Gilgamesh.
Written down according to the original and collated.
Palace of Ashurbanipal, King of the Universe, King of Assyria.'6

The diligence with which these written relics of the past were collected and the care with which they were preserved do honour not only to the scribes, but to the kings, their masters. Paradoxically, the Assyrians who caused so much destruction saved for posterity a great deal of the spiritual treasures of Sumer, Akkad and Babylon, and of their own country.

MESOPOTAMIAN SCIENCE

It is unlikely that Ashurbanipal's library was much used by the king himself. He might, for his lordly pleasure, have deciphered 'the stones from before the flood', or read the great epic tales— Gilgamesh, Etana, Adapa—but he hardly had the time or the inclination to read the thousands of tablets assembled on his orders. The palace library must have been accessible to the palace and temple scribes who could find there the reference document they required. It might have been part of an 'academy' (*bit mummi*, 'House of Knowledge'), such as flourished in various cities at various periods, perhaps founded to attract and fix in Nineveh the learned men of Mesopotamia. At their disposal were not only literary, historical and religious compositions in large number, but also philological works, lists of plants, animals and minerals, geographical lists, medical prescriptions, mathematical tables, astronomical observations, in a word, a corpus of scientific documents, an encyclopaedia, as it were, of Assyro-Babylonian knowledge. These documents are as invaluable to us as they were to the ancient scholars, though for different reasons, but while they call for a general survey of Mesopotamian science, alone they are insufficient for this purpose. We have therefore in this chapter made use of sources more recent or more ancient than the seventh-century Kuyunjik tablets, in particular scientific texts from Nippur, Tell Harmal, Assur and Uruk ranging from the end of the third millennium to approximately the third century B C.7

The Greeks who knew—and admired—the 'Chaldaeans' mostly as magicians and fortune-tellers have done considerable harm to their memory. It is true that magic in the broader sense of the term (i.e. words or actions purporting to influence supernatural forces) had always been closely associated with Sumero-Akkadian religion and that the diviner's art had been perfected and codified in Mesopotamia at a very early date,8 but the vulgarization of magical practices did not come into full play until the end of the pre-Christian era. Far from being the last word in Babylonian wisdom, witchcraft and popular astrology developed as a sign of decay in a declining civilization, and we now know for certain that Sumerians and Assyro-Babylonians alike were blessed with almost all the qualities required for a truly scientific attitude of mind. They had, first of all, an insatiable curiosity, the curiosity that prompted them to collect ancient tablets, establish museums of antiquities and bring home from distant countries rare species of plants and unknown animals. They had a patience, a devotion to detail apparent in all their activities, from the compilation of accounts to their works of art. They possessed an acute sense of observation, studied nature with intensity, recorded and correlated a vast amount of data, not so much for practical purposes as for the sake of pure knowledge, and, at least in some fields, went a long way on the road to discovery. Finally, their mathematics prove that they were capable of abstract thinking to a degree rarely found in pre-classical antiquity.

As soon as he went to school,9 the would-be Mesopotamian scribe had occasion to apply these inborn qualities. Teaching was essentially verbal—no textbook on any subject has ever been found—and therefore developed his auditive memory. Then, the intricacies of cuneiform writing, where each sign could be read as an ideogram or as a phonogram with several phonetic values, and the fact that two widely different languages—Sumerian and Akkadian—had to be mastered obliged him to embark at once upon fairly complex philological studies. Instead of an alphabet, he had to memorize long lists of signs with their names, their pronunciation and their meaning in both languages. Several of these 'syllabaries' have survived, most fortunately, since without them we could never have understood the Sumerian language.[10] In a second stage, the student made use of conjugation tables, of vocabularies—lists of objects, technical terms or expressions belonging to the same category—and of bi- or tri-lingual dictionaries including Sumerian dialects, Kassite, Hittite and, later, Greek. Of special interest are tablets engraved with archaic pictographic signs side by side with their Neo-Assyrian counterparts. Since pictograms had fallen into disuse about 2,600 years before these tablets were written and could hardly be of any practical value to the Assyrians, this is further proof of their love of pure research work. Science in general lay in the realm of the god Enki-Ea and was under the protection of the god Nabû, son of Marduk, while the goddess Nisaba, 'who in her hand holds the stylus', presided over the difficult and much honoured art of writing.

This system of education naturally inclined the Assyro-Babylonian scholar to record his observations and offer them to his colleagues and pupils in the form of lists. Mesopotamian zoology, botany and mineralogy, for instance, have come to us in vocabularies, sometimes disconcertingly arranged, nevertheless representing a serious effort towards the classification of a vast material.[11] Geographical texts consist mostly of lists of countries, mountains, rivers or cities, and of itineraries which are extremely useful to the modern historian, especially when they indicate in *bêru*, or 'double-hours' (approximately six miles) the distance between two towns. As far as we know, there were no actual maps, but plans of fields and cities have been recovered, the most interesting being a plan of Nippur which matches remarkably the survey of the ruins made by modern archaeologists. We also possess a rudimentary 'map of the world' on clay, dating from the sixth century BC: the earth is a flat surface bound by a circular 'Bitter River'; in the middle flows the Euphrates; unfamiliar countries at the four points of the compass are described in a few words, the northernmost being called 'land where the sun is never seen'—

which might suggest that the Babylonians had heard of the arctic winter night.[12] If we leave aside royal annals and building inscriptions which were really not historical but propaganda and votive texts, we see that history was also presented in tabular form: king lists, lists of eponyms and dynasties, synchronous lists, etc. Even Babylonian Chronicles, nearer to continuous historical narratives, are in fact no more than developed lists of events. In addition, we have mathematical and astronomical tables and, in medicine, lists of symptoms and prognoses—to say nothing of the lists of gods, temples, feasts, omens, etc. Indeed, Mesopotamian science has been called, somewhat derisively, 'a science of lists', but it must be emphasized that tuition being uniquely verbal, the documents that have survived are 'manuals' or 'vade-mecums' rather than textbooks. There is no doubt that the Assyro-Babylonians knew much more than it would appear: the transport and erection of huge blocks of stone, for instance, or the construction of long aqueducts postulate an advanced knowledge of several laws of physics; similarly, certain principles of chemistry, carefully hidden under secret recipes, were successfully applied in the preparation of drugs and pigments and the manufacture of coloured glass and enamelled bricks. Moreover, in at least two domains—mathematics and astronomy—we are able to understand the mental mechanism that presided over scientific development, and it is precisely in these fields that the Mesopotamians made their greatest strides.

MATHEMATICS AND ASTRONOMY

Our knowledge of Mesopotamian mathematics[13] is derived from two categories of texts: lists of numbers arranged in various ways (increasing and decreasing series, multiplication and division tables, etc.) and problems. Surprisingly, the majority of these problems are exercises for advanced students (or even possibly intellectual recreations) and not, as one would expect in a so-called 'primitive' or 'archaic' society, problems relating to architecture, land-surveying, irrigation and other matters of practical interest. The following examples are particularly demonstrative:

Problem No. 1

'I found a stone but did not weigh it; then I added one-seventh and I added one-eleventh. I weighed: one *mana*. What was the original weight of the stone? The weight of the stone was: 1 *mana*, 8 shekels and 22½ "lines".'14

Problem No. 2

'If somebody asks you thus: as much as the side of the square which I made I dug deep, and I extracted one *musaru* (603) and a half of volume of earth. My base (ground) I made a square. How deep did I go?

'You, in your procedure operate with 12. Take the reciprocal of 12 and multiply by 1,30,0,0 which is your volume. 7,30,0 you will see. What is the cube root of 7,30,0? 30 is the cube root. Multiply 30 by 1, and 30 you see. Multiply 30 by another 1, and 30 you see. Multiply 30 by 12, and 6,0 (360) you see. 30 is the side of your square, and 6,0 (360) is your depth.'15

The sentence introducing the first problem shows that it is purely hypothetical. The solution is given, but the way to reach it was, no doubt, verbally indicated by the teacher. In the second problem, on the contrary, the procedure is fully developed. It will be seen that Babylonian mathematicians were fully conversant with cube roots, and this as early as the seventeenth or eighteenth century BC, which is the date of this tablet. They also knew, of course, of square roots and were able to calculate the square root of 2 with only a very minute error (1·414213 instead of 1·414214). The calculations involved also point to the two main characteristics of Mesopotamian mathematics: they were based on the sexagesimal system and, while all systems of numeration used in antiquity (including the Roman system) were 'juxtapositional', they alone used a 'positional' system, that is to say a system where the value of a given numeral varies according to its position in the written number. (This is what we still do when we write, for instance, 3,333, the same numeral being worth 3,000, 300, 30 and 3 respectively.) Both the sexagesimal and the positional systems offered definite advantages for calculations, but unfortunately, the decimal system was also used within units of the sexagesimal, and the figure 'zero' was unknown until a very late date. The interpretation of Mesopotamian problems is therefore often fraught with difficulty, even for experts, and we must assume that, in many cases, the students were verbally supplied with the necessary indications.

Another point to be emphasized is that, without using symbols, Babylonian mathematicians operated by algebraical rather than by arithmetical methods. The terms of many of their problems show that they could only be solved by a process equivalent to the use of equations of the first or second degree. For instance, a problem like:[16]

'I have added 7 times the side of my square and 11 times its surface: the result is 6,15 (in sexagesimal numeration). Write down 7 and 11',

postulates the equation:

$$11x^2 + 7x = 6{,}15$$

It would also appear from some tablets that the Babylonians were familiar with functions and that their calculations occasionally involved serial, exponential and logarithmic relations. They thought in abstractions; they liked numbers for their own sake, not for their practical uses. For this reason, their geometry was much less advanced than their algebra. They were aware of some fundamental properties of the triangle, the rectangle and the circle, but failed in their attempts to demonstrate them and measured polygonal surfaces by rough approximation. When tablets are inscribed with geometrical figures, these are usually meant to illustrate arithmetical problems. Contrary to the Greeks, the Babylonians were less interested in the properties of lines, surfaces and volumes than in the intricate calculations suggested by their mutual relations.

Mathematics found in astronomy a wide field of application and gave this science a degree of precision unrivalled in antiquity.[17] The need for studying the movements of celestial bodies arose, in Mesopotamia, from a double preoccupation: metaphysical and chronological. The belief that what happened in heaven was reflected on earth, and the thought that, if planets and constellations were identified with gods, kings and countries, and if their mutual relations could be foreseen, it would be possible to predict the future alleviated, to some extent, the dramatic uncertainty which was at the root of Mesopotamian philosophy. Astrology, therefore, was the foundation of astronomy, although the system adopted was never rigid and left room for divine and human initiative, predetermination in the form of horoscopes appearing only during the Achaemenian period. On the other hand, the Mesopotamians had to solve the problem of the lunar calendar. As far as we can go back in the past, the cycle of the moon had been taken as a convenient means of measuring time. The year began on the first New Moon following the spring equinox, and was divided into 12 months of 29 or 30 days. Each day began at sunset and was divided into 12 'double-hours' (*bêru*), themselves divided into 60 'double-minutes'—a system which we still follow and owe to the Babylonians. Unfortunately, the lunar year is shorter than the solar year by approximately 11 days, so that, after 9 years, the difference amounts to one full season. Moreover, the lunar month began in the evening when the new moon was visible for the first time, but those who have lived in Iraq know that the Oriental sky is not always as clear as Europeans imagine and clouds, dust, or sandstorms may render this observation impossible. How then were the official astronomers to decide that the month had begun, and how could they calculate in advance the exact date and time at which any month would begin? What were, in other words, the laws of the lunar cycle and—since the motions of the moon are linked with those of the sun—what were the laws of the solar cycle?

The amazing results obtained by Mesopotamian astronomers in this field are not due, of course, to the perfection of their instruments—they had only the gnomon (a rudimentary sun-dial) the clepsydra (a clock worked by flow of water) and the polos (an instrument registering the shadow projected by a minute ball suspended over a half-sphere). They are due to constant, accurate observation and to the use of mathematics for the extrapolation of the data obtained. At an early date, the 'roads' of the sun and planets were determined and divided into twelve 'stations', themselves divided into thirty degrees (the origin of our Zodiac). We possess observations of Venus (Ishtar) written down under the First Dynasty of Babylon and detailed catalogues of stars from the eighth and seventh centuries BC. Soon, eclipses of the moon and, later, eclipses of the sun could be predicted with a fair degree of accuracy. For centuries the difficulty created by the

difference between the solar year and the lunar year was solved
arbitrarily, the king deciding that one or two intercalary months
should be added to the year, but in the eighth century BC, astronomers remarked that 235 lunar months made up exactly 19
solar years and, on their advice, King Nabû-nasir, in 747 BC,
decreed the intercalation of 7 extra months in 19 lunar years.
The 'Nabonassar calendar' became standardized between 388 and
367 BC.[18] Meanwhile, a considerable amount of work had been
done on the preparation of lunar, solar and stellar ephemerides.
The tables of new and full moons and of eclipses drawn by
Nabû-rimâni (the 'Naburianus' of Strabo) at the beginning of the
fourth century are incredibly accurate,[19] and the greatest of all
Babylonian astronomers, Kidinnu (Cidenas), who practised about
375 BC, gave the exact duration of the solar year with an error of
only 4 minutes and 32·65 seconds. His error in the value of the
motion of the sun from the node was actually smaller than that
made by the modern astronomer Oppolzer in 1887![20]

MEDICINE

No such precision can, of course, be expected from what is still
regarded as an art more than a science: medicine. Yet Mesopotamian medicine is worthy of a special study for three main
reasons: it is copiously documented, highly interesting and often
misunderstood.[21]

The Mesopotamians believed that disease was a punishment
inflicted by the gods upon men for their sins. The word 'sin'
should be taken here in a broad sense including not only crimes
and moral offences, but also small mistakes and omissions in the
performance of religious duties, or the unintentional breaking of
some taboo. The offended gods could strike directly. Thus, in the
Code of Hammurabi, the Babylonian boundary stones and the
political treaties of the ancient Near East, they are called upon
individually to send all kinds of 'grievous maladies' upon whoever would destroy or alter the document, and physicians as well
as priests recognized the 'hand' of various gods in the symptoms
exhibited by the patients. The gods could also allow demons to
take possession of the sick person, each demon attacking by
preference one part of the body, or they could let a man or

woman fall the victim of a spell cast by a sorcerer or witch.²²
Illness was therefore essentially an ethical defect, a black mark, a
condemnation which rendered man morally unclean as well as
physically unhealthy; and a moral ailment calling for a moral cure,
treatment was, in many cases, magical and religious. The *bâru*-
priest, or diviner, was asked to find out by all the methods at his
disposal the hidden sin responsible for the divine wrath, the
demons were exorcised by the *âshipu*-priest using magical rites
and incantations, and the gods were appeased through prayers
and sacrifices.

If Mesopotamian medicine had consisted of nothing but moral
catharsis, it would hardly deserve its name. But in recent years an
extensive study of the texts in our possession has shown it under
another, entirely different aspect. There were, in ancient Iraq,
true physicians who believed in the supernatural origin of most
diseases, but who also recognized the causative action of natural
factors such as dust, dirt, food or drink and even contagion; who
sometimes referred their patients to the *bâru* or the *âshipu*, but
who always observed the symptoms with extreme attention,
grouped them into diseases and applied chemical or instrumental
treatments. Side by side with the sacerdotal and magico-religious
medicine (*âshiputu*), there had always been, in Mesopotamia, a
rational and pragmatic medicine (*asûtu*).

The physician (*asû*) was neither priest nor witch-doctor, but a
professional man belonging to the upper middle-class of the
Assyro-Babylonian society. He spent years at school learning the
basic sciences of his time and further years with a senior colleague,
mastering his art. The Code of Hammurabi, where nine laws
concerning medicine (or rather, surgery) fix the price of certain
operations and pronounce mutilation and even death for professional faults (see above, page 170), gives the impression that
the medical profession was controlled by the state and throws
discredit on the ability of its members. But these laws are examples of judgements in exceptional cases, and there is no known
instance of their having ever been applied. In fact, physicians
were held in high esteem at all times and established their own
fees. Consultants of renown were in great demand, and we know
that royal courts exchanged doctors. Thus, Tushratta, King of
Mitanni in the fourteenth century, sent physicians to the pharaoh

Amenophis III, and medical experts from Babylon were despatched to the Hittite monarch Hattusilis III (1275–1250 BC).

We possess a considerable number of lists of symptoms and medical prescriptions written by physicians, and several letters addressed to or sent by doctors. From numerous tablets or fragments of tablets written between the eighth and the fifth centuries BC but belonging to the same series, Professor Labat has been able to reconstruct a complete 'treatise' of medical diagnosis and prognosis.[23] It comprised forty tablets and was divided into five 'chapters'. The first chapter, intended in fact for exorcists, gave an interpretation of the ominous signs which could be observed when proceeding to the patient's house. Thus:

'When the exorcist proceeds to the patient's house. . . . if he sees a black pig, this patient will die; (or) he will be cured after extreme suffering. . . . If he sees a white pig, this patient will be cured; (or) he will be in distress. . . . If he sees a red pig, this patient will [die?] on the 3rd month (or) on the 3rd day. . . .'[24]

Then came the description of a variety of symptoms grouped together by organs, by syndromes or diseases, and by order of occurrence. A last group of six tablets was devoted to gynaecological and infantile diseases. Throughout the treatise, emphasis was placed on prognosis rather than on diagnosis proper, and treatments were rarely indicated. Similar texts, or collections of texts, dealt with the diseases of certain organs only; others were more particularly concerned with therapeutics. Here are a few examples chosen among the diseases which can be easily identified:

Epilepsy
'If the (patient's) neck is constantly twisted to the left; if his hands and feet are outstretched; if his eyes facing the sky are wide open; if saliva drips from his mouth; if he snores; if he loses consciousness; if, at the end . . . it is an attack of *grand mal*; "hand" of Sin.'[25]

Vesical calculus
'If . . . for three days he has a stone of the bladder (*aban mushtinni*), this man will drink beer: (thus) the stone will dissolve; if this man, instead of drinking beer drinks much water, he will go to his destiny (i.e. die.)'[26]

Severe jaundice

'If the body of a man is yellow, his face yellow and black, and the surface of his tongue black, it is *ahhazu*. . . . For such a disease the physician should do nothing: this man will die; he cannot be cured.'[27]

While the diagnosis and prognosis of Mesopotamian physicians were a mixture of superstition and accurate observation, their therapeutics owed nothing to magic. The oldest 'pharmacopaeia' known to date is a collection of recipes dating from the Third Dynasty of Ur,[28] which describes the preparation of ointments, lotions and mixtures made from minerals and plants, and might have been written two or three hundred years ago. Drugs were administered in every possible way short of injections: mixtures, potions, inhalations, fumigations, instillations, ointments, liniments, poultices, enemas, suppositories. It is often impossible for us to identify some of the simples and salts which entered into their composition, but in many cases substances that have only recently fallen into disuse or that are still used in pharmacy can be recognized. In the following recipe, for instance, opium by mouth and emollients in local application are prescribed for urinary retention:

'Crush poppy seeds in beer and let the patient drink it. Grind some myrrh, mix it with oil and blow it into his urethra with a tube of bronze. Give the patient anemone crushed in *alappanu*-beer.'[29]

And here is the complex, though rational formula of a poultice to be applied in case of 'stricture of the lungs':

'Take . . . parts of the kidney of a sheep; $\frac{1}{2}$ *qa* of dates, 15 *kisal* of firtree turpentine, 15 *kisal* of pinetree turpentine, 15 *kisal* of laurel, 13 *kisal* of opopanax, 10 *kisal* of resin of galbanum, 7 *kisal* of mustard, 2 *kisal* of cantharis. . . . Grind these drugs in a mortar together with fat and dates. Pour the mixture on a gazelle's skin. Fold the skin. Put it on the painful area and leave it in place for three days. During that time the patient shall drink sweet beer. He shall take his food very hot and stay in a warm place. On the fourth day, remove the poultice, etc. . . .'[30]

In some cases, the physician acted instrumentally. In a letter to Ashurbanipal, the king's personal physician, Arad-Nanna, expresses his views on the treatment of epistaxis:

'As regards the nose-bleeding . . . the dressings are not properly applied. They have been placed on the side of the nose, so that they interfere with respiration and the blood flows into the mouth. The nose should be plugged up to its end that the air entry be blocked, and the bleeding will cease.'[31]

Modern physicians would not change a word of this procedure.

Finally, we must quote an amazing text recently published, because it proves that, contrary to general belief, the Mesopotamians had some notions of hygiene and preventive medicine. Zimri-Lim, King of Mari, who lived *circa* 1780 BC (see above, page 165) wrote to his wife Shibtu:

'I have heard that the lady Nanname has been taken ill. She has many contacts with the people of the palace. She meets many ladies in her house. Now then, give severe orders that no one should drink in the cup where she drinks, no one should sit on the seat where she sits, no one should sleep in the bed where she sleeps. She should no longer meet many ladies in her house. This disease is contagious (*sabtu*: literally 'catching').'[32]

Thus, Mesopotamian medicine, although still shrouded in superstition, had already some features of a positive science. Transmitted in part to the Greeks, together with Egyptian medicine, it paved the way for the great Hippocratic reform of the fifth century BC. Yet, in its two thousand years of existence, it made very little progress. The physicians of Mesopotamia, like her astronomers, founded their art upon metaphysical doctrines and thereby closed the door to a fruitful quest for rational explanations. They knew the answers to many of the 'when's' and 'what's', but they lacked the curiosity to ask themselves 'how?' and 'why?'. They never attempted to build up theories, but modestly—and perhaps wisely—devoted their efforts to the collection of data. It is only fair to say that, in their achievements, they often surpassed the other learned men of the ancient East.

CHAPTER XXIII

THE CHALDAEAN KINGS

I N 612 BC, less than thirty years after Ashurbanipal celebrated his triumph, the palaces of Nineveh collapsed in flames, and with them collapsed the Assyrian state. The Chaldaean kings of Babylonia, responsible with their allies the Medes for this sudden, violent and radical destruction, remained sole masters in Mesopotamia. Their rule witnessed a colossal amount of building work in southern Iraq, and Babylon—now the largest, most beautiful city in the Near East—became the centre of a movement of architectural, literary and scientific renaissance. It looked as though another Nineveh had been born, and indeed the campaigns of Nebuchadrezzar II in the West suggest that a Babylonian empire was on the verge of replacing the Assyrian empire. But the brilliant 'Neo-Babylonian period' was short-lived. The last great Mesopotamian monarch was succeeded by weak, irresponsible princes incapable of resisting the new, formidable enemy that had arisen in the East. In 539 BC, Babylon fell without resistance into the hands of the Persian conqueror Cyrus.

Such are, in their tragic simplicity, the events which fill the last chapter in the history of Mesopotamia as an independent country, and which must now be told in greater detail.

THE FALL OF NINEVEH

After 639 BC, the annals of Ashurbanipal come to an abrupt end, leaving in complete darkness the last eight years of his reign. The reason for this silence is unknown, but it seems to be due to a combination of civil strife and military setbacks. Herodotus practically our sole source of information for this period, tells us that Phraortes, King of the Medes, attacked the Assyrians but lost his life on the battlefield and was succeeded by his son Cyaxares

(*Uvarkhshatra*). Soon, however, the Medes were overpowered by the Scythians to whom they were forced to pay tribute for twenty-eight years. The wild horsemen also poured over the Zagros, raided Assyria, Syria and Palestine and would have entered Egypt if Psammetichus had not bribed them off. Eventually Cyaxares recovered his freedom by massacring their drunken chieftains at a banquet. The same author, referring to another war, states that a Median onslaught on Nineveh was relieved by a Scythian army—which is quite credible, since we know that Ashurbanipal had made an alliance with the Scythian chief Madyes (see page 275 above).[1] These events appear to have taken place between 653 (date of Phraortes' death) and 630 BC. How they affected Assyria, we are not told, but if Herodotus' account of the Scythian invasion is trustworthy, the fact that their hordes could ride across the entire empire and safely return home is eloquent proof of the extraordinary state of debility into which the Assyrian army had fallen. Without any doubt, the key to the final disaster of 614–609 BC lies in these obscure years.

The likelihood of civil strife is supported by the troubles which broke out in Assyria after the death of Ashurbanipal, in 631 BC. His son, Ashur-etil-ilâni,* had to crush one revolt in order to ascend the throne and yet another before his short reign ended. Otherwise, little is known of this king, except that he restored a few temples and occupied the so-called 'Burnt Palace' at Nimrud.[2] His brother, Sin-shar-ishkun,† who was probably crowned in 629 BC, also appears to have met with strong opposition from among his own countrymen,[3] while the political situation outside Assyria was rapidly deteriorating.

There was little to be feared from the North: Urartu was neutralized by its powerful neighbours, and the Cimmerians, now under Scythian domination, showed no signs of aggressiveness. But in Iran, Cyaxares was reorganizing his army, turning it into a powerful instrument of war. From Ecbatana (Hamadan), his capital city, he ruled over 'the three Medias', from lake Urmiah to the region of Teheran, and indirectly over the Persians established further south. In the West, the Phoenician cities seem to have severed their ties with Nineveh, and so ineffective was the

---

* 'Ashur, hero of the gods.'
† 'The god Sin has appointed the king.

Assyrian control over Palestine that Josiah, King of Judah, was able to promote his religious reform in the province of Samaria, former kingdom of Israel.4 The most immediate danger, however, lay in the south, where the Babylonians, taking advantage of Assyria's weakness, had resumed their traditional struggle for independence. Kandalanu, the governor appointed by Ashurbanipal in Babylon after the rebellion of Shamash-shum-ukîn, had already revolted. After his death, in 627 BC, the governor of the Sea-Land, Nabû-apal-uṣur ('Nabopolassar'), an Aramaean of the Kaldû tribe, became the leader of the insurrection. The Assyrian troops stationed in Nippur were unable to defeat him and, on 23rd November, 626 BC, after a year of guerilla-war,5 he sat on the throne of Babylon. From that day dates the official beginning of the Eleventh and last Babylonian dynasty or, as we call it, the 'Chaldaean' or 'Neo-Babylonian' dynasty. By a happy coincidence, 626 BC also marks the starting point of a series of Babylonian chronicles which enable us to follow step by step and almost day by day the history of Babylonia and include an invaluable account of the fall of Nineveh and other Assyrian cities.6

For eleven years (626–615 BC), the war between Babylonians and Assyrians consisted of a series of attacks and counter-attacks having as objective the network of fortified cities held by the Assyrians in southern Iraq. Nabopolassar eventually succeeded in taking Nippur and in liberating the whole of Sumer and Akkad. In 616 BC, he even marched along the Euphrates up to the district of Harran and along the Tigris as far as Arrapha (Kirkuk) and Assur, which he besieged without success. In order to win the friendship of the Elamites—who had by then recovered their freedom—he returned the statues of their gods held captive in Babylonia; but he failed to obtain their armed support and dared not launch, alone, a full-scale offensive against his rival. Sin-shar-ishkun, on the other hand, driven into the defensive and seeing his authority challenged within his own country, sought and obtained the alliance of the Egyptians who had not forgotten their narrow escape from the Scythian invasion and observed with alarm the progress being made by the Medes in Iran and Asia Minor. The fact that Egypt was now called to the rescue by her former conquerors is significant of the desperate straits in which Assyria now found herself. The Egyptians, however, did not actively support their allies until 612/611 BC, already much too late.

The Assyrians might have resigned themselves to accepting the autonomy of Babylonia and a compromise could perhaps have been reached if the Medes, acting independently, had not thrown their weight into the balance. At the end of 615 BC, they suddenly invaded Assyria and took Arrapha. During the following winter, they marched against Nineveh, but, instead of attacking it, moved southwards and fell upon Assur which they captured (614 BC):

'He (the Mede), says our Chronicle, made an attack upon the town ... and the city-wall (?) he destroyed. He inflicted a terrible massacre upon the greater part of the people, plundering it (the city) and carrying off prisoners from it.'7

The Babylonians arrived too late to take part in the action. Nabopolassar met Cyaxares (called by the Babylonians *Umakish-tar*) under the walls of Assur and 'they established mutual friendship and peace'. The alliance was later sealed by the marriage of Nabopolassar's son, Nebuchadrezzar, with Cyaxares' daughter, Amytis.8 From then on, Babylonians and Medes were to fight hand in hand, and Assyria was doomed.

The following year was spent by Nabopolassar in unsuccessful campaigns along the Euphrates, and it was not until the summer of 612 BC that the final assault was launched against Assyria's main city, Nineveh. The town was strongly defended and at first, Babylonians and Medes made very slow progress. After two months of siege, however,

'A strong attack they made against the city and in the month of *Ab* (July–August), the ... th day, the city was captured, a great defeat of the chief (people) was made. On that day Sin-shar-ishkun, the Assyrian king, [was killed?]. The great spoil of the city and temple they carried off and turned the city into a ruin-mound (*tilu*) and heaps of debris.'9

By the end of 612 BC, the three capital cities of Assyria–Assur, the religious metropolis, Nineveh, the administrative centre, and probably Nimrud, the military headquarters—as well as all the main Assyrian towns10 had been destroyed. Yet the ghost of an Assyrian kingdom survived for three years. Sin-shar-ishkun having been killed, one of his officers sat on the throne under the name of Ashur-uballiṭ, the same name, ironically, as that of the great monarch who, in the thirteenth century, had freed his country from the Hurri-Mitannians (see above page 213). Rallying what was left of the Assyrian army, he shut himself up in Harran, with a few Egyptian troops, at last sent to the rescue. In 610 BC, the Babylonians and the *Umman-manda* (Medes?)[11] marched against Harran. The Assyro-Egyptians abandoned it to take refuge beyond the Euphrates, and the city fell into the hands of the Medes. The following year, after an unsuccessful attempt to recover his stronghold, Assur-uballiṭ disappeared.

Thus ended miserably within the short space of three years the giant who, for three centuries, had caused the world to tremble with fear. In a few words Nabopolassar wrote his epitaph:

'I slaughtered the land of Subarum (Assyria), I turned the hostile land into heaps and ruins.

The Assyrian, who since distant days had ruled over all the peoples, and with his heavy yoke had brought injury to the people of the Land, his feet from Akkad I turned back, his yoke I threw off.'[12]

No one, as far as we know, sat on the ruins of Nineveh to write a lamentation.[13]

NEBUCHADREZZAR

The Medes do not appear to have laid claim to the kingdom which they had contributed to overthrow. Content with their share of booty, they withdrew behind the Zagros and turned their ambition towards Armenia and the rest of Asia Minor. The Babylonians remained in full possession of Assyria, but did not occupy it and made no attempt to repair the damage they had caused. All their efforts were devoted to the religious and cultural revival of southern Mesopotamia, and in the field of foreign policy to the protection of the Taurus frontier and the subjection of Syria-Palestine. The latter country had been rid of its Assyrian masters only to fall into Egyptian hands. In a belated and fruitless effort to save his allies, pharaoh Necho II had invaded it in 609 BC, defeating and killing Josiah, King of Judah, who foolishly tried to bar his way,[14] and now Egyptian troops held Karkemish and the crossing of the Euphrates. The possession of Karkemish and the control of the Phoenician coast and hinterland were even more important to the Babylonians than they had been to the Assyrians, since practically all their trade was with the West. The Chaldaean kings could forsake all hope of reconstructing the Assyrian empire; they could abandon the lands beyond the mountains to the Medes; but they could not accept being deprived of rich provinces, nor seeing their gateway to the Mediterranean blocked by the Egyptians. Their reigns are filled with repeated campaigns in 'the land of Hatti', and their so-called conquests were, in fact, nothing but an endless struggle to secure the vital sources of Babylonian prosperity.

After his final victory over the Assyrians, Nabopolassar, who was now ageing, relied more and more upon his son, Nabû-kudurri-uṣur ('Nebuchadrezzar') for the conduct of military operations. In 607 BC, the young and energetic crown prince was entrusted with the task of dislodging the Egyptians from Syria. After two years of unsuccessful attempts at establishing bridge-heads at other points of the Euphrates valley, Nebuchadrezzar mustered his army and attacked Karkemish (May–June 605 BC). The Egyptian garrison, reinforced by Greek mercenaries, put up strong resistance but was finally overwhelmed and massacred.

'As for the rest of the Egyptian army which had escaped from the defeat (so quickly that) no weapon had reached them, in the district of Hama the Babylonian troops overtook and defeated them so that not a single man escaped to his own country.'[15]

The whole of Syria-Palestine now lay open to the Babylonians who advanced as far as Pelusium, on the Egyptian border. It was then that Nebuchadrezzar heard of his father's death. Wasting no time—the death of an Oriental monarch was always a critical moment—he returned to Babylon 'in twenty-three days' and was crowned upon his arrival in the capital city (23rd September, 605 BC).

The Babylonians must have known that if invading Syria had been relatively easy, holding it would be extremely difficult. The northern Syrians would be generally submissive, but neither the Phoenicians, nor the Philistines, nor the Jews could whole-heartedly accept paying Babylon a tribute which they had just ceased paying—so reluctantly—to Nineveh. Moreover, Egypt, which had just seen her age-old dream of a Syrian 'colony' take shape and vanish, would now more than ever, throw oil on the fire. Soon Nebuchadrezzar found himself compelled to display his strength almost every year in the Mediterranean areas and to quell rebellion after rebellion, as Sargon and his successors had done. Twelve months after the battle of Karkemish, he was in Syria again, collecting tribute from Damascus, Tyre, Sidon and Jerusalem, but also destroying Ascalon whose ruler had revolted. In 601 BC, the Chronicle mentions a great, though inconclusive battle between the King of Babylon and the King of Egypt—'they fought with each other in close battle and inflicted grave havoc on each other'.[16] In 599 BC, from one of his Syrian camps, Nebuchadrezzar 'sent out his companies scouring the desert' against the Arabs of Qedar. During the winter of 598/97 BC, Jehoiakim, King of Judah, deaf to the warnings of Jeremiah the prophet, refused to pay tribute. Babylonian retaliation came swiftly. On March 16, 597 BC, Jerusalem was captured, another Jew, Zedekiah, was placed on the throne, and 3,000 Hebrews were deported to Mesopotamia.[17] An unfortunate gap in the series of Babylonian Chronicles deprives us of a continuous narrative covering the following years, but we know from other sources that Necho's successor, Psammetichus II, led an expedition to Syria (circa 600 BC) and that pharaoh Apries (595–570 BC) captured Gaza and attacked Tyre and Sidon.[18] The proximity of an Egyptian army and the belief that he could rely upon its assistance probably encouraged Zedekiah to revolt. From his headquarters at Riblah, near Homs, Nebuchadrezzar directed the operations. After a siege of 18 months, Jerusalem surrendered. Zedekiah, who had fled towards Jericho, was captured:

'So they took the king and brought him up to the King of Babylon to Riblah; and they gave judgment upon him. And they slew the sons of Zedekiah before his eyes, and put out the eyes of Zedekiah, and bound him with fetters of brass, and carried him off to Babylon.'[19]

Thousands of Jews were deported with their king, whilst others took refuge in Egypt. A native governor was appointed over Judah. Jerusalem was looted, its walls were 'broken down round about', and the House of the Lord, the temple that Solomon had built was burned. Thus, one hundred and thirty-five years after Israel, 'Judah was carried away out of the land' (June 587 BC).

The last action of Nebuchadrezzar in Syria, of which we have a record, is a siege of Tyre which lasted, we are told, no less than thirteen years and ended with the capture of the city and the replacement of its king by another. A fragmentary tablet in the British Museum alludes to a campaign against pharaoh Amasis, in 568 BC, and mentions an Egyptian town, but this cannot be regarded as sufficient proof that the Babylonians ever set foot in the Nile valley.[20] Ten years at least before the end of the reign, the Western districts were firmly in Nebuchadrezzar's hands, and mount Lebanon, that inexhaustible source of timber, was open to regular exploitation:

'I made that country happy by eradicating its enemy everywhere. All its scattered inhabitants I led back to their settlements. What no former king had done I achieved: I cut through steep mountains, I split rocks, opened passages and I constructed a straight road for the (transport of the) cedars. I made the inhabitants of Lebanon live in safety together and let nobody disturb them.'[21]

Meanwhile, the Medes were progressing in a north-westerly direction, invading successively Armenia—Urarțu was conquered and its towns destroyed by the Medes and the Scythians at the beginning of the sixth century—and Cappadocia. In 585 BC, when Cyaxares the Mede and Alyattes of Lydia found each other face to face at the 'Battle of the Eclipse' and unable to solve their conflict by arms, Nebuchadrezzar acted as referee, negotiated a truce between the two countries, and fixed their common frontier on the Halys River (Kizil Irmak).[22] But, either in agreement with his ally or as a precaution against a possible Median invasion from the north, he occupied Cilicia and fortified several towns 'along the border of Urarțu'. Contrary to the belief of some historians, there is no evidence that he ever conquered Elam.[23]

The last years of Nebuchadrezzar's reign are obscure. It ended, it seems, amidst internal disorders. His son, Awêl-Marduk ('Evil-Merodach' of the Old Testament) ruled for only two years (562–560 BC) and was replaced by a Babylonian general, a commoner who had married one of Nebuchadrezzar's daughters:

Nergal-shar-uṣur ('Neriglissar'). This king, formerly known only for his building activities, must now be credited with a victorious campaign in Cilicia.[24] After two months of reign, Neriglissar's son, Labâshi-Marduk, a mere child, was murdered, and in June 556 BC the Babylonians raised to the throne a high official of royal descent: Nabonidus. But already events were taking place in Iran, which were to change once again the face of the Ancient World.

THE FALL OF BABYLON

The last king of an independent Babylon, Nabû-na'id* or—as we call him after the Greeks—Nabonidus (556–539 BC) is one of the most enigmatic and fascinating figures in the long series of Mesopotanian monarchs. He was the son of a certain Nabû-balaṭsu-iqbi, 'wise prince and governor', and of a votaress of the god Sin in the city of Harran, both probably of royal blood. A man in his sixties when he ascended the throne, he had held important administrative functions under Nebuchadrezzar and Neriglissar. Extremely fond of his mother—she died in 547 BC, at the age of one hundred and four, and was buried with royal honours[25]—he had inherited from her a keen interest in religious affairs and a special, almost exclusive devotion for the god she had served all her life. After the death of Nabû-na'id the pro-Persians of Babylon, anxious to please their new sovereign, did everything in their power to sully his memory. In a libel known as 'the Verse Account of Nabonidus', they accused him of being a madman, a liar boasting of victories he had never won and, above all, a heretic who blasphemed Marduk and worshipped, under the name of Sin, 'a deity which nobody had ever seen in the country'[26]. These vicious accusations met with a success that their authors themselves could hardly have expected. Through a confusion of names they gave birth to the story of Nebuchadrezzar's madness as told in the Book of Daniel, and found an echo in a fragment of the famous Dead Sea Scrolls[27]. Even the most cautious of modern historians are obliged to admit that they contain a spark of truth. Some at least of Nabonidus' inscriptions suggest that Sin ranked higher in his esteem than the national god Marduk, and the sanctuaries of the moon-god throughout the country were the

* 'The god Nabû has exalted' (the king).

objects of his special attention: not only did he splendidly restore the ziqqurat and several temples of Ur, but the rebuilding of E.hul.hul, the temple of Sin in Harran, which had been destroyed by the Medes during the war against Assyria, appears to have been the *idée fixe* of his reign. To say, however, that Nabû-na'id for political and sentimental reasons wanted to replace Marduk by Sin at the head of the Babylonian pantheon is perhaps going too far. Other temples in Mesopotamia—including the great temple of Marduk in Babylon—also benefited from his zeal, and the eagerness with which, before building anew, he sought the *temenu*, or foundation-deposit, which authenticated the sacred ground testifies to his attachment to the religious traditions of Sumer and Akkad. On account of his lengthy excavations in search of these written documents, Nabonidus has been nick-named 'the royal archaeologist', though neither his aims nor his methods had anything to do with archaeology. Nevertheless, the king certainly shared with his subjects that passion for the study of the past which characterizes his epoch. During the Neo-Babylonian period—and indeed, during the following Achaeme-nian period—a number of ancient chronicles were copied, king lists compiled, and antiquities collected with fervour. To quote an amusing example: when Sir Leonard Woolley was excavating at Ur the palace of Bêl-shalti-nannar—Nabonidus' daughter and high-priestess of Sin—he was puzzled to find in the same building, in the same occupation-level, objects of widely different periods, such as a Kassite *kudurru*, a fragment of a statue of King Shulgi and a clay cone of one of the Kings of Larsa. Only later did he realize that he had been exploring Bêl-shalti-nannar's private museum![28]

In complete contrast with this devout and apparently weak monarch stands the formidable figure of Cyrus II, 'Great King, the Achaemenian, King of Parsumash and Anshan', who ascended the Persian throne in 559 BC, three years before Nabonidus was crowned.

The Persians—an Indo-European speaking people—had entered Iran at the end of the second millennium, at the same time as the Medes with whom they were closely related. Moving slowly along the folds of the Zagros, they had eventually reached and occupied the mountainous range still known as Fars, to the south of the Iranian plateau. At the close of the seventh century BC,

when their history becomes better known, they were divided into
two kingdoms ruled by the descendents of Teispes, son of
Achaemenes (*Hahamanish*). In Persia proper (*Parsa* or *Parsumash*),
i.e. the region between Isfahan and Shiraz, reigned the family of
Ariaramnes, elder son of Teispes, while further west, along the
border of Elam, the country of Anshan, or Anzan was ruled by the
family of Ariaramnes' brother, Cyrus I. Both kingdoms were
vassals of the Medes. For one or two generations, the House of
Ariaramnes held sway over the House of Cyrus, but Cyrus' son,
Cambyses I (*circa* 600–559 BC) reversed the situation and added
to his prestige by marrying the daughter of Astyages, his Median
overlord. From this marriage was born Cyrus II. At the beginning
of Nabonidus' reign, Cyrus (*Kurash*) from his palace at Pasargadae
ruled over a large but isolated district of Iran, paying tribute to his
grandfather. But the Persian prince lacked neither ambition nor
intelligence. He had already started reducing to obedience the
Iranian tribes of the neighbourhood and was slowly enlarging his
kingdom, when the King of Babylon himself gave him an
opportunity to acquire an empire.

We have seen that Nabonidus' most cherished dream was to
rebuild the temple of Sin in Harran. Not only was this sanctuary
dear to his heart, but the possession of the market-place and
strategic city commanding the roads from northern Mesopotamia
to Syria and Asia Minor was of extreme importance to the
economy and security of the Babylonian kingdom. Unfortunately, Harran had been in the hands of the Medes since 610 BC,
and against the Medes Nabonidus alone was powerless. Seeing in
the Persians the true successors of the Elamites upon whose
assistance the Babylonians had so often relied in the past, he called
upon Cyrus for help. Cyrus accepted. Astyages got wind of the
plot, summoned his grandson to Ecbatana, but met with a refusal
to obey. A bitter war ensued, ending with the victory of the
Persians. Betrayed by his own general, Astyages was captured by
Cyrus who, in one day, found himself the master of both the
Persian and the Median kingdoms (550 BC). This important event,
long known to us from the works of classical authors,[29] is also
mentioned in contemporary cuneiform texts. In one of his
inscriptions,[30] Nabonidus tells us that Marduk appeared to him
in a dream and ordered him to rebuild E.hul.hul in Harran. As

PLATE 30. Stele of
Esarhaddon, King
of Assyria (680–
669 BC), found at
Zenjirli, in the
Amanus mountains.
Taharqa, King
of Egypt (kneeling),
and Abdi-Milkuti,
King of Sidon
(standing), supplicate
Esarhaddon who
is holding them
captive.

PLATE 31.
The Assyrian
army at war.
In a moun-
tainous and
wooded
country,
foot-soldiers
and cavalry-
men, fighting
with bows,
lances and
slings, are
progressing.
A mounted
officer shouts
orders.
Relief from
Nineveh.
Reign of
Ashurbanipal
(668–631 B.C.)

the king objected that Harran was in the hands of the 'Umman-manda' (Medes), Marduk replied:

'The Umman-manda of whom you speak, they and their land and the kings who side with them no longer exist. In the coming third year I shall make Cyrus, King of Anzan, their young slave, expel them. With his few troops, he will disperse the widespread Umman-manda.

He (Cyrus) captured Astyages (*Ishtumegu*), King of the Umman-manda and took him prisoner to his country.'

Another, more precise account of the conflict is given in the so-called 'Nabonidus Chronicle':

'King Ishtumegu called up his troops and marched against Cyrus, King of Anshan, in order to meet him in battle. The army of Ishtumegu revolted against him and in fetters they delivered him to Cyrus.'[31]

Following his victory over the Medes, Cyrus embarked upon a series of brilliant military campaigns which, after ten years, gave him an empire considerably larger than anything the world had ever witnessed. His first objective was Lydia, where reigned the fabulously rich Croesus. Rather than cross the Armenian highlands, Cyrus led his troops along the road that ran parallel to the Taurus range, through the steppe of Jazirah. Crossing the Tigris below Nineveh and marching westward *via* Harran, he occupied Cilicia, then a vassal-state of Babylon, thereby breaking the alliance he had just formed with Nabonidus and throwing the Babylonians on the side of Lydia and her traditional allies, the Egyptians. But neither the Egyptians nor the Babylonians could send troops to the aid of Croesus, who met the Persians alone and was defeated at Pteryum (547 BC). Lydia absorbed, the Greek cities of Ionia fell one by one, and the whole of Asia Minor submitted to Persian rule. No sooner was the conquest achieved than Cyrus turned his weapon in the opposite direction. Successively, Parthia and Aria, kingdoms of eastern Iran, Sogdia and Bactria in Turkestan and Afghanistan, and part of India fell into his hands. The Persian empire now stretched from the Aegean to the Pamirs, a distance of almost three thousand miles. Confronted with such a giant, Babylon had no hope of survival.

During this time Nabonidus was in Arabia. We read in the Chronicle that, in his third year, he went to Syria, raised troops in 'the land of Hatti' (as Syria was then called), entered the Arabian desert and besieged Adumu (al-Jauf, 280 miles due east of Akaba), an important settlement once occupied by the Assyrians. Whether he returned home after this campaign is uncertain owing to an unfortunate break in the tablet, but the entries for the seventh to the eleventh years state that 'the king was in Temâ', with the result that the New Year Festival could not be celebrated in Babylon.[32] Temâ (Arabic Teima) is a large oasis in western Arabia, and from Temâ, Nabonidus could easily wander from oasis to oasis as far away as Iatribu (Yathrib, Medina), as we learn from an inscription recently discovered at Harran.[33] What the King of Babylon was doing in Arabia is one of the most vexing problems in the history of ancient Iraq. Various sugges- tions have been put forward,[34] the most plausible being that, having lost to the Medes (and Persians) the northern and eastern trade routes of Mesopotamia, he was endeavouring to secure the 'incense trade route' that ran from Yemen to Egypt and Palestine through Hejâz. The official reason, given in the Harran inscrip- tions, is that he voluntarily abandoned Babylonia in the throes of civil war and famine. Yet none of these explanations can account for those *ten* years of uninterrupted absence from the capital city, unless we suppose that Nabû-na'id was prevented by his enemies from returning to Babylon. He had left the government in the care of his son Bêl-shar-uṣur ('Belshazzar' of the Old Testament), a capable soldier but a poor politician whose authority was chal- lenged by an increasingly influential pro-Persian party. In almost every country which his victories had placed under Persian rule, it had been Cyrus' policy to win the goodwill of his new subjects rather than frighten them into obedience, to pose as liberator and treat his prisoners with mercy, to respect and even encourage local cults, traditions and customs. He was therefore extremely popular throughout the Near East, and among the Babylonians many thought that they would lose little by becoming the subjects of such a good prince. The writing was on the wall: Babylon would be an easy prey.

Cyrus attacked Babylonia in the autumn of 539 BC. Nabonidus, who had at last returned from Arabia, ordered Belshazzar to deploy his troops along the Tigris in order to cover the capital city. But the Persians had overwhelming numerical superiority. Moreover, Gubaru (Gobryas), governor of Gutium (i.e Assyria), who ought to have protected the left flank of Belshazzar's army, went over to the enemy. The subsequent events are described in detail in the Nabonidus Chronicle:35

'In the month of *Tashritu* (September–October), when Cyrus attacked the army of Akkad in Opis on the Tigris, the inhabitants of Akkad revolted, but he (Nabonidus) massacred the confused inhabitants.

The fifteenth day, Sippar was seized without a battle. Nabonidus fled.

The sixteenth day, Gubaru, the governor of Gutium, and the army of Cyrus entered Babylon without a battle. Afterwards, Nabonidus was arrested in Babylon when he returned (there).

Till the end of the month, the shield-carrying Gutians were staying within Esagila (the temple of Marduk), but nobody carried arms in Esagila and its buildings. The correct time (for a ceremony) was not missed.

In the month of *Arahsamnu* (October–November), the third day, Cyrus entered Babylon. Great twigs were spread in front of him. The state of 'peace' was imposed on all the city. Cyrus sent greetings to all Babylon . . .'

Belshazzar was killed in the battle at Opis and Nabonidus, probably in Babylon, although, according to other sources, Cyrus appointed him governor of Carmania (Central Iran).36 Far from being destroyed as its rival Nineveh had been, Babylon was treated with the utmost respect. From the first day of Persian occupation (October 12, 539 BC), care was taken not to offend the Babylonians in any way, and every effort was made to resettle them in their homes, to enforce law and order throughout the country. The gods of Sumer and Akkad, whom Nabonidus had brought into Babylon during the war, were reinstalled in their chapels, 'the places which make them happy', and even the gods of Assyria, once taken captive by the Medes, were returned, and their temples rebuilt. Cyrus made it known to all that he considered himself as the successor of the national rulers, that he worshipped Marduk and 'praised his great godhead joyously'. Indeed, we can believe the Persian conqueror when, in an inscription written in Akkadian on a clay cylinder,37 he declares that the Babylonians accepted his rule with enthusiasm:

'All the inhabitants of Babylon, as well as of the entire country of Sumer and Akkad, princes and governors, bowed to him (Cyrus) and kissed his feet, jubilant that he had received the kingship, and with shining faces happily greeted him as a master through whose help they had come to life from death and had all been spared damage and disaster, and they worshipped his name.'

CHAPTER XXIV

THE SPLENDOUR OF BABYLON

SHORT as it was, the rule of the Chaldaean kings has left deep traces in the records of history. Monuments, royal inscriptions, letters, legal and commercial documents in great number concur to help us form of the Neo-Babylonian kingdom a fairly complete and accurate picture, and from this collection of data, two main features emerge which give the whole period a character of its own: a religious revival, combined with extensive architectural activity, and a resurgence of the temples as major social and economic units.

Geography, circumstances and the will of her rulers had turned Assyria into an expanding military nation. The same factors, acting through a thousand years of political abeyance, had made Babylonia the heir and guardian of Sumero-Akkadian traditions, the 'sacred area' of Mesopotamia, acknowledged as such and generally respected by the Assyrians themselves. A Babylonian renaissance in the sixth century BC was therefore bound to take the form of a religious revival. To the rebuilding of sanctuaries, the restoration of age-old rites, the celebration of religious festivals with increased ceremonial display, the Chaldaean kings devoted much time, energy and money. In their official inscriptions the stress was constantly laid on their architectural rather than their warlike performances. They could have claimed, like their predecessors, kingship over 'the Universe' of 'the Four Quarters of the World'; they preferred to call themselves 'Provider (*zaninu*) of Esagila and Ezida'*—a title which appears on thousands of bricks scattered throughout southern Iraq. Their colossal work of reconstruction involved all the main cities of Sumer and Akkad, from Sippar to Uruk and Ur, but the capital city was given, as

---

* Respectively the temples of Marduk in Babylon and his son Nabû in Barsippa.

expected, preferential treatment: rebuilt anew, enlarged, fortified and embellished, Babylon became one of the world's marvels. Jeremiah the prophet, whilst predicting its fall, could not help calling it 'a golden cup in the Lord's hand, that made all the earth drunken', and Herodotus, who is believed to have visited it *circa* 460 B C, admiringly proclaimed: 'It surpassses in splendour any city of the known world'.[1]

Was this reputation deserved or was it, as in other instances, the product of Oriental exaggeration and Greek credulity? The answer to this question should not be sought in the barren mounds and heaps of crumbling brickwork which today form most of this famous site, but in the publications of R. Koldewey and his co-workers who, between 1899 and 1917, excavated Babylon on behalf of the Deutsche Orient Gesellschaft.[2] It took the Germans eighteen years of hard and patient work solely to recover the plan of the city in broad outline and unearth some of its main monuments, but we now possess enough archaeological evidence to complete, confirm, or amend Herodotus' classical description and, on many points, share his enthusiasm.

BABYLON, THE GREAT CITY

Without doubt, Babylon was a very large town by ancient standards. It covered an area of some 500 acres, contained we are told, 1,179 temples of various sizes, and whilst its normal population is estimated at about 100,000, it could have sheltered a quarter of a million people, if not more. The city proper, roughly square in plan, was bisected by the Euphrates, which now flows to the west of the ruins, and was surrounded by an 'inner wall'. But, 'in order that the enemy should not press on the flank of Babylon', Nebuchadrezzar had erected an 'outer wall', about 3 miles long, adding 'four thousand cubits of land to each side of the city'. The vast area comprised between these two walls was suburban in character, with mud-houses and reed-huts scattered amidst gardens and palm-groves, and contained, as far as we can judge, only two official buildings: Nebuchadrezzar's 'summer palace', whose ruins form the mound at present called Bâbil, in the north-eastern corner of the town, and perhaps the *bît akîtu*, or Temple of the New Year Festival, not yet exactly located.

The walls of Babylon[3] were remarkable structures, much admired in antiquity. Reinforced by towers and protected by moats, they were made of two thick walls of burnt bricks, one behind the other, joined together by a filling of brick rubble. The top of the outer wall, for instance, was thus more than 36 feet wide and could accommodate one or even two chariots of four horses abreast, enabling a rapid movement of troops from one end of the town to the other. This formidable defensive system, however, proved useless: whether or not they had accomplices in the city, the Persians entered Babylon through the bed of the Euphrates at low water and took it by surprise, proving that every armour has its faults and that the value of fortifications lies in the men behind them.

Eight gates, each of them named after a god, pierced the inner wall. The north-western gate, or Ishtar Gate, which played an important part in the religious life of the city, is, fortunately, the best preserved, its walls still rising some 36 feet above the present ground-level.[4] Like most city gates in the ancient Near East, it consisted of a long passage divided by projecting towers into several gateways, with chambers for the guard behind each gateway. But the main interest of Ishtar Gate resides in its splendid decoration. The front wall, as well as the entire surface of the passage, were covered with blue enamelled bricks on which stood out in relief red-and-white dragons (symbolic of Marduk) and bulls (symbolic of Adad), arranged in alternating rows. Even the foundations were similarly decorated, although not with enamelled bricks. The total number of animal figures has been estimated at 575. The passage was roofed over, and the sight of these strange creatures, shining in the dim light of torches and oil-lamps, must have produced the most startling, awe-inspiring effect.

Ishtar Gate was approached from the north through a broad, truly magnificent avenue called by the Babylonians *Ai-ibur-shabu*, 'may the enemy not cross it', but better known today as 'Procession Street'. The avenue, 63 feet wide, was paved with slabs of white limestone and red breccia and was bordered by two thick walls, no less impressive than those of Ishtar Gate for, on each side, sixty mighty lions (symbolic of Ishtar) with red or yellow manes were cast in relief on blue ceramic. Behind these walls were three large buildings called by the Germans 'Northern Citadel' (Nordburg), 'Main Citadel' (Hauptburg) and 'Advanced Work' (Vorwerk). All three formed part of the defensive system of the city, though the Hauptburg seems to have been used also as a royal or princely residence.5 Its ruins have yielded a number of inscriptions and sculptures ranging from the second millennium to the fifth century BC, among which the basalt statue of a lion trampling on a man, known as 'the lion of Babylon'. The origin of this colossal, roughly made piece of work is unknown but, foreign as it is to all that we know of Mesopotamian sculpture, it conveys such an impression of strength and majesty that it has become a symbol of the glorious past of Iraq. Beyond Ishtar Gate, Procession Street continued, somewhat narrower, through the city proper. It passed in front of the Royal Palace, crossed over a canal called *Libil hegalla* ('may it bring abundance'), skirted the vast precinct of the ziqqurat and, turning westwards, reached the Euphrates at the point where the river was spanned by a bridge of six piers shaped like boats. It divided the city into two parts: to the east lay the tangle of private houses (mound of Merkes6), to the west and south, were grandiose palaces and temples.

Immediately behind the city wall and close to Ishtar Gate lay the 'Southern Citadel' (Südburg), 'the House the marvel of mankind, the centre of the Land, the shining Residence, the dwelling of Majesty'—in simpler words, the palace built by Nebuchadrezzar over the smaller palace of Nabopolassar, his father.7 This very large building was entered from Procession Street through one single monumental gate, and comprised five courtyards in succession, each of them surrounded by offices, reception rooms and royal apartments. In contrast with the Assyrian palaces, no colossi of stone guarded the doors, no sculptured slabs or inscribed orthostats lined the walls. The only decoration—obviously intended to please the eye rather than inspire fear—consisted of panels of ceramic depicting animal figures, pseudo-columns and floral designs in yellow, white, red and blue. Of special interest was a peculiar construction included in the north-eastern corner of the palace. It lay below ground-level and was made of narrow corridors and small vaulted cellars. In one of the cellars was found an unusual well of three shafts side by side, probably used in connection with a chain-pump. It is extremely tempting to see in this construction the understructure of roof gardens, the famous 'hanging gardens of Babylon' described by several authors and erected—so one legend tells us—by Nebuchadrezzar for the pleasure of his wife, the Median princess Amytis.[8]

To the south of the royal palace, in the middle of a vast open space surrounded by a buttressed wall, rose the 'Tower of Babel', the huge ziqqurat called *E-temen-an-ki*, 'the Temple Foundation of Heaven and Earth'. As old as Babylon itself, damaged by Sennacherib, rebuilt by Nabopolassar and Nebuchadrezzar, it was, as will be seen, completely destroyed, so that only its foundations could be studied by the archaeologists. Any reconstruction of Etemenanki therefore rests essentially upon the meagre data yielded by these studies, upon the eye-witness description of Herodotus, and upon the measurements given, in rather obscure terms, in a document called 'the Esagila tablet'.[9] It was certainly a colossal monument, 300 feet wide at its base and perhaps 200 feet high, with no less than 7 storeys. On its southern side, a triple flight of steps led to the second storey, the rest of the tower being ascended by means of ramps. At the top was a shrine (*sahuru*) 'enhanced with bricks of resplendent blue enamel', which Herodotus describes as follows:

'In the last tower (= storey) there is a great shrine; and in it a great and well-covered couch is laid, and a golden table set hard by. But no image has been set up in the shrine, nor does any creature lie therein for the night, except one native woman, chosen from all women by the god, as say the Chaldaeans, who are priests of this god. The same Chaldaeans say—but I do not believe them—that the god himself is wont to visit the shrine and rest upon the couch . . .'[10]

Clearly, this description combines two different traditions: the occasional descent of the god from heaven to earth, using the *sahuru* as a resting-place, and the Sacred Marriage ceremony which, as we shall presently see, took place not on the ziqqurat, but either in the *bît akîtu* or in Esagila.

E-sag-ila, 'the Temple that Raises its Head', was the name given to the temple of Marduk, the tutelary god of Babylon and the supreme deity of the Babylonian pantheon since the reign of Hammurabi. It was a complex of large and lofty buildings and vast courtyards lying to the south of Etemenanki, on the other side of Procession Street and not at the foot of the ziqqurat, as did most Mesopotamian temples. All the kings of Babylon had bestowed their favours upon the greatest of all sanctuaries, and Nebuchadrezzar, in particular, had lavishly rebuilt and adorned the Palace of Heaven and Earth, the Seat of Kingship':

'Silver, gold, costly precious stones, bronze, wood from Magan, everything that is expensive, glittering abundance, the products of the mountains, the treasures of the seas, large quantities (of goods), sumptuous gifts, I brought to my city of Babylon before him (Marduk).

In Esagila, the palace of his lordship, I carried out restoration work. *Ekua*, the chapel of Marduk, Enlil of the gods, I made its walls gleam like the sun. With shining gold as if it were gypsum . . . with lapis-lazuli and alabaster I clothed the inside of the temple . . .

Du-azag, the place of the Naming of Destiny . . . the shrine of kingship, the shrine of the god of lordship, of the wise one among the gods, of the prince Marduk, whose construction a king before me had adorned with silver, I clothed with shining gold, a magnificent ornament . . .

My heart prompts me to rebuild Esagila; I think of it constantly. The best of my cedars, which I brought from Lebanon, the noble forest, I sought out for the roofing of *Ekua* . . . Inside (the temple), these strong cedar beams . . . I covered with shining gold. The lower beams of cedar I adorned with silver and precious stones. For the building of Esagila, I prayed every day.'[11]

The wealth of Esagila is also emphasized by Herodotus who, having described the ziqqurat, speaks of a 'lower temple':

'Where is a great golden image of Zeus (Marduk), sitting at a great golden table, and the footstool and chair are also of gold; the god of the whole was said by the Chaldaeans to be of 800 talents' weight (3 tons). Outside the temple is a golden altar. There is also another great altar, whereon are sacrificed the full-grown of the flocks. Only sucklings may be sacrificed on the golden altar, but on the greater altar the Chaldaeans even offer a thousand talents' weight of frankincense yearly . . .'[12]

Twenty-three centuries after Herodotus visited Babylon, however, the great temple of Marduk lay buried under more than 60 feet of earth and sand, making extensive excavations almost impossible. At the cost of a considerable effort, the Germans were able to unearth the main sanctuary ('Hauptbau'), where, among the many rooms symetrically arranged around a central courtyard, they identified *Ekua*, the shrine of Marduk, the smaller chapel of Marduk's consort, the goddess Sarpanitum, and chapels devoted to other deities, such as Ea and Nabû. Of an adjacent building ('Anbau'), only the outer walls and gates could be traced. Thoroughly plundered in antiquity, Esagila yielded practically no object of value. On top of the artificial hill that concealed it, the tomb of 'Amran ibn 'Ali, a companion of the Prophet, perpetuates for the Moslems the sacred character attached to that part of Babylon.

THE NEW YEAR FESTIVAL

Once a year, in the spring, the religiosity diffused throughout Sumer and Akkad crystallized in Babylon. For eleven days the thoughts of the entire population were focused on the ceremonies which took place in the capital city, because they offered an answer to the fears and hopes of every Mesopotamian. It was felt that mankind shared in the great renewal undergone by nature, that the past was abolished, that the cosmos momentarily reverted to chaos, that the fate of the country depended upon the judgment pronounced by the gods. Nothing short of a complex ritual loaded with magical virtues could solve the unavoidable crisis and put an end to the terrible uncertainty that overwhelmed the human race.

The New Year Festival, or *akîtu*, as celebrated in Babylon during the first millennium BC,[13] resulted from the confluence of two powerful currents of religious thought: an extremely ancient Fertility Cult, originally common to the whole prehistoric Near East, and a properly Sumerian cosmogony, comparatively more recent. We have already said (page 82) that in Sumer each city state ensured the fecundity of its own fields, flocks and people by means of a Sacred Marriage between the city-god and the city-goddess. We know from texts of the Ur III period, for instance, that such a marriage took place at Lagash between Ningirsu and

Baba, at Ur between Nanna and Gula, at Uruk between Anu and Inanna and at Nippur between Enlil and Ninlil. The ceremony, called in Sumerian *zagmuk*, 'New Year', was often performed twice a year, in the spring and in the autumn. It was arranged and directed by the local *ensi* or *lugal* who, at an early date, seems to have played the part of the male god in a human enactment of the divine union. Meanwhile, the theologians of Nippur had developed a cosmogony wherein the creation of the world was attributed to Enlil following his victory over Tiamat and the forces of Chaos. After the world was created, a general assembly of the gods presided by the 'Lord Wind' decreed the Destinies of the Land, the fate of humanity. Creation and the naming of Destiny were not unique and final, but annual and conditional. The great cosmic struggle was believed to take place every year and its outcome was unpredictable. In the Babylonian *akîtu*-festival, Sacred Marriage and Myth of Creation were harmoniously blended together, the passage of nature from want to fruitfulness being made to coincide with the restoration of divine order, and in this double drama the main roles were played by Marduk, who combined the personality of Enlil, champion and king of the gods, with his own personality of fertilizing city-god.

The *akîtu*-festival began at Babylon on the first day of Nisan (March–April) and lasted for eleven days.[14] The first eight days were days of bereavement, for Marduk was said to be held captive in the 'mountain' of the Netherworld.[15] From the first to the fourth of Nisan in Esagila, haunted only by the priests, prayers were said, hymns were sung and preparations were made for the subsequent ceremonies. On the fourth day, 'after the second meal in the late afternoon', the *urigallu*-priest recited the long poem *Enuma elish* (the Epic of Creation) in its entirety. The fifth day was devoted to purification: the *mashmashu*-priest sprinkled lustral water on the temple, beat the kettle-drum, recited incantations, burnt incense, and finally cut off the head of a ram, rubbing the temple walls with its blood, and threw head and body into the river, the 'scape-goat' being supposed to take away with him all the sins of the year. Rendered impure by these acts, the *mashmashu* left Esagila for the remainder of the festival. While these rites were performed, the people outside the temple expressed their emotion in a less formal way. We are ill informed on what went on in the streets of Babylon, but a much broken and apparently incoherent text[16] alludes to public wailing and mourning culminating in a state of anarchy: fighting broke out in various places, the chariot of Bêl (Marduk), without its driver, went 'speeding to the *bît akîtu*', a criminal disguised as a king seems to have been given free hand in the city ... Manifestations of mass hysteria, no doubt, but also perhaps an attempt to create an image of the chaos into which the god's disappearance had plunged the world.

On the fourth day of Nisan, the king proceeded to Barsippa (Birs Nimrud, 10 miles to the south of Babylon[17]) in order to fetch the god Nabû, who was to deliver his father Marduk from the grip of the Netherworld. Travelling by boat, he returned the next day and accompanied Nabû's statue to Esagila. At the gate of the temple, however, the king surrendered the insignia of kingship—the sceptre, the circle and the sword—to the *urigallu*-priest, who deposited them on a chair in front of Marduk, and then struck the king on the cheek:

'He (the priest), says the ritual to which we owe these details, shall accompany him (the king) into the presence of the god Bêl ... he shall drag him by the ears and make him bow down to the ground ... The king shall speak the following (only) once: "I did not sin, lord of the countries. I was not neglectful of your godship. I did not destroy Babylon; I did not command its overthrow ... The temple Esagila, I did not forget its rites. I did not rain blows on the cheek of a subordinate ... I did not humiliate them. I watched out for Babylon; I did not smash its walls ..."'

The priest reassured the king:

'Have no fear ... The god Bêl will listen to your prayer ... He will magnify your lordship ... He will exalt your kingship ... The god Bêl will bless you for ever. He will destroy your enemy, fell your adversary.'

The king was given back his insignia and struck once more:

'He (the priest) shall strike the king's cheek. If, when he strikes the king's cheek, the tears flow, (it means that) the god Bêl is friendly; if no tears appear, the god Bêl is angry: the enemy will rise up and bring about his downfall.'[18]

The symbolism of this humiliating ritual is clear: the king, scapegoat of the community, atoned for his sins and was reminded that he owed his powers to none but the gods. Purified and reinstated, he could enter the sanctuary and play in the ceremonies of the following days a part so important that, in his absence, the festival could not take place.

During the next two days, the gods of Sippar, Kutha, Kish, Nippur, Uruk and other cities arrived at Babylon, some by road, some by canal, while the king, in Esagila, performed various rites aimed at bringing Marduk back to earth. On the eighth of Nisan, Marduk was resurrected. The king entered the shrine of the god, 'took his hand'—a gesture which had come to summarize the royal participation in the festival—installed him in the great courtyard of Esagila, and introduced the other gods one by one. In this first divine assembly was proclaimed the sovereignty of Marduk, as stated in the Epic of Creation (see page 88). A great, solemn cortège was then formed, including the statues of all the gods and goddesses. Headed by Marduk on his chariot glittering with gold and precious stones and led by the king, it went down Procession Street across Babylon in an aura of incense, songs and music, while people were kneeling down in adoration as it passed by. Through Ishtar Gate, the cortège left the city and, after a short journey on the Euphrates, reached the *bît akîtu*, a temple filled with plants and flowers in the middle of a large park.[19] We lack details concerning the ceremonies which took place there. The triumph of Marduk over the forces of evil was certainly celebrated. Some scholars think that this was the place where the Sacred Marriage was consummated; others believe that it was consummated later in Esagila. In any case, the gods stayed in the *bît akîtu* for three days. On the eleventh of Nisan, they returned to Esagila where they assembled once more, this time to decree 'the Destinies of the Land'. What is meant by this vague expression, we do not know exactly. Perhaps oracles concerning definite events, such as wars, famines, inundations, etc., were pronounced; perhaps the gods simply reaffirmed their protection over the Babylonians and their monarch in general terms. The session ended in a huge banquet accompanied by music and prayers. On the twelfth of Nisan, all the gods who had come to Babylon returned to their respective cities, the priests to their temples, the king to his palace. The great New Year Festival was over.

ECONOMIC LIFE

From the lofty summits of religious thought to the mundane realities of economic life, the distance in Chaldaean Babylonia was not very great, since in many places the clergy cared for both the spiritual and material needs of the population. For instance, the archives of E-Anna, the great sanctuary of Uruk, show that the temple owned large estates which were partly let out to tenants, carried on extensive trade within and outside Mesopotamia and formed a social and economic unit almost independent of the central government.[20] These various activities were directed by an 'administrator' (*shatammu*), assisted by an 'overseer' (*qipu*) and by several priest-scribes. The temple employed a considerable number of people: free men (*mâr banûti*) engaged in various professions were at its service in one way or another; hired men and slaves ploughed and harvested its fields, dug and maintained its canals, grazed its cattle and flocks, and assured the transportation and storage of goods. Among the temple servants, special mention should be made of the *shirkê* (sing. *shirku*), literally 'consecrated', a new social class lying somewhere between free men and slaves, made up of men and women who had been 'offered' in perpetuity to the temple, performed various tasks, received no pay, but were fed and kept by the clergy.[21] The produce of the land, the profits of trade, the rent of fields and houses, taxes levied on the community, and part of the offerings and sacrifices—in theory optional, but in practice compulsory—constituted the revenues of the temple. A similar organization probably existed in other cities, though most of the documents published up to now from Babylon, Sippar, Nippur, Barsippa and Ur seem to deal with transactions between individuals.[22]

The importance assumed at least by some temples under the Chaldaean dynasty probably originated in the tenth and eleventh centuries BC. Prior to that date, the general trend in history had been towards a gradual reduction of the temples' privileges through the creation of large royal estates and the development of private property. But during the 'dark age' of Aramaean invasion, events took a different course. Despite the lack of written evidence, we may reasonably suppose that, while the invaders ransacked and occupied the open country, the Mesopotamian farmers and craftsmen took refuge in or immediately around the cities, and put themselves at the service of the only remaining authority, the local clergy. The temples then became the social, economic and cultural centres of southern Mesopotamia—a state of affairs reminiscent of the rôle played by the monasteries in our Middle Ages—with unlimited facilities for enlarging their domains. Under the Assyrian domination, when texts again become available, it appears that the wealth of Babylonia was concentrated in her 'holy cities'. The kings of Assyria, who relied a great deal upon the temples to maintain the political stability of Babylonia, bestowed their favours upon them and generally exempted them from taxes and duties. But they also kept them under tight administrative control and, on occasion, 'borrowed' from their treasures.[23] The collapse of Assyria freed the temples, to a great extent, from governmental interference, and if Nabopolassar and Nebuchadrezzar, out of personal devotion and faithfulness to a well-established tradition, materially rebuilt and adorned the sanctuaries, they abstained from interfering with their organization, and contented themselves with a twenty per cent return on their revenue. Nabonidus, however, attempted to bring the temples business under closer royal scrutiny. We know that he appointed two high officials—the 'Royal Officer Lord of the Appointment', and the 'Royal Officer over the King's Coffer'—over the E-Anna of Uruk, with instructions to supervise its transactions and ensure the regular collection of royal tithe. In all probability it was this, more than the king's 'heresy', which alienated the priests from him and threw them on Cyrus' side.

This new, unpopular policy was no doubt dictated by serious financial difficulties. Nebuchadrezzar had spent fabulous sums in the rebuilding of Babylon and other cities, and the 'archaeological' activities of Nabonidus himself were hardly less costly. In addition, the government had to support a large and permanent army. With the exception of Elam, all the northern and eastern countries were now practically closed to Mesopotamian trade, and if Syria-Palestine was still in Babylonian hands, frequent revolts made these distant provinces a burden more than an asset. Moreover, the Phoenician cities had lost much of their former wealth. The sixth century BC was precisely the great period of Greek maritime and colonial expansion, and the main commercial centres of the eastern Mediterranean were no longer on the Lebanese coast, but in Greece, Ionia, Lydia, Cilicia and Egypt. Increased expenditures and reduced income drained heavily on the royal treasury and deeply affected the general economy of Babylonia. A study of the hire and sale contracts reveals a marked increase in prices between the beginning and end of the Neo-Babylonian period. Thus, a male slave costing 40 shekels of silver about 600 BC, cost 50 shekels some 50 years later. Under Nebuchadrezzar, 1 shekel could buy from 2 to 4 *qa* of cultivated land, but only 1 to 2 *qa* under Nabonidus.[24] A similar increase affected foodstuffs, clothes and other daily necessities. For various reasons it is difficult to draw an exact scale of wages, but they seem to have remained fairly low throughout the period. The average monthly salary of an unskilled labourer, for instance, was about 1 shekel; with this, he could purchase 2 bushels of grain and 3 bushels of dates, just enough for him to feed his family. In consequence, people took to borrowing money on a long-term basis, and credit inflation rendered the Babylonian economy even more un-healthy.

The term 'money' here should not be taken in its ordinary sense, for minted coins—said to have been invented by the Lydians in the seventh century BC—did not circulate widely in the Near East before the reign of Darius I (521–486 BC). What the Babylonians had in their purses were bits of silver of various shapes and standardized weights: the *shiqlu* (shekel), weighing about three-tenths of an ounce; the *mana* (mine or pound) of 60 shekels, weighing about 18 ounces; and the *biltu* (talent) of 60 mines, weighing about 67 pounds. In current use were also the half-shekel and, occasionally, the *she*, literally a 'grain' of silver. The system was very old, since lingots of bronze stamped with some inscription or image which guaranteed their fineness appear in Mesopotamia as early as the second millennium BC, and the Assyrians used cast objects of lead and, later, copper as currency.

What was novel in the Neo-Babylonian period was the adoption of the silver standard, the ratio of silver to gold varying between 14 and 10 to 1. Standardized currency taken as a system of reference made accounting considerably easier and facilitated transactions, but the silver standard also encouraged the development of credit, for the simple reason that silver 'coins' were easy to store and manipulate. 'Usuary, mortgages and enslaved debtors followed the new medium of exchange wherever it was introduced.'[25] Private banking on a scale hitherto unknown suddenly flourished in Babylonia at the end of the sixth century BC, and while most of the population endured considerable hardship, a few 'dynasties of bankers'—such as the Egibi family in Babylon —made colossal fortunes simply by lending money at 20 to 30 per cent interest, and became even wealthier than the temples and, possibly, the State.

The emergence of a monetary system and the development of large-scale banking are phenomena the importance of which cannot be overstressed; but the resurgence of the temples as major social and economic units is equally important. Both help to explain what happened after Babylonia had lost her political autonomy. Economic depression contributed to the decline of the Mesopotamian civilization, but the temples kept it alive for almost 600 years. By a remarkable coincidence, this civilization was to die as it was born: under the wings of the gods.

CHAPTER XXV

DEATH OF A CIVILIZATION

NOT very long ago, the great city which we have just described lay buried beneath a thick blanket of earth, as did all the towns and villages of ancient Iraq. Here and there on these 'tells' could be seen a brick inscribed with a writing no scholar could read. Of the monuments of art, of the masterpieces of literature, of the works of science produced in Mesopotamia during three thousand years of history, almost nothing was known. The Mesopotamian civilization was dead and forgotten, and even today no one, when confronted with the most desolate of ruins, can help wondering when, how and why it died.

If the Persians had dealt with Babylon as the Medes and Babylonians had dealt with Nineveh, there would be no problem. The Near East offers, besides Assyria, other examples of nations and cultures which disappeared almost overnight, the victims of devastating wars—the Hittite kingdom of Boghazköy, Urartu and Phrygia, for instance. But the Persians did not destroy Babylon, nor did they destroy the other cities of Babylonia, and a number of monuments and inscriptions dating from the Achaemenian, Hellenistic and Parthian periods testify to a partial survival of the Mesopotamian civilization down to the first century AD. How then did it slowly decline and ultimately vanish?

There are, it seems, two main reasons why this extremely important question has not yet received all the attention it deserves. On the one hand, it encompasses three separate fields of scholarly research. Historians of the Semitic Near East, hebraists or assyriologists by training, are naturally reluctant to encroach on the domain of Greek and Iranian studies with which they are not fully conversant, while Hellenists and Iranologists, struggling with wider problems, tend to treat Mesopotamia as a secondary subject, beyond the normal scope of their work. On the other hand, the decline and fall of a civilization anywhere in the world is always a complicated process, dependent upon multiple political, ethnic, linguistic, religious, economic and even geographical factors which, in this particular case, are too often beyond the grasp of our knowledge. Nevertheless, we feel that, having described at length how the Mesopotamian civilization was born, we should at least endeavour to examine how it died. Carrying this work a few centuries beyond that fateful date of 539 BC, when Babylonia lost its independence for ever, we shall give here a condensed account of Mesopotamian history during the three relevant periods of foreign domination:

> the Achaemenian period (539–331 BC)
> the Hellenistic period (331–126 BC)
> the Parthian period (126 BC–AD 227)

THE ACHAEMENIAN PERIOD

To many Babylonians, the conquest of their country by the Persians may have appeared as a mere change of dynasty. Soon after Babylon was captured, life between the Tigris and the Euphrates resumed its normal course and business was carried on as usual, the only difference being that contracts were now dated in the years of 'Kurash, King of Babylon, King of the Lands', instead of in the years of Nabû-na'id. The government of Babylonia was first entrusted to Nabonidus' former general, Gobryas, but in Nisan 538 BC, Cyrus' own son, Cambyses (Kambuziya) 'took the hand of Bêl' in the New Year Festival[1] and from then on acted as viceroy, with headquarters in Sippar and a staff of native officials. In 530 BC, when Cyrus was killed on a distant battlefield, Cambyses, already associated with the throne, became King of Persia. We have very little information concerning this period, except that Babylonian soldiers were enrolled in the Persian army and took part in the conquest of Egypt, but whatever truth there may be in the story of the king's mad behaviour in the Nile valley, it seems certain that Babylonia enjoyed complete peace throughout his reign.

The death of Cambyses, early in 522 BC, marks the end of this honeymoon. Bardiya, his brother, who had usurped the throne, was defeated and slain eight months later by Darius;[2] but although Darius was of royal blood—he was a descendant of Ariaramnes and therefore belonged to the Achaemenian family—his authority was immediately challenged. Several of the satraps appointed by Cyrus refused to obey the new king, while a second Phraortes in Media and a pseudo-Bardiya in Persia rallied many supporters. The Babylonians, hitherto submissive, were not slow in joining the rebels, for among them were men in whose hearts the flame of freedom was still burning high. In the long cuneiform inscription in three languages—Old Persian, Babylonian, Elamite—carved in the rock at Behistun (near Kermanshah) to commemorate Darius' victories over his foes,[3] the Persian monarch himself tells us how a Babylonian called Nidintu-Bêl recruited an army by declaring that he was 'Nebuchadrezzar, son of Nabonidus' and seized kingship in Babylon. Darius in person marched against him, routed the Babylonians on the Tigris and on the Euphrates and pursued the rebel to his capital city where he was captured and executed. According to dated contracts, 'Nebuchadrezzar III' reigned from October to December 522 BC. In August 521 BC, while Darius was fighting for his throne in Media and Persia, the Babylonians 'broke the truce for the second time'. The pretender —who also claimed to be 'Nebuchadrezzar, son of Nabonidus'— was an 'Armenian' (Urartian), Arakha, son of Haldita. Against him, Darius dispatched one of his generals, Vindafârna:

'I said to him: "Go forth! Fight this Babylonian army which does not declare itself for me!" Vindafârna marched against Babylon with the (Persian) army. Ahuramazda lent me his assistance. By the will of Ahuramazda, Vindafârna fought the Babylonians and took them captive. Twenty-two days of the month Margazana had elapsed when he captured Arakha and the nobles, his main followers. Whereupon, I gave an order: 'This Arakha and the nobles, his main followers, shall be impaled in Babylon!'"'[4]

'Nebuchadrezzar IV' was put to death on November 27, 521 BC. At the beginning of 520 BC, Darius, finally rid of all his enemies, was recognized king throughout most of the Near East and immediately set out to promote a number of major reforms aimed at consolidating his power and cementing together the various regions of his vast empire. The administrative system was reshaped, largely on the Assyrian model. The number of satraps was increased and their authority further limited by the creation of military governors, tax collectors and royal inspectors. Royal couriers rode swiftly from the Aegean to the Persian Gulf on an admirable network of roads. A common law, reminiscent in style of the Code of Hammurabi, was imposed upon all subject peoples. The monetary systems were unified and based on a gold standard, the coinage used in trade and banking now being the gold *daric*, worth twenty shekels of silver. Reorganized, cleared of corruption, heavily taxed and subjected to tight royal control, Babylonia remained quiet during the rest of Darius' long reign (520–485 BC).

In the fourth year of Xerxes, however, the Babylonians made a last attempt at recovering their freedom (482 BC). Contracts from Dilbat, Barsippa and Babylon show that Bêl-shimanni and Shamash-eriba were successively accepted as kings, the former in August, the latter in September, while we learn from other sources that the satrap Zophyrus was killed and that Xerxes, greatly angered, sent his brother-in-law Megabysus to crush the revolt.5 The repression was brutal, the rebels were tortured and slain, but the exact amount of damage inflicted upon Babylon itself is difficult to assess. If Herodotus really visited, some twenty years later, the city which he describes, we may conclude that it had suffered very little harm—indeed, the 'Father of History' merely states that Xerxes took from Esagila the colossal golden statue of Marduk. Yet Arrian, Ctesias and Strabo suggest that the city walls were dismantled and the temples razed to the ground. Since Esagila and other sanctuaries are mentioned in later texts, it is probable that they were only partly damaged and that they fell into ruin through lack of maintenance in the course of the following centuries, rather than through violent destruction.

The failure of the Babylonians to restore a national monarchy had consequences that went far beyond a simple loss of prestige. From time immemorial, the Mesopotamian kings had been responsible to the gods for the welfare of their subjects. The cities owed to them their temples, their palaces, their fortifications and often their parks and gardens. They had never failed to ensure that canals were dug, kept open and extended, that dykes and dams were built, that land rights were safeguarded. In a country like ancient Iraq these functions were of vital importance. No matter what the temples could achieve in their own spheres, only a king residing permanently in the country and constantly aware of its needs could raise the funds and mobilize the labour required for such undertakings on a nation-wide scale. Without her own rulers Mesopotamia was, to a great extent, paralysed. Sooner or later, it could be predicted, buildings left unattended would crumble down, canals would become silted up and part of the land would revert to desert.

The first Persian kings, conscious of their duties towards one of their richest and most civilized provinces, carried out some of the royal tasks traditional in Mesopotamia. We know, for instance, that Cyrus restored the precinct of the temple of Sin at Ur, that he and Darius repaired the E-Anna of Uruk. In Babylon, his winter residence, Darius built an arsenal, a palace for the crown prince and an *apadana* (i.e. a hall supported by columns, in the Persian style) for his own palace.[6] But Xerxes and his successors, engaged in an endless and costly war against Greece, do not seem to have cared much for their Babylonian satrapy. The entire period between the accession of Xerxes (485 BC) and the conquest of Alexander (331 BC) is exceedingly poor in architectural remains and building inscriptions. In southern Iraq, business documents found *in situ*[7] prove that Babylon, Barsippa, Kish, Nippur, Uruk and Ur—to mention only the main cities—were alive, some of them even fairly prosperous, but none of their monuments appears to have been rebuilt or repaired. As for the North, it was still suffering from the great destructions of the years 614–609 BC. Xenophon, who marched through Assyria in 401 BC with ten thousand Greek mercenaries, describes Nimrud (which he calls 'Larissa') as 'deserted', and did not even recognize the walls of Nineveh in the 'large undefended fortifications' which he saw near Mescila (Mosul?).[8] With the exception of Erbil, all the cities of Assyria lay in ruins or had become small villages.

Adverse economic conditions perhaps contributed to the decline of the Mesopotamian civilization. The main artery of the Persian empire, the 'Royal Road' from Sardis to Susa, ran at the foot of the mountains and bypassed Babylon. Trade with India and the East in general was monopolized by the Persians, nearer to these countries. Syria had been detached from Mesopotamia by Darius or Xerxes. Babylonia and Assyria, forming together the ninth satrapy, were grossly overtaxed: they paid to the Crown an annual tribute of one thousand talents of silver and supplied the Persian court with food during four months of the year. In addition, they had to bear the full burden of a greedy local administration. If we are to believe Herodotus, the satrap of Babylonia received daily the content of an *artaba* (about 100 pints) of silver and kept 800 stallions and 16,000 mares, while his Indian dogs were fed by four villages!9 For all these reasons, the upward trend of prices already noticed during the Neo-Babylonian period continued under the Achaemenians: within the century following the death of Darius, the cost of living doubled, without corresponding increase in wages, and the rent of an average house passed from fifteen shekels per month under Cyrus to forty shekels under Artaxerxes I (465–424 BC).10 Naturally, the great bankers and usurers benefited from these conditions. The Murashu family of Nippur, for instance—a powerful financial firm operating between 460 and 400 BC—owned and hired out canals, cattle and fisheries and held in mortgage most of the land around the city. Their main source of income was from the money which they lent, at 40 to 70 per cent interest, to the landowners of Nippur to enable them to pay their taxes to the government.11

No less important were the ethnic and linguistic changes brought about by the Achaemenian domination. The population of Babylonia, already mixed with Medes, Arabs, Jews, Egyptians, Urartians and other foreigners in Assyrian and Babylonian times received a strong influx of Persian blood under Darius and Xerxes: many Persians were granted estates by the king; others were appointed judges or given major or minor administrative posts. With these men, the gods of Iran entered the Tigris-Euphrates valley. There is, it is true, no evidence that they were at this time the object of an organized cult, and the decree of Xerxes12 forbidding the worship of deities other than Ahuramazda was never obeyed; but the mere fact that a number of Babylonians changed their Semitic name for a name composed with Aryan gods betrays a certain dwindling of private devotion. For all these people of various origins and tongues, there could be only one common language: Aramaic. Already widely spoken in Western

Asia, easy to learn, eminently suitable for writing on papyrus or parchment, officially adopted by Darius as the *lingua franca* throughout the empire, Aramaic replaced Babylonian in the homes, streets and shops. Only learned men and temple scribes could still read and write the Akkadian and Sumerian languages in their cuneiform script. The numerous literary, religious and historical texts copied during the Achaemenian period, as well as the remarkable works of astronomers such as Nabû-rimani and Kidinnu (see above, page 305) are proof that the traditional culture of Mesopotamia was still very much alive in these restricted circles. But for the great majority of the population, inscriptions on clay were meaningless, and history tells us that a nation which forgets its language forgets its past and soon loses its identity.

Oppressed, impoverished and partly 'denationalized', such was Mesopotamia, it would appear, in the last decades of the fourth century BC, when Alexander came to give her a new, though entirely different life.

THE HELLENISTIC PERIOD

The battle of Gaugamela (near Erbil), on October 1, 331 BC, opened for Alexander the road to Babylonia and Persia, as the battle of Issus, two years before, had opened for him the road to Syria and Egypt. The Persian troops stationed in Babylon surrendered without fighting, and the Macedonian conqueror made a triumphal entry into the old Semitic metropolis. Realizing, like Cyrus, that he could never rule over 'a hundred different nations' unless he won their hearts, he made sacrifice to Marduk and ordered the rebuilding of the temples thought to have been destroyed by Xerxes—a gigantic task which was never to be completed.[13] The Babylonians hailed him as their liberator and immediately acknowledged his kingship. After a month's stay in Babylon, he proceeded to Susa, and thereafter embarked upon the great armed expedition to the East which took him as far as the river Ganges. When he returned, nine years later, his mind was full of grandiose projects: Babylon and Alexandria in Egypt were to become the twin capital cities of his empire; they would be linked by sea around the Arabian peninsula, shortly to be conquered; the coasts of the Indian Ocean would be explored; the Euphrates would be rendered navigable up to the Persian Gulf; a great port would be built at Babylon and another at the mouth of the river. But most of these plans remained a dead letter: on June 13, 323 BC, Alexander died in Babylon, probably of malaria, at the age of 32.

At that date, Alexander's only son, the future Alexander IV, was not yet born, and it was his brother, Philip Arrhideus, who was proclaimed king in Macedonia. But the authority of this young and mentally retarded prince remained purely nominal. The real power lay in the hands of Alexander's generals—the *Diadochi*—who, having divided the empire between themselves, struggled for forty-two years to prevent each other from reconstructing it. During this period—one of the most complex in the history of antiquity—Babylon changed hands several times. At first the seat of a military junta presided over by the regent Perdiccas, it was allotted to Seleucus, chief of the Macedonian cavalry, by his colleagues in 321 BC, after they had murdered Perdiccas. In 316 BC, Antigonus, the ambitious satrap of Phrygia, dislodged Seleucus from Babylon, forcing him to take refuge with Ptolemy in Egypt. But Seleucus came back in 312 BC, recovered his satrapy, and for four years successfully protected it from repeated attacks launched by Antigonus and his son Demetrius. It was a fierce and bitter war which brought terrible suffering upon Babylon and its territory—'there was weeping and mourning in the land' repeats, as a leit-motif, a Babylonian chronicle describing these events.[14] Finally, Antigonus was defeated and killed at Ipsus, in Phrygia (301 BC), and Seleucus added to Babylonia the satrapy of Syria and the eastern half of Asia Minor. The war, however, continued, this time in the West, between Seleucus, Ptolemy, Demetrius and the Macedonian ruler of Thrace, Lysimachus. In September 281 BC,[15] a few months after he had defeated Lysimachus at Korupedion (near Sardis), Seleucus was stabbed to death by a son of Ptolemy. He had taken the title of king in 305 BC, but for the Babylonians, the 'years of *Silukku*', the Seleucid era, began on the first New Year's Day following his return from Egypt: April 3, 311 BC. It was the first time that a continuous numerical dating system was used in Mesopotamia.

After Ipsus, Seleucus ruled directly or indirectly over a huge territory extending from the borders of India to those of Egypt, and from the Black Sea to the Persian Gulf. But this empire lacked cohesion and started disintegrating almost as soon as it was formed. By 200 B C, the descendants of Seleucus had lost practically all their provinces and protectorates beyond the Taurus and the Zagros, and after Babylonia had been conquered by the Parthians (126 B C), all that remained was a small state in northern Syria, torn apart by dynastic crises, which fell an easy prey to the Romans in 63 B C. In actual fact, ever since Seleucus founded Antioch on the Orontes, in May 300 B C, and made it his favourite residence, the Seleucid kingdom had always been essentially a Syrian kingdom. If we except an unsuccessful attempt made by Antiochus III (223–187 B C) to recover the Eastern districts, the diplomatic and military activities of its rulers were almost entirely absorbed in an endless conflict with the Ptolemies of Egypt for the possession of the Phoenician ports and hinterland. This meant peace for the Babylonians, who must have been relieved to see the ravages of war removed from their own country to '(the country) across the river' (ebir nâri), as they now called Syria.[16] But it also meant that Babylon lost the privileged position it would have held had it remained the capital city of the Macedonian dominion, as geography and history destined it to be. For many years to come, the world's political, cultural and economic centre had shifted from the banks of the Euphrates to the shores of the Mediterranean.

Undoubtedly the most durable achievement of Alexander and his successors was the foundation, in Egypt and Western Asia, of numerous cities, organized on the model of the Greek *poleis* and populated by Greco-Macedonian settlers, as well as by Oriental subjects. Whether, by so doing, they merely wished to create a network of political and military strongholds, or aimed at promoting the Greek culture and way of life in the Orient is a much debated problem.[17] But the results obtained are obvious: the Near East became 'hellenized' in various degrees, and the pattern of urban life in these regions was profoundly altered. We know of at least a dozen such cities in Mesopotamia[18] alone, from Edessa-Antioch in the extreme north, to Alexandria-Charax on or near the Persian Gulf. They were, as a rule, built beside or on top of ancient towns and villages, though their layout and architectural characteristics were entirely new. Seleucia-on-the-

Tigris (Tell 'Umar, opposite Ctesiphon), founded by Antiochus I
in 274 BC, probably on the site of Semitic Upâ (Opis), was the
largest city, not only of Mesopotamia, but of the whole Seleucid
kingdom, with a population of about 600,000. Aerial photographs
clearly show its 'grid-plan', the blocks of habitations being
separated by straight avenues and streets crossing each other at
right angles. Two brief campaigns of excavations have yielded
numerous clay figurines, statuettes, coins, and other objects
typically hellenistic in style, but the few buildings unearthed
belonged to a Parthian occupation-level superimposed on the
hellenistic level. A similar situation confronted archaeologists at
Dura-Europus (Salahiych, on the Euphrates, 30 miles upstream
of ancient Mari), though here, remains of Greek monuments—a
fortress, a palace, and at least one temple—could be traced underneath the Parthian buildings.[20]

These hellenistic cities were all situated on the great trade
routes which linked Central Asia with the Mediterranean, and
thrived on transit operations. Seleucia, in particular, was the
meeting point of two land routes coming from India (one through
Bactria and the north of Iran, the other through Persepolis and
Susa), of the important sea route from India through the Persian
Gulf, and of several tracks crossing the Arabian peninsula. From
Seleucia, gold, ivory, spices, incense, and precious stones, as well
as the products of Mesopotamia itself—wheat, barley, dates,
woollens and bitumen—were transported to Syria, either along
the Euphrates *via* Dura-Europos, or along the Tigris and across
Jazirah *via* Nisibin(Antioch in Mygdonia) and Edessa. Commercial
intercourse between Europe, Asia and part of Africa was extremely
active in hellenistic times, and there is little doubt as to the
prosperity of the Seleucid kingdom in general—at least during the
third century BC. Our information on Babylonia is regrettably
scanty, but the few commercial texts published (mainly from
Uruk) show that a fair amount of business was carried out even
within the older towns, and that prices had fallen much below the
levels they had reached in Achaemenian times.[21]

The new economic and demographic conditions prevalent in
Seleucid Mesopotamia exerted a deep, though varied influence
upon the older cities. Thus Nimrud owed to its situation on the
Tigris route its revival as a small but prosperous village. Similarly,

Nineveh, Mari and Arslan-Tash were reoccupied after long years of abandonment.[22] Ur died slowly, probably killed by competition from Alexandria-Charax as much as by hydrographic changes in the region. Babylon was severely affected. It is true that sporadic efforts were made by the Macedonian rulers to revive and modernize the half-ruined city. In the last royal inscription in Akkadian that we possess, Antiochus I (280–262 BC) calls himself 'provider of Esagila and Ezida', like the Chaldaean kings, and declares that he 'formed with his august hands' and brought from 'Hatti' (Syria) the first bricks of these temples.[23] A tablet dated in the reign of Seleucus III (226–220 BC) shows that regular offerings were still made to a number of Babylonian gods in their own shrines. Remains of hellenistic architecture were discovered on the mound of Bâbil and on the site of Nebuchadrezzar's palace. Under Antiochus IV (151–143 BC)—the king who did most to propagate the Greek culture—Babylon received a gymnasium and a remarkable Greek theatre, later enlarged by the Parthians.[24] Yet not only was Babylon no longer the seat of the royal government, but it was already partly deserted, a great number of its inhabitants having been transferred to Seleucia when that city was founded.[25] We do not know what happened in Sippar, Kish and Nippur, but Uruk seems to have enjoyed considerable prosperity, judging from the impressive monuments erected during the Seleucid period. A huge terrace constructed around the E-Anna ziqqurat completely transformed the aspect of the sacred area, while in other parts of the city were built two large temples: *Irigal* (or, better, *Esh-gal*), dedicated to Ishtar, and the so-called *Bît rêsh*, dedicated to Anu.[26] Both had the conventional features of Babylonian temples, but a long inscription on glazed bricks which ran on the walls of the cult-room of Irigal was, significantly, in Aramaic script and language. Equally typical of the period are the Greek names conferred by the kings to the two city magistrates who built these temples: Anu-uballit Nicarchus and Anu-uballit Kephalon. A study of contracts on clay tablets and of *bullae*★ bearing Greek or Aramaic inscriptions shows that Uruk (called by the Greek *Orchoi*) gave shelter to an important Greek community, but retained its ancient laws and

★ Small balls of clay attached by a string to official documents on papyrus or parchment.

customs and was exempted from certain royal taxes. Most of the
business transactions were carried out by the temple organization,
in the activities of which ordinary citizens could be financially
interested by means of a system not very different from our
modern shareholding.[27] The existence of semi-independent
temple-states is well attested in Asia Minor in hellenistic times,
and it is probable that Uruk owed a similar status to the liberal
policy of the Seleucids.

It was in temples like those of Uruk, Sippar, Babylon and
Barsippa that the Sumero-Akkadian culture was preserved.
Throughout the Seleucid period, temple astronomers and
astrologers continued to record on tablets the motions of celestial
bodies, while temple scribes wrote down contemporary history
in the form of chronicles and copied a number of very ancient
myths, rituals, hymns and omens. It would seem *a priori* that the
much advanced Greek culture which flourished in cities such as
Seleucia must have exerted a strong attraction on the less con-
servative members of the Babylonian *intelligentsia*; but if a long
list of Greek authors native from Mesopotamia can be compiled,[28]
it is often difficult to distinguish between those who were of pure
Greco-Macedonian descent and those who, born Babylonian, had
adopted a Greek name. In fact the evidence available seems to
indicate a movement in the opposite direction: the Greeks became
interested, not so much in Mesopotamian history and literature,
as in the scientific and pseudo-scientific works of the 'Chaldaeans'.
In the second and third centuries BC, the Babylonian Sudinês
translated into Greek the writings of Kidinnu and other astronomers, and Berossus, priest of Marduk, wrote in Greek that strange
mixture of astrology and historical narratives called *Babyloniaca*,
which he dedicated to Antiochus I.[29] Limited as they were, these
cultural contacts saved for posterity some of the most remarkable
achievements of Mesopotamian scientists, while the most objec-
tionable end-product of the Mesopotamian belief in Destiny,
astrology, permeated and corrupted the religions of the West.

THE PARTHIAN PERIOD

The Parthians—a branch of the Scythians—appear for the first
time in history *circa* 250 BC, when Arsaces led his nomadic tribes-

men out of the steppes of Turkestan to settle in the north-eastern corner of Iran. By 200 B C, the 'Arsacids' were firmly established along the southern shore of the Caspian sea. Between 160 and 140 B C, Mithridates I conquered the Iranian plateau in its entirety and, reaching the Tigris, pitched his camp at Ctesiphon, opposite Seleucia. The Seleucid Demetrius II succeeded in recovering Babylonia and Media for a short period, but in 126 B C, Artabanus II reasserted his authority over these regions, and from then on the Tigris-Euphrates valley remained in Parthian hands—save for two brief periods of Roman occupation under Trajan and Septimus Severus—until it fell under Sassanian domination with the rest of the Parthian kingdom, in A D 227.

To govern their empire, the Arsacids could only rely upon a small, if valorous, Parthian aristocracy, but they had the intelligence to use for their own benefit the social organizations created by the Seleucids, or those which had grown upon the ruins of the Seleucid kingdom. They encouraged the development of hellenistic cities and tolerated the formation of independent vassal kingdoms, such as Osrhoene (around Edessa-Urfa), Adiabene (corresponding to ancient Assyria) and Characene (near the Persian Gulf). Towards the beginning of the Christian era, Hatra —one of the few cities which they had founded—acquired its autonomy and became the centre of a small state known as Araba.[30] The Arsacids and their vassals were rich, since they controlled practically all the trade routes between Asia and the Greco-Roman world, with the result that the second and first centuries B C were marked, in Mesopotamia, by intensive building activities resulting from governmental or regional initiative. Not only were Seleucia, Dura-Europus and, presumably, other prosperous market-places provided with a large number of new monuments, but towns and villages which had been lying in ruins for hundreds of years were reoccupied. In southern Iraq, traces of Parthian occupation were found in almost every site excavated, in particular Babylon, Kish, Nippur, Uruk and even forgotten Lagash.[31] In the North, Assyria was literally resurrected: Nuzi, Kakzu, Shibanniba were inhabited again, and Assur, rebuilt anew, became at least as large a city as it had been in the heyday of the Assyrian empire.[32] But it must be emphasized that the revived settlements had very little in common with their Assyrian or

Babylonian precursors. Several of them, if not all, had straight streets, often lined with columns, a citadel, usually built on top of the old ziqqurat, an agora. Walls of stone or ashlar masonry replaced the traditional walls of mud bricks, and the buildings themselves, with their lofty vaulted chambers wide open on one side (*iwan*), their elegant peristyle and their decoration of moulded stucco, differed from the buildings erected by Mesopotamian architects as markedly as the Greco-Iranian statues of the rulers of Hatra differed from those of Gudea or Ashurnasirpal.

These archaeological data, combined with textual evidence, point to a massive influx of foreign population. The Greek and Macedonian settlers, probably not very numerous at the beginning, had lived side by side with the Babylonians with relatively few social contacts; they had preserved their nationality, their institutions, their art, their language, their 'Greekhood' in a word, and were still keeping it under the protection of enlightened monarchs who called themselves 'philhellen'. But the newcomers—mostly Aramaeans, Arabs and Iranians—settled in Mesopotamia in very large numbers, and mixed with the native population more easily, since they were of Oriental, often Semitic stock and spoke the same language. Each city, old or new, gave shelter to several foreign gods. At Dura-Europus, for instance, were brought to light two Greek temples, an Aramaean sanctuary, a Christian chapel, a synagogue and a Mithreum, let alone the shrines of local deities and of the gods of Palmyra. Similarly, the Sumero-Akkadian god Nergal, the Greek god Hermes, the Aramaean goddess Atar'at and the Arabian deities Allat and Shamiya had their temples in Hatra, around the majestic sanctuary of Shamash, the sun-god common to all Semites. Even at Uruk, the ancestral home of Anu and Ishtar, can still be seen a charming little temple, more Roman than Greek in style, dedicated to the Iranian god Gareus, and the remains of an extraordinary absidal building believed to be a temple of Mithra.[33]

This human flood submerged what was left of the Sumero-Akkadian civilization. A handful of tablets, about two hundred astronomical or astrological texts, and two or three very fragmentary chronicles and Babylonian-Greek vocabularies constitute all the cuneiform literature in our possession.[34] The last cuneiform text known so far—an astronomical 'almanac'—was written in

PLATE 32. The Assyrian army at rest. In the upper register, soldiers are eating and drinking; one of them is feeding a horse. The lower register probably represents a distribution of water (in goatskins) to prisoners of war. Relief from Nineveh. Reign of Ashurbanipal.

PLATE 33

A. Tablet inscribed with the Babylonian Chronicle for the years 619–609 BC, including an account of the capture and destruction of Nineveh by the Medes and Babylonians: 'The great spoil of the city and temple they carried off and turned the city into a ruin-mound and heaps of debris.'

B. A mathematical tablet from Tell Harmal, dating from the nineteenth century BC. Written fifteen hundred years before Euclid, it deals with an Euclidian theorem on the properties of similar triangles.

AD 74–5.35 It is quite possible that the Babylonian priests and astronomers continued to write in Aramaic on papyrus or parchment for several generations, but no work of this kind is likely to be found. We know that some of the ancient temples were restored, that Ashur was worshipped in his home town, that a cult was rendered to Nabû in Barsippa until, perhaps, the fourth century AD. But there is no evidence that Esagila, the temple of the former national god Marduk, was kept in repair. Indeed, Babylon probably suffered more damage in the repression which followed the revolt of a certain Hymeros in 127 BC, or in the civil war between Mithridates II and Orodes in 52 BC, than in the hands of Xerxes. When Trajan, in AD 115, entered the once opulent city, it was not to 'take the hand of Bêl', but to sacrifice to the *manes* of Alexander. Eighty-four years later, Septimus Severus found it completely deserted.36

Very little is known of the administrative, social and economic status of Mesopotamia under the Sassanians (AD 227–636). We learn from Greek and Latin authors that the northern part of the country was ravaged by four centuries of almost uninterrupted war between Romans (or Byzantines) and Persians, and that Assur was destroyed by Shapur I, in AD 256, as radically as it had been destroyed by the Medes. At Ctesiphon can be admired the remains of a magnificent palace attributed to Chosroes I, while the more modest residence of another Sassanian king has been excavated at Kish.37 At Uruk, nor far from the city wall originally built by Gilgamesh, a local ruler (?) was buried with his crown of golden leaves.38 Sherds of Sassanian pottery testify to the occupation or reoccupation of other ancient sites, and we read in the Talmud that important colonies of Jews lived in Babylon and Nippur. But, at the beginning of the seventh century AD, shortly before the Islamic conquest, the usual combination of military setbacks, internal strife and economic difficulties brought about the decline of the Sassanian kingdom and the ruin of Mesopotamia. Many canals left unattended dried up; the rivers, unchecked, could meander freely; people abandoned the towns deprived of water, scattering to outlying villages, and the ancient cities of Iraq were rapidly buried beneath the sand of the desert and the silt of the valley.

EPILOGUE

THUS perished one of the oldest and most remarkable civilizations of the ancient world. Brutally destroyed in Assyria at the end of the seventh century BC, it survived in Babylonia for about six centuries to disappear with the last cuneiform inscription at the beginning of the Christian era. Born during the Uruk and Proto-Literate periods (*circa* 3300–2800 BC), it had lasted for more than three thousand years.

In its slow decline (500 BC–AD 100), economic conditions played a smaller part than is sometimes believed, and the geographical changes—the wandering of the Twin Rivers, the silting-up of canals, the salinization of the soil—responsible for the abandonment of many ancient towns and villages and the depopulation of vast areas did not assume large-scale proportions until the end of the Sassanian period (fifth–sixth centuries AD). All considered, the decay and death of the Mesopotamian civilization can be ascribed to three main causes: the absence of a national government, the foundation by Alexander and his successors of new cities competing with and eventually superseding the older settlements and, above all, the profound ethnic, linguistic, religious and cultural changes introduced by successive waves of invaders—Persians, Greeks, Aramaeans, pre-Islamic Arabs—who could be neither kept at bay nor assimilated. In the course of her long history, Mesopotamia had been invaded many times. Guti, Amorites, Hurrians, Kassites and Aramaeans had found in the Tigris-Euphrates valley a young and vigorous culture immensely superior to their own, and had invariably adopted it. But to the highly civilized Greeks of the third century BC, to the disciples of Plato and Aristotle, the Babylonians had little to offer beside the abstruse works of their astronomers, and nothing was less suited to the requirements of the cosmopolitan society then taking roots in Iraq than the intricate cuneiform script which the Babylonians themselves were giving up. What the

Greco-Macedonian and Oriental settlers found in that country was a culture in many ways antiquated and 'ossified', perpetuated by a few priests in a few temples. Spontaneity and creativeness were absent from literature since the time of Hammurabi; sculpture had died with the Assyrians; architecture, under the Chaldaean and Seleucid dynasties, still produced some impressive monuments but adhered to traditional blue-prints; as for the various sciences, they had apparently reached their limits, with the notable exception of mathematics and astronomy. Attachment to tradition, which was perhaps the dominant character of the Sumero-Akkadian civilization, had ensured its cohesion and continuity for three millennia, but it had now become a handicap rather than an asset. The crucial period for Mesopotamia, the hellenistic period, can be compared with the sixteenth-century Renaissance or, indeed, with our own age. The new world heralded by Alexander was a fast changing world marked by extensive commercial intercourse, bursting with curiosity, eager to re-appraise most of its religious, moral, scientific and artistic values. There was no room in such a world for a literature which none but a few scholars could read, for an art which drew its inspiration from outdated ideals and models, for a science which evaded rational explanations, for a religion which did not admit scepticism. The Mesopotamian civilization, like its Egyptian counterpart, was condemned. If it were permissible to enclose a highly complex phenomenon into one single and necessarily inaccurate formula, one could say that it died of old age.

Civilizations, however, rarely die without leaving any trace and even we, men of the twentieth century, must acknowledge our debt towards the ancient inhabitants of Mesopotamia.[1] While we are harnessing the atom and preparing ourselves to explore the stars, it is appropriate to remember that we owe the Babylonians the basic principles of our mathematics and astronomy, including our 'positional' numeration and the sexagesimal system by which we still divide our circle and our clocks. We also owe them—though this is of more doubtful value—the bulk of an astrology which, judging from the number of modern publications devoted to this pseudo-science, has lost nothing of its appeal to the masses. To this heritage must be added the rudiments of an efficient administration (undoubtedly a creation of the Assyrians), some institutions, such as the coronation of our kings, a number of symbols mainly used in religious art (the crescent, the Maltese cross, the 'tree of life', for instance), a few words that have come to us through the channels of Greek or Arabic—e.g. cane (Akkadian *qânu*), alcohol (*guhlu*), dragoman (*targumanu*), gypsum (*gaṣṣu*), myrrh (*murru*), saffron (*azupiranu*), naphtha (*naptu*) in English, or corne (*qarnu*) and mesquin (*mushkênu*) in French—and, last but not least, the Mesopotamian elements detectable in the Bible. All this may appear exceedingly light compared with the enormous weight of our Greco-Roman heritage, but lists of this kind, even when they are exhaustive, fall short of doing full justice to the importance assumed by the Sumero-Akkadian civilization in the history of mankind. To reckon only with those Mesopotamian elements that have survived up to now is like counting the pieces of furniture inherited from remote ancestors, forgetting that these ancestors have shaped the lives of our forefathers and, indirectly, our own life. Classical scholars, long dazzled by the so-called 'Greek miracle', have now come to realize the full impact of oriental influences upon the formative phase of Greek thought, art and ethics—and the Orient, throughout most of pre-classical antiquity, was to a great extent culturally dependent upon Mesopotamia. Long before Alexander brought Greece into Asia, the Aegean countries were in direct contact with the Hittite lands and in commercial relations by sea with Canaan and Egypt. Merchants, craftsmen, ambassadors, princes, royal couriers, physicians and even priests travelled widely within and outside the Near East. We know that, already in the third millennium BC, there were Assyrian colonies in the heart of Asia Minor; between 1500 and 1200 BC, Mycaenean traders lived in Ugarit, on the Syrian coast and, perhaps, West Semitic traders in the Messara plain of Crete,[2] while Mesopotamian epics and myths were copied on the banks of the Nile in their original cuneiform script. We should not be surprised, therefore, to find that the Greek civilization was 'built upon East Mediterranean foundations'[3] largely made up of Mesopotamian material. It has already been suggested that Assyro-Babylonian medicine paved the way for the great Hippocratic reform of the fourth and fifth centures BC,[4] and it is highly probable that early Greek mathematicians, such as Pythagoras (sixth century BC), drew largely upon the work of their Babylonian predecessors. The analysis of oriental influences upon Greek art and literature is fraught with difficulties, since it is not always easy to distinguish between stimulus, parallel though independent creation, and sheer borrowing. Yet, to quote only undisputable examples, it is now generally recognized that the Aesopian fable had Sumero-Akkadian antecedents and that Gilgamesh was the prototype of both Heracles and Ulysses,5 while a glance at the archaic statues and figurines of continental and insular Greece reveals at once strong affinities with earlier or contemporary Mesopotamian works.

If Mesopotamia can be shown to have influenced Greece, it is not unreasonable to believe that she exerted an even greater influence upon other Near Eastern countries. The case has been repeatedly proven with regards to the Hittites, the Hebrews, Canaan, Urarṭu, Media and Achaemenian Persia. But what of the Mesopotamian heritage in later oriental civilizations? What of Parthian and Sassanian Iran, of Hellenistic, Roman and Byzantine Anatolia? What of Arabia? What of the Islamic religion and institutions? What of Iraq itself, from Parthian times down to the present day? Going even further afield, Professor Rostovtzeff— one of the few scholars equally at ease in the hellenistic and oriental worlds—could write, twenty-two years ago: 'We are gradually learning how great was the influence of Babylonian and Persian Art on the artistic development of India and China.'6 The material available is already substantial, if scattered; yet no one, it seems, has undertaken to study it from this particular point of view. So much has still to be done in the fields of assyriology and Mesopotamian archaeology, so many chapters in the history of ancient Iraq require completion that this delicate but fascinating and very useful task must be reserved for scholars of future generations.

LIST OF ABBREVIATIONS USED IN THE BIBLIOGRAPHY

AAA	*Annals of Archaeology and Anthropology*, Liverpool.
AAO	H. FRANKFORT, *The Art of Architecture of the Ancient Orient*, Penguin Books, Harmondsworth, 1954.
AAS	*Annales Archéologiques de Syrie*, Damascus.
AASOR	*Annual of the American Schools of Oriental Research*, New Haven.
AfO	*Archiv für Orientforschung*, Berlin/Graz.
AJ	*Antiquaries Journal*, London.
AJA	*American Journal of Archaeology*, Concord, New Haven.
AJSL	*American Journal of Semitic Languages and Literature*, Chicago.
AM	A. PARROT, *Archéologie Mésopotamienne*, Paris, 1946–53.
ANET	*Ancient Near Eastern Texts Relating to the Old Testament* (edited by J. B. PRITCHARD), Princeton, N.J., 1950, 2nd edition, 1955.
ARAB	D. D. LUCKENBILL, *Ancient Records of Assyria and Babylonia*, Chicago, 1926–27.
ARM	*Archives Royales de Mari* (edited by A. PARROT and G. DOSSIN), Paris, 1950 ss.
BASOR	*Bulletin of the American Schools of Oriental Research*, New Haven.
BBS	L. W. KING, *Babylonian Boundary Stones*, London, 1912.
BHT	S. SMITH, *Babylonian Historical Texts*, London, 1924.
Bi.Or.	*Bibliotheca Orientalis*, Leiden.
Bo.Stu.	*Boghazköy Studien*, Leipzig.
CAH	*Cambridge Ancient History*, Cambridge.
EA	J. A. KNUDZTON, *Die El-Amarna Tafeln*, Leipzig, 1915.
HBS	S. N. KRAMER, *History Begins at Sumer*, Doubleday, New York, 1959. 1st edition, 1956.
ILN	*Illustrated London News*, London.
Iraq	*Iraq*, London (British School of Archaeology in Iraq).
ISA	F. THUREAU-DANGIN, *Les Inscriptions de Sumer et d'Akkad*, Paris, 1905.
JAOS	*Journal of the American Oriental Society*, New Haven.
JCS	*Journal of Cuneiform Studies*, New Haven.
JNES	*Journal of Near Eastern Studies*, Chicago.

JRAS	*Journal of the Royal Asiatic Society*, London.
JSOR	*Journal of the Society of Oriental Research*, Chicago.
JSS	*Journal of Semitic Studies*, Manchester.
JWH	*Journal of World History* (=Cahiers d'Histoire Mondiale), Paris.
KAH	*Keilschrifttexte aus Assur, Historischen Inhalts*, Leipzig, 1911, 1922.
KB	*Keilinschriftliche Bibliothek*, Berlin, 1889 ss.
KING, *Chronicles*	L. W. KING, *Chronicles Concerning Early Babylonian Kings*, London, 1907.
MAO	G. CONTENAU, *Manuel d'Archéologie Orientale*, Paris, 1927–47.
MDOG	*Mitteilungen der deutschen Orient-Gesellschaft*, Berlin.
MDP	*Mémoires de la Délégation en Perse*, Paris.
MDVG	*Mitteilungen der deutschen vorderasiatische Gesellschaft*, Berlin.
MVAG	*Mitteilungen der vorderasiatisch-aegyptischen Gesellschaft*, Berlin.
NBK	S. LANGDON, *Die neubabylonischen Königinschriften*, Leipzig, 1912.
OIC	Oriental Institute Communications, Chicago.
OIP	Oriental Institute Publications, Chicago.
Orientalia	*Orientalia*, Rome (Pontifical Biblical Institute).
PSBA	*Proceedings of the Society of Biblical Archaeology*, London.
RA	*Revue d'Assyriologie*, Paris.
RB	*Revue Biblique*, Jérusalem/Paris.
CRAE	LEROY WATERMAN, *Royal Correspondence of the Assyrian Empire*, Ann Arbor, 1930–36.
RISA	G. A. BARTON, *The Royal Inscriptions of Sumer and Akkad*, New Haven, 1929.
RLA	*Reallexikon der Assyriologie*, Berlin.
SKL	T. JACOBSEN, *The Sumerian King List*, Chicago, 1939.
Sumer	*Sumer*, Baghdad (Directorate-General of Antiquities).
Syria	*Syria*, Paris.
UE	*Ur Excavations*, London, 1927 ss.
UET	*Ur Excavations Texts*, London, 1928 ss.
UVB	*Uruk vorlaüfiger Berichte* (= Vorläufiger Berichte über die . . . Ausgrabungen in Uruk-Warka), Berlin.
VDI	*Vestnik Drevney Istorii* (=Journal of Ancient History), Moscow.
WISEMAN, *Chronicles*	D. J. WISEMAN, *Chronicles of Chaldaean Kings* (626–556 BC), London, 1956.

WVDOG   *Wissenschaftliche Veröffentlichungen der deutschen Orient-Gesselschaft*, Leipzig.

ZA   *Zeitschrift für Assyriologie*, Leipzig/Berlin.

ZZB   D. O. EDZARD, *Die Zweite Zwischenzeit Babyloniens*, Wiesbaden, 1957.

BIBLIOGRAPHY AND NOTES

CHAPTER I

1. No detailed study of the geography of Iraq in general has yet been published. Excellent maps of the country in antiquity can be found in M. Beek, *Atlas of Mesopotamia*, London, 1962.
2. B. LANDSBERGER, *Die Fauna des alten Mesopotamien*, Leipzig, 1935; R. CAMPBELL THOMPSON, *A Dictionary of Assyrian Botany*, London, 1949.
3. K. W. BUTZER, *Quaternary Stratigraphy and Climate of the Near East*, Bonn, 1958.
4. HERODOTUS, II, 5.
5. Put forward by PLINY, *Hist. Nat.*, VI, xxxi, 13, as early as the first century AD, this theory was codified by de MORGAN in *MDP* I (1900), pp. 4–48.
6. G. M. LEES and N. L. FALCON, The geographical history of the Mesopotamian plains, *Geogr. Journal*, CXVIII (1952), 1, pp. 24–39.
7. A. HOLMES, *Principles of Physical Geology*, London, 1949, pp. 417–18.
8. G. ROUX, Recently discovered ancient sites in the Hammar-Lake district, *Sumer*, XVI (1960), pp. 20–31.
9. This method consists of a systematic survey of all ancient settlements which are dated by means of their surface pottery and plotted on maps. Since practically all towns and villages were on the banks of rivers or canals, it is thus possible to reconstruct the courses of waterways at a given period. See: TH. JACOBSEN, Mesopotamian mound survey, *Archaeology*, VII (1954), pp. 53–54; R. M. ADAMS, Settlements in ancient Akkad, *Archaeology*, X (1957), pp. 270–3; Survey of ancient watercourses and settlements in Central Iraq, *Sumer*, XIV (1958), pp. 101–4; TH. JACOBSEN, The waters of Ur, *Iraq*, XXII (1960), pp. 174–83.
10. M. S. DRAWER, Perennial irrigation in Mesopotamia, in *A History of Technology*, London, 1955, I, pp. 545–55; P. BURINGH, Living conditions in the lower Mesopotamian plain in ancient times, *Sumer*, XIII (1957), pp. 30–46.
11. In the opinion of some scholars, the extensive salinization which took place in southern Iraq between 2400 and 2100 BC was the reason for the decline of the political power of the Sumerians. See: TH. JACOBSEN, Summary of report by the Diyala Basin

Archaeological Project, *Sumer*, XIV (1958), pp. 79–89; TH. JACOBSEN and R. M. ADAMS, Salt and silt in ancient Mesopotamian agriculture, *Science*, CXXVIII, pp. 1251–8.

12. M. IONIDES, *The Régime of the Rivers Euphrates and Tigris*, London, 1937.

13. B. LANDSBERGER, Jahreszeiten in Sumerisch-Akkadischen, *JNES*, VII (1949), pp. 248–97.

14. HERODOTUS, I, 193; STRABO, XVI, 14.

15. TH. JACOBSEN, *Sumer*, XIV (1958), p. 81.

16. V. SCHEIL, De l'exploitation des dattiers dans l'ancienne Babylonie, *RA*, X (1913); A. H. PRUESSNER, Date culture in ancient Babylonia, *AJSL*, XXXVI (1920), pp. 212–32; V. H. DOWSON, *The Cultivation of the Date-palm on the Shatt-el-'Arab*, London, 1921; H. DANTINE, *Le Palmier-dattier et les Arbres Sacrés*, Paris, 1937.

17. J. LASSØE, Reflexions on modern and ancient Oriental waterworks, *JCS*, VII (1953), pp. 5–26.

18. On this desert in general, see: C. P. GRANT, *The Syrian Desert*, London, 1937 (with copious bibliography).

19. See the introductory remarks in M. E. L. MALLOWAN, The excavations at Tall Chagar Bazar, *Iraq*, III (1936), pp. 2–5.

20. W. THESIGER, The Ma'dan or marsh dwellers of southern Iraq, *J. Roy. Centr. Asian Soc.* XLI (1954), pp. 3–25; The marshmen of southern Iraq, *Geogr. Journal*, CXX (1954), pp. 272–81; S. WESTPHAL-HELLBUSCH, Die Kultur der Ma'dan in Gegenwart und Vergangenheit, *Sumer*, XII (1956), pp. 66–75; H. ST. J. PHILBY, The eastern marshes of Mesopotamia, *Geogr. Journal*, CXXV (1959), pp. 65–9.

21. R. J. FORBES, *Bitumen and Petroleum in Antiquity*, Leiden, 1936; *Studies in Ancient Technology*, I, Leiden, 1955, pp. 1–118.

22. On the origin and commerce of metal, see: S. N. BROMEHEAD and R. J. FORBES in *A History of Technology*, London, 1955, I, pp. 558–99; H. LIMET, *Le Travail du Métal au Pays de Sumer au Temps de la IIIe Dynastie d'Ur*, Paris, 1960; W. F. LEEMANS, *Foreign Trade in the Old Babylonian Period*, Leiden, 1960.

23. J. LEWY, Studies in the historic geography of the ancient Near East, *Orientalia*, XXI (1952), pp. 1–12; 265–92; 393–425; A. GOETZE, An Old Babylonian itinerary, *JCS*, VII (1953), pp. 51–72. Cf. L. LE BRETON, P. GARELLI and TH. JACOBSEN, in *RA*, LII (1958), p. 110 ss.

24. SIR ARNOLD T. WILSON, *The Persian Gulf*, London, 1954.

CHAPTER II

1. On Mesopotamian archaeology in general, cf.: v. CHRISTIAN, *Altertumskunde des Zweistromlandes*, Leipzig, 1940; G. CONTENAU, *Manuel d'Archéologie Orientale*, 4 vols., Paris, 1927–47; A. PARROT, *Archéologie Mésopotamienne*, 2 vols., Paris, 1946–53; H. FRANKFORT, *The Art and Architecture of the Ancient Orient*, Penguin Books, Harmondsworth, 1954.

2. Up to the end of the third millennium B C, temples and palaces were, with rare exceptions, made of sun-dried bricks. Baked bricks were almost exclusively used for the pavement of open courtyards, bathroom floors and drains. In many buildings of later periods, only the lower part of the walls was built of kiln-baked bricks.

3. The Akkadian (Assyro-Babylonian) word is *tilu*. Sentences such as: 'I turned this town into a mound (*tilu*) and a heap of ruins (*karmu*)' are frequently found in Assyrian royal inscriptions.

4. More details on the technique of excavations can be found in: W. F. BADE, *A Manual of Excavations in the Near East*, Berkeley, 1935; SIR LEONARD WOOLLEY, *Digging up the Past*, Penguin Books, 1952 and SIR MORTIMER WHEELER, *Archaeology from the Earth*, Penguin Books, 1956. Cf. also: A. PARROT, *AM* II, pp. 15–78.

5. M. DUNAND, *Les Fouilles de Byblos*, I, Paris, 1939, Chapter 2.

6. *ANET*, pp. 269–70.

7. *ANET*, p. 271.

8. *ARAB*, II, p. 434.

9. For instance, the list of the kings of the dynasty of Larsa published by F. THUREAU-DANGIN in *RA* XV (1918), pp. 1–58.

10. TH. JACOBSEN, *The Sumerian King List*, Chicago, 1939.

11. E. FORRER, Zur Chronologie der neuassyrischen Zeit, *MDVG* XX (1916), p. 3; A. UNGNAD, *RLA* II, 1938, p. 412 ss.

12. For a general survey of this complicated problem, cf.: A. PARROT, *AM* II, pp. 332–438. We have adopted here for Hammurabi the dates 1792–1750 B C proposed by SIDNEY SMITH in *Alalakh and Chronology*, London, 1940, and accepted by an increasing number of scholars (cf. now, M. B. ROWTON, The date of Hammurabi, *JNES* XVII (1958), pp. 97–111).

13. F. E. ZEUNER, *Dating the Past*, London, 1958, pp. 341–46.

14. For details, cf. A. PARROT, *AM* I, 1946; S. A. PALLIS, *Early Explorations in Mesopotamia*, Copenhagen, 1954, and SETON LLOYD, *Foundations in the Dust*, Penguin Books, 1955.

15. XENOPHON, *Anabasis*, iii, 4. Cf. G. GOOSSENS, L'Assyrie après l'Empire, *Comptes-Rendus de la 3 ème Rencontre Assyriologique Internationale*, Leiden, 1954, p. 93.

16. STRABO, XVI, 5.
17. On this question, see: C. H. FOSSEY, *Manuel d'Assyriologie*, I, Paris, 1904; A. PARROT, *AM* I, pp. 109–121; S. N. KRAMER, *Sumerian Mythology*, Philadelphia, 1944; M. RUTTEN, *La Science des Chaldéens*, Paris, 1960, pp. 19–29.

CHAPTER III

1. Further details on general prehistory in a not too technical form can be found in: L. S. B. LEAKEY, *Adam's Ancestors*, London, 1953; K. P. OAKLEY, *Man the Tool-Maker*, London, 1958 and W. E. LE GROS CLARK, *History of the Primates*, London, 1958. See also: S. COLE, *The Neolithic Revolution*, London, 1959.
2. F. E. ZEUNER, *Dating the Past*, London, 1958, p. 145.
3. H. E. WRIGHT Jnr., The Geological Setting of Four Prehistoric Sites in North Eastern Iraq, *BASOR* 128 (1952), pp. 11–24; Geologic Aspects of the Archaeology of Iraq, *Sumer* XI (1955), pp. 83–90.
4. NAJI-AL-'ASIL, Barda Balka, *Sumer* V (1949), pp. 205–6.
5. H. E. WRIGHT, Jnr. and B. HOWE, Preliminary Report on Soundings at Barda Balka, *Sumer* VII (1951), pp. 107–10.
6. D. A. E. GARROD, The Palaeolithic of Southern Kurdistan: Excavations in the Caves of Zarzi and Hazar Merd, *Bulletin No. 6, Amer. School of Prehist. Research*, New Haven (1930).
7. R. SOLECKI's reports on Shanidar Cave have appeared in *Sumer* VIII (1952), pp. 37–44 and 127–60; IX (1953), pp. 60–93 and 229–32; XI (1955), pp. 14–35; XIII (1957), pp. 165–70; XIV (1958), pp. 104–8; XVII (1961), pp. 71–91.
8. R. SOLECKI, *Sumer* XIII (1957), p. 59; T. D. STEWART, First views of the restored Shanidar I skull, *Sumer* XIV (1958), pp. 90–6.
9. *ILN* 7-5, 1960, pp. 772–5.
10. R. J. BRAIDWOOD, From Cave to Village in Prehistoric Iraq, *BASOR* 124 (1951), pp. 12–18. R. J. BRAIDWOOD and B. HOWE, *Prehistoric Investigations in Iraqi Kurdistan*, Chicago, 1960.
11. R. J. BRAIDWOOD, *Sumer* X (1954), pp. 120–38.
12. The term 'Ground Stone age' is now obsolete.
13. R. J. BRAIDWOOD, *Sumer* X (1954), pp. 128–9.
14. Professor R. J. BRAIDWOOD's excavations at Jarmo have been published in the form of preliminary reports or articles in: *AJA* LIII (1949), pp. 49–51; *Antiquity* XXIV (1950), pp. 189–95; *BASOR* 124 (1951), pp. 12–18; *ILN* 15-12-1951, pp. 992–5 and 28-4-1956, pp. 410–11.

15. W. F. LIBBEY, *Radiocarbon Dating*, Chicago, 1955, p. 79; F. E. ZEUNER, *Dating the Past*, 1958, p. 345; K. M. KENYON, *Journal Royal Anthrop, Inst.* 89 (1958), pp. 35-43.

16. K. M. KENYON, *Digging up Jericho*, London, 1957, pp. 51-76.

17. R. J. BRAIDWOOD, L. BRAIDWOOD, J. G. SMITH, C. LESLIE, Matarrah, a southern variant of the Hassunan assemblage, excavated in 1948, *JNES* XI (1952), pp. 1-75.

CHAPTER IV

1. On Proto-history in general, see: A. MOORTGAT, *Die Entstehung der Sumerischen Hochkultur*, Leipzig, 1945; A. L. PERKINS, *The Comparative Archaeology of Early Mesopotamia*, Chicago, 1949; R. J. BRAIDWOOD, The earliest village communities of southwestern Asia, *JWH* I (1953), pp. 278-310; A. PARROT, *AM* II (1953), pp. 107-331; H. FRANKFORT, *The Birth of Civilization in the Near East*, London, 1954; V. G. CHILDE, *New Light on the Most Ancient East*, London, 1958; J. MELLAART, and M. E. L. MALLOWAN in *The Dawn of Civilization* (ed. by S. PIGGOTT), London, 1961, pp. 41-96.

2. SETON LLOYD and FUAD SAFAR, Tell Hassuna, *JNES*, IV (1945), pp. 255-89.

3. C. S. COON, Three skulls from Hassuna, *Sumer* IV (1950), pp. 93-6.

4. E. E. HERTZFELD, *Die Ausgrabungen von Samarra*, V, Berlin, 1930.

5. R. DU MESNIL DU BUISSON, *Baghouz, l'ancienne Corsôtê*, Leiden, 1948; R. J. BRAIDWOOD and al., New chalcolithic material of Samarran type and its implications, *JNES* III (1944), pp. 48-69.

6. M. FREIHERR VON OPPENHEIM, *Der Tell Halaf*, Leipzig, 1931. Detailed publication: *Tell Halaf*, I, *Die prähistorischen Funde*, Berlin, 1943.

7. R. CAMPBELL THOMPSON and M. E. L. MALLOWAN, The British excavations at Nineveh, *AAA* XX (1933), p. 71 ss.

8. M. E. L. MALLOWAN and C. ROSE, Prehistoric Assyria. The excavations at Tall Arpachiyah, 1933, *Iraq* II (1935), pp. 1-78.

9. M. E. L. MALLOWAN, The excavations at Tall Chagar Bazar, *Iraq* III (1936), pp. 1-86; IV (1937), pp. 91-117.

10. For a general survey of this material, see: D. J. WISEMAN, *Cylinder-seals of Western Asia*, London, 1959.

11. R. DUSSAUD in *Syria* XX (1931), pp. 92-5.

12. On this question, see: M. E. L. MALLOWAN, *Twenty-five years of Mesopotamian Discovery*, London, 1956, pp. 1-11; R. W. EHRICH, *Relative Chronologies in Old World Archaeology*, Chicago, 1954.

13. D. E. MCCOWN, *The Comparative Stratigraphy of early Iran*, Chicago, 1942, pp. 36–9.
14. H. R. HALL and C. L. WOOLLEY, *Al-'Ubaid*, London, 1927 (*UE* I).
15. H. LENZEN, *UVB* IX (1938), p. 37 ss.; XI (1940), p. 26 ss.; C. ZIEGLER, *Die Keramik von der Qal'a des Haggi Mohammed*, Berlin, 1953.
16. SETON LLOYD and FUAD SAFAR, Eridu, *Sumer* III (1947), pp. 84–111; IV (1948), pp. 115–27; VI (1950), pp. 27–33.
17. This question has recently been discussed by J. OATES in his article: Ur and Eridu, the prehistory, *Iraq* XXII (1960), pp. 32–50.
18. At Nippur, however, in the campaign of 1960–61, it was found that the earliest temple of Inanna (Early Dynastic I) was built on top of *private houses* of the Proto-literate period (R. C. HAINES, *ILN* 9–9, 1961, pp. 408–11). For earlier excavations of this temple, see V. E. CRAWFORD, *Archaeology* XII (1959), pp. 74–83.
19. A. J. TOBLER, *Excavations at Tepe Gawra*, II, Philadelphia, 1950.
20. Only four copper objects were discovered at Tepe Gawra: a blade, an awl and a ring in level XVII, a button in level XII. Arpachiya has yielded a copper blade. It is possible that copper objects were used in southern Iraq, but were not preserved owing to the humidity of the soil. Note the presence of gold in Mesopotamia during the Ubaid period: a twisted gold wire at Ur, and fluted gold beads at Tepe Gawra.
21. A. J. TOBLER, *op. cit.*, p. 113.

CHAPTER V

1. According to W. F. ALBRIGHT (*AJA* 55 (1951) p. 210), the Uruk pottery has strong affinities with the grey ware of Beth-Shan, Megiddo and Far'ah in Palestine dated 3300–3100 BC. For the synchronisme Proto-Literate—Early Pharaonic in Egypt, cf. below, note 12.
2. The results of the German excavations at Uruk-Warka (1928–39 and 1953 onwards) are published in a series of preliminary reports known as *Uruk Vorlaüfiger Berichte* (abbreviated *UVB*). In addition, volumes of monograph (*Ausgrabungen der Deutschen Forschungsgemeinschaft in Uruk-Warka*) deal with particular aspects of the excavations (cf. notes 5, 7 and 11 below). An excellent summary in English is given by R. NORTH: Status of Warka excavations, *Orientalia* 26 (1957), pp. 185–256.
3. H. LENZEN, Die Tempel der Schicht Archaisch V in Uruk, *ZA* 49 (1949), pp. 1–20.

4. SETON LLOYD and FUAD SAFAR, Tell Uqair, *JNES* II (1943), pp. 131–58.

5. H. LENZEN, *Die Entwicklung der Zikkurat*, Leipzig, 1942.

6. For a general description of this ceramic, see SETON LLOYD, Uruk pottery, *Sumer* IV (1948), pp. 39–51.

7. Published by A. FALKENSTEIN, *Archaische Texte aus Uruk*, Leipzig, 1942. List of other archaic texts in G. CONTENAU, *MAO* I, 1927, pp. 207–10.

8. A. FALKENSTEIN, *op. cit.*, p. 64; *Das Sumerische*, Leiden, 1959, pp. 10–11.

9. E. MACKAY, *Report on Excavations at Jemdet Nasr, Iraq*, Chicago, 1931; H. FIELD and R. A. MARTIN, Painted pottery from Jemdet Nasr, *AJA* 39 (1935), pp. 310–18.

10. For a critical study of this term, see A. PARROT, *AM* II, pp. 272–78. The Proto-Literate period, as defined by P. DELOUGAZ (*OIP* LVIII, p. 8), includes all the architecture (Warka levels V–IV) described here as belonging to the Uruk culture and reduces the latter to the pottery found in the deep sounding under the archaic 'Limestone Temple' (Warka levels XIV–VI). With H. LENZEN and others, we believe that the parting line should pass between Warka level IV (first tablets) and Warka level III. Moreover, we think that the whole of Warka XIV–II (i.e. Uruk-Proto-Literate) represents one single great cultural phase with two sub-divisions: before and after the appearance of writing.

11. H. HEINRICH, *Kleinfunde aus den archaischen Tempelschichen in Uruk*, Leipzig, 1936, pp. 15–16, pl. 2–3, 38. Hunt stele in *UVB* V (1934), pp. 11–13, pl. 12–13. Woman's head in *UVB* XI (1940), frontispiece.

12. For details and bibliography, cf. H. FRANKFORT, *The Birth of Civilization in the Near East*, London, 1954, pp. 100–10.

13. A. PARROT, *Mission Archéologique de Mari, I, Le Temple d'Ishtar*, Paris, 1956, pp. 7 and 187.

14. M. E. L. MALLOWAN, Excavations at Brak and Chager Bazar, Syria, *Iraq* IX (1947): *Twenty-five Years of Mesopotamian Discovery* London, 1956, pp. 24–38.

15. On the Gawra and Ninevite periods, A. L. PERKINS, *The Comparative Archaeology of Early Mesopotamia*, Chicago, 1949, pp. 162–97.

16. Summary of the problem and bibliography in A. PARROT, *AM* II, pp. 308–31.

17. There is still considerable uncertainty as regards the meaning of KI.EN.GI. A number of scholars think that *Shumer* and *Kengi/Kengi(r)* are different pronunciations of the same word in the two

Sumerian dialects, *emeku* and *emesal*. Others believe that KI.EN.GI is a 'compound ideogram' (for this term, see below, Chapter VIII, note 13) meaning 'Country (*KI*) of the Lord (*EN*) of the Reed (*GI*)', i.e. 'Country of the god Enki'. On this, cf. E. SOLLBERGER, in *RA* XLV (1951), pp. 114–15.

18. The question of the early contacts between Sumerians and Akkadian Semites has been discussed at the IXth 'Rencontre Assyriologique Internationale', 1960. See the papers by D. O. EDZARD, W. VON SODEN, I. J. GELB, S. N. KRAMER and P. AMIET in *Genava* VIII (1960), pp. 241–314.

19. Skulls of Kish (S. LANGDON, *Excavations at Kish*, Paris, 1924, pp. 115–25), of Ubaid (*UE* I, 1927, pp. 214–40), of Ur (*UE* II, 1934, pp. 400–7) and of Eridu (*Sumer* V (1949), p. 103). Cf. A. PARROT, *AM* II, pp. 316–22.

20. For a different opinion, see S. N. KRAMER, *AJA* (1948), pp. 156–64 and *Proceed. Amer. Philos. Soc.*, 90 (1946), pp. 120–30.

21. FUAD SAFAR, *Sumer* III (1947), p. 104.

22. H. FRANKFORT, *Birth of Civil.*, p. 50, n. 1.

CHAPTER VI

1. On the Sumerian and Assyro-Babylonian religion in general, see: E. DHORME, *Les Religions de Babylonie et d'Assyrie* ('Mana' I, 2), Paris, 1949; N. SCHNEIDER, *Die Religion der Sumerer und Akkader*, Vienna, 1951; J. BOTTERO, *La Religion Babylonienne*, Paris, 1952; S. H. HOOKE, *Babylonian and Assyrian Religion*, London, 1953.

2. Our knowledge of Sumerian religious ideas has been immensely enriched by the work of S. N. KRAMER (of the University of Pennsylvania) who, in recent years, has discovered, deciphered and published a number of very important Sumerian myths. See, in particular, his *Sumerian Mythology*, Philadelphia, 1944; *From the Tablets of Sumer*, Indian Hills, Colorado, 1956; *History Begins at Sumer*, New York, 1959, and his contribution to *Mythologies of the Ancient World*, New York, 1961. The great Sumerian and Assyro-Babylonian hymns and prayers have been published in German translation by A. FALKENSTEIN and W. VON SODEN: *Sumerische und Akkadische Hymnen und Gebete*, Zurich/Stuttgart, 1953.

3. H. and H. A. FRANKFORT, J. A. WILSON, TH. JACOBSEN, and W. A. IRWIN, *The Intellectual Adventure of Ancient Man*, Chicago, 1946. (Published as a Penguin Book under the title *Before Philosophy*, Harmondsworth, 1951.)

4. Utu was born from Nanna and his consort, the goddess Ningal (E. DHORME, *Religions*, p. 60); Nanna was the son of Enlil and Ninlil (S. N. KRAMER, *Sumer. Mythol.*, pp. 43–7).

5. See, for instance, H. ZIMMERN, *Der Babylonische Gott Tamuz*, Berlin, 1909; S. LANGDON, *Tammuz and Ishtar*, London, 1914; A. MOORT-GAT, *Tammuz*, Berlin, 1949; E. O. JAMES, *Myth and Ritual in the Ancient Near East*, London, 1958.

6. Translations in *ANET*, pp. 50–2 (Sumerian version) and pp. 106–109 (Babylonian version). Cf. S. N. KRAMER, *JCS* V (1951), pp. 1–17.

7. See the discussion by A. FALKENSTEIN in *Compte-Rendu de la 3ème Rencontre Assyriologique Internationale*, Leiden, 1954 and the remarks by S. N. KRAMER in his article: Death and Netherworld according to the Sumerian literary texts, *Iraq* XXII (1960), pp. 59–68. Also: *Mythologies of the Ancient World*, pp. 102–7 ss.; *City Invincible*, Chicago, 1960, p. 89 (KRAMER) and 94 (JACOBSEN).

8. TH. JACOBSEN in *Intellectual Adventure*, p. 138.

9. Possibly in the first centuries of the Early Dynastic period, after Enmebaragesi, king of Kish had built the temple of Enlil in Nippur. (S. N. KRAMER, *Genava* VIII (1960), p. 277, note 25).

10. TH. JACOBSEN in *Intellectual Adventure*, p. 140 ss.

11. Hymn to Enlil, *HBS*, pp. 93–4.

12. KRAMER has recently proposed to see in Enki-Ea (and Inanna-Ishtar) Semitic dieties incorporated early to the Sumerian pantheon (*Genava* VIII (1960), pp. 272–83), but his arguments are not very convincing.

13. Myth 'Enki and the World Order' (S. N. KRAMER, *Sumer. Mythol.*, pp. 64–8).

14. On these legends, see A. HEIDEL, *The Babylonian Genesis*, Chicago, 1942, and *ANET*, pp. 99–100.

15. W. THESIGER, *Geogr. Journal* CXX (1954), p. 276.

16. The main translations of *Enuma elish* are those of: S. LANGDON, *The Babylonian Epic of Creation*, Oxford, 1923; E. EBELING in *Altorientalische Texte zum alten Testament*, Berlin, 1926, p. 108 ss.; R. LABAT, *Le Poème Babylonien de la Création*, Paris, 1935; A. HEIDEL, *op. cit.*, and E. A. SPEISER in *ANET*, pp. 60–72, from which we quote.

17. As suggested by TH. JACOBSEN in *Intellectual Adventure*, p. 170. Others see in *mummu* an epithet of Tiamat: 'mother Tiamat', 'creator Tiamat', or the like (cf. A. HEIDEL, The meaning of *mummu* in Akkadian literature, *JNES* VII (1948), pp. 98–105).

18. W. G. LAMBERT, *Babylonian Wisdom Literature*, Oxford, 1960, p. 41.

19. W. G. LAMBERT, *op. cit.*, p. 101.

20. The Gilgamesh Epic, Old Babylonian version, III, iv, 6–8. (Transl. E. A. SPEISER, *ANET*, p. 79.)

21. On after-life, see: A. HEIDEL, *The Gilgamesh Epic and Old Testament Parallels*, Chicago, 1949, pp. 137–223 and S. N. KRAMER in *Iraq* XXII (1960), pp. 59–68.

22. 'Inanna's Descent to the Netherworld', Obv. 8–11 (Transl. A. HEIDEL).

23. '*Ludlul bêl nemeqi*,' II, 36–42, 48 (W. G. LAMBERT, *op. cit.*, p. 41).

CHAPTER VII

1. Myth 'Enki and Ninhursag', cf. S. N. KRAMER, *Sumer. Mythol.*, pp. 54–59; *ANET*, pp. 37–41; *HBS*, p. 83.

2. P. B. CORNWALL, On the location of Dilmun, *BASOR* 103 (1946), pp. 3–11.

3. cf. S. N. KRAMER, *HBS*, pp. 108–9, and A. HEIDEL, *Babyl. Genesis*, pp. 64–72.

4. Recent translations of the Adapa legend by A. HEIDEL, *op. cit.*, pp. 147–53 and E. A. SPEISER, *ANET*, pp. 101–3.

5. G. ROUX, Adapa, le vent et l'eau, *RA* LV (1961), pp. 13–33.

6. E. EBELING, *Tod und Leben nach den Vorstellungen der Babylonier*, Berlin & Leipzig, 1931, p. 27a.

7. TH. JACOBSEN, Primitive democracy in ancient Mesopotamia, *JNES* II (1943), pp. 159–72; Early political development in Mesopotamia, *ZA* LII (1957), pp. 91–140.

8. TH. JACOBSEN, *The Sumerian King List*, Chicago, 1939.

9. *Bad-tibira* has now been definitely identified with Tell Medain, near Telloh (V. E. CRAWFORD, *Iraq*, XXII (1960), pp. 197–9). *Larak* might be Tell el Wilaya, near Kut-el-Imara (*Sumer* XV (1959), p. 51). *Sippar* is modern Abu Habba, about 20 miles S.W. of Baghdad, partly excavated by H. RASSAM in 1881–2, by V. SCHEIL in 1894 and by W. ANDRAE and J. JORDAN in 1927 (cf. *AM* I, pp. 101, 159, 326). *Shuruppak* is Tell Fara, about 40 miles S.E. of Diwaniyah, excavated by the Germans in 1902–3 (H. HEINRICH and W. ANDRAE, *Fara*, Berlin, 1931) and by the Americans in 1931 (E. SCHMIDT, *Museum Journal* XXII (1931), pp. 193–245).

10. 'Gilgamesh', tablet XI, 9–196 (quotations from A. HEIDEL's translation). See also: E. SOLLBERGER, *The Flood*, London, 1962.

11. Usually identified with mount Pîr Omar Gudrun, 9000 feet, in the Zagros range, south of the Lower Zab (E. A. SPEISER, *AASOR* VIII (1928), pp. 18, 31).

12. cf. *ANET*, pp. 42–4 and 104–6.

13. SIR LEONARD WOOLLEY, *AJ* IX (1929), pp. 323–30; X (1930), pp. 330–41; *Ur of the Chaldees*, London, 1950, p. 29; *Excavations at Ur*, London, 1954, pp. 34–36; *UE* IV, p. 15 ss.

14. cf. A. PARROT, *Déluge et Arche de Noé*, Neuchâtel, 1953 (English translation, London, 1955).

15. G. CONTENAU, *Le Déluge Babylonien*, Paris, 1941, pp. 115–29; W. F. ALBRIGHT, *From the Stone Age to Christianity*, Baltimore, 1946, p. 128.

16. A. W. NIEUWENHUIS, Die Sintflutsagen als kausallogische Naturs-chöpfungsmythen, *Festschrift P. W. Schmidt*, Vienna, 1928.

17. *Kish* (el-Uhaimir) was excavated by the French in 1912 (H. DE GENOUILLAC, *Fouilles Françaises d'el-Akhymer*, Paris, 1924–5) and by an anglo-american mission from 1923 to 1930 (L. C. WATELIN and ST. LANGDON, *Excavations at Kish*, 4 vols., Paris, 1924–34).

18. TH. JACOBSEN, The assumed conflict between Sumerians and Semites in early Mesopotamian history, *JAOS* LIX (1939), pp. 485–95.

19. The translation of the Etana legend by E. A. SPEISER in *ANET*, pp. 114–18 supersedes all previous translations.

20. 'Gilgamesh and Agga', cf. S. N. KRAMER, *AJA* LIII, p. 1 ss.; *ANET*, pp. 44–7; *HBS*, pp. 29–34.

21. S. N. KRAMER, *Enmerkar and the Lord of Aratta*, Philadelphia, 1952. See also: *HBS*, pp. 17–28, 204–7, 222–5 (Enmerkar) and 207–11 (Lugalbanda).

22. For a localization in Iranian Kurdistan, near lake Urmiah, see E. I. GORDON, *Bi.Or.* XVII (1960), p. 132, n. 63.

23. On the Sumerian cycle of Gilgamesh, see *HBS*, pp. 174–81 and 190–9; *ANET*, pp. 45–52; *Gilgamesh et sa Légende*, Paris, 1960.

24. The main translations of the Gilgamesh epic are those of A. SCHOTT, *Das Gilgamesch Epos*, Berlin, 1934; A. HEIDEL, *The Gilgamesh Epic and Old Testament Parallels*, Chicago, 1946 and E. A. SPEISER in *ANET*, pp. 79–99, from which we quote.

CHAPTER VIII

1. More recent excavations were conducted at Telloh by H. DE GENOUILLAC and A. PARROT for the Louvre Museum between 1929 and 1933. On the site in general, see: A. PARROT, *Tello*, Paris, 1948.

2. F. THUREAU-DANGIN'S *Les Inscriptions de Sumer et d'Akkad*, Paris, 1905 (abbreviated *ISA*) remains fundamental. Cf. also G. A. BARTON,

The Royal Inscriptions of Sumer and Akkad, New Haven, 1929 (abbreviated *RISA*).

3. C. J. GADD, *UE* I, p. 126; *RISA*, p. 2.

4. D. O. EDZARD, Enmebaragesi von Kish, *ZA* 53 (1959), pp. 9–26.

5. S. N. KRAMER in *Gilgamesh et sa Légende*, Paris, 1960, pp. 59–63. The document mentions the various Sumerian rulers who built or restored the temple called Tummal in Nippur.

6. Assuming that the Proto-Literate period ended between 2900 and 2800 BC, this leaves from 100 to 200 years in which to place the first two phases of the Early-Dynastic period as defined by H. FRANKFORT from the excavations at Tell Asmar and Khafaje in the Diyala valley (*OIC* 20 (1936), pp. 25–39). According to FRANKFORT, historical texts do not appear before ED III. ED I and ED II are purely archaeological and 'prehistoric'.

7. H. FRANKFORT, Town planning in ancient Mesopotamia, *Town Planning Review*, 21 (1950), p. 104; I. M. DIAKONOFF, On the area and population of the Sumerian city-state, *VDI* (1950), 2, pp. 77–93.

8. W. ANDRAE, *Die archaischen Ischtar-Tempel in Assur*, Leipzig, 1922; *Das wiedererstandene Assur*, Leipzig, 1938, pp. 72–8.

9. On Mari in general, see *AM* I, pp. 495–513. The Pre-Sargonic Ishtar temple is described in A. PARROT, *Le Temple d'Ishtar*, Paris, 1956. For the monuments discovered in post-war excavations, cf. *Syria* 29 (1952) ss. and *AAS* (1953) ss.

10. Preliminary reports on *OIC* 13 (1932), 16 (1933), 17 (1934), 19 (1935) and 20 (1936). Several volumes of detailed reports have also been published. For the Early-Dynastic period, see in particular: H. FRANKFORT, *Sculptures of the Third Millennium B.C. from Tell Asmar and Khafaje*, Chicago, 1940 (*OIP* XLIV); P. DELOUGAZ, *The Temple Oval at Khafaje*, Chicago, 1940 (*OIP* LIII); P. DELOUGAZ and SETON LLOYD, *Pre-Sargonid Temples in the Diyala Region*, Chicago, 1942 (*OIP* LVIII); H. FRANKFORT, *More Sculptures from the Diyala Region*, Chicago, 1943 (*OIP*, LX) and H. FRANKFORT, *Stratified Cylinder-Seals from the Diyala Region*, Chicago, 1955 (*OIP* LXXII).

11. A. FALKENSTEIN, La cité-temple sumérienne, *JWH*, I (1954), pp. 784–814. C. J. GADD, The cities of Babylonia, *CAH* I (revised edition), ch. 13 (1962).

12. Cf. M. LAMBERT, La vie économique à Shuruppak, *Sumer* IX (1953), pp. 198–213; X (1954), pp. 150–90; Textes commerciaux de Lagash, *RA* XLVII (1953), pp. 57–69 and 105–20. *Archiv Orientální* XXIII (1955), pp. 557–74.

13. For the reading *ensi*, cf. A. FALKENSTEIN, *ZA* 42 (1947), p. 152. In Sumerian, certain words made of several signs could be written and pronounced in two different ways. Thus, the two signs for mouth (*KA*) and bread (*NINDA*), when put together, meant 'to eat' and were pronounced *KÚ* and not *KA-NINDA*. The reading of such 'compound ideograms' is only known from texts where they are written in full, e.g. PA.TE.SI: *en-si*.

14. Kish: E. MACKAY, *A Sumerian Palace and the 'A' Cemetery at Kish*, Chicago, 1929. Eridu: FUAD SAFAR, *Sumer* VI (1950), pp. 31-3.

15. *AJ*, VII (1927); VIII (1928); IX (1929); *Ur Excavations*, vol. II, *The Royal Cemetery*, London, 1934; *Ur of the Chaldees*, Penguin Books, 1929; *Digging up the Past*, Penguin Books, 1930; *Excavations at Ur*, London, 1954.

16. Mes-kalam-dug and A-kalam-dug are not mentioned in the King List, probably because they were not considered as having ruled over the whole country of Sumer.

17. References in C. J. GADD, The spirit of living sacrifices in tombs, *Iraq*, XXII (1960), pp. 51-8.

18. *ANET*, p. 51 (cf. S. N. KRAMER, *Iraq*, XXII (1960), pp. 59-68).

19. *ISA*, p. 58; *RISA*, p. 53.

20. *ISA*, p. 69 ss.; *RISA*, p. 79 ss.; A. DEIMEL, *Orientalia*, II (1920), pp. 6-8; M. LAMBERT, *RA* L (1956), p. 169 ss. (but cf. I. M. DIAKONOFF, *RA* LII (1958), p. 1 ss.); S. N. KRAMER, *HBS*, pp. 45-50.

21. Sources: Stele of the Vultures (*ISA*, p. 25 ss.; *RISA*, p. 23 ss.) and inscriptions of Entemena (*ISA*, p. 62 ss.; *RISA*, p. 57 ss.; M. LAMBERT, *RA* L (1956), pp. 141-6; S. N. KRAMER, *HBS*, pp. 35-44). Photographs of the stele in A. PARROT, *Sumer*, Paris, 1960, pls. 163-6.
    Umma (Jokha) has not yet been excavated. For a description of the site, cf. L. KING, *History of Sumer and Akkad*, London, 1923, pp. 21-3.

22. E. I. GORDON, Mesilim and Mesannepadda, are they identical?, *BASOR*, 132 (1953), pp. 27-30.

23. The site of *Akshak* has not been identified with certainty, but inscriptions of Kings of Akshak have been found at Tell 'Umar (ancient Upâ-Opis or Seleucia), opposite Ctesiphon (cf. *AM* I, p. 388).

24. Excavated by the University of Chicago in 1903-4. E. J. BANKS, *Bismya, or the Lost City of Adab*, New York, 1912.

25. *ISA*, p. 90 ss.; *RISA*, p. 89 ss.; L. KING, *op. cit.*, pp. 189-90.

26. *ISA*, p. 218 ss.; *RISA*, p. 97 ss.; TH. JACOBSEN, *ZA* 52 (1957), pp. 135-6.

CHAPTER IX

1. Condensed information on the Semites in general can be found in: S. MOSCATI, *The Semites in Ancient History*, Cardiff, 1959.

2. Discussion in R. J. FORBES, *Studies in Ancient Technology*, II, Leiden, 1955, pp. 187–203.

3. The most informative work on the nomads in Mesopotamia is that of J. R. KUPPER, *Les Nomades en Mésopotamie au temps des Rois de Mari*, Paris, 1957.

4. S. N. KRAMER, *Genava*, VIII (1960), p. 277.

5. A. GUILLAUME, *Prophecy and Divination among the Hebrews and other Semites*, London, 1938.

6. On this question, cf. *AM* II, 1953, pp. 308–31.

7. I. J. GELB, *Old Akkadian Writing and Grammar*, Chicago, 1952; *Genava*, VIII (1960), pp. 265–7.

8. L. W. KING, *Chronicles Concerning Early Babylonian Kings*, II, London, 1907, pp. 87–96; E. A. SPEISER, in *ANET*, p. 119.

9. Inscriptions (or copies of inscriptions) of Sargon in *RISA*, pp. 101–19; cf. also *ANET*, pp. 267–8.

10. *Dêr*, 16 miles S.W. of Baghdad, has been suggested, but Iraqi excavations made there in 1941 have rendered it 'improbable that the ruins could be associated with a capital-city' (TAHA BAQIR and MOHAMMED ALI MUSTAFA, *Sumer*, I (1945), p. 37). There is some possibility that the site of Agade might be, in fact . . . Babylon.

11. G. G. CAMERON, *History of Early Iran*, Chicago, 1936, p. 28.

12. M. E. L. MALLOWAN, The bronze head of the Akkadian period from Nineveh, *Iraq*, III (1936), p. 104 ss.; A. PARROT, *Sumer*, pls. 206, 208.

13. W. ALBRIGHT, The epic of the King of the Battle, *JSOR*, VII (1923), p. 1 ss.

14. J. NOUGAYROL, Un chef d'oeuvre inédit de la littérature babylonienne, *RA* XLV (1951), p. 169 ss.

15. KING, *Chronicles*, II, p. 3 ss.

16. A. GOETZE, Historical allusions in Old Babylonian omen texts, *JCS* I (1947), p. 256, No. 13.

17. *SKL*, p. 112, n. 249.

18. *RISA*, pp. 129–31.

19. I. J. GELB, *Hurrians and Subarians*, Chicago, 1944, p. 55; E. A. SPEISER, Some factors in the collapse of Akkad, *JAOS* LXXII (1952), p. 98.

20. H. FRANKFORT, *Kingship and the Gods*, Chicago, 1948, pp. 224–6.

21. *UET* I, No. 275; *ANET*, p. 268.

22. *Iraq* IX (1947), pp. 63–8.
23. Rock sculpture of Darband-i-Gawr in s. SMITH, *History of Early Assyria*, London, 1928, p. 97. Stele of Narâm-Sin: J. DE. MORGAN, *MDP* I (1900), p. 144 ss.; v. SCHEIL, *MDP*, II (1900), p. 53 ss.; A. PARROT, *Sumer*, pls. 212–13.
24. So-called because it was written on an apocryphal stele allegedly deposited in Kutha (Tell Ibrahim). Cf. O. GURNEY, *Anatolian Studies*, V (1955), pp. 93–113.
25. *SKL*, VII, 1–7.
26. *MDP* IV, pl. XI; *ISA*, p. 246 ss.; *RISA*, p. 151.
27. s. PIGGOTT, *Antiquity* XVII, pp. 169–82; SIR MORTIMER WHEELER, *Ancient India*, 3, (1947), pp. 78–80. Commercial relations with the Indus valley were already established during the Early Dynastic period (*UE* II, p. 397 ss.).
28. A 5-foot high pyramidal block of diorite covered with an Akkadian inscription in 69 columns and known as the 'obelisk of Manishtusu' refers to the purchase by the king of a large estate in central Mesopotamia. Translation by v. SCHEIL, *MDP* II (1900), pp. 1–52.
29. A. FALKENSTEIN, *JWH* I (1954), p. 808.

CHAPTER X

1. Royal inscriptions in *RISA*, pp. 171–3 and 300. On the Guti in general, s. SMITH, Notes on the Gutian period, *JRAS* (1932), pp. 296–308, and E. A. SPEISER, Some factors in the collapse of Akkad, *JAOS*, LXXII (1952), pp. 97–101.
2. Inscription of Utu-hegal: F. THUREAU-DANGIN, La fin de la domination gutienne, *RA* IX (1912), pp. 111–20; X (1913), pp. 98–100. English translation in C. J. GADD, *A Sumerian Reading-Book*, London, 1924, pp. 65–73.
3. On the reign of Ur-Nammu, cf. G. CASTELLINO, Ur-Nammu, three religious texts, *ZA*, 18 (1957), pp. 1–57.
4. S. N. KRAMER and A. FALKENSTEIN, Ur-Nammu law code, *Orientalia*, 23 (1954), pp. 40–51; E. SZLECHTER, Le code d'Ur-Nammu, *RA*, XLIX (1955), pp. 169–77.
5. SIR LEONARD WOOLLEY, *Ur Excavations* V, *The Ziggurat and its Surroundings*, London, 1939; *Excavations at Ur*, London, 1954, pp. 125–35.
6. The only known exception is the ziqqurat of *Choga-Zambil*, near Susa, built in the thirteenth century BC. The first storey comprises several chambers accessible only from above, the purpose of which is not clear.

7. H. LENZEN, *Die Entwicklung der Zikkurat*, Leipzig, 1941.
8. These theories are developed in A. PARROT, *Ziggurats et Tour de Babel*, Paris, 1949, pp. 200–17.
9. A. PARROT, *Tello*, 1948, pp. 147–207; *Sumer*, pls. 251–66.
10. The quotations given here are from: Cylinder A, translation M. LAMBERT and R. TOURNAY, *RB* 55 (1948), pp. 403–23 (cf. A. L. OPPENHEIM in *ANET*, p. 268); Statue E, translation M. LAMBERT, *RA* XLVI (1952), p. 81.
11. S. N. KRAMER, *Iraq* XXII (1960), p. 60.
12. The date-lists of the Third Dynasty of Ur are given by A. UNGNAD in *RLA* II (1938), pp. 136–47. Urbillum is modern Erbil; Simurrum is probably Altun Köprü, on the Lower Zab; Lullubum has not been identified.
13. G. G. CAMERON, *History of Early Iran*, Chicago, 1936, pp. 48–50.
14. A. GOETZE, *JCS* I (1947), p. 261, Nos. 29–31.
15. Description in *AJ* XI (1931), p. 343 ss. and *Excavations at Ur*, pp. 150–9.
16. CH. F. JEAN, L'Elam sous la dynastie d'Ur, *RA* XIX (1922), pp. 1–44.
17. Bibliography up to 1948 in A. L. OPPENHEIM, *Catalogue of the Cuneiform Tablets in the W. Eames Babylonian Collection*, New Haven, 1948, pp. 215–24. For subsequent publications, see T. B. JONES and J. W. SNYDER, *Sumerian Economic Texts from the Third Ur Dynasty*, Minneapolis, 1961, pp. 347–62.
18. T. FISH, The Sumerian city Nippur in the period of the Third Dynasty of Ur, *Iraq* V (1938), p. 164.
19. A. FALKENSTEIN, *JWH* I (1954), p. 791.
20. On this institution, cf. W. HALLO, A Sumerian amphictyony, *JCS* XIV (1960), pp. 88–114.
21. F. R. KRAUS, Le rôle des temples depuis la Troisième Dynastie d'Ur jusqu'à la Première Dynastie de Babylone, *JWH* I (1954), pp. 530–1.
22. E. SOLLBERGER, Byblos sous les rois d'Ur, *AfO* XIX (1959–60), pp. 120–2.
23. See now: D. O. EDZARD, Neue Inschriften zur Geschichte von Ur III under Shusuen, *AfO* XIX (1959–60), pp. 1–32.
24. On the Amorites in general, see J. R. KUPPER, *Nomades*, pp. 146–96.
25. E. CHIERA, *Sumerian Epics and Myths*, Chicago, 1934, Nos. 58 and 112.
26. E. CHIERA, *Sumerian Texts of Various Contents*, Chicago, 1934, No. 3.
27. TH. JACOBSEN, The reign of Ibbi-Suen, *JCS* VII (1953), pp. 36–44.
28. See the letter from Ibbi-Sin to Puzur-Numushda, governor of Kazallu, transl. S. N. KRAMER in *ANET*, pp. 480–1.

29. Ibbi-Sin lamentation in A. FALKENSTEIN and W. VON SODEN, *Sumer. und Akkad. Hymnen und Gebete*, Zurich, 1953, No. 37, pp. 189–92.

30. Lamentation over the destruction of Ur, transl. S. N. KRAMER in *ANET*, pp. 459–60.

CHAPTER XI

1. H. FRANKFORT, *AAO*, pp. 54–8.

2. F. R. KRAUS, *JWH* I (1954), p. 535.

3. *Isin* is Ishân Bahriyat, 16 miles S. of Nippur; *Larsa* is Sankara, 30 miles N.W. of Diwaniyah. Isin has not yet been excavated. Larsa was briefly excavated by the French in 1933 (A. PARROT, *RA* XXX (1933) pp. 169–82), but there is still much to be done on this important site.

For details on the 'Isin-Larsa period', see F. R. KRAUS, Nippur and Isin nach altbabylonischen Rechtsurkunden, *JCS* III (1951), and D. O. EDZARD, *Die Zweite Zwischenzeit Babyloniens*, Wiesbaden, 1957.

4. A. FALKENSTEIN and W. VON SODEN, *Sumer. und Akkad. Hymnen und Gebete*, Zurich, 1953, p. 85 ss.

5. A. L. OPPENHEIM, The seafaring merchants of Ur, *JAOS* 74 (1954), pp. 6–17.

6. Published by F. R. STEELE in *AJA* 52 (1958), pp. 425–50. Cf. *ANET*, (1950), pp. 159–61 and E. SZLECHTER, *RA* LI (1957), pp. 57–82, 177–196 and LII (1958), pp. 74–89.

7. KING, *Chronicles*, II, pp. 12–16. On the substitute King, cf. H. FRANKFORT, *Kingship and the Gods*, Chicago, 1955, pp. 262–5.

8. *Marad* is Wannah-es-Saadun, 15 miles N. of Diwaniyah.

9. The history of Eshnunna is developed in H. FRANKFORT and TH. JACOBSEN, *The Gimilsin Temple and the Palace of the Rulers at Tell Asmar (OIP* XLIII), Chicago, 1940, especially pp. 196–200.

10. A. GOETZE, *Sumer* IV (1948), pp. 63–102; *ANET*, pp. 161–3; *The Laws of Eshnunna*, New Haven, 1956.

11. TAHA BAQIR, Tell Harmal, *Sumer* II (1946), pp. 23–30; IV (1948), pp. 137–8.

12. *Assur* (Qal'at Sherqat) was excavated by a German expedition under W. ANDRAE between 1903 and 1914. Detailed reports are still being published. For a short account of the excavations, cf. W. ANDRAE, *Das viedererstandene Assur*, Leipzig, 1938.

13. A. POEBEL, The Assyrian King List from Khorsabad, *JNES* I (1942), pp. 247–306; 460–95.

14. It is generally believed that Narâm-Sin, King of Assur, is identical with Narâm-Sin, King of Eshnunna, who occupied Assur for a short period.

15. *ARAB* I, §§ 25–38.

16. D. O. EDZARD, *ZZB*, pp. 90–2.

17. *ARM* I, 3.

18. G. DOSSIN, L'inscription de fondatiþn de Iahdun-Lim, roi de Mari, *Syria* XXXII (1955), pp. 1–28. For other military exploits of this king, see the year-names in *Studia Mariana*, Leiden, 1950, pp. 52–3.

19. B. LANDSBERGER, Assyrische Königliste und 'dunkles Zeitalter', *JCS* VIII (1954), pp. 34–5. J. R. KUPPER, *Nomades*, pp. 207–13.

20. *ARAB* I, § 45.

21. Up to now, eight volumes of French translations have been published by G. DOSSIN and co-workers (J. BOTTERO, G. BOYER, CH. F. JEAN, J. R. KUPPER) under the title: *Archives Royales de Mari*, Paris, 1950 ss. (abbreviated *ARM*). Volumes I, IV and V deal with the correspondence of Shamshi-Adad and his sons. The other volumes contain letters to and from the 'national' king Zimri-Lim and his officials, as well as legal and administrative texts.

22. *ARM* I, 124.

23. *ARM* IV, 70.

24. *ARM* I, 61.

25. *ARM* I, 69. 'To kill the dâwîdum' is probably an expression meaning 'to win a victory' (J. R. KUPPER, *Nomades*, pp. 60–2).

26. J. R. KUPPER, *Les Nomades en Mésopotamie au temps des rois de Mari*, Paris, 1957.

27. *ARM* II, 118.

28. This is the same name as that of the Israelite tribe of Benjamin, although there is no evidence of a connection between the two. On the Bene-Iamina, see G. DOSSIN, Benjaminites dans les textes de Mari, *Mélange Dussaud* II, Paris, 1939, pp. 981–96.

29. *ARM* V, 6.

30. *ARM* I, 24, 46, 77. G. DOSSIN, Iamhad and Qatanum, *RA* XXXVI (1939), pp. 46–54. *Qatna*, modern Mishrifeh, 11 miles N.E. of Homs, was excavated by the French from 1924 to 1929 (R. DU MESNIL DU BUISSON, *Le Site Archéologique de Mishrifé-Qatna*, Paris, 1935).

31. *ARM* IV, 88.

32. *ARM* I, 93; IV, 5, 14.

33. *ARM* V, 56.

CHAPTER XII

1. L. W. KING, *The Letters and Inscriptions of Hammurabi*, London, 1900. F. THUREAU-DANGIN, La correspondance de Hammurabi avec Shamash-hasir, *RA* XXI (1924), pp. 1–58. On the reign in general, see: TH. DE LIAGRE BOHL, King Hammurabi of Babylon in the setting of his time, in *Opera Minora*, Leiden, 1953, pp. 339–63, and H. SCHMÖKEL, *Hammurabi von Babylon*, Oldenbourg, 1958.

2. See, for instance, the stone head of (possibly) Hammurabi in the Louvre museum, *AAO*, pl. 63; A. PARROT, *Sumer*, pl. 375.

3. From then on, the Akkadian language develops into (Old) Babylonian and (Old) Assyrian.

4. All dates according to SIDNEY SMITH's chronological system (see above, chapter II, note 12).

5. The date-formulae of Hammurabi are given in German translation by UNGNAD in *RLA* II, pp. 178–82. English translation by A. L. OPPENHEIM in *ANET*, 1950, pp. 269–71.

6. *ARM* IV, 20.

7. Zimri-Lim date-formula No. 1.

8. Most of Zimri-Lim's correspondence is to be found in *ARM* II, III and VI. Another important source for the reign is the date-formulae published by G. DOSSIN in *Studia Mariana*, Leiden, 1950, pp. 54–9. They are not, however, in chronological order.

9. Zimri-Lim date-formula No. 6: 'Year when Zimri-Lim killed the dâwîdum of the Bene-Iamina in Sagarâtim and killed their kings.'

10. Zimri-Lim date-formulae Nos. 20 and 32.

11. *ARM* II, 43; VI, 54.

12. *ARM* VI, 66.

13. *ARM* II, 68, 71.

14. *ARM* II, 33, 72.

15. Marduk, in Sumerian AMAR-UTU, 'bullock (or son) of the Sun-god', seems to have been a solar deity. On this god, cf. E. DHORME, *Religions*, pp. 139–50.

16. Code of Hammurabi, Prologue, I, 1–30.

17. Code of Hammurabi, Prologue, I, 32–9.

18. The Code of Hammurabi has been translated into several languages and copiously commented. The most recent English translations are in *ANET*, (1950,) pp. 163–80 (TH. J. MEEK) and in G. R. DRIVER and J. C. MILES, *Babylonian Laws*, Oxford, 1955–6. Vol. I: Legal Commentary; vol. II: Translation and Philological Commentary.

19. G. R. DRIVER and G. C. MILES, *Babylonian Laws*, p. 48 ss.; F. R. KRAUS, Ein zentrales Problem des altmesopotamischen Rechtes: was ist

der Codex Hammu-rabi? *Genava* VIII (1960), pp. 283–96; J. J. FINKELSTEIN, Ammiṣaduqa's edict and the Babylonian 'Law Codes', *JCS* XV (1961), pp. 91–104; D. J. WISEMAN, The Laws of Hammu-rabi again, *JSS* VII (1962), pp. 161–72.

20. Part of the stele was erased in antiquity, resulting in the loss of five to seven columns of text and approximately thirty-five laws. Fragments of the Code on clay tablets help to fill the gap.

21. E. A. SPEISER, Mushkênum, *Orientalia* XXVII (1958), pp. 19–28. The *mushkênum* is already mentioned in the Laws of Eshnunna, §§ 12, 13, 24, 34, 50.

22. The Babylonian marriage was essentially a contract (*CH* § 128). Before the ceremony, the future husband presented his father-in-law with a 'bridal gift' (*terhatum*), and the bride's father gave her a dowry (*sheriqtum*) of which she had perpetual possession.

23. Neither the Laws of Eshnunna nor the Sumerian Laws (Ur-Nammu, Lipit-Ishtar) mention the *ilkum* which might have been introduced by Hammurabi as a political measure. Note, however, that the absence of this institution in these Law Codes could be due to the fact that they are not so well preserved as the Code of Hammurabi.

24. Code of Hammurabi, Epilogue, xxiv, 30–59 (transl. TH. J. MEEK).

CHAPTER XIII

1. In these scenes, the owner of the seal, accompanied by his 'personal god', presents offerings to a deity. Examples in *AAO*, p. 61.

2. Street chapels of PA.SAG, Ninshubur and unidentified minor gods at Ur: SIR LEONARD WOOLLEY, *AJ* X (1930), pp. 368–72; *Excavations at Ur*, pp. 190–2; D. J. WISEMAN, The goddess Lama at Ur, *Iraq* XXII (1960), pp. 166–71.

3. Examples: temple of Hani and Nisaba at Tell Harmal (*Sumer* II (1946), pp. 23–4); temple of Ishtar-Kititum at Ishchâli (*OIC* XX (1936), pp. 74–98).

4. Temple of the goddess Nin-gal at Ur: *AJ* V (1925), pp. 371–6; VI (1926), pp. 366–75; *Excavations at Ur*, pp. 166–74.

5. For the development of temples in Mesopotamia, see: H. LENZEN, Mesopotamien Tempelanlagen . . . *ZA* XVII (1955), pp. 1–36.

6. For details on temples, clergy and cult see: B. MEISSNER, *Babylonien und Assyrien*, II, Heidelberg, 1925, pp. 53–101; E. DHORME, *Religions*, pp. 174–257.

7. F. THUREAU-DANGIN, *Rituels Accadiens*, Paris, 1907.

8. F. THUREAU-DANGIN, *op. cit.*, p. 10 ss. (Cf. *ANET*, pp. 334–8). This ritual dates, in fact, from the Hellenistic period, but it certainly reproduces a much older original.

9. For instance, were high-priestesses of Nin-gal at Ur: En-he-du-anna, daughter of Sargon of Akkad, Enannatum, daughter of Ishme-Dagan of Isin, and Bel-shalti-Nannar, daughter of Naboni-dus of Babylon.

10. G. R. DRIVER and G. C. MILES, *Babylonian Laws*, I, pp. 358–83.

11. The priests received part of the offerings and of the animals sacrificed in proportions fixed by royal decree. See, for instance, the stone-tablet of Nabû-apal-iddina, king of Babylon, in *BBS*, pp. 120–7.

12. The palace of Kish and the palace (?) of Eridu, in Early Dynastic times, measured 270 × 140 and 135 × 200 feet respectively. The *E-har-sag* building of Ur (perhaps the royal palace) was only 167 feet square (*AJ* VI (1926), p. 382).

13. Preliminary reports in *Syria* 1936 ss. Final publication by A. PARROT, *Mission Archéologique de Mari*, III, *Le Palais*, 3 vols. Paris, 1958–9.

14. H. VINCENT, *RB* (1939), p. 156.

15. *Syria* XVIII (1937), pp. 74–5.

16. PARROT assumes that the royal throne was on the lower pedestal (*Palais*, I, p. 111).

17. A. PARROT, *Mari, une Ville Perdue*, Paris, 1938, p. 161.

18. *ARM* I, 64; IV, 79.

19. Modern Tell Ashâra, on the Euphrates, 45 miles N. of Mari.

20. *ARM* III, 62.

21. G. DOSSIN, Une révélation du dieu Dagan à Terqa. *RA* XLII (1948), pp. 125–34.

22. A town on the lower Khabur, probably Tell Fedain.

23. Examples taken from *ARM* II, 106; VI, 43; I, 89; II, 112 respectively.

24. This was the usual opening sentence for letters. The sender spoke to the scribe who was to read the letter to the addressee.

25. *AJ* VII (1927), pp. 386–99; XI (1931), pp. 359–68. *Excavations at Ur*, pp. 175–94. Most of the houses date back to the Ur III period and were rebuilt along the same lines in Isin-Larsa and Old Babylonian times. They were abandoned in the 12th year of Samsu-iluna, Hammurabi's son and successor.

26. Cemeteries outside the town seem to have fallen into disuse during the Third Dynasty of Ur.

27. *AJ* XI (1931), pp. 364–6. *Excavations at Ur*, pp. 186–7.

28. A. L. OPPENHEIM, *JAOS* 74 (1954), p. 15, 17. W. F. LEEMANS, *The Old Babylonian Merchant*, Leiden, 1950, pp. 78–95; *Foreign Trade in the Old Babylonian period*, Leiden, 1960.

CHAPTER XIV

1. On the Indo-Europeans in general: G. V. CHILDE, *The Aryans*, London, 1926; C. S. COON, *Races of Europe*, New York, 1939; A. MEILLET, *Introduction a l'étude comparative des langues Indo-Européennes*, Paris, 1949.
2. C. F. HAWKES, *The Prehistoric Foundations of Europe*, London, 1940; G. V. CHILDE, *The Dawn of European Civilization*, 5th ed., London, 1950; *Prehistoric Migrations in Europe*, Oslo, 1950.
3. *The Cambridge Ancient History*, vols. I–VIII, Cambridge, 1924 ss.; A. J. WACE, *Mycenae*, Princeton, 1949; G. GLOTZ, *La Civilization Egéenne*, 2nd ed. Paris, 1952; J. FORSDYKE, *Greece before Homer*, London, 1956.
4. See J. CHADWICK, *The Decipherment of Linear B*, Cambridge, 1959.
5. A. PENDLEBURY, *The Archaeology of Crete*, London, 1939.
6. E. MACKAY, *Early Indus Civilizations*, 2nd ed., London, 1948; S. PIGGOTT, *Prehistoric India*, Harmondsworth, 1950; SIR MORTIMER WHEELER, *The Indus Civilization*, Cambridge, 1953.
7. SETON LLOYD, *Early Anatolia*, Harmondsworth, 1956. A. GOETZE, *Kleinasien*, 2nd ed., Munich, 1957; J. MELLAART, Anatolia c. 4000–2300 BC *CAH* (revised edition), I ch. 18 (1962).
8. B. LANDSBERGER, *Assyrische Handelskolonien in Kleinasien*, Leipzig, 1925; SETON LLOYD, *op. cit.*, pp. 112–26.
9. G. CONTENAU, *La Civilisation des Hittites et des Hourrites du Mitanni*, Paris, 1948; O. R. GURNEY, *The Hittites*, Harmondsworth, 1954; Anatolia c. 1750–1600 BC *CAH* (revised edition), II, ch. 6 (1962).
10. E. A. SPEISER, Ethnic movements in the Near East in the second millennium BC, *AASOR* XIII (1933), pp. 13–54; I. J. GELB, *Hurrians and Subarians*, Chicago, 1944; R. T. O'CALLAGHAN, *Aram Naharaim*, Rome, 1948, p. 37 ss.
11. D. J. WISEMAN, *The Alalakh Tablets*, London, 1953, p. 9. For a slightly different opinion, cf. I. J. GELB, *JCS* XV (1961), p. 39.
12. *Nuzi* (sometimes written *Nuzu*) is modern Yorgan Tepe, 8 miles S.W. of Kirkuk. American excavations from 1925 to 1931 (R. F. STARR, *Report on the Excavations at Yorgan Tepe, near Kirkuk*, Cambridge (Mass.), 1937–9. Thirteen volumes of texts, mostly legal and economic, have been published by E. CHIERA, E. LACHEMAN,

TH. MEEK and R. H. PFEIFFER. For a vivid account of their content, see C. H. GORDON, *Adventures in the Near East*, London, 1957, pp. 105–20.

13. For Tepe Gawra, see above, chapter IV, note 18. Tell Billa (Assyrian *Shibbaniba*), near Bashiqa (10 miles N.E. of Mosul), was also excavated by the Americans from 1930 to 1933. Reports in *BASOR* Nos. 40 to 60. The Hurrian level there has yielded houses and pottery, but no text.

14. E. A. SPEISER, The Hurrian participation in the civilizations of Mesopotamia, Syria and Palestine, *JWH*, I (1953), pp. 311–26.

15. For a general account of the early history of Syria, cf. P. K. HITTI, *History of Syria*, London, 1951.

16. *The Cambridge Ancient History*, vols. I–III, Cambridge, 1924 ss.; E. MEYER, *Geschichte des Altertums*, Stuttgard, 1913, 1928; E. DRIOTON and J. VANDIER, *L'Egypte*, Paris, 1952, and SIR ALLAN GARDINER, *Egypt of the Pharaohs*, Oxford, 1961, can be used as introductions to the vast domain of Egyptian history.

17. *Alalah* is modern Tell Atchana, between Aleppo and Antioch. British excavations in 1936–9: SIR LEONARD WOOLLEY, *Alalakh*, London, 1955; *A Forgotten Kingdom*, 2nd ed., Harmondsworth, 1959. Texts published by D. J. WISEMAN, *The Alalakah Tablets*, London, 1953.

18. *Ugarit* (modern Ras-Shamra, 7 miles N. of Lataqiah) is, with Mari, the most important archaeological site in Syria. The French excavations under CL. F. SCHAEFFER, started in 1929 and are still in progress. Preliminary reports in *Syria* 1929 ss. Texts published by C. VIROLLEAUD, J. NOUGAYROL *et al.* in the series *Mission de Ras Shamra, Le Palais Royal d'Ugarit*, Paris 1955 ss. Cf. also the series *Ugaritica*, Paris, 1939 ss.

19. W. A. WARD, Egypt and the East Mediterranean in the early second millennium BC. *Orientalia XXX* (1961), pp. 22–45; 129–155.

20. W. F. ALBRIGHT, *The Archaeology of Palestine*, Harmondsworth, 1954, p. 80.

21. R. DE. VAUX, Les patriarches hébreux et les découvertes modernes, *RB* 53 (1946), pp. 321–48; 55 (1948), pp. 321–47; 56 (1949), pp. 5–36.

22. J. BOTTERO, *Le Problème des Habiru à la 4ème Rencontre Assyriologique Internationale*, Paris, 1954. M. GREENBERG, *The Hab/piru*, New Haven, 1955.

23. SIR ALLAN GARDINER, *op. cit.*, p. 156.

CHAPTER XV

1. Apart from a considerable number of economic texts, contracts and letters, the main sources for the history of Samsu-iluna and his successors are the year-names of each reign published by A. UNGNAD in *RLA* II, pp. 182–92 (cf. A. GOETZE, The year-names of Abi-eshuh, *JCS* V (1951), pp. 98–103, and S. I. FEIGNIN, The date-list of . . . Samsu-ditana, *JNES* XIV (1955), pp. 137–60) and the Babylonian chronicle published by KING, *Chronicles* II, pp. 15–24.

2. Inscription of Esarhaddon: *ARAB* II, § 576.

3. TH. DE LIAGRE BOHL, Ein Brief des Königs Samsu-iluna von Babylon, *Bi.Or.* VIII (1951), pp. 50–60.

4. A *Kashtiliash* whose name appears among the Semitic rulers of Hana is probably the same person as the second successor of *Gandash* who founded the Kassite dynasty outside Babylon during the reign of Samsu-iluna.

5. See, in particular, the very important 'decision of justice' published by F. R. KRAUS, *Ein Edikt des Königs Ammi-ṣaduqa von Babylon*, Leiden, 1958.

6. J. GARSTANG and O. GURNEY, *The Geography of the Hittite Empire*, London, 1959, p. 63.

7. Inscription of Telepinus (c. 1500 BC). Cf. F. HROZNY, Eine Inschrift des Königs Telepinus, *BoStu*, III (1919), pp. 202–4.

8. KING, *Chronicles*, II, p. 22.

9. K. BALKAN, *Kassitenstudien*, I, *Die Sprache der Kassiten*, New Haven, 1954.

10. F. EL-WAILLY, Synopsis of royal sources of the Kassite period, *Sumer* X (1954), pp. 43–54.

11. Published by F. E. PEISER and H. WINCKLER in *KB* I (1889), pp. 194–203.

12. Inscription of Agum-Kakrime published by P. JENSEN in *KB* III (1892), pp. 134–53.

13. *Synchr. History*, I, 5–7 (correct Burnaburiash in Ulamburiash, the synchronism with Puzur-Ashur being assured by the Assur list, *ANET*, p. 273). A similar agreement was later passed between Kara-Indash and Ashur-bêl-nishêshu (*ibid.* I, 1–4).

14. J. JORDAN, *UVB* I (1930), p. 30; *AAO*, pp. 63–4, pl. 70a.

15. TAHA BAQIR, Excavations at 'Aqar Quf, *Iraq*, Supplement 1944–5 and *Iraq* VIII (1946), pp. 73–92.

16. S. N. KRAMER, TAHA BAQIR, S. J. LEVY, Fragments of a diorite statue of Kurigalzu in the Iraq Museum, *Sumer* IV (1948), p. 1 ss. S. N. KRAMER, *ANET*, pp. 57–9.

17. *ARM* I, 50; II, 123; IV, 38; V, 20. On the horse in the Near East in general, see now A. SALONEN, *Hippologica Accadica*, Helsinki, 1956.

18. Most Kassite kudurrus are published by L. KING in *Babylonian Boundary Stones*, London, 1912.

19. T. BERAN, Die Babylonische Glyptic der Kassitenzeit, *AfO* XVIII (1958), pp. 255–87.

20. W. J. LAMBERT, *Babylonian Wisdom Literature*, Oxford, 1960, pp. 184–5.

CHAPTER XVI

1. See, in particular: R. T. O'CALLAGHAN, *Aram Naharaim*, Rome, 1948, and S. SMITH, *Early History of Assyria*, London, 1928. Egyptian texts in English translation in J. H. BRESTEAD, *Ancient Records of Egypt*, Chicago, 1906–7 and in *ANET*, pp. 234–58.

2. *ARAB* I, §§ 47–59.

3. Note that the Egyptian word Naharin, obviously derived from West Semitic *naharaim*, 'rivers', applies to the region from the Orontes to the Euphrates rather than to the region between Euphrates and Tigris.

4. Recent American (1940) and German (1955–56) excavations at Tell Fekheriyeh, near Ras-el-'Ain, on the Khabur, have failed to confirm the traditional identification of this site with Washukkanni. See A. MOORTGAT, *Archäologische Forschungen der Max Freiherr von Oppenheim-Stiftung in nördlischen Mesopotamien*, Köln, 1957–59.

5. S. SMITH, *The Statue of Idrimi*, London, 1949. Tablet from Nuzi: A. L. OPPENHEIM, *BASOR*, 93 (1944), p. 16.

6. R. F. STARR, *Nuzi*, II, pl. 118, 1.

7. Treaty between Mattiwaza and Suppiluliumas, Rev. 8–10 (E. WEIDNER, Politische Dokumente aus Kleinasien, *BoStu* VIII (1923), p. 39.

8. *EA* 29.

9. *EA* 17, 29.

10. O. R. GURNEY, *The Hittites*, p. 27.

11. This correspondence (abbreviated *EA*) was found at Tell-el-'Amarna (ancient Akhetaton), the ephemeral capital-city of Egypt under Amenophis IV, but the tablets are now dispersed in various museums. They were first gathered and published by J. A. KNUDTZON, *Die El-Amarna Tafeln*, Leipzig, 1915. English transla-

tion: S. A. MERCER, *The Tell el-Amarna Tablets*, Toronto, 1939. Except for one letter in Hurrian and two in a Hittite dialect, the letters, numbering over 350, were all written in Akkadian with occasional Canaanite glosses. In addition, the Egyptian royal archives contained copies of Sumero-Akkadian myths and epics such as 'Adapa', the 'Epic of the King of the Battle', etc.

12. For a general survey of the period, cf. E. CAVAIGNAC, *Subbiluliuma et son Temps*, Paris, 1932.

13. *EA* 1–5.

14. *EA* 7, lines 69–72.

15. *EA* 7, lines 53–4.

16. *EA* 14.

17. Treaty between Suppiluliumas and Mattiwaza, Rev. 50 (*BoStu* VIII (1923), p. 17). Mattiwaza's flight to Babylon is contested by O'CALLAGHAN, *Aram Naharaim*, pp. 89–90.

18. *EA* 15–16.

19. *Synchr. Hist.* I, 8–17. Also the so-called 'Chronicle P', I, 9–14. (Outdated English translation by TH. G. PINCHES in A. H. SAYCE, *Records of the Past*, V, London, 1891.)

20. *Chronicle P*, III, 10–19.

21. Identified with Tell Kazel, north of Tripoli (M. DUNAND and N. SALIBY, *AAS*, VII (1957), pp. 3–16).

22. *ANET*, pp. 199–203.

23. J. FRIEDRICH, *Der Alte Orient*, XXIV, 3 (1925), p. 26.

24. *Synchr. Hist.* I, 18–23.

25. *ARAB* I, § 73.

26. *Synchr. Hist.* I, 24–31 (War between Adad-nirâri and Nazi-Maruttash).

27. *ARAB* I, § 116.

28. See now: W. G. LAMBERT, Three unpublished fragments of the Tukulti-Ninurta Epic, *AfO* 18 (1957–58), pp. 38–51. E. WEIDNER, *Die Inschriften Tukulti-Ninurtas I und seiner Nachfolger*, Gratz, 1959.

29. *ARAB* I, § 145.

30. *Chronicle P*, IV, 8–9 (Cf. *ARAB* I, § 141).

31. *ibid.* IV, 9–13. *Kâr-Tukulti-Ninurta* (modern Tulul Akir), one mile north of Assur, on the left bank of the Tigris, was excavated by the Germans in 1913–14: W BACHMANN, *MDOG* 53, pp. 41–57; W. ANDRAE, *Das wiedererstandene Assur*, pp. 121–5.

32. G. G. CAMERON, *History of Early Iran*, Chicago, 1936, pp. 109–111.

1. Later, the *Parsua* moved to the south-western part of Iran, occupied a district in the Bakhtiari mountains close to Elam and gave it their name: *Parsu(m)ash*, Persia, Fars. (See R. GHIRSHMAN, *Iran*, Harmondsworth, 1954, pp. 91 and 119).

2. W. F. ALBRIGHT, *From the Stone Age to Christianity*, 2nd ed., New York, 1957, pp. 13 and 255.

3. I Kings i–xi; II Chronicles i–ix.

4. CL. F. A. SCHAEFFER, *Ugaritica I*, Paris, 1939, pp. 45–6.

5. I Kings v. 1–12; vii. 13 ss.; ix. 11–14; II Chronicles ii. 3–16; iv. 11–18.

6. G. CONTENAU, *La Civilisation Phénicienne*, 2nd ed., Paris, 1939 (to be supplemented with the reports on excavations at Ras-Shamra); D. HARDEN, *The Phoenicians*, London, 1962.

7. On the alphabet, cf. G. R. DRIVER, *Semitic Writing*, Oxford, 1948; D. DIRINGER, *The Alphabet*, London, 1948; J. G. FEVRIER, *Histoire de l'Ecriture*, Paris, 1948; I. J. GELB, *A Study of Writing*, London, 1952.

8. For a general survey of this literature, cf. C. H. GORDON, *Ugaritic Literature*, Rome, 1949, and *Ugaritic Manual*, Rome, 1955.

9. O. R. GURNEY, *The Hittites*, Harmondsworth, 1952, pp. 39–46; SETON LLOYD, *Early Anatolia*, Harmondsworth, 1956, pp. 156–76.

10. SETON LLOYD, *op. cit.*, pp. 177–82. Good summary in the articles by I. J. GELB and M. J. MELLINK in *Bi.Or.* VII (1950), pp. 129–50.

11. On recent excavations at *Arpad* (Tell Rifa'at, 23 miles N. of Aleppo), see M. V. SETON WILLIAMS, *Iraq* XXIII (1961), pp. 68–82.

12. On the Aramaeans in general, cf. S. SCHIFFER, *Die Aramäer*, Leipzig, 1911; E. G. KRAELING, *Aram and Israel*, New York, 1918; R. T. O'CALLAGHAN, *Aram Naharaim*, Rome, 1948, pp. 93–130; A. DUPONT-SOMMER, *Les Araméens*, Paris, 1949, and J. R. KUPPER, *Nomades*, pp. 112–45.

13. Deuteronomy xxvi. 5.

14. *ARAB* I, § 166.

15. *KAH* II, No. 63, III, 4–5; No. 71, 19.

16. S. MOSCATI, The Aramaean Ahlamû, *JSS* IV (1959), pp. 303–7.

17. M. FREIHERR VON OPPENHEIM, *Der Tell Halaf*, Leipzig, 1931, pp. 71–198, and *Tell Halaf* II, *Die Bauwerke*, Berlin, 1950; III, *Die Bildwerke*, Berlin, 1955.

18. See now: A. POEBEL, *The Second Dynasty of Isin according to a New King List Tablet*, Chicago, 1955.

19. Quoted by G. G. CAMERON, *History of Early Iran*, Chicago, 1936, p. 132.

20. L. KING, *BBS* No. VI, pp. 29–36.
21. *ARAB* I, § 257 (Inscription of Tiglathpileser I).
22. *ARAB* I, § 287; *ANET*, p. 275.
23. *ARAB* I, §§ 300–3; *ANET*, pp. 274–5.
24. *ARAB* I, § 309. Cf. E. WEIDNER, Die Feldzüge und Bauten Tiglatpilesers I, *AfO* XVIII (1958), pp. 342–60.
25. *ARAB* I, §§ 247–8.
26. Stone tablet of Nabû-apal-iddina (885–852 BC), Col. I, 4–5. (L. KING, *BBS*, p. 121).
27. J. R. KUPPER, *Nomades*, p. 115 ss.
28. KING, *Chronicles*, II, pp. 143–79; *Synchr. Hist.*, II, 29–36.
29. KING, *Chronicles*, II, pp. 81–83.

CHAPTER XVIII

1. Exactly since Ninurta-apal-ekur (1192–1180).
2. No monography on the Assyrian empire has been published since A. T. OLMSTEAD's *History of Assyria*, New York, 1923. The main sources for the political history of the period are: (1) the royal inscriptions published by D. LUCKENBILL in *ARAB*, Chicago, 1926; (2) the royal correspondence from Nineveh published in English by LEROY WATERMAN, *Royal Correspondence of the Assyrian Empire*, Ann Arbor, 1930–6 (abbreviated *RCAE*); (3) the royal archives from Nimrud published by D. J. WISEMAN, H. W. SAGGS and B. PARKER in *Iraq* XII (1950) ss.; (4) the Old Testament (II Kings, II Chronicles, Prophets).
3. *ARAB* I, §§ 355–84, 396–9.
4. *ARAB* I, § 360. *Synchr. Hist.*, III, 1–21.
5. *ARAB* I, §§ 400–434.
6. D. G. HOGARTH, *The Ancient Near East*, London, 1950, p. 25.
7. *ARAB* I, §§ 466, 501–2. The talent (*biltu*) was worth about 67 lbs.; the mina (*manû*), 18 oz. A *gur* was about 2 bushels.
8. See A. T. OLMSTEAD, *op. cit.*, pp. 530–2.
9. *AAO*, pl. 82; A. PARROT, *Assur*, Paris, 1961, pls. 22–3.
10. Inscriptions of Ashurnaṣirpal in *ARAB* I, §§ 436–552. Also: E. MICHEL, Die Texte Assur-naṣir-aplis II, *Die Welt der Orient* II (1954), pp. 313–21, 404–7.
11. *ARAB* I, § 443.
12. *ANET*, p. 276; *ARAB* I, §§ 479, 518.
13. *Tushhan* is Kurkh, 20 miles south of Diarbekr. *Kar-Ashurnaṣirpal* and *Nibarti-Ashur*, facing each other on either side of the Euphrates,

are probably Zalabiyah and Halabiyah, between Raqqa and Deir-ez-Zor.

14. *ARAB* I, §§ 433, 445, 455, 472.

15. *ARAB* I, § 489.

16. A. H. LAYARD, *Nineveh and its Remains*, London, 1849; *Nineveh and Babylon*, London, 1882.

17. Detailed reports in *Iraq* XII (1950) ss. Summary of the excavations by M. E. L. MALLOWAN, *Twenty-five Years of Mesopotamian Discovery*, London, 1956, pp. 50–64. Numerous articles in *ILN* since 1950.

18. D. J. WISEMAN, A new stela of Assur-naṣir-pal, *Iraq* XIV (1952), pp. 24–39.

19. *AAO*, pl. 93.

20. D. OATES, Fort Shalmaneser. An interim report, *Iraq* XXI (1959), pp. 98–129; The excavations at Nimrud, 1960, *Iraq* XXIII (1961), pp. 1–14. J. LAESSØE, A statue of Shalmaneser III, from Nimrud, *Iraq* XXI (1959), pp. 147–57.

21. L. KING, *Bronze Reliefs from the Gates of Shalmaneser*, London, 1915, pls. 91–92. *AAO*, pls. 91–2. A. PARROT, *Assur*, pls. 121–8.

22. To the inscriptions published in *ARAB* I, §§ 553–612, add now: G. G. CAMERON, The annals of Shalmaneser III, a new text, *Sumer* VI (1950), pp. 6–26; FUAD SAFAR, A further text of Shalmaneser III, *Sumer* VII (1951), pp. 3–21; J. LAESSØE, Building inscriptions from Fort Shalmaneser, *Iraq* XXI (1959), pp. 38–41. Critical study: E. MICHEL, Die Assur-Texte Salmanasars III, *Die Welt der Orient* II (1947)—116 (1952). Poetic version of the campaign in Urartu: W. G. LAMBERT, The Sultantepe tablets, VIII, Shalmaneser in Ararat, *Anatolian Studies* XI (1961), pp. 143–58.

23. French excavations 1929–31: F. THUREAU-DANGIN and M. DUNAND, *Til-Barsib*, Paris, 1936.

24. *ARAB* I, § 611; *ANET*, p. 279. Note that this is the first historical mention of the Arabs.

25. *ARAB* I, § 681. Cf. II Kings viii. 7–15.

26. *BBS*, pp. 120–27.

27. *ARAB* I, § 624. *Synchr. Hist.* III, 22–35.

CHAPTER XIX

1. Inscriptions of Shamsi-Adad V in *ARAB* I, §§ 713–28. On the wars against Babylon, cf. E. WEIDNER, Die Feldzüge Samsi-Adads V gegen Babylonien, *AfO* IX (1933–4), pp. 89–104.

2. Memorial stele of Sammuramat in *ARAB* I, § 731. Cf. *ARAB* I, § 745.

3. A. T. OLMSTEAD, *History of Assyria*, p. 158. Legend of Semiramis in HERODOTUS I, 184; STRABO XV, 1, 5, ii, 5; XVI, i, 2; DIODORUS SICULUS II, 4–20.

4. G. GOOSENS, Communication at the 6th Rencontre Assyriologique Internationale, Paris, 1956.

5. Inscriptions of Adad-nirâri III in *ARAB* I, §§ 732–48. Cf. also *Iraq* XV (1953), p. 135 ss.

6. F. THUREAU-DANGIN, L'inscription des lions de Til-Barsib, *RA* XXVII (1930), pp. 1–21.

7. The reigns of these three kings are mostly known from the lists of eponyms (*ARAB* II, § 1197).

8. L. KING, *Chronicles*, II, p. 154.

9. American excavations at Hasanlu, south of lake Urmiah: R. H. DYSON, *Expedition* I, 3 (1959), pp. 4–17 and II, 3 (1960), pp. 2–11.

10. *ARAB* I, §§ 749–60.

11. On early excavations in Turkish Armenia, SÉTON LLOYD, *Early Anatolia*, 1956, pp. 183–90. Recent excavations in USSR Armenia summarized by R. D. BARNETT and W. WATSON in *Iraq* XIV (1952), pp. 132–47 and by B. PIOTROVSKY *et al.* in *Ourartou* . . . Paris, 1954. Urartian inscriptions published by F. W. KOENIG, *Handbuch der Chaldischen Inschriften*, I, Gratz, 1955. Numerous articles (in Russian) on Urartian history by I. M. DIAKONOFF, G. A. MELIKISHVILI, S. M. BATSIEVA etc. in *VDI*, 1951 ss. (summary in French in *RA* LII (1958) and LIII (1959).

12. E. FORRER, *Die Provinzeinteilung der assyrischen Reiches*, Leipzig, 1920, p. 49 ss. Cf. also H. W. SAGGS, *Iraq* XXI (1959), pp. 176–9.

13. *ARAB* I, §§ 770, 772, 795, 806.

14. *RCAE*, No. 327.

15. To the royal inscriptions published in *ARAB* I, §§ 761–821, add now the fragments from Nimrud published by D. J. WISEMAN in *Iraq* XIII (1951), p. 21 ss. and XVIII (1956), p. 117 ss. Other source: the so-called 'Babylonian Chronicle' (F. DELITZCH, *Die Babylonische Chronik*, Leipzig, 1906).

16. *ARAB* I, § 772; II Kings xv. 19–20.

17. French excavations in 1928: F. THUREAU-DANGIN, A. BARROIS, G. DOSSIN, M. DUNAND, *Arslan-Tash*, Paris, 1931.

18. R. GHIRSHMAN, *Iran*, Harmondsworth, 1954, p. 94.

19. Nimrud letter No. XII in *Iraq* XVII (1955), p. 128.

20. *ARAB* I, § 816; II Kings xv. 29–30; II Chronicles xxviii. 5–8.

21. Nimrud letters, *Iraq* XVII (1955), pp. 21–56. Cf. *ARAB* I, §§ 792–4, 806; *Babyl. Chronicle*, I, 17–23.

22. II Kings xvii. 4–6. On this problem, see now: H. TADMOR, The campaigns of Sargon II of Assur, *JCS* XII (1958), pp. 22–40; 77–100.

23. Inscriptions of Sargon: *ARAB* II, §§ 1–230. Prism from Nimrud: C. J. GADD, Inscribed prisms of Sargon from Nimrud, *Iraq* XVI (1954), pp. 172–201. Annals edited by A. G. LIE, *The Inscriptions of Sargon II, King of Assyria, I, The Annals*, Paris, 1929. H. TADMOR'S article *supra* is essential for the chronology of the reign.

24. So-called 'Assur Charter', *ARAB* II, §§ 132–5.

25. *Babyl. Chronicle* I, 33–7. C. J. GADD, Inscribed barrel cylinder of Marduk-apal-iddina II, *Iraq* XV (1953), pp. 123–34.

26. *ARAB* II, § 5; *ANET*, p. 285.

27. *ARAB* II, §§ 30, 62; *ANET*, p. 286. Cf. H. TADMOR, *ibid.*, pp. 83–4.

28. *RCAE*, esp. Nos. 101, 123, 145, 148, 251, 380, 381, 424, 444, 515. Nimrud letters: H. W. SAGGS, *Iraq* XX (1958), pp. 182–212.

29. F. THUREAU-DANGIN, *Une Relation de la Huitième Campagne de Sargon*, Paris, 1912. *ARAB* II, §§ 139–89. On the so-called 'Letters to the Gods', see A. L. OPPENHEIM, The city of Assur in 714 BC, *JCS* XIX (1960), pp. 133–47.

30. F. THUREAU-DANGIN, *op. cit.*, p. 7.

31. A. G. LIE, *op. cit.*, p. 61. Allusions to the war in *RCAE*, Nos. 436, 542, 571.

32. *ARAB* II, §§ 44, 70, 186.

33. French excavations in 1843–4 and 1852–4: P. E. BOTTA and E. FLANDIN, *Les Monuments de Ninive*, Paris, 1849–50; V. PLACE, *Ninive et l'Assyrie*, Paris, 1867–70. American excavations in 1930–5: G. LOUD, *Khorsabad*, Chicago, 1936–8.

34. *ARAB* II, § 89.

CHAPTER XX

1. D. D. LUCKENBILL, *The Annals of Sennacherib* (*OIP* II), Chicago, 1924; *ARAB* II, §§ 231–496; A. HEIDEL, The octagonal prism of Sennacherib in the Iraq Museum, *Sumer* IX (1953), pp. 117–88.

2. *RCAE*, Nos. 146, 197.

3. H. R. HALL, *The Ancient History of the Near East*, London, 1950, pp. 486–8.

4. The siege of Lachish is depicted in a famous bas-relief from Nineveh (*AAO*, pl. 101), but not mentioned in Sennacherib's annals.

5. II Kings xviii. 13–xix, 34; II Chronicles xxxii. 1–22; Isaiah xxxvi. 1–xxxvii. 38.
6. *ARAB* II, § 240 (Cf. *ANET*, p. 288).
7. II Kings xix. 35; HERODOTUS, II, 141; BEROSSUS in JOSEPHUS, *Jewish Antiquities*, X, i, 4–5.
8. *ARAB* II, § 242.
9. *ARAB* II, §§ 246–7, 318–22, 350, 353.
10. Tell 'Umar, on the Tigris, south of Baghdad.
11. *Babyl. Chronicle* II, 32–III, 16 (*ANET*, pp. 301–2).
12. *ARAB* II, §§ 253–4, but see *Babyl. Chronicle* III, 16–18. Hallule has not been located.
13. After *ARAB* II, §§ 339–41. The *Babyl. Chronicle* (III, 22, 28) simply says: 'The city was taken' and 'For eight years, there was no king in Babylon'.
14. *Babyl. Chronicle* III, 34; II Kings xix, 36–7; Rassam cylinder of Ashurbanipal, *ARAB* II, §§ 795–6 (*ANET*, p. 288). On this debated question, cf. E. A. KRAELING, The death of Sennacherib, *JAOS* LIII (1933), pp. 335–46; M. VIEYRA, Notes d'histoire, *RA* LIV (1960), pp. 41–2, and the works of CAMPBELL THOMPSON and HIRSCHBERG cited below, note (19).
15. Nebi-Yunus is built up and has hardly been touched by archaeologists. Kuyunjik has been the object of several campaigns of excavations since the pioneer work of LAYARD, in 1847. For a general description of the site, cf. R. CAMPBELL THOMPSON, *A Century of Exploration at Nineveh*, London, 1929.
16. *ARAB* II, § 366.
17. TH. JACOBSEN and SETON LLOYD, *Sennacherib's Aqueduct at Jerwan* (*OIP* XXIV), Chicago, 1935.
18. W. BACHMANN, *Felsreliefs in Assyrien*, Leipzig, 1927. L. W. KING, Some unpublished rock inscriptions of Sennacherib on the Judi-Dâgh, *PSBA* XXXV (1913), pp. 66–94.
19. *ARAB* II, §§ 497–761; R. CAMPBELL THOMPSON, *The Prisms of Esarhaddon and Ashurbanipal*, London, 1931; R. BORGER, *Die Inschriften Asarhaddons, König von Assyrien*, Graz, 1956; A. HEIDEL, A new hexagonal prism of Esarhaddon, *Sumer* XII (1956), pp. 9–37. H. HIRSCHBERG, *Studien zur Geschichte Esarhaddons*, Berlin, 1932.
20. *ANET*, pp. 289–90.
21. *ARAB* II, §§ 639–87. (Cf. J. NOUGAYROL, *AfO* XVIII (1958), pp. 314–18).
22. *Babyl. Chronicle* IV, 34–37 and the so-called 'Esarhaddon Chronicle' (s. SMITH, *Babylonian Historical Texts*, London, 1924, pp. 1–21; *ANET*, p. 303), Rev. 12–13.

23. Treaty between Esarhaddon and Ba'alu of Tyre: R. BORGER, *op. cit.*, pp. 107–9.
24. Excellent summary in D. J. WISEMAN, The vassal-treaties of Esarhaddon, *Iraq* XX (1958), especially pp. 9–13.
25. *ARAB* II, §§ 518a, 536, 551; *ANET*, pp. 291–2. On the Arabs at that period, cf. T. W. ROSMARIN, Aribi und Arabien in den Babylonisch-Assyrischen Quellen, *JSOR* XVI (1932), p. 1 ss.
26. Zenjirli stele, *ANET*, p. 293. Statues of Taharqa and of the Egyptian goddess Anuqet were recently found in Esarhaddon's palace at Nineveh (Nebi Yunus) (v. VIKENTIEV, *Sumer* XI (1955), pp. 111–14 and XII (1956), pp. 76–9).
27. *RCAE*, No. 1239.
28. *ARAB* II, §§ 762–1129; T. BAUER, *Das Inschriftwerk Assurbanipals*, Leizig, 1933; A. C. PIEPKORN, *Historical Prism Inscriptions of Ashurbanipal*, Chicago, 1933.
29. *ANET*, pp. 294–5 (cf. *ARAB* II, § 772).
30. J. H. BREASTED, *Ancient Records of Egypt*, Chicago, 1906–7, IV, p. 919 ss.
31. *RCAE*, No. 1391 (cf. L. F. HARTMANN, *JNES* XXI (1962), pp. 25–37).
32. *ARAB* II, § 855.
33. HERODOTUS, II, 152.
34. *ARAB* II, § 785.
35. *AAO*, pl. 114.
36. *RCAE*, No. 301.
37. *BHT*, pp. 22–6.
38. *ANET*, p. 299.
39. *ARAB* II, §§ 810–11.
40. According to II Chronicles xxxiii. 11, the Assyrians took Manasseh, King of Judah, and 'carried him to Babylon'. This event is not mentioned in the (incomplete) Assyrian records.
41. Nahum iii. 7, 15, 19.

CHAPTER XXI

1. See C. H. W. JOHNS, *Assyrian Deeds and Documents*, 2nd ed., Cambridge, 1924; J. KOHLER and A. UNGNAD, *Assyrische Rechtsurkunden*, Leipzig, 1913. Assyrian 'Code of Laws', dating to the second millennium: G. E. DRIVER and J. C. MILES, *The Assyrian Laws*, Oxford, 1935; *ANET*, 180–8 (TH. J. MEEK). Economic documents from Nimrud published by D. J. WISEMAN and B. PARKER in *Iraq* XX (1950) ss.

2. C. PREUSSER, *Die Wohnaüser in Assur*, Berlin, 1955, pp. 15–60. G. LOUD and CH. B. ALTMAN, *Khorsabad*, II, Chicago, 1938.

3. On this subject in general, cf. R. LABAT, *Le Caractère Religieux de la Royauté Assyro-Babylonienne*, Paris, 1939, and H. FRANKFORT, *Kingship and the Gods*, Chicago, 1948.

4. *ARAB* II, § 986.

5. A. HALLER, *Die Gräber und Grüfte von Assur*, Berlin, 1954, pp. 170–80.

6. K. F. MULLER, Das assyrische Ritual, *MVAG* XLI, 3, Berlin, 1937; R. LABAT, *op. cit.*, pp. 82–7; H. FRANKFORT, *op. cit.*, p. 247.

7. R. FRANKENA, *Tâkultu*, Leiden, 1954 (in Dutch with summary in English). J. LAESSØE, *Studies on the Assyrian Ritual and Series bît rimki*, Copenhagen, 1955.

8. H. FRANKFORT, *op. cit.*, p. 259.

9. *RCAE*, No. 437 (R. LABAT, *op. cit.*, p. 359; H. FRANKFORT, *op. cit.*, p. 264).

10. For a general introduction to this vast subject, cf. G. CONTENAU, *La Divination chez les Assyriens et les Babyloniens*, Paris, 1940 (with bibliography).

11. *RCAE*, No. 1237.

12. *RCAE*, No. 137.

13. H. DILLON, *Assyro-Babylonian Liver-Divination*, Rome, 1932, p. 38.

14. B. PARKER, The Assyrian civil-service, *Sumer* XVI (1960), pp. 32–8.

15. On the Assyrian society in general, B. MEISSNER, *Assyrien und Babylonien*, I, Heidelberg, 1920; L. DELAPORTE, *La Mésopotamie*, Paris, 1923, pp. 297–344; S. SMITH in *CAH*, III (1929), pp. 95–9.

16. An up-to-date monography of the Assyrian army is needed. The only detailed study available so far is: W. MANITIUS, Das stehende Heer der Assyrer Könige und seine Organisation, *ZA* XXIV (1910), p. 97 ss.; 185 ss.

17. E. CAVAIGNAC, Le code Assyrien et le recrutement, *RA* XXI (1924), p. 64.

18. Example in *RCAE*, No. 1237.

19. Pieces of equipment and weapons were found in 'Fort Shalmaneser' at Nimrud: D. STRONACH, Metal objects from the 1957 excavations at Nimrud, *Iraq* XX (1958), pp. 169–81. Also *ILN*, 17-1-1959, p. 99.

20. *AAO*, p. 84.

21. A. WALTER, *Kultrelief aus dem Brunnen des Assur Tempels zu Assur*, Leipzig, 1931; *AAO*, pl. 72.

22. The two most important collections of Assyrian reliefs are those in the British Museum (C. J. GADD, *The Assyrian Sculptures*, London,

1934; S. SMITH, *Assyrian Sculptures in the British Museum*, London, 1938) and in the Louvre Museum (*Encyclopédie Photographique de l'Art*, L'art de la Mésopotamie Ancienne au Musée du Louvre, fasc. VI, Paris, 1936). All general histories of art contain reproductions of the main reliefs. Good selection in *AAO*, pls. 77, 83–114, R. D. BARNETT and W. FORMAN, *Assyrian Palace Reliefs*, London, 1960 and A. PARROT, *Assur*, Paris, 1961.

23. A. WALTER, *Farbige Keramik aus Assur*, Berlin, 1923. G. LOUD and CH. B. ALTMAN, *Khorsabad*, II, Chicago, 1938, pl. 89.

24. Traces of mural paintings were found at Eridu, Uruk, Tepe Gawra and Tell Uqair.

25. A. PARROT, *Assur*, frontispiece and pp. XIII–XVI, pls. 1, 109–19, 266, 336–48.

26. A. PARROT, *Mission Archéologique de Mari*, I, *Le Temple d'Ishtar*, Paris, 1956, pp. 148, 152, 154, 156.

27. To the 550 pieces published in R. D. BARNETT, *A Catalogue of the Nimrud Ivories . . . in the British Museum*, London, 1957, must be added the ivories found in the course of practically every campaign of excavations since 1953 and published by M. MALLOWAN and D. OATES in *Iraq* and *ILN*. A number of the Nimrud ivories are in the Iraq Museum, Baghdad.

CHAPTER XXII

1. SETON LLOYD, *Foundations in the Dust*, Harmondsworth, 1955, p. 154.

2. C. BEZOLD, *Catalogue of the Cuneiform Tablets . . . in the British Museum*, London, 1889–99 (with supplement by L. KING, 1914).

3. *RCAE*, IV, p. 213, No. 6 (transl. E. CHIERA, *They Wrote on Clay*, Chicago, 1938, p. 174). Cf. also *RCAE*, Nos. 18, 255, 688.

4. Preliminary reports by SETON LLOYD and O. R. GURNEY in *Anatolian Studies*, III (1953) ss. Texts published by O. R. GURNEY and J. J. FINKELSTEIN, *The Sultantepe Tablets*, I, London, 1957.

5. D. J. WISEMAN, Assyrian writing-boards, *Iraq* XVII (1955), pp. 3–13.

6. A. HEIDEL, *The Gilgamesh Epic*, Chicago, 1946, p. 93.

7. Recent works on Mesopotamian sciences in general: O. NEUGE-BAUER, *The Exact Sciences in Antiquity*, Providence, Rhode Island, 1957. R. LABAT, La Mésopotamie in *La Science Antique et Médiévale*, *Histoire Générale des Sciences*, I, Paris, 1957, pp. 73–138. In spite of its date, B. MEISSNER, *Babylonien und Assyrien*, II, Heidelberg, 1925, is still extremely useful.

8. E. DHORME, *Les Religions de Babylonie et d'Assyrie*, 'Mana' I, Paris, 1945, pp. 259–98.

9. On schools (Sumer. é.dub.ba, Akkad. *bît tuppi*, 'House of Tablets') in Mesopotamia, see C. J. GADD, *Teachers and Students in the Oldest Schools*, London, 1956.

10. Examples in B. MEISSNER, *op. cit.*, pp. 346–60. Syllabaries and Vocabularies are now published by B. LANDSBERGER, *Materialen zum Sumerischen Lexikon*, Rome, 1937 ss.

11. B. LANDSBERGER, *Die Fauna des alten Mesopotamien*, Leipzig, 1934. R. C. THOMPSON, *A Dictionary of Assyrian Chemistry and Geology*, Oxford, 1936; *A Dictionary of Assyrian Botany*, London, 1949. M. LEVEY, *Chemistry and Chemical Technology in Ancient Mesopotamia*, Amsterdam, 1959.

12. B. MEISSNER, *op. cit.*, p. 378. The Mesopotamians might have heard of the Scandinavian countries through amber traders or through the Phoenicians who sailed at least as far as the coasts of England.

13. Good summary on mathematics by R. CARATINI in R. LABAT, *op. cit.*, pp. 103–37 (with bibliography) and in *A History of Technology*, I, Oxford, 1954, pp. 785–804 (O. NEUGEBAUER). Important texts from Tell Harmal published and commented by TAHA BAQIR, A. GOETZE, E. M. BRUINS and W. VON SODEN in *Sumer* VI (1950) ss.

14. R. LABAT, *op. cit.*, p. 112.

15. TAHA BAQIR, *Sumer* VII (1951), p. 30.

16. R. LABAT, *op. cit.*, p. 113.

17. The capital work on astronomy remains that of F. X. KRUGER, *Sternkunde und Sterndienst in Babel*, Münster, 1907–10. Summaries in R. LABAT, *op. cit.*, pp. 123–37 and O. NEUGEBAUER, The history of ancient astronomy, *JNES* IV (1945), pp. 2–38.

18. R. A. PARKER and W. H. DUBBERSTEIN, *Babylonian Chronology*, Providence, Rhode Island, 1956, pp. 1–3.

19. A. T. OLMSTEAD, *History of the Persian Empire*, Chicago, 1948, p. 206.

20. A. T. OLMSTEAD, *op. cit.*, p. 457.

21. On Mesopotamian medicine in general, cf. G. CONTENAU, *La Médecine en Assyrie et en Babylonie*, Paris, 1938; H. E. SIGERIST, *A History of Medicine*, Oxford, 1951, I, pp. 377–497; R. LABAT, *La Médecine Babylonienne*, Paris, 1953.

22. G. CONTENAU, *La Magie chez les Babyloniens et les Assyriens*, Paris, 1947.

23. R. LABAT, *Traité Akkadien de Diagnostics et Pronostics Médicaux*, Leiden, 1951.

24. R. LABAT, *Traité*, p. 3.

25. R. LABAT, *Traité*, p. 81.
26. R. LABAT, *Traité*, p. 173.
27. F. KUCHLER, *Beiträge zur Kentniss der Assyrisch-Babylonischen Medizin*, Leipzig, 1904, p. 60.
28. S. N. KRAMER, *HBS*, pp. 60–4; *ILN*, 26-2-1955, p. 370.
29. R. C. THOMPSON, Assyrian prescriptions for diseases of the urine. . . . *Babyloniaca* XIV (1934), p. 124.
30. R. C. THOMPSON, Assyrian prescriptions for diseases of the chest and lungs, *RA* XXXI (1934), p. 23. |
31. *RCAE*, No. 108.
32. A. FINET in *Annales Inst. Philol. et Hist. Orient. et Slaves*, Bruxelles, XIV, 1957.

CHAPTER XXIII

1. HERODOTUS I, 102 ss. Cf. DIODORUS SICULUS II, 26, 1–4.
2. A. T. OLMSTEAD, *History of Assyria*, New York, 1923, p. 627. Inscriptions in *ARAB* II, §§ 1130–1135; *Iraq* XX (1957), p. 11; *AfO* XIX (1959–60), p. 143.
3. Inscriptions of Sin-shar-ishkun in *ARAB* II, §§ 1136–65.
4. II Kings xxiii. 4, 15–19; II Chronicles xxxiv. 6.
5. Reference in the 'Chronicle of the Years BC 680–625' (S. SMITH, *BHT*, p. 26.)
6. The very important chronicle B.M. 21901, first published by C. J. GADD, *The Fall of Nineveh*, London, 1923 (*ANET*, pp. 303–5), and again, with four new tablets, by D. J. WISEMAN, *Chronicles of Chaldaean Kings*, London, 1956. For the 'Nabonidus Chronicle', see below, note 31. The Neo-Babylonian royal inscriptions are published in German translation by S. LANGDON, *Die neubabylonischen Königinschriften*, Leipzig, 1912.
7. D. J. WISEMAN, *Chronicles*, p. 57.
8. Discussion by C. J. GADD, *The Fall of Nineveh*, pp. 10–11.
9. D. J. WISEMAN, *Chronicles*, pp. 59–61.
10. Istambul stele of Nabonidus, *NBK*, p. 219; *ANET*, p. 309.
11. The term *Umman-manda*, loosely used elsewhere to designate the Cimmerians and/or the Scythians, seems here to apply to the Medes (cf. D. J. WISEMAN, *Chronicles*, p. 16).
12. *NBK*, p. 61; A. T. OLMSTEAD, *History of Assyria*, p. 640.
13. Joyful reactions in Judah: Zephaniah ii 13 ss.; Nahum ii ss.; Ezekiel, xxxi 3 ss.; xxxii, 22 ss.
14. II Kings xxiii. 29; II Chronicles xxxv 20; Jeremiah xlvi. 2; HERODOTUS, II, 159.

15. D. J. WISEMAN, *Chronicles*, pp. 68–9. Accounts of JOSEPHUS and BEROSSUS, *ibid.*, pp. 23–6.
16. D. J. WISEMAN, *Chronicles*, p. 71.
17. II Kings xxiv. 17; Jeremiah xxxvii. 1; JOSEPHUS, *Antiq. Jud.*, X, 6; D. J. WISEMAN, *Chronicles*, pp. 32–5, 73.
18. Cf. A. GARDINER, *Egypt of the Pharaohs*, pp. 360–1.
19. II *Kings*, xxv, 6–7 (cf. II Chronicles xxxvi. 13–20; Jeremiah xxxiv. 1–18).
20. D. J. WISEMAN, *Chronicles*, pp. 30, 94–5.
21. From an inscription of Nebuchadrezzar in Wadi-Brissa, Lebanon: *NBK*, p. 175; *ANET*, p. 307.
22. HERODOTUS, I, 74.
23. G. G. CAMERON, *History of Early Iran*, p. 220 (but see D. J. WISEMAN, *Chronicles*, p. 36).
24. D. J. WISEMAN, *Chronicles*, pp. 37–42, 75–77.
25. Harran inscription of Nabonidus' mother: *NBK*, pp. 289–95; *ANET*, pp. 311–12; C. J. GADD, The Harran inscriptions of Nabonidus, *Anatolian Studies* VIII (1958), pp. 46–57.
26. *BHT*, pp. 27–97; *ANET*, pp. 312–15.
27. Daniel iv. 28–33. J. T. MILIK, 'Prière de Nabonide' et autres écrits d'un cycle de Daniel, *RB* LXIII (1956), p. 408.
28. SIR LEONARD WOOLLEY, *Excavations at Ur*, London, 1954, p. 237.
29. HERODOTUS I, 127–30; STRABO XV, 3, 8; DIODORUS SICULUS II, 34, 6.
30. *NBK*, p. 221.
31. Nabonidus Chronicle I, 22–II, 2 (*BHT*, pp. 98–123; *ANET*, pp. 305–7).
32. Nabonidus Chronicle II, 5–25.
33. C. J. GADD, *Anatolian Studies* VIII (1958), pp. 57–89.
34. They are discussed in R. P. DAUGHERTY, *Nabonidus and Belshazzar*, New Haven, 1929.
35. Nabonidus Chronicle III, 12–22 (Cf. XENOPHON, *Cyropaedia* VII, 5, 20–36).
36. JOSEPHUS, *Contra Apionnem*, I, 21; EUSAEBIUS, *Preaep. Evang.* IX, 41.
37. F. H. WEISSBACH, *Die Keilinschriften der Achaemeniden*, Leipzig, 1911, p. 2 ss.; *ANET*, pp. 315–16.

CHAPTER XXIV

1. Jeremiah li. 7; HERODOTUS, I, 178. For a critical study of HERODOTUS' account, cf. O. E. RAVN, *Herodotus' description of Babylon*, Copenhagen, 1942.

2. Summary of the excavations in R. KOLDEWEY, *Das wieder erstehende Babylon*, Leipzig, 1913, 4th ed., 1925 (English translation: *The Excavations at Babylon*, London, 1914). Detailed results published in the volumes of the *Wissenschaftliche Veröffentlichungen der Deutsche Orient-Gesellschaft (WVDOG)* listed below.

3. F. WETZEL, *Die Stadtmauern von Babylon (WVDOG* 48), Leipzig, 1930.

4. R. KOLDEWEY, *Das Ischtar-Tor in Babylon (WVDOG* 32), Leipzig, 1918. Excellent photographs of the gate as reconstructed in the Berlin Museum in A. PARROT, *Assur*, Paris, 1961, pls. 220–222.

5. R. KOLDEWEY and F. WETZEL, *Die Königsbürgen von Babylon*, II (*WVDOG* 55), Leipzig, 1932.

6. O. REUTHER, *Merkes, die Innenstadt von Babylon (WVDOG* 47), Leipzig, 1926.

7. R. KOLDEWEY and F. WETZEL, *Die Königsbürgen von Babylon*, I (*WVDOG* 54), Leipzig, 1931.

8. DIODORUS SICULUS, II, 10; STRABO, XVI, i, 5; QUINTUS CURTIUS, *Hist. Alex.*, V, i, 31–5; BEROSSUS in JOSEPHUS, *Antiq. Jud.*, X, 226–7; *Contra Apionnem*, I, 19.

9. F. WETZEL and F. WEISSBACH, *Das Hauptheiligtum des Marduk in Babylon. Esagila und Etemenanki (WVDOG* 59), Leipzig, 1938. Voluminous literature on the 'Tower of Babel'; see, in particular, TH. DOMBART, *Der Babylonische Turm*, Berlin, 1930; A. PARROT, *Ziggurats et Tour de Babel*, Paris, 1949.

10. HERODOTUS, I, 182–3.

11. *NBK*, pp. 125–7.

12. HERODOTUS, I, 183.

13. The New Year Festival can be reconstructed from various texts, the most important being the *akîtu*-ritual dating to the Seleucid period published by F. THUREAU-DANGIN, *Rituels Accadiens*, Paris, 1921, pp. 127–54 (*ANET*, pp. 331–4). Descriptions and studies in: A. PALLIS, *The Babylonian Akîtu Festival*, Copenhagen, 1926; R. LABAT, *Le Caractère Religieux* . . . pp. 166–76; H. FRANKFORT, *Kingship and the Gods*, pp. 313–33. Important article by A. FALKEN-STEIN, *akiti-*Fest und *akiti-*Festhaus, in *Festschrift Johannes Friedrich*, Heidelberg, 1959, pp. 147–82.

14. Outside Babylon, New Year Festivals were celebrated in Assur, Nineveh, Erbil, Harran, Dilbat and Uruk, but at different dates.

15. This might be the origin of the appellation 'tomb of Bêl' given by STRABO (XVII, 5) and DIODORUS (XVII, 112) to the ziqqurat of Babylon.

16. S. LANGDON, *The Babylonian Epic of Creation*, Oxford, 1923, pp. 34-49.

17. Partially excavated by the Germans in 1902 (R. KOLDEWEY, *Die Tempel von Babylon und Borsippa (WVDOG 15)*, Leipzig, 1911, pp. 50-59). Important remains of the ziqqurat and of the temple.

18. *ANET*, p. 334.

19. The *bît akîtu* of Assur, described by Sennacherib (*ARAB* II, §§ 434-51c) has been excavated (*RLA* I, p. 188; *AM* I, pp. 228-230). Excavations at Uruk (*UVB*, 1956, pp. 35-42) have yielded the plan of its *bît akîtu*. According to A. FALKENSTEIN (*op. cit.*), there were three *akîtu*-temples in Babylon during the Neo-Babylonian period.

20. Cf., in particular, C. E. KAISER, *Letters and Contracts from Erech*, New Haven, 1918; H. F. LUTZ, *Neo-Babylonian Administrative Documents from Erech*, Berkeley, Calif., 1927; R. P. DOUGHERTY, *Archives from Erech*, New Haven, 1923 and 1933. On the temple administration, H. W. F. SAGGS, Two administrative officials at Erech in the sixth century BC, *Sumer* XV (1959), pp. 29-38, and *The Greatness that was Babylon*, London, 1962, pp. 261-8.

21. R. P. DOUGHERTY, *The shirkûtu of Babylonian Deities*, New Haven, 1923.

22. O. KRÜCKMANN, *Neubabylonische Rechts- und Verwaltungstexte*, Leipzig, 1933; H. H. FIGULLA, *Business Documents of the New Babylonian period (UET IV)*, London, 1949.

23. A. T. OLMSTEAD, *History of Assyria*, pp. 526-7.

24. W. H. DUBBERSTEIN, Comparative prices in later Babylonia, *AJSL* LVI (1930), pp. 20-43. 1 *qa* was worth 10 *gar*, or 675 square feet.

25. G. CHILDE, *What Happened in History*, Harmondsworth, 1942, p. 193.

CHAPTER XXV

1. Nabonidus Chronicle III, 24-8.

2. For a discussion of the events leading to the 'usurpation' of Darius, see A. T. OLMSTEAD, *History of the Persian Empire*, Chicago, 1948, pp. 107-13.

3. Published by F. H. WEISSBACH, *Die Keilinschriften der Achaemeniden*, Leiden, 1911, and, more recently, by F. W. KONIG, *Relief und Inschrift des Koenigs Dareios I am Felsen von Bagistan*, Leiden, 1938.

4. Behistun, § 50. On the chronology, see R. A. PARKER and W. H. DUBBERSTEIN, *Babylonian Chronology (626 BC-AD 75)*, Providence, Rhode Island, 1956, pp. 15-16; G. G. CAMERON, Darius and Xerxes in Babylonia, *AJSL* LVIII (1941), pp. 314-25.

5. R. A. PARKER and W. H. DUBBERSTEIN, *op. cit.*, p. 17. HERODOTUS, I, 183; STRABO, XVI, i, 5; ARRIAN, *Anabasis*, VII, xvii, 2; DIODORUS, II, ix, 4 ss.; CTESIAS, *Persica*, Epit. 52–3. F. M. TH. DE LIAGRE BOHL, Die Babylonischen Prätendenten zur Zeit Xerxes. *Bi.Or.* XIX (1962), pp. 110–14.

6. SIR LEONARD WOOLLEY, *Excavations at Ur*, pp. 225, 244 ss. Uruk: *UVB* XII–XIII (1956), pp. 17 and 28–31. Babylon: F. WETZEL, E. SCHMIDT, A. MALLWITZ, *Das Babylon der Spätzeit* (*WVDOG* 62), Berlin, 1957, pp. 25–7.

7. A. T. CLAY, *Legal and Commercial Transactions dated in the Assyrian, Neo-Babylonian and Persian Periods*, Philadelphia, 1908; A. TREMAYNE, *Records from Erech, Time of Cyrus and Cambyses*, New Haven, 1925. Cf. also Ch. XXIII, note 20.

8. XENOPHON, *Amabasis*, III, 4.

9. HERODOTUS, I, 192.

10. A. T. OLMSTEAD, *op. cit.*, pp. 299–301.

11. G. CARDASCIA, *Les Archives des Murashû*, Paris, 1951.

12. *ANET*, pp. 316–17.

13. ARRIAN, *Anabasis*, III, xvi, 4; VII, xvii, 2; STRABO, XVI, i, 5.

14. S. SMITH, A Chronicle concerning the Diadochi, *BHT*, pp. 129–49.

15. A. J. SACHS and D. J. WISEMAN, A Babylonian King List of the hellenistic period, *Iraq* XVI (1954), pp. 202–11.

16. S. SMITH, Historical account of the reign of Antiochus I Soter, *BHT*, pp. 154–7.

17. Discussion in M. ROSTOVTZEFF, *The Social and Economic History of the Hellenistic World*, Oxford, 1941, I, pp. 499–504.

18. The term 'Mesopotamia' is taken here in its broader sense. During the Seleucid period, the country was divided into three satrapies: Mesopotamia in the north, Babylonia in the south, and Parapotamia along the Euphrates.

19. American excavations 1927–32 and 1936–37: LEROY WATERMAN, *Preliminary Report on the Excavations at Tell Umar, Iraq*, Ann Arbor, 1931; *Second Preliminary Report* . . ., Ann Arbor, 1933; C. HOPKINS, A bird's eye view of Opis and Seleucia, *Antiquity* XIII (1939), pp. 440–8; separate publications on pottery (N. C. DEBEVOISE), coins and inscriptions (R. H. MCDOWELL) and figurines (W. VAN INGEN).

20. French excavations 1922–23; American excavations, 1928–39. Several Preliminary and Final Reports published. For a general account of the excavations, M. ROSTOVTZEFF, *Dura-Europos and its Art*, Oxford, 1938.

21. A. T. CLAY, *Legal Documents from Erech dated in the Seleucid Era*, New Haven, 1913. O. KRUCKMANN, *Babylonische Rechts- und Verwaltungsurkunden aus der Zeit Alexanders und der Diadochen*, Weimar, 1931 (with bibliography).

22. Nimrud: D. and J. OATES, Nimrud, 1957: the Hellenistic Settlement, *Iraq* XX (1958), pp. 114–57. Seleucid graves at Mari: A. PARROT, *Syria* XVI (1935), pp. 10–11; XXIX (1952), pp. 186–7; XXXII (1955), pp. 189–90. Remains of a Greco-Oriental temple at Arslan-Tash, F. THUREAU-DANGIN, *Arslan-Tash*, Paris, 1931.

23. *ANET*, p. 317.

24. F. WETZEL et al., *op. cit.*, pp. 3–22.

25. PLINY, *Naturalis historia*, VI, 122; PAUSANIAS, *Descriptio Graeciae*, I, xvi, 3.

26. R. NORTH, Status of the Warka Excavation, *Orientalia* XXVI (1957), pp. 206–7, 228–33, 237–41 (with bibliography).

27. M. RUTTEN, *Contrats de l'Epoque Séleucide conservés au Musée du Louvre*, Paris, 1935. A. AYMARD, Une ville de la Babylonie Séleucide d'après les contrats cunéiformes, *Revue des Etudes Anciennes*, XL (1938), pp. 5–52.

28. E. MEYER, *Blüte und Niedergang des Hellenismus in Asien*, Berlin, 1925, p. 24.

29. R. CAMPBELL THOMPSON, *CAH* III, pp. 246–50. SIR WILLIAM TARN and G. T. GRIFFITH, *The Hellenistic Civilization*, London, 1959, p. 295 ss.

30. German excavations, 1903–14 (W. ANDRAE, *Hatra*). Iraqi excavations, 1951–5, partly published in *Sumer* VIII (1952) ss.

31. A. PARROT, *Tello*, Paris, 1948, pp. 309–14.

32. H. LENZEN, *Die Partherstadt Assur* (*WVDOG* 57), Leipzig, 1933.

33. *UVB* VI (1935), pp. 33–6; XI (1940), pp. 28–31; XII–XIII (1956), pp. 32–4; XIV (1958), pp. 18–20; XVI (1960), pp. 13–21.

34. J. N. STRASSMAIER, Arsakideninschriften, *ZA* III (1888), pp. 129–42. TH. J. PINCHES and H. SAYCE, *PSBA* (1902), p. 108 ss. TH. J. PINCHES, *The Old Testament in the Light of the Historical Records of Assyria and Babylonia*, London, 1902, pp. 481–6. J. KOHLER and A. UNGNAD, *100 äusgewählte Rechtsurkunden der Spätzeit des babylonischen Schrifttums*, Leipzig, 1909. A. J. SACHS and J. SCHAUMBERGER, *Late Babylonian Astronomical and Related Texts*, Providence, Rhode Island, 1955.

35. A. J. SACHS and J. SCHAUMBERGER, *op. cit.*, No. 1201 (mentioned but not published).

36. DION CASSIUS, LXXI, 2; AMMIANUS MARCELLINUS, XXIII, vi, 34; ZONARAS, XI, 22; XII, 2.

37. S. LANGDON, Excavations at Kish and Barghutiat, *Iraq* I (1934), pp. 113–22.

38. H. LENZEN, Ein Goldkranz aus Warka, *Sumer* XIII (1957), pp. 205–6. On this tomb, the date of which has not been determined with certainty, cf. *UVB* XV (1959), pp. 27–34; XVI (1960), pp. 23–9.

NOTES TO THE EPILOGUE

1. A very thorough survey of our Mesopotamian heritage is presented by H. W. F. SAGGS in *The Greatness that was Babylon*, London, 1962, pp. 483–504.

2. According to Professor Cyrus H. Gordon, of Brandeis University, Massachusetts, the 'Linear A' writing of Crete, dated about 1500–1400 BC, expressed a West Semitic language. For a brief exposé of this much discussed theory, see now: C. H. GORDON, *Before the Bible*, London, 1962, pp. 206–17 and 300–2.

3. C. H. GORDON, *op. cit.*, pp. 9 and 302.

4. J. FILLIOZAT, Pronostics médicaux akkadiens, grecs et indiens, *Journal Asiatique* CCXL (1952), pp. 299–321; M. SANDRAIL, *Les Sources Akkadiennes de la Pensée et de la Méthode Hippocratiques*, Toulouse, 1953.

5. R. GRAVES, *Greek Mythology*, Harmondsworth, 1957, II, p. 89. For a detailed study, see C. H. GORDON, *op. cit.*, pp. 49–97 and 218–77.

6. M. ROSTOVTZEFF, *The Social and Economic History of the Hellenistic World*, Oxford, 1941, I, p. 84.

I. PREHISTORY

BC		Northern Iraq	Southern Iraq
600000	*Lower Palaeolithic*		
		Barda-Balka	
120000	*Middle Palaeolithic*		
		Hazar-Merd	
60000		**Shanidar D**	
35000	*Upper Palaeolithic*	Shanidar C Zarzi Palegawra	
10000	*Mesolithic*	Shanidar B Karim-Shehir Mlefaat	
7000	*Neolithic*	**Jarmo**	
		Hassuna	
5000	*Chalcolithic*	Matarrah	
		Hassuna-Samarra Period	
4500			Eridu Qal'at Hajj Muhammed
		Halaf Period	
4000		**Northern Ubaid**	**Ubaid Period**
3500		Gawra Culture	
			Uruk Period
3000		Nineveh Culture	**Proto-Literate Period**

II. EARLY DYNASTIC PERIOD (c. 2700–2400 BC)

BC	KISH	URUK	UR	LAGASH	AKSHAK	OTHER DYNASTIES
2750	*DYN. I* / *21 kings from the "Flood" to*	*DYN I* / Mes-ki-agga-sher / **Enmerkar**	"*Royal Cemetery*" / (*Mes-kalam-dug* / *A-kalam-dug*)			
		Lugalbanda				
2700	**En-me-barage-si**	Dumuzi	*DYN. I*			
	Agga	**Gilgamesh**	**Mes-anne-padda**	Gurshar		
2650	*DYN. II* / SHU-... / Dadasig	Ur-nungal				
2600	Magalgalla	Utu-kalamma / Laba–...IR / E-nun-dara-anna / Mes-HE	A-anne-padda	Gunidu / Ur-Nanshe		
	Kalbum					
	She-è	Melam-anna / Lugal-ki-tun	Mes-kiag-nunna	Akurgal		
2550	GA-SHUB-nunna		Elulu	**Eannatum**	Unzi	**DYNASTY OF AWAN** / **DYNASTY OF HAMAZI**
	Enbi-Ishtar					

		(Uruk / Akkad)		(Lagash)	(Mari)	
	DYN. III Lugal-mu	*DYN. II* En-shakush-anna	Balulu	Enannatum I **Entemena**	Undalulu Ur-ur Puzur-Nirah	**DYNASTY OF ADAB** Lugal-anne-mundu
2500						**DYNASTY OF MARI** *(6 kings, 136 years,* *according to the* *Sumerian King List)*
	DYN. IV Ku-baba Puzur-Sin	*DYN. III* **Lugal-kinishe-dudu** **Lugal-kisal-si**	**Lugal-kinishe-dudu** **Lugal-kisal-si**	**Enannatum II** Lugalanda	Ishu-Il	
2450					Shu-Sin	
2400	Ur-Zababa	*DYN. III* **Lugal-zagge-si** (c. 2400–2371)	. . . . . . gi	**Urukagina**		
	Simu-dár	**AKKAD** **Sharru-kin (Sargon)** (2371–2316)	Ka-kug			
2350	Usi-watar Ishtar-muti Ishme-Shamash					
	Nannia	Rimush (2315–2307) →				
2300						

III. DYNASTIES OF AKKAD, GUTIUM AND UR III (2400–2000 BC)

BC	AKKAD	URUK III		LAGASH
2400		Lugal-zagge-si (circa 2400–2371)		Urukagina (circa 2415–2400)
	Sharru-kin (Sargon) (2371–2316)			
				Akkadian domination
2350				
	Rimush (2315–2307) Manishtusu (2306–2292) Narâm-Sin (2291–2255)			
2300				
		URUK IV (5 kings, Circa 2260–2230)		
2250	Shar-kali-sharri (2254–2230)		**DYNASTY OF GUTIUM**	Gutian domination
	Anarchy		21 kings, 91 years (2211–2120) according to the Sumerian King List,	
2200				

	UR III	URUK V	ISIN DYNASTY	DYNASTY OF LARSA	
					Ur-Baba *but probably ruled since about 2250*
2150		**Utu-hegal** (2120–2114)			**Gudea** (?)
2100	**Ur-Nammu** (2113–2096)				Ur-Ningirsu
	Shulgi (2095–2048)				Ugme
2050	Amar-Sin (2047–2039)		**Ishbi-Irra** (2017–1985) →	**DYNASTY OF LARSA** Nablânum (2025–2005)	*Several minor rulers*
	Shu-Sin (2038–2030)				
	Ibbi-Sin (2029–2006)			Emisum (2004–1977) →	*(Lagash under Gungunum of Larsa in 1926 BC)* →
2000	*Ur overthrown* (2006)				

B C	ISIN DYNASTY	LARSA DYNASTY	UR III DYNASTY (since 2113)
2050			
	Ishbi-Irra (2017–1985)	Nablânum (2025–2005)	Ibbi-Sin (2029–2006)
2000		Emiṣum (2004–1977)	Ur overthrown (2006)
	Shu-ilishu (1984–1975) Iddin-Dagan (1974–1954)	Samium (1976–1942)	
1950	Ishme-Dagan (1953–1935)	Zabaia (1941–1933)	
	Lipit-Ishtar (1934–1924) Ur-Ninurta (1923–1896)	Gungunum (1932–1906)	BABYLON DYNASTY
1900		Abisarê (1905–1895)	
	Bûr-Sin (1895–1874)	Sumu-El (1894–1866)	Sumu-abum (1894–1881) Sumu-la-ilum (1880–1845)
	Lipit-Enlil (1873–1869) Irra-imitti (1868–1861) Enlil-bâni (1860–1837)	Nûr-Adad (1865–1850)	
1850		Sin-idinnam (1849–1843)	
	3 kings (1836–1828) Sin-magir (1827–1817)	3 kings (1842–1835) Warad-Sin (1834–1823) Rîm-Sin (1822–1763)	Sabium (1844–1831) Apil-Sin (1830–1813)
	Damiq-ilishu (1816–1794)		Sin-muballiṭ (1812–1793)
1800	Isin overthrown (1794)		Hammurabi (1792–1750)
	SEALAND DYNASTIES	Larsa overthrown (1763)	
1750	Iluma-ilu (independent in 1742)	KASSITES Gandash (c. 1746–1731)	Samsu-iluna (1749–1712)
		Agum I	
1700	Damiq-ilishu	Kashtiliash I	Abi-eshuh (1711–1684)
		Ushshi Abirattash	Ammi-ditana (1683–1647)
	Gulkishar		
		Tashigurumash	
1650	Peshgal-daramash	Harbashipak	Ammi-ṣaduqa (1646–1626)
	Aidarkalama	Tiptakzi	Samsu-ditana (1625–1595)
1600		Agum II (1602–1585)	Hittite raid (1595)

BABYLONIAN PERIODS (2000–1600 BC)

ASSYRIA	MARI	ESHNUNNA	ANATOLIA	EGYPT
Zariqum		Ilshu-ilia		**MIDDLE KINGDOM** *DYNASTY XI* (*since circa* 2160)
Puzur-Ashur I		Nurahum Kirikiri	*Assyrian trade colonies in Asia Minor*	
Shalim-ahum		**Bilalama**		*DYNASTY XII* Amenhemet I (1991–1962) Senusret I (1971–1928)
Ilushuma				
		Ur-Ninmar		Amenhemet II (1929–1895)
				Senusret II (1897–1877)
		Adbi-Erah	Pitkhanas Anittas	
Erishum I				Senusret III (1878–1843)
Sargon I				
		Ibal-pî-El I		
Ilâ-kabkabû	Iaggid-Lim	**Ipiq-Adad II** Narâm-Sin		Amenhemet II (1842–1797)
	Iahdun-Lim			
Shamshi-Adad I (1814–1782)		**Dadusha**		
	Iasmah-Adad (1796–1780)	**Ibal-pî-El II** (1790–1761)		Amenhemet IV (1798–1790)
Ishme-Dagan (1781–1742)	**Zimri-Lim** (1779–1761)			Sebeknofru (1789–1786) *DYNASTIES XIII–XIV*
	Mari overthrown (1761)	*Eshnunna overthrown* (1761)	**OLD HITTITE KINGDOM** Tudkhaliyas I (*circa* 1740–1710)	
Assur-dugul *5 kings*			Pu-sarrumas	
Adasi			Labarnas I	
Several minor rulers in succession				
				HYKSOS PERIOD *DYNASTIES XV–XVII* (*circa* 1660–1580)
			Hattusilis I (*circa* 1650–1621)	
			Mursilis I (1620–1590)	
↓			↓	↓

BC	BABYLONIA	ASSYRIA	MITANNI	HURRI
1600	*KASSITE DYNASTY* Agum II (1595–1585) Burnaburiash I			
1550	*About 9 rulers* *(chronology uncertain)*	Erishum III Ishme-Dagan II		
1500		Ashur-nirâri I		
			Paratarna	
1450	Kashtiliash II **Ulamburiash**	Puzur-Ashur III *Mitannian* *domination*	**Shaushatar**	
	Kara-Indash	Ashur-bêl-nisheshu	Artatama I	
1400	Kurigalzu I	Eriba-Adad	Shuttarna I **Tushratta**	Artatama I
1350	**Burnaburiash II** (1375–1347) **Kurigalzu II** (1345–1324) Nazi-Maruttash	**Ashur-uballiṭ I** (1365–1330) Enlil-nirâri Arik-dên-ilu	Mattiwaza *Mitanni overthrown*	Shuttarna
1300	Kadashman-Turgu **Kadashman-Enlil II** (1279–1265) Kashtiliash III	Adad-nirâri ï **Shalmaneser I** (1274–1245)		Shattuara I Washashatta Shattuara II *Hurri overthrown*
1250		**Tukulti-Ninurta I** (1244–1208)		
	Assyrian rule *(7 years)*	Ashur-nadin-apli Ninurta-apal-Ekur		
1200	*Elamite invasion* (1171)	Ashur-dân I (1179–1134 ?) ↓		

HITTITES	SYRIA	EGYPT	ELAM
OLD HITTITE KINGDOM (*since circa* 1740) Hantilis (1590–1560)		**NEW KINGDOM** *DYNASTY XVIII*	
		Ahmes I (1580–1550)	
Zidantas I (1560–1550)			
		Amenophis I (1550–1528)	
Telepinus (1525–1500)	*Egyptian campaign*	Tuthmosis I (1528–1510) Tuthmosis II	
		Tuthmosis III (1490–1436)	
HITTITE EMPIRE Tudkhaliyas II	*Egyptian conquest*		
	Mitannian influence in N. Syria		
Arnuwandas I			
Hattusilis II		Amenophis II (1436–1413)	
Tudkhaliyas III	*"El-Amarna period"* (c. 1400–1350)	Tuthmosis IV **Amenophis III** (1405–1367)	
Arnuwandas II **Suppiluliumas** (1375–1335)	*Hittite conquest*	**Amenophis IV** (1367–1350)	
		Tut-ankh-Amon (1347–1339)	Hurpatila
Mursilis II (1334–1306)		Horemheb (1335–1308 ?) *DYNASTY XIX*	
Mutawallis (1306–1282)		Ramesses I Seti I (1308–1291)	Pahir-ishshan
Urhi-Teshup **Hattusilis III** (1275–1250)	*Battle of Qadesh* (1285) *Egypto-Hittite Treaty* (1269)	**Ramesses II** (1290–1224)	Humban- numena
Tudkhaliyas IV			**Untash-GAL**
Arnuwandas IV	*Moses. Israelite Exodus*	Merenptah (1224–1214)	Kidin-Hutru
Phrygian invasion (c. 1190)	*Invasion of the "People of the Sea"* *Philistines in Palestine*	*DYNASTY XX* **Ramesses III** (1182–1151) ↓	**Shutruk- nahhunte** Kutir- nahhunte ↓

VI. MIDDLE-ASSYRIAN AND MIDDLE-BABYLONIAN PERIODS (1200–750 BC)

BC	BABYLONIA	ASSYRIA	HEBREWS	ARAMAEANS AND PHOENICIANS
1200	*Kassite dynasty since 1595.* *Overthrown by Elamites 1174–1171*	Ninurta-apal-Ekur (1192–1180) Ashur-dân I (1179–1134 ?)		
	DYN. IV. Marduk-kabit-ahêshu (1170?–1152) Itti-Marduk-balatu (1151–1143)			
1150		Ashur-rêsh-ishi (1131–1116)	*Israelites conquer Canaan (Judges)*	*Aramaeans established in Syria*
1100	**Nebuchadrezzar I** (1124–1103) Marduk-nadin-ahhê	**Tiglathpileser I** (1115–1077)		*Tiglathpileser I conquers Syria*
	Marduk-shapik-zêrmâti	Ashur-bêl-kala (1074–1057)		*Aramaeans invade Mesopotamia (circa 1077–911)*
	Adad-apal-iddina (1067–1046)			
1050	DYN. V. Shimmash-shipak (1038–1022) 2 kings	Ashurnasirpal I (1049–1031) Shalmaneser II (1030–1019)	Saul	
	DYN. VI. 3 kings (1015–997)	Ashur-râbi II (1010–970)	**David** (c. 1010–955)	*Neo-Hittite and Aramaean kingdoms in N. Syria Beginning of Phoenician prosperity* Hiram I of Tyre (980–936)
1000	DYN. VII. 1 king (996–991) DYN. VIII. Nabû-mukin-apli (990–955)			

Date	Babylon	Assyria	Israel / Judah	Syria / West
	Mar-bîti-ahhê-iddin (953–942)	Tiglathpileser II (966–935)	**Solomon** (c. 955–935)	
950	Shamash-mudammiq (941–901)			
			ISRAEL **JUDAH**	Ben–Hadad I of Damascus
		Ashur-dân II (934–912)	Jeroboam Roboam	
900		**Adad-nirâri II** (911–891)	(931–910) (931–915)	Aramaeans expelled from Assyria
		Tukulti-Ninurta II (890–884)		
	Nabû-apal-iddina (885–852)	Ashurnasirpal II (883–859)	**Omri** (885–874)	Assyrian campaigns in Syria (against Hama and Damascus)
			Ahab (874–853)	Battle of Qarqar (853)
850	Marduk-zakir-shumi (852–828)	**Shalmaneser III** (858–824)	**Jehu** (841–814)	Hazael of Damascus
	Marduk-balatsu-iqbi	Shamshi-Adad V (823–811)		Ben–Hadad III of Damascus
800		**Adad-nirâri III** (810–783)		Phoenicians found Carthage (814)
	Eriba-Marduk (782–763)	Shalmaneser IV (782–772)		Adad-nirâri III takes Damascus
		Ashur-dân III (771–754)	Azariah (766–740)	
750	Nabû-shum-ishkun (762–747)	Ashur-nirâri V (753–746)	Menahem (752–741)	
	→	→	→	

BC	ASSYRIA	BABYLONIA	ASIA MINOR
750			
740	Tiglathpileser III (745–727)	DYN. IX. Nabû-nâṣir (746–734)	Sardur III (Urarṭu)
730	Shalmaneser V (726–722)	DYN. X. Ukîn-zêr (732–730)	Rusas I (Urarṭu)
720	Sargon II (721–705)	Marduk-apal-iddina (721–711)	
710		Sargon vice-regent (710–705)	Argistis II (Urarṭu)
700	Sennacherib (704–681)	Bêl-ibni (702–700) Ashur-nadin-shum (699–694) Mushezib-Marduk (693–689)	
690		Sack of Babylon (689)	Rusas II (Urarṭu)
680	Esarhaddon (680–669)		Gyges (Lydia)
670	Ashurbanipal (668–631)	Shamash-shum-ukîn (668–648)	
660			
650		Kandalanu (647–627)	Sardur III (Urartu) Ardys (Lydia)
640			
630	Ashur-etil-ilâni Sin-shar-ishkun (629–612)		Sadyattes (Lydia)
620		DYN. XI. Nabopolassar (626–605)	
610	Ashur-uballiṭ II Assyria overthrown (614–609)		
600		Nebuchadrezzar II (605–562)	
590			Alyattes (Lydia) Urartu overthrown (c. 585)
580			
570			
560		Awêl-Marduk/Neriglissar/ Labâshi-Marduk	Croesus (Lydia)
550		Nabonidus (556–539)	(560–547) Lydia overthrown (547)
540		Babylon captured by Cyrus (539)	
530			

NEO-BABYLONIAN KINGDOM (745–739 BC)

MEDES	PERSIANS	SYRIA-PALESTINE	EGYPT
			Pi'ankhy (751–730)
Daiakku (Deioces)		*Assyrians attack and conquer Neo-Hittite kingdoms in N. Syria (745–720)*	Tafnekt (730–720)
Cyaxares I		*Samaria captured (722)*	Bocchoris (720–716) Shabako (716–695)
	Achaemenes	Hezekiah (Judah) (715–686)	Shebiktu (695–690)
		Manasseh (Judah) (686–640)	**Taharqa** (689–664)
Phraortes (675–653)	Teispes (675–640)		*Assyrian invasions (671–669)*
Cyaxares II (653–585) *Scythian rule for 28 years (?)*	Cyrus I (640–600)		**Psammetichus** (663–610) *Assyrians expelled (c. 655)*
Ashurbanipal overthrows Elam (639)		Josiah (Judah) (637–608)	
Medes attack Assyria (614)		*Battle of Karkemish (605)*	**Necho** (610–595)
Astyages (585–550)	Cambyses I (600–559)	*Jerusalem captured (587)*	Apries (595–570)
		Tyre captured (571)	Amasis (570–526)
	Cyrus II (559–530)		
Medes overthrown (550)			
	Cambyses II (530–522) ↓		↓

O

VIII. LATE PERIODS

BC	IRAN ACHAEMENIANS	GREECE	MAIN EVENTS IN MESO-POTAMIA
550	(since *c.* 700 BC)		*Babylon captured by Cyrus* (539)
	Cambyses II (530–522)		**ACHAEMENIAN PERIOD** (539–331 BC)
	Darius I (521–485)		Revolts of Nebuchadrezzar III and IV (522–521)
500		*Persian War* (499–449)	
	Xerxes I (485–465)		Revolts of Bêl-shimanni and Shamash-eriba (482). Sack of Babylon
	Artaxerxes I (465–424)		
450		*Athens under Pericles* (443)	*Murashu bankers at Nippur* (*c.* 460–400)
	Darius II (424–404)		
400	Artaxerxes II (404–358)		*Xenophon in Mesopotamia* (401)
350	Artaxerxes III (358–337)	Philippus II in Macedonia (359–336)	**HELLENISTIC PERIOD** (331–126 BC)
	Darius III (335–330)	**Alexander-the-Great** (336–323)	*Alexander enters Babylon* (331) *Alexander dies in Babylon* (323)
		THE DIADOCHI **Seleucus I** (305–281)	Seleucid era (from 311 BC)
300		**THE SELEUCIDS** **Antiochus I** (281–261) Antiochus II (261–246)	*Foundation of Seleucia* (274) *Last royal inscription in Akkadian* (*Antiochus I*)
250	**PARTHIANS** Arsaces (250–248) Tiridates I (248–211)	Seleucus II (246–226) **Antiochus III** (220–187)	
	Artabanus I (211–191)		
200	Priapatius (191–176) **Mithridates I** (171–137)	**Antiochus IV** (174–154)	*Greek theatre in Babylon* *Mithridates I founds Ctesiphon*
150		Demetrius II (146–126)	
	Phraates II (137–128) Artabanus II (128–124) Mithridates II (123–88)	Antiochus VIII (125–95) (*The Seleucid Dynasty ended in 63 BC*)	*Artabanus II conquers Mesopotamia* **PARTHIAN PERIOD** (126 BC–AD 227)
100			

INDEX

Modern Geographical names are in italics. The names of deities are followed by an asterisk.

INDEX

INDEX

MAPS

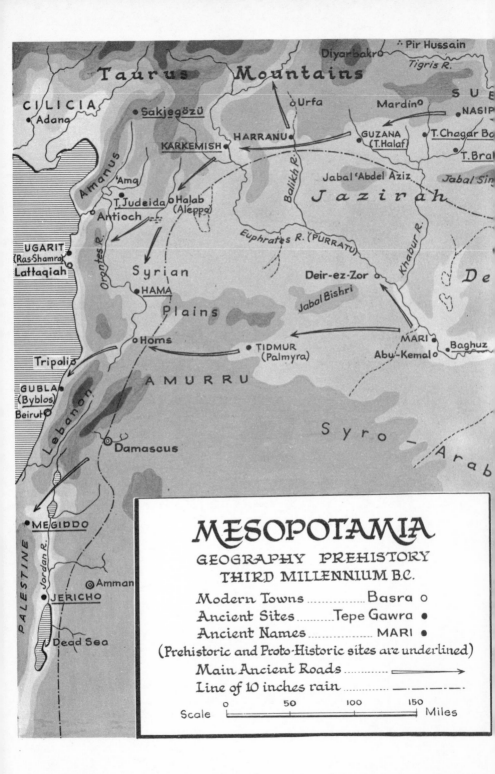

MESOPOTAMIA

GEOGRAPHY   PREHISTORY
THIRD MILLENNIUM B.C.

Modern Towns .... Basra o
Ancient Sites .... Tepe Gawra •
Ancient Names .... MARI •
(Prehistoric and Proto-Historic sites are underlined)
Main Ancient Roads .... ⊏══⟶
Line of 10 inches rain .... —·—·—·—·

Scale ⊢ 0 ——— 50 ——— 100 ——— 150 ⊣ Miles

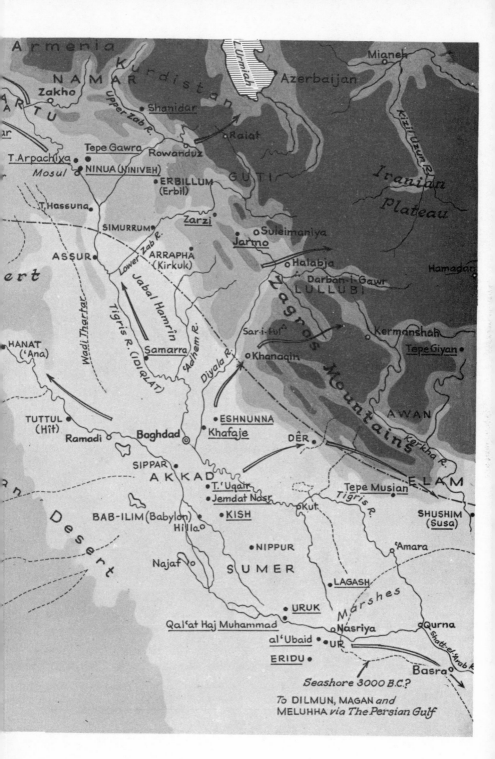

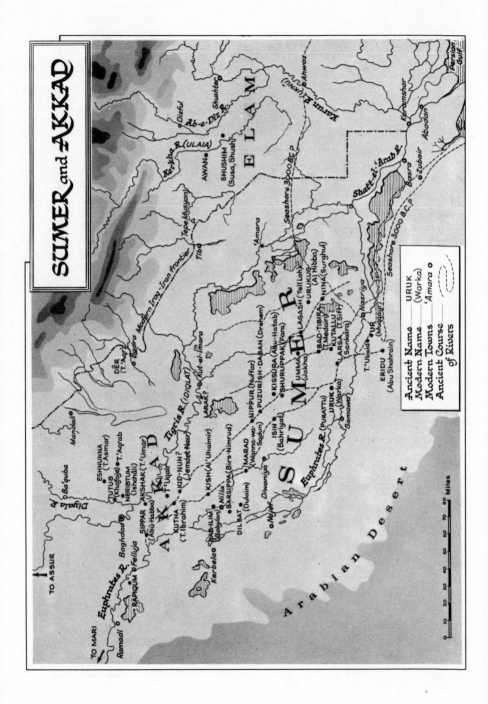

SUMER and AKKAD

Ancient Name........ URUK
Modern Name........ (Warka)
Modern Towns..... Amara ○
Ancient Course ...... ⟨⟨⟨⟩⟩⟩
of Rivers

Persian Gulf

ELAM

Seashore 3000 B.C.?

Shatt-el-'Arab R.

Karun R. (KVU)

Ab-e-Diz R.

Kerkha R. (ULAIA)

AWAN●

SHUSHIM
(Susa, Shush)

Tepe Musyan○

Tibo

'Amara

Modern Iraq-Iran frontier

DĒR
(T.'Aqar)

Elgara

Kut-el-'amara

LARAK?
(Jemdet-Nasr)

Tigris R. (IDIQLAT)

KID-NUN?

NIPPUR (Nuffar)

PUZURISH-DABAN (Dreham)

SHURUPPAK (Fara)

UMMA (Jokha)

KISSURA (Abu-Hatab)

LAGASH (Telloh)

URUKUG (Al Hibba)

NINA (Surghul)

BAD-TIBIRA (T.Medain)

KUTALLU (T.Sifr)

LARSA (Sankara)

Samawa

UR (Muqayyir)

T.'Ubaid○

ERIDU (Abu Shahrain)

a Nasriya

Seashore 3000 B.C.?

Kerbumshar

Zubair○

Basra

Abadan

Seashore 3000 B.C.?

TO ASSUR

Diyala R.

Ba'quba○

Baghdad●

RAPIQUM ○Felluja

Ramadi ○

TO MARI

Euphrates R.

ESHNUNNA (T.Asmar)
TUTUB (Khafaje)● ●T.'Aqrab
NERIBTUM (Ishchali)

AKSHAK(T.'Umar)

SIPPAR (Abu-Habba)

KUTHA T.'Uqair

KISH (A1 'Uhaimir)

BAB-ILIM (Babylon) Hilla

BARSIPPA (Birs-Nimrud)

DILBAT (Dulaim)

Kerbela○

MARAD (Wanna-wa-Sadun)

ISIN (Bahriyat)

URUK (Warka)

PURATTU

Euphrates R.

○Nejef

Diwaniya

AKKAD

SUMER

Arabian Desert

0 10 20 30 40 50 60 70 80 Miles

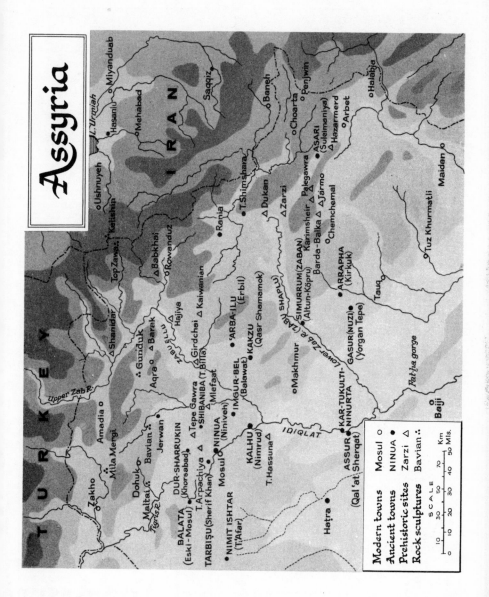

Assyria

TURKEY

IRAN

Zakho ⚬
Amadia ⚬
Mila Mergi ⚬∴
Dohuk ⚬
Maltai ∴⚬
Tigris R.
BALATA (Eski-Mosul) ⚬
T.Arpachiya △
TARBIŞU (Sherif Khan) ⚬
DUR-SHARRUKIN (Khorsabad) ⚬
Jerwan ⚬
Bavian ∴
T.Billa) △
SHIBANIBA (T.Billa) △
Tepe Gawra △
Aqra ⚬
Barek △
Guniduk ∴
ZAB-ELLU
Girdchei △
Hajiya △
Kaiwanian △
Babkhai △
Rowanduz ⚬
Top Zawa ∴
Shanidar △
Ushnuyeh ⚬
Kellishin ∴
Hasanlu ⚬
L. Urmiah
Miyanduab ⚬

NIMIT ISHTAR (T.'Afar) ⚬
Mosul ⚬
NINUA (Nineveh) ⚬
Mlefaat ⚬
IMGUR-BEL (Balawat) ⚬
'ARBA-ILU (Erbil) ⚬
KAKZU (Qasr Shamamok) △
Rania ⚬
T.Shimshara ●
T.Dukan △
Zarzi △
Mehabad ⚬
Saqqiz ⚬
Baneh ⚬
Penjwin ⚬
Choarta ⚬
Halabja ⚬

KALHU (Nimrud) ⚬
T.Hassuna △
Makhmur ⚬
SHAPLU
SIMURRUM (ZABAN) (Altun-Köpru) ●
Karimsheir △ Palegawra △
Barda-Balka △ Jarmo △
Chemchemal ⚬
ASARI (Suleimaniya) ⚬
Hazarmerd △
Arbet ⚬

ASSUR (Qal'at Sherqat) ⚬
IDIQLAT
KAR-TUKULTI-NINURTA ⚬
GASUR (NUZI) (Yorgan Tepe) ●
ARRAPHA (Kirkuk) ⚬
Tauq ⚬
Maidan ⚬
Tuz Khurmatli ⚬

Hatra ⚬
Fat'ha gorge
Beiji ●

Upper Zab R.

LOWER ZAB R. (ZAB)

Key

Modern towns	Mosul ⚬
Ancient towns	NINUA ●
Prehistoric sites	Zarzi △
Rock sculptures	Bavian ∴

SCALE

Km
0 10 20 30 50 70

Mls.
0 10 20 30 40 50

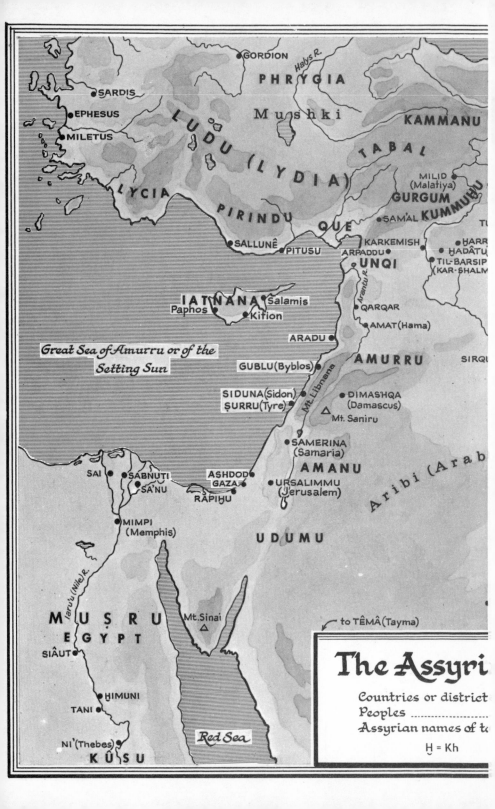

GORDION

Halys R.

PHRYGIA

SARDIS

EPHESUS

Mushki

MILETUS

KAMMANU

LUDU (LYDIA)

TABAL

MILID
(Malatiya)

GURGUM

KUMMUHU

LYCIA

PIRINDU

SAM'AL

QUE

TU

SALLUNÊ

PITUSU

KARKEMISH

HARR

ARPADDU

HADÂTU

UNQI

TIL-BARSIP
(KAR-SHALM

Arantu R.

IATNANA

Salamis

QARQAR

Paphos

Kition

AMAT (Hama)

ARADU

AMURRU

SIRQI

Great Sea of Amurru or of the
Setting Sun

GUBLU (Byblos)

Mt. Libnana

SIDUNA (Sidon)

DIMASHQA
(Damascus)

SURRU (Tyre)

Mt. Saniru

SAMERINA
(Samaria)

AMANU

SAI

SABNUTI

ASHDOD

URSALIMMU

Aribi (Arab

SA'NU

GAZA

(Jerusalem)

RAPIHU

MIMPI
(Memphis)

UDUMU

Iaru'u (Nile) R.

to TÊMÂ (Tayma)

MUSRU

Mt. Sinai

EGYPT

SIÂUT

The Assyri

HIMUNI

Countries or district

TANI

Peoples

Assyrian names of to

NI' (Thebes)

Red Sea

Ḫ = Kh

KÛSU

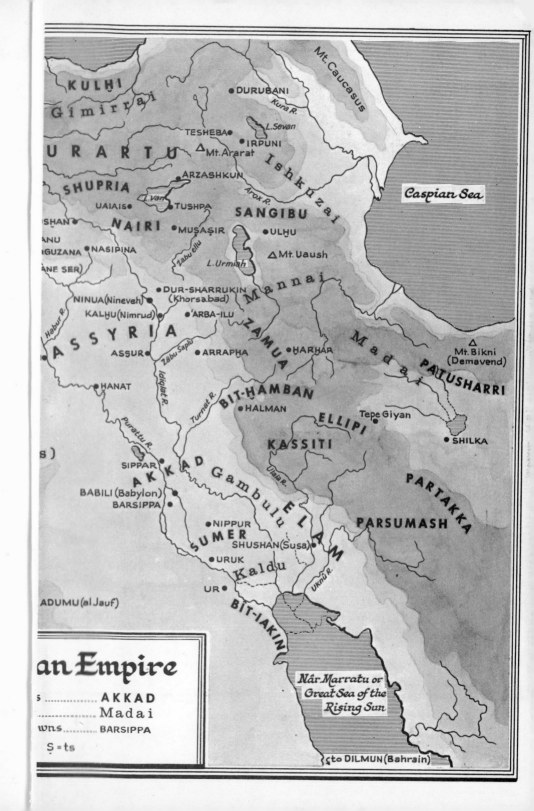

KULHI

Gimirrai

DURUBANI

Mt. Caucasus

Kura R.

L. Sevan

TESHEBA

IRPUNI

URARTU

Ishkuzai

△ Mt. Ararat

Caspian Sea

SHUPRIA

ARZASHKUN

Arox R.

SANGIBU

L. Van

UAIAIS

TUSHPA

NAIRI

MUSASIR

ULHU

SHAN

△ Mt. Uaush

ANU

L. Urmiah

Mannai

GUZANA

NASIPINA

Zabu ellu

ANE SER)

NINUA (Nineveh)

DUR-SHARRUKIN
(Khorsabad)

Madai

ZAMUA

'ARBA-ILU

KALHU (Nimrud)

△ Mt. Bikni
(Demavend)

Habur R.

ASSYRIA

ASSUR

HARHAR

PATUSHARRI

Zabu Saplu

ARRAPHA

Idiqlat R.

BIT-HAMBAN

Tepe Giyan

HANAT

ELLIPI

HALMAN

Turnat R.

SHILKA

KASSITI

Purattu R.

PARTAKKA

AKKAD Gambulu

SIPPAR

Uaia R.

ELAM

PARSUMASH

BABILI (Babylon)

BARSIPPA

NIPPUR

SUMER

SHUSHAN (Susa)

ADUMU (al Jauf)

URUK

Kaldu

Ukni R.

UR

BIT-IAKIN

an Empire

s .... AKKAD

.... Madai

wns .... BARSIPPA

S = ts

Nâr Marratu or
Great Sea of the
Rising Sun

ç to DILMUN (Bahrain)

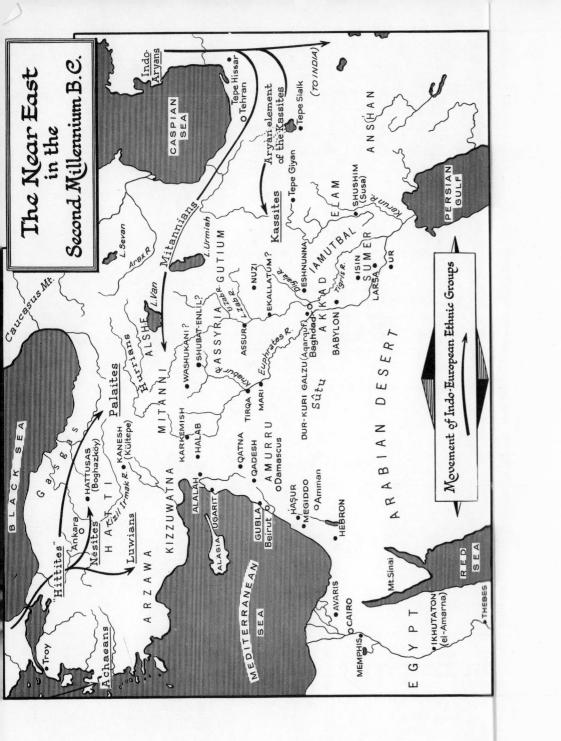

The Near East in the Second Millennium B.C.

Movement of Indo-European Ethnic Groups